MURDER IN THE SYNAGOGUE

MURDER IN THE SYNAGOGUE

by

T. V. LoCicero

PRENTICE-HALL, Inc. Englewood Cliffs, N.J.

Murder in the Synagogue
by T. V. LoCicero

ISBN 0-13-606590-2

Library of Congress Catalog Card Number: 74-104045

Printed in the United States of America *T*

Prentice-Hall International, Inc., London
Prentice-Hall of Australia, Pty. Ltd., Sydney
Prentice-Hall of Canada, Ltd., Toronto
Prentice-Hall of India Private Ltd., New Delhi
Prentice-Hall of Japan, Inc., Tokyo

Grateful acknowledgment is made to Joyce Carol Oates and *The Detroit Free Press* for permission to quote from "Richard Wishnetsky: Joyce Carol Oates Supplies a Missing View" (*Detroit Magazine,* March 6, 1966); to *Jewish Heritage* for permission to quote from "The Rabbi: 1966" by Rabbi Morris Adler (*Jewish Heritage,* Vol. 8, no. 4, Spring, 1966), and to Crown Publishers, Inc., for permission to quote from *May I Have a Word with You?* by Rabbi Morris Adler. © 1967 by B'nai B'rith. (Crown Publishers, Inc., New York: 1967)

For my father

CONTENTS

The young man standing opposite me smiled. Then he dropped on his knees and with a dreamy look on his face told me: "There has never been a time in which I have been convinced from within myself that I am alive. You see, I have only such a fugitive awareness of things around me that I always feel they were once real and are now fleeting away. I have a constant longing, my dear sir, to catch a glimpse of things as they may have been before they show themselves to me. I feel that then they were calm and beautiful. It must be so, for I often hear people talking about them as though they were."

Franz Kafka, Conversation with the Supplicant

INTRODUCTION

On a Saturday morning that was Lincoln's Birthday 1966, in front of a gathering of over seven hundred people, including his parents, sister, and grandmother, Richard Wishnetsky, aged twenty-three, stood on the altar of massive Shaarey Zedek Synagogue in suburban Detroit and read a short statement condemning the congregation as a "travesty and an abomination," after which he used a sawed-off .32 Colt revolver to send a bullet into the head of Rabbi Morris Adler, one of the nation's prominent religious leaders. He then placed the barrel of the gun over his own right ear and shot himself through the head.

When the shooting occurred, I was at work on a novel in my home only three miles from Shaarey Zedek. But before I read about them in the Sunday newspapers, I knew nothing of Rabbi Adler or Richard Wishnetsky. I am not Jewish and had not encountered the rabbi or known of his extensive reputation in the community. As for Richard, our paths had nearly crossed in Ann Arbor where we had gone to school and had a couple of mutual friends. He was two years younger than I.

On the following Wednesday Richard died. A day earlier both Detroit dailies had published articles containing writing that he had been doing in the last few weeks of his life, including an apologia for his fantasized murder of the Secretary of Defense, Robert McNamara. Rabbi Adler died three weeks later, and thousands mourned him in a funeral described as the largest in the city's history.

The idea of doing a book on what seemed a bizarre yet significant story first occurred to me some months after I had written

"The Murder of Rabbi Adler," an article published by *Commentary* in June 1966. Sources in the Jewish community offered encouragement for a more extensive study of the subject, and when response to the article included queries from a number of publishers, I decided to leave my novel and my teaching position and attempt a book on the assassination-suicide.

From the beginning of my inquiry it seemed that one who seriously considered the matter would be led into a labyrinth of questions, facts, opinions, answers, and inevitably more questions. As I finally conceived of it, the framework within which I hoped to formulate and explore the right questions consisted of a biography of Richard as complete and accurate as possible, dictated by those who knew him and by what he wrote about himself and his world; a portrait of Rabbi Adler in the same fashion but with less detail; and a description of the milieu within which their lives converged and tragically ended.

The basic problem in a description of milieu was one of definition or demarcation of limits. Both Rabbi Adler and Richard were part of Congregation Shaarey Zedek and the world Jewish community, simultaneously residents of Detroit in the second third of the twentieth century, and knowledgeable inheritors of the accumulated traditions of Western civilization. They were at times more intimately aware of the ancient communities of Babylonia or Greece than they were of the streets of suburban or northwest Detroit. Thus, while the line I drew encircled the immediate community and its contemporary history, reference to points in time and space beyond this line was frequent.

As might be expected I had little difficulty finding a large number of people who would talk readily about their experience with Rabbi Adler. I began with Mrs. Adler, who was immediately gracious, courageous, and most helpful and remained so throughout my work on the project. Fortunately, the rabbi was a man with love and reverence for the spoken and written word. Of great assistance were his book on the Talmud and especially his posthumous collection of essays and occasional pieces entitled *May I Have a Word with You?* He has been called "America's most quotable rabbi," and I have often quoted from his works in an effort to present the man, his ideas, attitudes, and values and to relate these to Richard.

The reconstruction of Richard's relatively short life was another matter. By his final act he had made himself (quite consciously and purposely, it seemed) a public person, legally and morally subject to investigation. Yet at the same time a thorough study would inevitably involve the privacy of many whose lives had been traumatically shattered by his final outburst of violence. Some would be either unwilling or unable to sort out their feelings, thoughts, and memories of Richard for a stranger, or indeed for anyone. Some might feel with or without reason that they had something to hide, others that their roles were bound by various professional oaths not to divulge information. Consideration had to be given to those who still had to live their lives and who might suffer psychological difficulty as a result of the study's publication.

Nonetheless, the lists of interviewees I compiled for several different points of focus in Richard's life continued to grow, and the frequently contradictory reports I received confirmed my notion that I must talk to as many as possible. Richard made a large number of contacts and presented many different faces, and so the number of interviews I conducted rose to over two hundred. With few exceptions, those I approached were most cooperative once they understood what I was doing and why, and they combined to produce a considerable amount of useful information and a number of significant documents belonging or relating to Richard.* To these people I am deeply grateful, not only for their information and insights but also, in so many cases, for their encouragement and inspiration.

Generally, the only important sources with whom I was not successful were Richard's family and the psychiatrists who treated him professionally. On three separate occasions I approached the Wishnetskys, initially through the kind offices of Mrs. Adler, who along with her husband had known the family for years. Each time I received a negative response. The response of the doctors was generally that though wanting to help, they felt it improper to comment on the matter because of the obligation of confidentiality. Clearly then, a thorough psychoanalytic approach was out of the question.

A survey of recent psychiatric literature, however, reinforced my notion that a close look at Richard's experience in late childhood, adolescence, and young adulthood should not be considered

* In several cases I supplied pseudonyms for those involved; in a few instances I changed certain background facts to further insure anonymity.

of negligible value simply because a deep and intimate knowledge of his early years was missing. Even if Richard's early childhood could not be documented in its vital detail, the study might fruitfully concentrate primarily on his later emotional and intellectual development and the impact of his social and cultural experience.

One of the few things that seemed clear when I first considered what Richard Wishnetsky said and did on February 12, 1966, was that he was a young man in pain—a deep and complex pain seemed etched in every word and every movement. About the time Richard graduated from high school in 1960, his future victim, Rabbi Adler, wrote a short but insightful essay on pain. In it he speaks of pain as a "many-faceted and multidimensional phenomenon," never localized, always involving the total being of the sufferer, mentally, emotionally, and spiritually. "To deal with the problem of pain," he wrote, "with any degree of adequacy, one would have to bring together several disciplines that have man as the object of their specialized study. Physician, psychologist, psychiatrist, sociologist, religious counsellor—all have a particular interest in this field, and each has a specific contribution to make toward our understanding of the problem of pain."

From the beginning of my work it seemed that only the kind of multilateral approach Rabbi Adler described could adequately analyze the events leading to his death and Richard's suicide. From the start, what I found most significant about the assassination-suicide was that it seemed the culmination of an extended series of apparent failures involving nearly all the basic institutions of modern society: the law, education, medicine, religion, fellowship, and the family. Underlying each of these apparent failures, of course, was the essential failure of a young man (seemingly marked for a valuable and enduring kind of success) to make the most basic decision for life and against death. The undeniable fact remained that neither the legal framework of society nor education of reputed quality nor psychiatry (three hospitals and a number of doctors) nor personal contact with prominent religious minds (Rabbi Adler and others) nor the apparent offer of significant human relationship (from a number of intelligent and concerned people) was able to prevent Richard from plunging with determination into the abyss.

An attempt to fix guilt, to define the essence of failure, to assign cause or causes in a case like this would have been naïve and absurd. Perhaps, however, one could legitimately attempt to describe the configuration of failure, collect the external evidence of internal conflict, and relate that conflict to the society which could do so little for or about it. Such an effort had even more importance, I felt, in the face of Richard's calculated attempt to announce to the world through his final act that he saw himself as a significant representative of a society which he declared totally bankrupt.

T. V. LoCicero

Oak Park, Michigan

PART I

Just born and already he enjoys the longest genealogical record in the Western world. Was he not admitted to the "Covenant of Abraham"? So-called blue bloods and their Social Register *are upstarts and parvenus alongside this little fellow. And the list of his ancestors is studded with the prominent names of creative spirits who enriched the life of all mankind. He seems a little frail to bear so great a patrimony.*

Yet what possibilities he represents. He is without fanatic loyalty or assimilationist tendencies. He has a capacity for such attachment to Jewish traditions as to enhance his life and to acquire a sense of deep companionship with Jews everywhere. He can be a good American imbued with profound democratic sensitivities and a fine awareness of the interdependence of all men. He is qualified to join in beautiful synthesis the two currents of influence in his life, the Judaic and the American. The past and present can unite to prepare him to work for a desirable and realizable future.

—RABBI MORRIS ADLER

ONE

Richard Steven Wishnetsky was born in the Bronx on July 1, 1942, in a land whose soil was never touched by the violence then wracking much of the globe. He was only three years old when the killing stopped, and he knew none of its thirty million victims. Yet as a Jew he would find special significance in the fate of a certain six million of these people. And as an American he would grow up with the specter wrought by a single capsule of pent-up energy dropped on each of two Japanese cities in August 1945.

Although the effects of war may not always be immediately visible, the first consequence of World War II for Richard was quite obvious: he was without a father for the first two or three years of his life. As he grew out of infancy with his mother in the Bronx, his father fought thousands of miles away with the 101st Airborne Division. Then with Richard established in the miniature universe of the two- or three-year-old, his father's return suddenly produced a new, large, and pervasive presence to deal with on intimate terms.

Richard very rarely spoke about his early years to his friends; when he did so, he generally restricted himself to the remark that he was not a very happy child. Upon his return from the war Mr. Wishnetsky worked for his father in the wine business (Richard later mentioned to friends that his dad was a real connoisseur of fine wines), and the family continued their residence in the Bronx. Richard's immediate family grew larger about the time he enrolled in the public-school system of the Bronx, when his mother brought home a new little sister named Terry. Three years later when Richard was eight, another daughter entered the family and was named Ellen. According to one of his first girl friends in high school, Richard did indicate that at one point during his first eleven years in New York, he had experienced some psychological disturbance apparently serious enough to bring him into contact with a psychiatrist.

One afternoon in the middle of November 1952, Richard, then aged ten, was brought to the Workmen's Circle School No. 16 off Allerton Avenue in the Bronx at some distance from his family's residence. For ninety minutes three or four times a week for the remainder of the school year, he attended sessions at the Yiddish secular school after a full day of regular public-school classes. The class at Workmen's Circle was taught by Emanuel Mark, a young man who would turn up again by chance in Richard's life a few years later and hundreds of miles distant. Mr. Mark remembers that Richard was well behind the other children upon arriving but almost immediately caught up:

"He stood out clearly very soon and was obviously very bright, always making comments and asking questions, always very interested. It was a secular rather than a religious school, and in order to give them some sense of their Jewish heritage, the children were taught Yiddish and a little Hebrew along with some Jewish history, music, literature, customs, and celebrations. We had some dramatics—we put on some plays in Yiddish—and some singing of Jewish songs."

Thus Richard gained some cultural notion of who his parents and grandparents were and where they had come from. In the process he was embarking on what would be a lifelong involvement with the puzzling question "What is a Jew?"

As Rabbi Morris Adler pointed out in an article he wrote for *Harper's* two years before he died, a satisfying answer is difficult to come by. A Jew, he said, has not gained his identity, his Jewishness, by assenting to a religious creed or a rigid formula, by virtue of his belonging to a "race" or a "civilization" or a "subculture." All these ways of definition, he said, finally disappoint the Jew. "So he feels frustrated. He still asks: 'What am I?' And perhaps in the process he has provided the best answer possible at present: 'A Jew is a person who is always asking 'What am I?' Certainly this definition is as authentic and comprehensive as any other."

Asking frequently "What is a Jew?" or as Rabbi Adler suggests, "What am I?" has led some to a strong sense of identity and deep insight. The toll taken, however, in the attempt to provide answers to these questions has at times been more than others like Richard Wishnetsky could afford to pay. In the paradox and ambiguity of Jewish history, one finds a remarkable story of endurance and achievement which cannot be told, however, without frequent and appalling reference to centuries of massacre, expulsion, isolation, and repression. A history of such accomplishment and victimization may impose an especially stern task on the young Jew who examines the past in an effort to understand himself.

In the past one hundred years the world Jewish community has experienced three of the most significant events in all its history: the uprooting and emigration of millions of Jews from Europe, beginning in the latter part of the last century; the murder of the six million; and the establishment of the state of Israel in 1948. Each of these three events has had sometimes indirect, often profound effects on most Jews, and Morris Adler and Richard Wishnetsky do not seem exceptions.

Morris Adler and his family, as well as both of Richard's grandfathers, arrived in America after the turn of the century during the most active phase of immigration in which more than two million Jews came to the United States, primarily from Russia and Poland. They came from the formerly compact and homogeneous society of the shtetl, which had already begun to disintegrate when mass emigration began in the last quarter of the nineteenth century. Previously life in the ghetto or small town had been a closely knit fabric of Yiddish culture, and these were people who lived with a powerful daily sense of Jewish identity and the unity of Israel. Yet long-standing conflicts intensified and deepened rifts within the society, pitting one religious sect or political group against another, rich against poor, class against class.

With emigration spurred by vicious pogroms in Russia, these conflicts generally resolved into the twin streams of religious Orthodoxy and secularism. Secularism under whatever banner—nationalism, Zionism, socialism, or the labor movement—was heavily represented among the Jews who found their way to America. The Orthodox Jew struggled to live his religion as he had in the old country, while the secularist went about the business of institutionalizing his particular ideology. Both groups however, settled primarily in the large urban centers. Both retained a strong sense of their own Jewishness and were thrown together in the new hostile urban ghettos where jobs were terribly scarce and living conditions often miserable. Yet only a decade or so into the new century it had become increasingly possible for the East European immigrant to move rather quickly into the American middle class. Both the Orthodox religious and secular Jew could share the feeling that America finally seemed to be paying off some of its promises.

In 1912 Rabbi Joseph Adler arrived in New York from the town of Slutsk in Russia to join relatives who had preceded him and had been urging him to sample the freedom and opportunities for a full life. One day a few years later, as Morris Adler would recall, the rabbi called his sons to him and said:

"Children, I first heard of America when I was about your age. I was living in a small, remote village far across the sea. America was a word I heard, its meaning or even location I did not know. One day a visitor came and I listened with fascination to the stories he told of the New World. I found a little book that told of the life of Abraham Lincoln. I listened eagerly as my parents read letters from fortunate relatives who had made their way to the land of freedom. I dreamed of America where all are free, where there are no Siberias, no pogroms, no persecution.

"This morning, dear children, I was sworn in as a citizen. I feel as if I have finally come home. I no longer feel like an outsider, an eternal alien, a stranger. I am part of the great fraternity of freedom of which I have dreamed these many years."

The labor-radicals among the immigrant population soon established their own secular Yiddish schools (like Workmen's Circle), their own press and theater, and their own welfare agencies. The aim and purpose of these institutions was nothing more and nothing less than the perpetuation of their community of Yiddish culture. The relationship between Richard's grandfather, William Hordes, and Jewish secularism in general (Zionism in particular) was perhaps not atypical.

Born in 1893 in the small town of Cholni near Bobruisk in White Russia, he was raised and educated by his Orthodox family who were members of the Habad, a philosophical and rationalizing branch of the Hasidic movement. In the face of this strict religious upbringing, Hordes in his youth turned to the Zionist Labor movement, embraced secular perhaps even antireligious ways and brought his hopes and attachments with him to the United States in 1910. Working on various jobs and in factories while he learned

English, Mr. Hordes finally settled in Detroit, entered the insurance business, established an agency, married, and raised a family of two sons and a daughter. Assuming a prominent position in the Farband Labor Zionist Order, he helped to establish Zionist-oriented Jewish folk schools in Detroit along with Michigan's first Jewish summer camp; relief fund-raising projects for Israel claimed his active interest as did the American political scene. The considerable success of his agency enabled him to pursue the tradition-honored activity of a generous philanthropy; because of his frequent contributions to the Jewish National Fund, he was known to many Detroit Jews as Mr. J.N.F. At his death in 1964 he was eulogized as a "one-man social service movement." Late in his life Mr. Hordes returned to the religion of his early youth and rejoined the Habad movement. He also became one of the most important people in the life of his grandson, Richard.

Moses Wishnetsky, Richard's paternal grandfather, was born in Russia in 1889. Coming to the United States about the same time Mr. Hordes did, he took up residence in the Bronx, became a merchant, married, and also raised two sons and a daughter. Eventually he acquired a Manischewitz wine franchise and was also involved in the company's export business. As it did to William Hordes, American success came generously to Mr. Wishnetsky. He is described as "a leader in organized Jewish life and in Jewish culture," a self-made man of very strong personality and ego, "a real live-wire, a tremendous conversationalist," whose conversations, however, are apt to be considerably one-sided even as he holds forth on a wide range of topics with verve and intelligence. "All the Wishnetsky men are like that—it seemed to be passed on directly from grandfather to father to son," said one who was acquainted with all three. Now nearing eighty, Moses Wishnetsky, still vigorous and sharp-witted, lives with his wife, "a quiet and reserved little woman," in their Westchester, New York, home.

Briefly, then, the first generation of Richard's family in the New World was secular, self-made, and successful in the American fashion; vigorously active in the community, adapting to the American scheme of things without excluding an ongoing sense of Jewish identity. If Richard's grandparents suffered anguish, anxiety, and alienation in the uprooting process, in retrospect these common factors seem to have been dealt with effectively and are not particularly visible.

In a book that became a favorite of Richard's, Will Herberg wrote about the development of the three great religions in America—Protestant, Catholic, and Jewish. About the Jews he says at one point:

> Because religion and immigrant culture were so thoroughly fused as to seem almost indistinguishable, the East European immigrants came up against a shattering crisis as they confronted the second generation, their American sons and daughters. The second generation, desperately anxious to become unequivocally American, was resentful of the immigrant culture which the older generation seemed so eager to transmit to it.

Thus, says Herberg, this second generation became the "weakest link in the chain of Jewish continuity." In the case of Richard's family, however, this crisis seems to have been mitigated. Because his grandparents arrived in a more hospitable America after the turn of the century, because of their strong secular bent, and because of their effective adaptation, they gave their children little to rebel against or reject in the terms employed by Professor Herberg. Richard's father attended Yiddish schools in New York, and subsequently there seems to have been no serious disaffection, rejection, or breaking away. Mr. Wishnetsky remained in the Bronx to help his father run the Manischewitz franchise and later, when he moved his family to Detroit, took a position in his father-in-law's insurance agency. The Yiddish culture of their parents perhaps seemed less relevant to Edward and Evelyn Wishnetsky, Richard's parents, than the American institutions they became active in, such as Democratic politics. But while they are certainly Americans first of all, they have not renounced their roots or a self-identification as members of the Jewish community.

At the time Richard was taking his afternoon classes at Workmen's Circle, the Wishnetskys were living in a solidly middle-class neighborhood in the upper Bronx. It was a predominantly Jewish area lined with apartment complexes, one of which served Richard and his family. In the summer in which he became eleven (1953) and after he had finished the fifth grade in the Bronx, the Wishnetskys moved to Detroit to occupy a new home on Manor Road on the city's heavily Jewish northwest side.

During the years in which Richard started his formal education and became slowly more aware of the larger realities around him, the world was learning for the first time what a global cold war was, and television perfected itself as an agent of societal metamorphosis in time to present a daily diet of the horses, guns, and fisticuffs of Ken Maynard and Hoot Gibson to a generation of entranced kids. In 1948 a nation called Israel had been born in violence; subsequently numbers of American Jews, including Richard's uncle, Herb Hordes, again cast their lot with emigration and traveled to share the uncertain fate of the new homeland.

TWO

The new neighborhood in Detroit was thoroughly middle-class, its quiet well-paved streets lined with a variety of private homes, most of them built within the previous twenty-five years. At one end of the block that included the new Wishnetsky home was a Lutheran church, and at the other end was a Catholic elementary school, its ample fenced-in playground only a few quick steps from Richard's door. A sign, however, on the large gate said, "Private Playground for Presentation Children Only." It was a rather well apportioned block—approximately one-third Jewish, one-third Catholic, and one-third Protestant. At the time, there were only a few widely scattered Negro families living in the area.

Manor Road, about a half mile from the city's northern limits at Eight Mile Road, was near the heart of Detroit's Jewish community; the area was then one-quarter to one-half Jewish. Within walking distance were synagogues, the Jewish Community Center, and the Jewish shops, stores, day schools, and delicatessens that line Seven Mile Road in the vicinity of the Royal Theater. With large elms joining from both sides to form a lush green canopy in the summer Manor was a cool, shady, and pleasant street. The sun seeped through the trees to sparkle lightly on well-tended green lawns in front of the white-frame and red-brick colonials that predominated on the Wishnetskys' block.

Richard's new home, two-story and square-faced in orange brick with tan trim and large shutterless windows, stood out as the only one of its design on the block; neat landscaping helped to give it a cheerful, open, and salutary appearance. Traffic on the street was light because Manor ended a few doors down from the Wishnetskys, at the Presentation playground. The public schools in the area had the reputation of being among the best in the city. Mr. Wishnetsky was only minutes away from the office where he took his new position in his father-in-law's insurance agency. His wife was back in her hometown among old and easily made new friends and only a short distance from her parents. The neighborhood was generally safe, quiet, and attractive. For the task of raising children while leading a comfortable, secure, and stable life, middle-class America seemed to offer little that was better.

Less than 4 percent of the three million people who were living in the metropolitan area at mid-century were Jewish, but researchers found that the number of Jews holding professional or white-collar jobs or who were self-employed was unproportionately high, that the Jewish median income was considerably higher than the non-Jewish, and that the educational level of the Jewish group was much higher than that of other groups.

Soon after Labor Day in that first September in Detroit, Richard began the sixth grade at Edward Alexander MacDowell School, three short blocks from his home. MacDowell was a large two-story orange-brick building which served over twelve hundred children in the primary grades, with thirty-five to thirty-eight youngsters in each of its neon-lit classrooms. That first day Richard sat in a homeroom class composed almost entirely of Jewish children; there were only one or two non-Jews evident as Miss Carvener called the roll. As she neared the end, she called, "Richard . . ." then paused for a second, whereupon Richard announced loudly, "It's *Wish* and *net* and *sky.*"

Phyllis Carvener, an experienced teacher with a good reputation among former students, recalls Richard quite vividly: "He was a very bubbly, friendly, outgoing little boy. Extremely eager in the classroom, really dying to answer questions, with legs and arms all going in different directions in the attempt to get my attention so he would be allowed to answer. I used to kid him about not being able to talk without his flamboyant arm gesturing."

Richard had Miss Carvener in homeroom for math, English, Spanish, and spelling, for about half of each school day. To her he seemed happy, affectionate, and bright, but he was only one in a group of very precocious children: "I thought there were others in the class who were brighter than he. But he was so eager! He would rush to get an answer out of his mouth and fall all over his tongue, which was quite comical at times. Then he would have to slow down to get the answer out."

Richard's classmates were grinding their own lenses for telescopes, reading widely on their own, and doing a considerable amount of outside work; a number of them were over the twelfth-grade reading level and could not be charted properly. To some extent many were allowed to work on their own and at their own pace in the classroom. Students who skipped a half or a full grade were not uncommon at MacDowell. Miss Carvener recalls: "I didn't think of Richard as a particularly creative child, at least not in my terms. . . . I had a number of kids writing stories and doing creative writing of sorts, but Richard didn't contribute this kind of thing. He seemed to learn effortlessly. He did seem to find it difficult to accept mistakes, but I never had any trouble with him, and he appeared to be comfortable with the other kids in the group."

One recurring episode in the classroom involved Richard's sister, Terry, then in the second grade at MacDowell. Says Miss Carvener: "She was a very cute, chubby-cheeked little girl and she used to come into our room every so often with a message for her big brother. The class would stop when Terry came in to announce that she had something to tell Richard, and everyone would wait and listen as she went down the aisle to her brother's desk to say something like, 'Richard, Mamma wants you to stop at the grocery store and buy a loaf of bread.' Richard would suffer through all of this patiently, knowing that everyone was watching and smiling or laughing a bit."

Richard's parents took an active interest in his progress in school and along with Mr. and Mrs. Hordes, Richard's grandparents, came to an open house that first year at MacDowell. They were told their son's work was always well done and on time, that he was good-natured and had a very special enthusiasm. Says Miss Carvener: "I expected the very best things for Richard. I found really no hint at all of future trouble. There were a number of kids at the time who were disturbed, some of them seeing psychiatrists, and once in a while someone would break into tears in the classroom. I remember vaguely tears of frustration coming to Richard on a couple of occasions, but it was certainly nothing out of the ordinary."

Miss Carvener liked Richard very much. Testimony from his

friends indicates that he was very fond of Miss Carvener, which perhaps helps to explain why he took great pleasure in teaching his teacher. "Richard corrected me in class on one or two occasions and got a terrific boot out of it," recalls Miss Carvener. "I tried to answer with humor, saying something like, 'Well, that's the first mistake I ever made in my life.' But I remember distinctly the excited timbre of his voice as he corrected me."

Julie Lieberman (pseud.) is a pretty, brown-haired and brown-eyed wife and mother now, and must have been a petite and attractive girl of eleven or so when she met Richard for the first time in the sixth grade. Their acquaintance began in class and on their walks home from school and became a lifelong friendship. Julie still has a photograph of Richard and her, taken during his first year in Detroit at a class picnic or summer outing. In the picture Richard is a skinny little boy in white short-sleeved shirt and short pants, his thin right arm nestled firmly—and, it seems, rather proudly—around Julie, who appears to be enduring the momentary possession quite stoically.

Julie remembers that Richard didn't always get along with his other teachers as well as he did with Miss Carvener. In particular there was a sixth-grade science teacher who had considerable difficulty with him; Richard was always wisecracking and chatting in his classroom. Once Richard presented a class report which apparently went rather thoroughly into some technical detail on the subject of atom smashing. When Richard had finished, however, the teacher remarked, "What kind of report is that? No one can understand it." To which Richard replied haughtily, gesturing to his classmates, "Well, these people can understand it. You're just too stupid to understand it." The man promptly marched him down to the principal's office and demanded that Richard be removed from his classroom. The Wishnetskys were called and informed of their son's behavior before he was allowed to return to the class.

According to Julie, Richard's good sense of humor and ready laugh made him well liked among his classmates, though he had few close friends outside of school. Often finishing an assignment ahead of time in class, he was easily bored and would constantly talk with those around him, sometimes getting himself into trouble. Though serious, he was very outgoing, not at all shy or introverted, always in love with conversation.

He and Julie would talk on the way home from school or during the summer, and were soon great pals. They often talked about school and their families; Richard described his grandfathers and said he liked both of them very much. Julie and his other classmates were sure he was going to become a scientist. She remembers walking home one day while Richard explained, for her educational benefit, what he said was Einstein's theory of relativity.

As are most youngsters at the strange and inconclusive age of twelve, Richard was in a great hurry to grow up. In the summer following his first year at MacDowell he was given a birthday party prepared by his mother in their home. A number of classmates and friends were invited, both boys and girls, including Julie. "Perhaps it was a bit too formal." she recalls, "arranged with candles on the table for a kind of grown-up dinner party." Richard was apparently under the impression that his mother and all other adults would disappear once the party got under way, but this didn't happen. He got very upset because his mother would not leave them alone, finally broke into tears, and left in some humiliation for his bedroom. He remained there crying until someone managed to persuade him to come back down and join the party.

But Julie also remembers lighter moments. One Saturday afternoon in the seventh grade, the two of them went to the movies, a matinee at the Royal Theater. Richard always loved the movies and in later years became an addicted cinemaphile who might experience a particular film as a highly significant event. No larger importance seems attached to this one, however—a typical matinee billing dramatizing the quaint Hollywood horror of various unfortunate people who grew into giant pea pods, or vice versa. Julie became thoroughly terrified and decided to sit on the floor under her seat. Richard, however, enjoyed himself immensely, laughing and teasing her throughout. Years later they would often refer to this episode and share giggles.

When Richard and his classmates moved on to the seventh grade at MacDowell, they were instructed in English and history by Mrs. Jeanne Harris, a calm and experienced teacher with adolescent children of her own. What Phyllis Carvener had to say about Richard and his mates is echoed by Mrs. Harris with some elaboration:

"Richard was not by any means the brightest boy in the class. Many of these Jewish children were brilliant, but also very nervous, uneasy, and at times very emotional. Richard was all these things and not at all unique . . . quite typical, in fact.

"At times these youngsters were difficult to work with, but generally Richard was a delightful boy and very pleasant to have in the classroom. Some of the boys, including Richard, could be disruptive, drumming on desks, doing a lot of fidgeting, a lot of visiting and talking with their neighbors. Sometimes parents were called in to help settle a child down.

"Mrs. Wishnetsky was very proud of Richard and very interested in his progress. Most of these children were intensely competitive and generally pushed by parents who were most concerned that their children achieve a very high level of success in their schoolwork."

The children often set their own standard in the classroom, and many of them forced their teacher to move ahead more quickly with the material at hand, to attempt projects that she would not ordinarily consider. MacDowell was generally a good school, according to Mrs. Harris, primarily because of the caliber of its students and because of the interest exhibited by their parents.

For Mrs. Harris, Richard was extremely industrious and always prepared. He handled himself well in the classroom and was very vocal. As in Miss Carvener's class, some of the brighter pupils were allowed to proceed on their own at times in small groups, and Richard could run a group effectively. Good-natured and fun-loving, according to Mrs. Harris he related well to his classmates but didn't seem very interested in girls. The teacher concluded:

"Richard was certainly not as creative as some of the others. But he was very well read for his age and brought a lot of background information to the discussions we had in class. He seemed very interested in government and politics, which is a bit unusual at this stage. He was very good verbally, could stand on his feet and express himself and did so often, but I can't remember anything he wrote."

Walking home one afternoon from school, Richard, as he was very apt to do, struck up a conversation with a fellow student. The boy was a grade ahead at MacDowell and, like Julie, would become a long-term friend. The boys discovered they lived a few blocks from one another and had mutual friends; they were soon into a discussion which continued off and on for the next dozen or so years. "We were sort of budding intellectuals even then," says Fred Baskin. "We would talk a lot, I'd go over to play Ping-Pong at his house, and the friendship struck up."

Fred Baskin is a second-generation Jew of less than medium height and slight build, with wavy brown hair over a high forehead and a goatee which gives him a pleasant, slightly devilish air. He has learned well, as have most in the group of young intellectuals of which Richard became more or less a part, the subtler techniques of youthful debate—the sweeping, dazzling display of jargon, the frequent and casual reference to the makers of intellectual history, the furrowed frown of mild contempt or the odd blank stare of incomprehension as an opponent struggles for the right word. This is Fred speaking about his friend:

"In grade school Richard was an easily piqued person (quite normally and properly so I thought at the time), very enthusiastic, crude, extroverted, intellectual, sensitive, and unhappy, particularly with his family (especially his father), religion, and a number of other things. I wouldn't say he was *extraordinarily* unhappy, but there were a number of things he didn't like and was very open to say he didn't like.

"Once he got to know me better he had no qualms about talking about personal things like his family. The important thing is that he had no reluctance whatsoever to say reasonably cynical things about his likes, dislikes, and beliefs. We were all forming our opinions at that time, and I'd say he was much more idealistic even than I and very unhappy with what evidence of nonidealism he found. He was no martyr or saint himself, and would fully admit faults and inadequacies in himself."

If Richard did in fact feel disaffection toward his family it would seem to have been linked on the surface to what Fred calls "evidence of nonidealism," and as such not uncommon. If one has grown up denouncing the values of one's parents, one has indeed traveled a well-beaten path. Yet youthful idealism seems never before to have been so thoroughly self-conscious, so often analyzed, romanticized, and in a certain sense prescribed. Frequently the very terms of genuine approval applied to Richard's parents by their many friends and acquaintances became terms of derision in the mouths of Richard and some of his friends.

Having married relatively young and because of wartime disruption, the Wishnetskys were not college-educated; included in their wide circle of friends, however, are a number of professional people, doctors, lawyers, judges, and city officials. Their tastefully decorated home on Manor had walls hung with original oils and shelves lined with the best books of the day. Community organizations often claim the Wishnetskys as active members, and the family has continued the philanthropic activity of Richard's grandparents.

Evelyn Wishnetsky is described by friends as a petite and attractive woman, gracious, tactful, and culturally aware, with a pleasant ability to make people comfortable by doing and saying what is socially called-for. She is well liked and popular, always well dressed in a tasteful and understated fashion, active in social, cultural, and religious work in the community, and described as very devoted to her children. "Richard," said one of his longtime friends, "was the apple of his mother's eye."

Mr. Wishnetsky, known to his friends as Eddie, is a man of imposing physique. With a reputation for being an impeccable dresser, his clothes are perfectly cut by a personal tailor, his appearance invariably immaculate. Said one acquaintance, "You sense that he judges others by the same standards of appearance he sets for himself." He is also described as a proud man not given to displays of feeling or emotion, who loves to relax in the semiprivate solitude of the golf course. At times direct and blunt in his speech, he is also known as a genial host and convivial wit, "a great punster who loves to play with words." Thought of as stubborn, intelligent, practical, and successful in business, Mr. Wishnetsky is pictured by some friends as a strong personality with perhaps a touch of the cynic. He was always very proud of Richard during his son's exceptional progress through school and was very apt to describe for a friend Richard's latest achievement. At the same time a firm disciplinarian of the old school, he apparently found it rather difficult to express or demonstrate this pride to his son.

The antagonism that developed between them was evident to many of Richard's closer friends. It likely had long-standing and unconscious roots, though its surface appearance was that of the almost classic confrontation of the hard-boiled, practical father and the sensitive, idealistic son. One of Richard's young intellectual pals who was often in the Wishnetsky home on Manor and who naturally sided with Richard recalls:

"Richard's father was the paradigm of the relatively intelligent and successful businessman. There was a good life which involved being only so conventional that your society would respect you and allow you to make money. And I'm sure he would have liked his son to be successful in some broad sense so he could be proud of him. Yet he wouldn't have been particularly proud for his son to become a Nobel Prize-winning author. The mother had a little of that mystique, hoping that her son would rise above the merchant class, but the father definitely didn't. He wouldn't even indicate hope that his son would be successful in business. I don't know, I never quite plumbed the full antagonism between them.

"The mother generally stood as a buffer between father and son. Richard always considered her a fence-sitter and thought she wouldn't stick up for him. And, of course, he was always unhappy about just how middle-class she was and about the very role she played. She believed very strongly that you never ask a question which would make anybody feel bad or antagonize them, and this bothered him."

There are contradictions, exaggerations, and unwarranted assumptions here, but these are to be expected. Complete accuracy isn't to be supposed from one who likely received only Richard's complaints and probably had less access to happier moments in the home. Yet if the details sound rather petty and commonplace, the situation was nonetheless real and troubling for Richard and his parents.

According to Fred Baskin, Richard had not yet decided what he wanted to be: "One of his principle interests then was science (astronomy, physics), but then for any of us kids who were intelligent, science was always connected with intelligence, never the humanities or social sciences at all; we were given this prejudice that intelligence was almost equated with being a scientist. We were also, however, beginning to read the newspaper for the first time. That was about the only nonscience intellectual thing anyone was interested in besides religion; even at that time I can remember us discussing the major events of the times."

Richard told Fred that he did not enjoy going to synagogue and resented going to Hebrew school for his Bar Mitzvah training. "He was very impressed," says Fred, "with the fact that I wasn't going to Hebrew school and was not going to have a Bar Mitzvah. It shook him up a little. His reasons were probably typical—he would have rather gone home after school at MacDowell and played catch or whatever. I became a profound atheist in about the seventh grade, and for Richard this was something new. When we would argue about religion, he for the first time found himself acting as the God-advocate and, I'm sure, found himself very unused to the role. Since he was not doing very well, he finally retreated to the position that one must have complete skepticism on all religious views with the possible exception of the existence of God. And he was pretty sure that an anthropomorphic God was ruled out. We more or less left it at that until we addressed the issue again later in high school."

The attitudes and ideas that any single witness may attribute to Richard cannot, of course, be automatically accepted. At one time or another most of us are apt to color the expression of our opinions to effect a favorable response. A remark from Richard that might please Julie Lieberman (for example, how highly he thought of his grandparents) might call forth only scorn if uttered in front of his young, rough-and-ready intellectual friends. In any case it will occasionally seem important to wonder why Richard said what to whom.

The discussions and arguments between Richard and Fred contained an element never really spoken of, but which took on increasing importance as their relationship developed: "There were a number of semicomic aspects to our arguments. I never took Richard seriously intellectually, and neither did any of my friends. When we got together in a group, he was someone whom you put your tongue in your cheek with. You know, a good stout fellow, but nobody really paid any attention to him. Though for all that I would always say that he was an extremely intelligent fellow."

Some of the friction between Richard and his parents perhaps involved the resentment he apparently felt over his Hebrew school experience. For an hour and a half each Monday through Thursday after classes at MacDowell, Richard attended one of the afternoon schools on Seven Mile Road where training normally covers four or five years and is primarily aimed at the Bar Mitzvah performance. Religious customs and ceremonies are examined, but primary emphasis is placed on language study to enable students to read the Torah in Hebrew. One of Richard's friends who shared the experience remarked, "It was a place generally for fun and games. Kids didn't feel that bad about attending them, because most of your friends were Jewish and attending with you. A great many go to Hebrew school for those first five years, but you don't really have time to learn the language and get a solid foundation."

Along with his previous Yiddish school study in the Bronx, Richard had two years of religious instruction in Detroit before the Sabbath preceding his thirteenth birthday, the time traditionally established for the Bar Mitzvah ceremony. The ritual took place at the synagogue of Conservative Congregation Avas Achim just off Seven Mile Road and a half mile from the Wishnetsky home. Rabbi Adler, with whom William Hordes, Richard's grandfather, had been friends for years, and Congregation Shaarey Zedek, Detroit's most prominent Conservative congregation, might have been the Wishnetskys' choice, but Shaarey Zedek required at least four years of instruction. The choice of Avas Achim was made because William Hordes was a member of the congregation and also because Avas Achim, apparently in this case at least, did not require four or more years of religious training. Thus, Richard pronounced his Jewish manhood, reading from the Torah, chanting from the Prophets, and announcing his dedication to the highest ideals of his faith as a responsible Bar Mitzvah ("man of duty").

The Bar Mitzvah experience is intended to promote a meaningful Jewish identity, and this is part of the reason that the ceremony has held such great importance for many American Jewish parents, particularly at a time of much talk about a breakdown of Jewish continuity after thousands of perilous years. "We've managed to survive centuries of privation and persecution," begins the standard cry. "But how are we going to keep them interested and committed when they're sitting in the lap of affluence and security?" For many Jewish families the occasion calls for much proud celebration at a large party after the ceremony. The young man is feted and often presented with gifts to the extent that he may still be dipping into his "Bar Mitzvah money" a decade later upon leaving college. The gaudy extravagance of some such parties has been widely noted, but the Wishnetskys reportedly held an evening reception at home for their son—nothing extraordinary. Still Richard may have quarreled with what he considered the materialistic trappings of a supposedly spiritual event for which in any case he had no strong concern or feeling.

In distinct contrast to his first two homeroom teachers at MacDowell, the woman who played a similar role in Richard's eighth-grade year had only slight memory of him: "Really I don't remember much about him except that he was bright and that he wasn't as pleasant to have in class as some of the others."

Near the end of Richard's last term at MacDowell, the eighth-grade class held a series of elections and contests. The results were published in the graduation edition of the school newspaper, a modest mimeographed enterprise begun the year before by Miss Carvener with Fred Baskin as its first editor. Richard was the newspaper's second editor and also a member of the election committee. Julie Lieberman, much to her delight at the time, won the contest for the cherished title of the class's Prettiest Girl. Later, however, Richard informed her that she owed him a debt of gratitude, since he had stuffed the ballot box for her. Julie recalls with a smile, "I felt very badly at that point and wished he hadn't told me."

Most appropriately Richard himself was elected Junior Professor and the Most Talkative Boy in Class. In the list of eighth-grade class honors, Richard was mentioned as a member of the Graduation Song and Dance Committees and an alternate on the Student Council. The newspaper also published prophecies for individual members of the class. "Richard Wishnetsky," his classmates predicted at that time, "will be the first person to fly to the moon in an atom bomb."

Couched in typical eighth-grade frivolity, the prophecy, according to Julie, refers to the expectation that Richard's major scholastic interest would lead him to become some kind of space scientist. But perhaps someone also saw something more in Richard's future: a commitment to the highest of human aspirations which carried with it an inevitably unhappy fate.

Richard had received many A's on his MacDowell report cards and left most of his teachers with the reputation of having that rare combination of talent and enthusiastic industry. The Joseph Faumans, who lived across the street from the Wishnetskys and also had a son at MacDowell, recall Mrs. Wishnetsky describing Richard at that time as "very moody, introspective, and unpredictable"; she worried sometimes about his violent fits of temper. At least a couple of teachers at MacDowell had found him a gloomy, sharp-tongued little personage whom they wouldn't particularly miss, but others like Miss Carvener and Mrs. Harris thought highly of Richard and followed his progress through the rest of his academic career.

THREE

A Jewish child growing up in a predominately Jewish area, with Jews for most of his friends and acquaintances, may reach college before he ever encounters what he would characterize as an anti-Semitic episode. Then again he may not.

For example, one day late in the summer after his graduation from MacDowell, Richard Wishnetsky was playing tennis with a newly made friend named David Roth (pseud.) on the courts at Mumford High School where they would soon be starting the ninth grade. Richard loved to play tennis; it was one of the few modes of relaxation he ever allowed himself and he would continue to play the game throughout his years in school and college. Many of his friends report playing tennis with him and most agree that he was a pretty fair match, making up with speed, endurance, and enthusiastic effort what he lacked in style, form, and coordination.

"Richard was a very exuberant and vociferous player," recalls David, "running all over the court, shouting and cheering good shots. Finally someone in the adjacent court, a fellow older than we were, started mocking Richard and his style and making anti-Semitic remarks. Richard stopped and got into an enormous argument with the fellow about Jews and anti-Semitism. That's the first real memory I have of Richard."

From the start at Mumford, David remembers Richard as a very outgoing and bold young man who always had something to say and never hung back from saying it. "He was loud and argumentative at times and had heated discussions in class, especially with teachers, some of whom thought him a challenge and recognized him as the sharpest kid in the class. They liked to provoke him into a running battle."

But Richard needed no provoking. Julie Lieberman, who moved on to Mumford along with most of Richard's other classmates at

MacDowell, recalls, "Richard was always reading extra material, and he always seemed to make it a kind of contest between himself and whatever teacher he had." He seemed particularly bent on showing up his teachers and, according to Julie, managed to do so occasionally. He always wanted to exhibit his extra work, asking numerous questions, adding point after point to those made by the teacher. If the teacher brought up another author, Richard invariably had something to say about him and three or four others he would throw in at the same time.

Richard was now attending a school larger than many colleges. At the time, Samuel C. Mumford High had nearly 4,500 students, 75 percent of whom were Jewish. About the same percentage (twice the national average) were headed for college, for Mumford was then generally recognized as the finest high school in the city. Or as Fred Baskin puts it, "Ten percent of the people there were worthwhile as opposed to the 2 percent in other schools."

Utilizing an area of five city blocks, the large and unattractive three-story building in blue and gray is set back from Wyoming Avenue (about a mile and a half from the city limits on the north); in front is a lot used for driver training, and in the back are large athletic fields. Directly across Wyoming at the time stood the Hordes Agency owned by Richard's grandfather and operated in part by his father.

About a third of the teachers at Mumford were Jewish, and one of these, a man who has taught at the school for over fifteen years, talked about a shift in student attitudes which had occurred shortly before Richard's arrival. Formerly students had been working primarily for grades, he thought, with little real concern for learning:

"These kids were primarily the children of upper-middle-class and well-to-do families, and the change came when more lower-class and middle-class people moved into the area. These middle-class kids, like the others predominately Jewish, were both bright and ambitious and were concerned with learning and really bettering themselves. As a result the school changed much for the better. There was a lot of competition among the kids, but the ambitions were generally good and so was the competition, which was stimulating and not stifling. There were few awards, rankings, or special prizes given to students so the motivation was primarily internal."

Richard's classmates generally agree that the atmosphere at

Mumford was intensely competitive, but also maintain that for most students, grades were still of primary importance as the index of success in competition. Still there seems to have been some real political, social, and intellectual awareness at Mumford, probably not to be found in most American high schools of the fifties.

Fred Baskin talks about his fellow Mumfordites: "Everybody was going into one or another of the professions that paid off. A few were going into business, but they were really no more materialistic than those going into medicine, for example—just a little slower.

"Very few people from the wealthier third-generation homes wanted to do more than their fathers had done. That was one of our pet theories. Richard and I used to talk about the third- versus second-generation complex. With the third-generation kid, if the father was a doctor, the kid guessed he also would be a doctor. And the kid whose father was a successful businessman sort of figured that he would get a college education and probably take over the business when his father died. So this was something Richard and I were very critical of, since we very much believed in the Protestant ethic and that people who were bright should train themselves to the fullest of their abilities and should go out and be as creative as possible.

"I used to call Richard a paradox because I didn't think he fit into my theory about second- versus third-generation kids. Originally I had explained it all in terms of economic insecurity, but Richard disagreed and added a refinement. He pointed out that the concept should be broadened to include people who were insecure for any number of reasons. Obviously even a twelfth-generation Anglo-Saxon Protestant who was ugly and unpopular might get some recognition in school and become an intellectual out of that motivation. Richard was always well organized and enthusiastic about his study . . . very worried about doing badly and very grade conscious."

At the time, Mumford was one of two or three schools in the city that had a Science and Arts program, a special honors curriculum with advanced work, and smaller classes for students who ranked in the top few percent of their class. Richard was not in this program but did take "pilot" courses for students selected by teachers as capable of dealing with "enriched" material. One of many extracurricular groups, the Current Affairs Club (of which

Richard became a member) met weekly to discuss political, economic, and social problems of the day and sponsored educational programs, such as mock elections and visits from area politicians.

"There were generally four groups at Mumford," said one of Richard's classmates. "The Jews from the wealthier neighborhoods east of Livernois [Avenue], the Jews [like Richard] from the middle-middle-class homes west of Livernois, a relatively small number of Gentile kids, and a scattering of Negroes. Dating among the Jews was generally along geographic lines. The class leaders mostly stuck to their own kind east of Livernois, and were marked most conspicuously by their cars and cashmere sweaters. There was a rumor going around about something called the Twenty Club, an exclusive collection of kids who supposedly owned twenty or more cashmere sweaters.

"There was little or no interaction between Jews and Gentiles except for some of the very bright Gentile kids who you sort of forgot were Gentiles. Most of the kids were liberal Democrats like their parents; a few said they were radicals but there were no 'beats' at Mumford at the time. The Jews certainly dominated the place, and on Rosh Hashanah and Yom Kippur the school almost closed down. They put classes together and had study halls."

According to the reports of most of Richard's friends, smoking, drinking, and sexual activity (at least sex that was talked about) were not common at Mumford; marihuana and drugs were virtually unknown. Said one girl: "You heard vague, somewhat unreal stories about someone who had been to bed with someone, and once a story about boys in a club who had supposedly hired the services of a girl. But generally nothing too wild was going on because the community was so cohesive and closely knit. Everybody's parents knew everybody else's parents and this generally acted as a kind of sentinel."

With heavy emphasis on social activities, academics, politics, and the arts, there was little room left for a concern with athletics. With the exception of a good football squad in Richard's junior year and a perennially strong tennis team, most of Mumford's athletic teams were marked by weakness or mediocrity, sparking little interest in the student body. As one of Richard's friends put it, "To be captain of the football team was to be virtually unknown."

Throughout his years at Mumford, Richard shared a locker with Julie Lieberman. As they had at MacDowell, Julie and Richard often walked home together after school; now the trip was over a mile. Their talks grew longer, deeper, and more personal, but though Richard cherished an idealistic love for Julie, according to Fred Baskin, their friendship remained quite platonic. She says:

"We dated once in a while when we were stuck for dates or when I wasn't going with someone, which I usually was. If we did go out, it was usually to the movies. He always studied very hard and always had all of his work done the day before an exam. Then he would tease me by saying, 'Hey, I'll take you to the show,' knowing, of course, that I had a lot more studying to do and wouldn't be able to go. He often did go to the movies the night before final exams. He said it relaxed him and he could think more clearly."

The only time Richard really seemed shy, says Julie, was in the presence of the opposite sex, particularly at parties. He told her once that he was afraid of being turned down by girls he might ask; actually he did very little dating before the twelfth grade. Though always neat and clean, he seemed more or less oblivious to the way he dressed, which was usually not in step with the latest fad. Often he'd wear the same clothes repeatedly. He was allergic to wool and in a school abounding in cashmere sweaters, Richard had perhaps one or two that his mother had lined for him.

Often on their walks home Julie and Richard would talk about the Jewish community, and often he was extremely critical of certain members and institutions. Some insist this particular perspective was fostered by his Grandfather Hordes, whom they describe as a critical and outspoken leader in the community. In any case Richard was ardently Jewish-minded, and in Julie's words, "He thought the Jews were the greatest people in the world, with the greatest accomplishments and achievements."

As for many Detroit Jews, however, he had decided they were nothing but show and extravagance. He was always concerned about what he deemed the hypocritical attitude of these people and was particularly upset by those who, he said, gave to charity just to see their names in the paper. Though Richard himself was not often one to shun the academic or intellectual spotlight, he rendered harsh judgment on anything materially pretentious or ostentatious. Says Julie, "We would often talk about other kids at Mumford with their flashy clothes and cars and how they showed off and tried to act important, and Richard of course disliked those people and could get upset about them."

There were times on their walks home and on other occasions when Richard gave the impression that he thought himself a brilliant and at least potentially important young man, perhaps marked for greatness. And there were subtle indications that he certainly didn't consider Julie and himself on equal ground and entertained the thought that he was quite superior to most everyone else he knew.

When Richard was in the tenth grade, a new family with a daughter in the same year at Mumford moved in near the Wishnetskys on Manor. Susie Goodman (pseud.) was a tall soft-spoken brunette with a shy awkward grace and a melancholy gaze in her large brown eyes. Not knowing anyone, she felt a bit strange in her new neighborhood for the first couple of weeks. She noticed a boy who lived a few houses down the street and learned something about him from her father, who knew that Mr. Hordes's grandson lived on the block. Seeing him walk down the street a number of times, she remarked on his peculiar, accentuated gait: those long, ambitious, almost aggressive strides of his, head bobbing a bit, all purpose—at times like a little boy straining to match the stride of a tall, swift-moving father, at other times carrying himself proudly in a free, open, and engaging way.

One day about two weeks after moving in, Susie found herself walking down her front walk at the same time Richard was walking down his. She recalls: "As we met, Richard said, 'Well, we might as well break the ice,' and introduced himself. He was really almost too nice for somebody in the tenth grade . . . extremely courteous and cordial . . . so adult and poised. From that point on I suppose I had a crush on Richard." Susie was "something of a loner" in high school, and if she had a crush on Richard she was the only one who knew about it. They played tennis once on the courts next to the Royal Theater but never really dated; every so often he would drop over to her house and talk, especially to her parents, whose conversation he seemed to enjoy.

People in the neighborhood generally liked Richard and thought him an intelligent, responsible, considerate boy—he seemed to have mellowed a bit in high school. The Fauman kids—the older boy and girl about the ages of Richard's sisters and the younger daughter a preschooler—found him "extremely nice." When the Faumans went out, they occasionally hired him as a baby-sitter for the children.

Not long after he started at Mumford, Richard made a series of new friends very quickly when he joined the Louis D. Brandeis A.Z.A. chapter of the B'nai B'rith Youth Organization. (The A.Z.A. for boys aged fourteen to twenty-one and its counterpart, B'nai B'rith Girls, together comprising over 32,000 Jewish young people, promote a concern with the meaning and preservation of Jewish identity.) There were about thirty boys in the Brandeis chapter—one of several at Mumford—who took active part in a program of athletics, religious seminars, dances, parties, oratorical and musical events, and charity projects.

As usual, Richard struck different people in the A.Z.A. in different ways. According to a number of reports, he was an amicable fellow member, who made friends easily and helped new members feel especially welcome. Several recall Richard as a good listener who seemed interested enough in others to give advice and counsel very freely. "You could talk personally with him about anything very easily," said one.

Another member, who years later got rather close to Richard, had a somewhat different view: "I first thought of Dick as rather insensitive and not particularly aware of other people . . . oblivious to what they might be doing or thinking. In fact I didn't think him that bright in high school—I thought his grades were probably the result of a lot of hard work and memorization. If Dick liked you he had to know all about you right away, asking rapid-fire questions about what you were doing, who your friends were. Sometimes I thought that his excessive interest might be a way of making up for his previous insensitivity when he'd been wrapped up in himself for some reason or other. Actually he was always something of an enigma. People didn't know quite how to take him and his intensity and his studiousness. As a result he faced a bit of ridicule once in a while."

The first time Richard introduced himself at a B.B.Y.O. city council session, one of his chapter friends at the meeting called out, "God bless you!" It was a standing joke among Richard's friends to react to the pronunciation of his surname as if it were a sneeze.

Effectively developing his verbal talents in various B.B.Y.O. contests, Richard quickly gained a reputation for his oratory. Thus, though rarely interested in running for office himself, he was much in demand to give nominating speeches for friends with such ambitions. At the same time, word quickly got to new members that Richard was to be avoided as a double-date partner. He wasn't much fun on a date. So intense and serious, he would only get into some kind of intellectual discussion and not let one relax and make time with one's date. Richard might insensitively exclude the girls or talk their heads off and scare them away. He just wasn't sexually aggressive, ran the warning, and maybe not really interested in girls at all.

Melvin Goldstein, who was president of the A.Z.A. city council in his senior year when Richard was a junior, remembers him as a constant champion of social and philanthropic causes, always presenting ideas at chapter meetings and council sessions. One project Richard got very excited about was the Peanuts for Polio campaign, and he wanted all Detroit area A.Z.A. members—a total of about four hundred—to go out and sell peanuts for money to be used in the fight against polio. As president Mel had to turn down Richard's proposal: "The rest of the group simply didn't get that enthusiastic about Richard's idea. It's not that the idea wasn't feasible—if everyone had felt as Richard did, we might have made a couple thousand dollars. But given the attitudes of most of the others it was unrealistic." Richard also got enthused about the Pennies for UNICEF program in which kids asked for donations on Halloween for the United Nations Children's Fund. When some high-ranking city officials came out publicly against the idea, saying it would spoil the kids' Halloween, Richard appeared before the Common Council of Detroit to defend the program and urge its endorsement. The fact that the UNICEF Halloween project has become something of a tradition in the city can perhaps be attributed in some small part to Richard's efforts.

Usually in his promotion of projects, however, there was a frustrating lack of success. Said Mel Goldstein, "After a while it became rather upsetting. Richard's earnestness and his passion for projects which did not enlist the favor of most of the others became almost painful to witness."

Yet many of his friends in the Brandeis chapter keep lists of "Richard stories," depicting him as a bit awkward, naïve, good-natured, and humorous. Richard could be amusing and fun to be around. Though without an abiding interest in sports, he would take part in an A.Z.A. softball game with great enthusiasm. Though he couldn't judge or catch a fly ball as well as some, he would always play center field because of his speed afoot, cavorting with a kind of reckless abandon. A typical Wishnetsky play involved a fly to center, Richard misjudging the ball badly but somehow racing to it in time for it to sail through his hands and hit him on the head, then bounce off and hit him on the arm before finally surrendering to his grasp.

Said a Brandeis member who was two years behind Richard at Mumford: "He could be uproariously funny. I remember a statewide convention in Detroit at Christmas time during his senior year when they held a mixer and a square dance. There was a group of four or five of us including Richard, all dressed in western outfits. We were supposed to be the leaders of the convention, but we acted silly all evening; we hadn't been drinking but we acted like it. . . . One of the fellows was blowing a whistle all night, and afterward Richard was driving very recklessly one hand or no hands on the wheel, going eighty miles an hour down the left side of Seven Mile Road. A car full of laughing, screaming convention leaders and Richard was right in the middle of it."

FOUR

In a tenth-grade history course at Mumford, Richard constantly contended with his teacher, a man in the habit of asking extremely esoteric questions. Said one girl: "I think they both had a lot of respect for each other, but their exchanges could get a bit heated. Richard usually did answer his questions, much to the man's chagrin, it seemed at times."

At Mumford, as had been the case at MacDowell, there were times when he could be anything but docile in the classroom. At least one incident occurred when Richard became enraged by a point a teacher made in a lecture and began arguing the issue effectively—or at least vociferously—enough to get the man upset. The teacher dismissed him from class and reportedly asked for his suspension from school.

Generally, however, Richard's experience with eleventh-grade

English teacher Mrs. Jane Morris seems to have been more typical. She remembers Richard as a "young man concerned about hypocrisy in the world." Of course, she says, many young people are very concerned about hypocrisy and find it very difficult to come to terms with—"it's one of their favorite themes. But this was particularly so with Richard.

"He was a boy you warmed to quite naturally. He was eager and responsive and you couldn't help but enjoy having him in your classroom. I wouldn't say he was the brightest student I ever had, but he was a fine student always with his assignments prepared and an intelligent comment to make. He seemed most interested in philosophy and certainly had read well beyond what most kids are familiar with at that stage."

Richard once told Mrs. Morris that he wanted very much to go to Israel, to live there, and to share in the pioneering work involved in the development of the new nation. He also spoke enthusiastically about the diplomatic service, but told Mrs. Morris at one point he was afraid that, being Jewish, he would have little opportunity to win any sort of advance or promotion even if he did manage to enter the field. Mrs. Morris suggested he write to Russell Barnes, a foreign news analyst for the Detroit *News,* who had responded helpfully to letters from some of her former students. Richard apparently took the advice; later he informed Mrs. Morris that he had received a letter from Barnes, who maintained that being a Jew was not necessarily a drawback in the foreign service.

"Some time before the end of the year," says Mrs. Morris, "I told Richard that I was recommending him for the pilot English course for his senior year. I was surprised that Richard wasn't in Science and Arts and I thought he must have missed out on the program because of some error or unfortunate circumstance when he took the tests. When I told Richard, he thanked me very much and was very polite, but said he was going to turn it down, because he felt the system was undemocratic, and he didn't feel he should be set apart in an elite group to receive special treatment."

Ron Burns, who shared an interest in the foreign service with Richard maintains that in the three-, four-, and five-cornered discussions he had with Richard, Fred Baskin, and others, "Fred was often out to put Richard down; in turn Richard patronized me, and I in turn was always out to vindicate myself. In those arguments, Richard was always a very intense and bellicose young man . . . an intellectual roughneck."

According to Larry Bernstein, another who sat in on these battles, Richard was well known as a peculiar kind of personality and rigidly idealistic scholar. "When he read Plato's *Republic* in high school," said Larry, "it became a kind of bible for him, almost a divine book. Richard was referred to in our group as 'Jesus Christ' because he would go to any length to defend his idealism. He'd make no concession to personalities. For example, Baskin would play rock 'n' roll music and Richard would protest violently and insist we listen to classical."

In the opinion of Ron Burns, "Richard tended to live off someone like Fred. In fact I would say that Richard was in awe of Fred and owed Fred for having shaped his ideas in high school." Baskin himself says, "Richard always considered me quite a bit brighter than himself, which wasn't the case. If anything he was a bit more intelligent than I. It was just that I was a year older and a little less orthodox and therefore able to do a little better in an argument."

In high school the two had become much closer friends, and there were periods of months when they would see each other daily, almost always in the recreation room of Richard's home. They would talk or argue until late at night, literally until they were both hoarse, breaking off only once in a while for a quick game of Ping-Pong. Their discussions now ranged from sex and dating to God and politics, and Richard's thinking was abstract, idealistic, and usually derived from his books. Not having read as widely or as deeply, Fred simply took up political or philosophical questions as they might occur to him:

"Of course I was very arrogant and very quick to come to opinions without having read anything, whereas he had a tendency to be extremely impressed by whatever he had last read and to answer everything in terms of it. It was a standing joke between Ron and I that we could always tell what Richard had just read after talking with him for five minutes on any subject, the classic case being the time I correctly predicted he had read *The Ugly American* even though I hadn't and we were discussing the weather or something." As to the substance of their talks, here's Fred again:

On politics: "His politics were always what I would call 'Leftist Reasonable' as opposed to some people who were much more radical. He was like most of us, sort of a Roosevelt leftist. Civil rights had not yet crept into people's consciences, except that needless to say we had no prejudices about anything racial or national. We were all a little unhappy about nationalism as such. We all felt some sort of responsibility by the U. S. to correct all sorts of evils in the world.

"I can remember going to one socialist meeting late in high school and the two of us coming away about equally satisfied that this was an older generation of sixty-five-year-olds who were not likely to produce any significant social change. Nor were their arguments, nor their ideas, nor their reasoning power particularly impressive . . . it was just an experiment for us to see what these people were like."

On religion and Israel: "As we became a bit more sophisticated about religion in high school, Richard became a Transcendentalist because we all read *Walden* and Emerson. When pressed he said he had pretty much settled on belief in a nonanthropomorphic God—he could discuss this with a little more language now—and that he only had a literary interest in all of the rest of conventional religion. There were some good ideas there—Christ had a few, Moses had a few—but he saw little value in—in fact, was pretty antagonistic toward—orthodox religion merely because he considered it a waste of time which would be better spent reading books.

"Actually Richard always had some respect for Orthodox Judaism, for those in Judaism who really kept the faith. We always argued that in the various levels of hell, obviously those who pretend to be religious and aren't are the worst; at that time I think we agreed that those who thought they weren't and weren't were the best. But at least these old Orthodox people have to be considered, though perhaps a bit to be humored, really a pretty good class of people.

"We always considered it a positive that one should work hard in Israel and build a nation, but we always tended to ignore the fact that Israel was Jewish. This was a beautiful social experiment. One of the reasons for his liking Israel was that it seemed to break the stereotyped image of the intellectual Jew. This was the only thing about him which made him antiintellectual, his feeling that these people should get out and experience life."

On sex and dating: "He would ask for advice on intellectual things, but I can never remember him asking for advice on anything personal. I remember arguing about sex, both of us arguing that premarital sex was immoral and giving a number of sociopsychological reasons to rationalize this. But he took this right down the line to say therefore all forms of necking and petting were strictly immoral. And I argued no, there was a qualitative as well as quantitative difference there. His dating was limited in part by his disdain for the relatively materialistic people who were around him. But there were a few kindred souls around, and these girls he dated."

One girl Richard apparently viewed as a "kindred soul" was Debbie Rossman (pseud.), a small and comely brunette with large dark eyes and pretty face and figure. In the words of one of Richard's friends, "Debbie was considered one of the sexiest prizes available; she was much sought after by all the conventional class leaders and very heavily dated. I was rather shocked that he was going out with her."

To Debbie, Richard was a very warm, well-mannered, and gentle young man, all of which she appreciated: "I think each of us at the time reinforced the image we wanted to have of ourselves. I suppose I liked being treated with reverence for the softness and purity and everything Richard thought I was." Debbie was almost always going steady with someone else, though once in a while, at a time when it seemed to matter greatly whom you were seen with, she would work in dates with Richard. Some of her friends considered him rather a "square," an "egghead," very naïve, and out of the social whirl. Yet when Mumford's big Snowball Dance arrived, Richard was Debbie's escort. They danced to the slow music and sat out the fast, and friends on both sides were generally confounded.

"Richard was so skinny back then," recalls Debbie. "But I still remember the quality of his voice . . . very calm and pleasing and soft. He was always very concerned about prettiness, always wanting me to be as pretty as possible when I was out with him, and taking the trouble to make sure my scarf was just so. At the most we might have kissed good night once or twice, but he always wanted to hold my hand. And his hand was always on your shoulder or your waist guiding you around."

They used to talk at length, and often their subject was "great men," what it takes to be one and whether a woman could achieve greatness. Richard enjoyed teasing Debbie about being a female, who might contribute to a man's greatness but of course wouldn't be able to achieve the quality herself. As for his own prospects, he seemed to have a firm notion that he was destined for some sort of eminence. They also discussed the teen-age couple's favorite topics:

"He was very idealistic about sex and love and marriage . . . very clear on the idea that he was going to be a virgin when he got married, and he expounded on the beauty of the situation in which both partners are virgins before marriage. I hadn't thought much about that possibility for myself, but the idea sounded pretty good when he talked about it.

"One time later Richard came to me extremely upset and said that he had heard that I had been sleeping with boys, that I was no longer a virgin. And he began to lecture me intensely. I finally had to talk a long time to convince him that I really was still a virgin. I think he finally was convinced, but always after that I had a very vague feeling that somehow Richard considered me something of a tramp no matter what."

As he had in previous summers, between his junior and senior years at Mumford Richard spent eight weeks at Camp Farband, a secular summer camp founded as the first Jewish camp in the state by a group of sponsors which included Richard's Grandfather Hordes more than forty years ago and owned and operated by the Labor Zionist Institute in Detroit. Occupying 132 acres, the campsite is set in a scenic wooded and rolling area of southeastern Michigan about an hour and a half from Detroit. In the early years there were classes in Yiddish and Jewish music, literature, and drama, but as the decades passed the Zionist and Jewish emphases diminished. When Emanuel Mark (Richard's former teacher at the Workmen's Circle School in the Bronx) took over as director in 1957, he placed more emphasis on the more typical camp activities of athletics, hiking, swimming, boating, and horseback riding.

About 150 campers (ages five to fifteen) were accommodated; boys and girls were segregated in a dozen or so white sideboard cabins in a U-shaped arrangement around a center flagpole and facing the large white barnlike structure which included an ample dining hall, kitchen facilities, and offices. The camp was proud of its much better than typical camp food, and Richard, though skinny, was known at Farband as a good eater.

In the summer of 1959 Richard celebrated his seventeenth birthday at camp; since his arrival a week earlier, he had been employed in one of his first paying jobs as a junior counselor. He was assigned to a cabin presided over by senior counselor Henry Shevitz, whom he had first met at Farband in 1950 when both were eight-year-old campers (Richard having come all the way from the Bronx for the summer).

Richard had also been assigned to Henry the year before as a counselor-in-training. Henry, who was a half year older but a full year ahead of Richard at Mumford and a rung higher on the ladder of authority at camp, remembered that Richard had seemed to resent Henry's superior position. Now the resentment seemed closer to the surface, and during their first two weeks together there was almost constant bickering and a number of disagreements over how to discipline the boys in their cabin. On Richard's first day off, Henry arranged to have him transferred out of the cabin and got himself another junior counselor. That evening Henry led his group on a hike, and they were sitting around a campfire when Richard returned to learn the news. Says Henry: "He controlled himself and wasn't angry, but he was disappointed. It was kind of a dirty trick, but for the rest of the time at camp we got along a little better. And he seemed to do all right with the other fellow he was under."

When Emanual Mark moved from New York to Detroit, he took a position with the Labor Zionist Institute and assumed direction of the camp along with his wife, Naomi, a pleasant and vivacious woman who "grew up at Camp Farband" because her father was a former director. Both of the Marks remember Richard, though not unpopular, as never having many close friends at camp. "Richard was something of a braggart," said Mr. Mark, and in his description of Richard is a hint of the antagonism that marked Richard's relations with some of his male teachers:

"He seemed to have a very strong ego. Sometimes he was just plain overbearing, very argumentative, always pouring a million facts at you. You never had a discussion with Richard or a conversation; it was always an argument or a lecture. The friends he did have were all somewhat the same way. No weak egos in that group! They were all pretty sharp kids, all very bright, talented, and successful. Richard was by no means the sharpest of the bunch."

The camp's caretaker, Brad Mason (pseud.), was a tall black-haired man from Kentucky; in his forties, he vaguely resembles Fess Parker. You don't notice any stiffness about him until he tells you that he lost a leg a few years back as the result of a tractor accident. The machine turned over on him one day, breaking his leg; later when an infection set in, Brad spent a year in the hospital and was visited by Richard and many of the other campers and counselors he had befriended.

"Every time he looked at you he had a smile on his face," recalls Brad. "He was such a friendly kid even though he seemed to stay clear of everybody. But Richard liked me and I liked him, and we used to walk around this place all the time and point things out to one another like the trees and birds and animals. I remember one time I started to recite this poem by William Cullen Bryant called 'Thanatopsis.' He was really surprised and he said, 'Brad, how did you learn that?' and I said, 'Since Bryant took so long to write it, I thought the least I could do was to sit down and learn it.' 'Gee,' he said, 'that must be awful hard. I don't think I could do it.' But the next summer Richard came back and he had memorized the poem, too."

Richard always seemed to enjoy participating in all of the camp's sports programs. Underweight and somewhat frail through much of high school, he was concerned about building himself up physically, but as always, he was also reading voraciously and pursuing his studies. Friends remember Richard reviewing algebra from a book used in a course he had already taken and being ridiculed for his obsessive studiousness. The Ninth of Ab, a minor Jewish holiday commemorating the destruction of the First and Second Temples in Jerusalem, usually occurs while camp is in session. One summer in preparation for an observance of the holiday, Richard read extensively for a presentation on conditions in the Warsaw Ghetto. "He told story after story," said Mrs. Mark, "all of them dripping with the most horrid and gory details."

The highlight of each camping season at Farband was a special eight-day program of competition called Blue and White Week. The camp was divided into Blue and White teams for competition at every level in nearly all the camp's activities—various athletic events and literary, art, and music contests, including an operetta which each team wrote, produced, and performed. Richard, according to Mr. Mark, was never popular enough to be appointed a general for one of the two teams: "He just wasn't enough of a leader. He didn't have the kind of connection it takes with the other kids to make plans, direct, and inspire them. But, of course, both teams always wanted Richard on their side because he was such a hardworking guy who hated to lose."

Henry Shevitz, in the summer he had Richard removed from his cabin, was made general of the Blue team; Richard worked with the White entrants in the literary contest. The Blues won the overall competition quite handily, but Richard's group of campers scored an overwhelming victory. Years later Henry and Richard would still boast to one another of their respective roles. Competition was to continue, in fact, as a mark of their relationship. Henry was a top student in high school, graduating third in his class as a Merit Scholarship finalist and winning honors in two departments at Mumford. He recalls:

"One day we happened to be talking about school—I was going off to Ann Arbor for my freshman year and Richard was going back to Mumford for his last year. Somehow we must have gotten on my accomplishments at Mumford because at one point he said, 'If you think *you* did well, when I graduate Mumford I'm going to make them forget all about you; I'm going to better every one of your records!' It seemed so uncalled-for. This was before Blue and White Week, and I had never even thought of competing against Richard."

The following year in the summer before he went off to college Richard was a senior counselor managing his own cabin. Of that cabin's spotless condition the Marks still have vivid memories. Richard himself was always well scrubbed, his clothes always immaculate; he did his own laundry, not sending it home as did most of the others. He was handling twelve-year-old campers who generally liked him and still recall him telling ghost stories in the darkened cabin after lights-out. Apparently he could tell an effective tale of his own or would dramatically read an Edgar Allan Poe story with the aid of a flashlight. (It was a tradition begun at Farband by Henry Shevitz.)

Camp Farband was never dull with Richard around. "He was always protesting something even here," recalls Mr. Mark, "always making his presence felt." One year Mark initiated a program in which the campers lined up in front of their cabins in the morning and did a few minutes of calisthenics. Richard objected vehemently —it was too militaristic, he insisted. On another occasion Mark thought it might be interesting to set up a small rifle range, buy a couple of .22's, and teach riflery: "Just teach the kids a skill—five shots apiece once a week for those who wanted to try it. Well, when Richard got wind of that he came charging up to me completely incensed. What was the meaning of this? he wanted to know. What purpose could possibly be served by having weapons in the camp? What great Jewish ideals were going to be advanced? Peace? The brotherhood of man? Richard was really upset. And he wouldn't have anything to do with it. Nor would he let any of his campers have anything to do with it. None of his kids ever took part."

FIVE

By the time he reached his senior year, Richard's academic success and extroverted personality had made him a well-known figure around Mumford. His bright-minded affability produced a positive reaction in most cases, as exemplified by a young man who claimed that Richard was not only the most intelligent fellow he'd ever known, but the acquaintance he had most admired in high school. Generous and friendly, Richard was an eternal optimist, he said.

But some who had only slight contact with Richard saw only his competitiveness, differentness, and rigid idealism; they disliked him and muttered about conceit, pretention, or possible homosexuality (the most common of teen-age allegations). A few who knew him more extensively refused to acknowledge (or thought less than genuine) his politeness, tolerance, and concern for others. One girl maintained, for example, that he always had a rather obnoxious way of presenting himself. She always considered him an unhappy person who found it difficult to communicate on his level with others, always defensive and rigid in his ideas and attitudes. Richard, she thought, was a bit naïve and blind to the realities of human nature, genuine in his sincerity but too self-centered to open his eyes to others.

Another girl described a preexam study session in which Richard took part: "We met at someone's home and sat around the dining-room table discussing our reports. Richard was one of the first and gave his very quickly—in three minutes it was over and Richard sat down. None of us had really understood what he said, but we went on. Richard soon decided that we were going too slow for him. He was bored and impatient and finally ended up sitting under the dining table, petting the dog, reading, or just lying there waiting. At one point later he got up, went outside for a while, and came back to tell us he had run around the block."

At Mumford one day Richard and Ron Burns heard about a lecture to be given at Wayne State by a United States foreign-service officer. Richard needed a ride so the two drove down together. The lecture was held in a rather small room which quickly became very crowded. As soon as all the seats were taken and a woman walked in looking for a place to sit, Richard immediately jumped up, went over to the woman, and ushered her gallantly to his seat. "He was very impressed with the speaker," said Ron, "and afraid that he himself would never be able to measure up to the demands of the job. On the way home I remember he criticized my driving; I was going about forty miles per hour, but he thought it was much too fast. 'What if you hit a child, Ron!' he said with that over-dramatic sincerity of his.

"Actually Richard was almost too sincere to believe. He was so flamboyant about everything that people either held him in awe or took him with a grain of salt."

In further contrast is the opinion of Fred Baskin who was probably as close as anyone to Richard throughout high school: "The fact that my mother didn't particularly like Richard—and wasn't very happy that he was my friend at this time—was largely a function of his not being particularly tolerant of people around him (with what I consider to be a healthy intolerance). He was relatively sarcastic and he didn't bother to say 'Hello, Mrs. Baskin' or 'Good-bye, Mrs. Baskin.' And he was a bit loud, particularly famous for a very loud laugh, and something of a backslapper."

These reports may tell us more about the people who are providing them than about Richard. In any case, the most frequently repeated opinion indicates that although he was generally quite popular, Richard seemed without any true bosom pals. Also, a pattern begins to emerge at this point: his younger friends—like some of those he made in the A.Z.A., a year or two or three behind Richard at Mumford—tend to praise him in the most unreserved terms. Years later he had become purely admirable, almost legendary in their memories. With acquaintances his own age and in the same year in school, he seemed to have a normal variety of relations, ranging from amity (with most) to antipathy (with a few). Older friends like Fred Baskin and Henry Shevitz he usually idolized or antagonized, at times seeming to combine the extremes in subtle ambivalence. It seems that where Richard could see himself in a father-teacher role (as with his younger friends), he was apt to be more consistently kind, helpful, and tolerant than when the roles were reversed or not clearly defined in father-son, teacher-student terms.

As he had in grade school, Richard imparted comments about his family life infrequently, and to only a few closer friends. Except for Fred Baskin and a few others, he did not often play host in his parents' home. Said Fred, "Richard and his father would argue about what should or could be done about some newspaper event, the Negro situation, or whatever, and one of his father's favorite banters was, 'What can you do? You're still wet behind the ears.' "

Richard's mother, according to Julie Lieberman, "was crazy about him . . . often talked about him and his accomplishments and seemed very proud of him." Another girl remembering Mrs. Wishnetsky from her appearance at a Mumford visitors' day remarked, "I thought to myself what a nice-looking, normal motherly-type person she seemed to be to have such an extraordinary son." Opinions diverge again on Richard's relations with his sisters. To Julie he seemed very fond of both girls; to Fred Baskin he appeared to have little interest in them, "because they were just kids." In any case Fred maintains that Richard did become much closer to Terry and Ellen after he left home for college.

And then there is the reaction of a young man a year behind Richard at Mumford and only a casual acquaintance, who recalls a convention for United Synagogue Youth in Detroit in 1959 and a discussion among eight or so young people in the Wishnetsky home. Richard, who was not a member of U.S.Y. (his sisters were), led the discussion very ably on a topic of current Jewish interest. Richard's parents took some part in the proceedings, and he got along with them very well, giving the impression that his familial situation was excellent, even enviable.

The young man said: "His parents seemed so concerned, so involved, and were able to take part in the discussion with no indication of rebellion against them on Richard's part. It seemed to be about as close to an ideal situation as you could get, and I compared it to my own home where I'd get scolded if I bought an extra book."

Richard's senior year at Mumford was a busy and important time. Extracurricular activities with the A.Z.A. and Current Affairs Club grew more intense and demanding. Competition for honors raced to its climax; tests had to be taken and decisions made in the great American game of getting into the "right" college. Dates, dances, parties, and proms offered Richard at last chance at a bona fide high-school sweetheart.

Academic work, however, always came first, and he burdened himself with an especially heavy class load and, as usual, much diligent study. Richard and his friend David Roth "crammed" one night for an English exam, and Richard demonstrated that he had memorized not only the usual "To be or not to be" soliloquy but much if not all of Shakespeare's *Hamlet*. It was not that Richard was particularly brilliant, insisted David, or even that he had an extraordinary memory. He had simply spent an enormous amount of time studying. Their teacher had a reputation for giving "impossible" exams as a challenge to his best students, and Richard wanted to be able to answer every question perfectly.

Richard's literary tastes were Romantic, Transcendental, and Gothic; his particular favorites were the Romantic poets Wordsworth, Shelley, Keats, and especially Byron. He seemed greatly attracted by the Romantic temper's concerns and obsessions: the appeal of the strange and the supernatural, the fascination of the forbidden, the erotic longing for death, man's striving for the infinite ("the desire of the moth for a star"), the solitary protagonist with an apocalyptic vision exiled from a society he has rejected or which has renounced him. The hero of Byron's *Manfred,* for example, is a man whose "aspirations/Have been beyond the dwellers of the earth," a violator of convention who is proudly unrepentant even in death, proclaiming, I "was my own destroyer, and will be/My own hereafter."

Richard's first-term senior English class was occasionally conducted by one of the students. When Richard's turn came, he opened the session by reading a poem which sang of philosopher-kings and power politics and which, he said, had been written by Byron. Richard led a lively discussion of the poem and its implications and explained it so well that at least one of his classmates thought it was Byron's best poem. "That was the first time I had ever really understood Byron," he recalls. At the end of the class the teacher, sitting in the back of the room, said, "Richard, I don't remember that poem at all. It isn't really Byron's, is it?" Richard smiled and admitted that he had written it himself.

In his last term at Mumford Richard decided to take the pilot English course which he had told Mrs. Morris he would not enter because the arrangement was not democratic. Apparently he had changed his mind. The course was his introduction to modern literature and called for the reading of twenty novels, authored by the likes of Dostoevski, Kafka, Wolfe, and Camus, far from typical high-school fare. He got most excited about the Russian classic *Crime and Punishment,* which he read and reread, pondering the implications as he would for years to come.

The novel's hero, Raskolnikov, is a young Russian fired by an intense desire to grow into a life that is extraordinary, valuable, and meaningful. To attempt anything less, he feels, would be to "accept one's lot humbly as it is, once for all and stifle everything in oneself, giving up all claim to activity, life, and love!" Disturbed by inner conflict involving a self-sacrificing mother and sister, driven by a compulsive self-loathing, and obsessed with a grandiose rationale for murder, he finally takes an ax to an old pawnbroker and her daughter, then attempts unsuccessfully to live with his guilt. In formulating the plan which leads to the bloody double slaying he begins by deciding that all men can be roughly divided into two groups: the masses, made up of common follower types, and the elite, those extraordinary few destined to lead. The extraordinary man has the right (he thinks the duty) to transgress any law or principle if by doing so he may lead the rest of mankind to something better. The only criteria for such action are an unconventional conscience and success. No sacrifice of innocence or guilt would be too great if the end were achieved; any act of transgression might be right and lawful for a superman.

Fred Baskin, who was now in his freshman year at Wayne State but still living at home and seeing a lot of Richard, recalls: "He would quote things right out of Dostoevski; when he read him late in high school it did have a big influence. It (Raskolnikov's theory) was an extremely and morbidly attractive concept because we all were taken with ourselves as perhaps being great men and this was the test. Ignoring the fact of insanity entirely, it was always an attractive concept. He never mentioned any particular desire to himself repeat the experiment, but he did consider it very interesting."

Another demanding last-term course forced Richard to cope with Aaron Gornbein's high standards in Contemporary Affairs, the texts for which were the daily newspapers and various news journals, such as *The Nation, The New Republic, Time,* and *Newsweek.* Mr. Gornbein, quickly named by his former students as one of the best teachers in the school, got along well with Richard and was no doubt a potent influence in his desire to study politics and enter the foreign service. Said the teacher:

"Richard was probably the best student in the classes he had with me, very concerned about what was going on in the world around him and ill at ease if he hadn't read the newspaper that morning . . . passionately concerned with liberal causes, especially civil rights. He couldn't understand and was very upset by what he considered the very unfair decision of the Supreme Court affirming the separate but equal idea."

In class Richard was as usual very vocal but, according to Gornbein, seemed quite gentle when critical of another's position. He would frequently employ a line that continued to be one of his favorites: "Well, maybe someday you'll see my point of view." Unlike more contentious students, he would not argue an unpopular position just for the sake of arguing. Richard was a creative student in Gornbein's terms, one who would not accept the word of a teacher on a particular issue before arriving at his own decision.

Richard's interest in political and social issues did not end with discussions in the classroom or with his friends. Perhaps taking his cue from his family's active concern with politics, Richard worked on the successful campaign of Detroit's congressman John Dingell and organized classmates to knock on doors and work for the passage of a Detroit school millage issue. Once he invited friends to a tea which his parents hosted in their home for incumbent governor John Swainson. He continued to be highly critical of the Jewish community and might, when sufficiently aroused, write a letter to *The Jewish News* (published weekly in Detroit) sharply indicting the leadership of the community.

His political bent also expressed itself in the spring of 1960 when he helped to research and organize Mumford's mock Democratic Convention sponsored by the Current Affairs Club. A member of the platform committee, Richard took great pride in the very liberal document finally adopted. As for candidates, he was a passionate backer of Chester Bowles, who was near the top of his list of high-school heroes. He had frequently urged on his friends one of Bowles's numerous books on foreign affairs which suggested an organization similar to the Peace Corps, an idea Richard got very excited about. In convention maneuvering, however, Richard and his cohorts backing Bowles were forced to make a deal with the Kennedy partisans. A Kennedy-Bowles ticket ultimately won the nomination.

On the senior trip to Washington, D. C., soon afterward, Richard was not interested in visiting the Kennedy campaign headquarters. He toured, however, in one of the nine buses serving about half of Mumford's graduating class, and wrote a long letter home to Julie (who had wanted to come but couldn't) describing his appreciation for the beauty of the city. On the train ride home he got into a long late-night discussion with Jerry Levitt (pseud.), who marked his close friendship with Richard from that night on. The two seventeen-year-olds spoke with typically intense idealism of human relationships and the beauty of love. It was, says Jerry, an inspiring and uplifting conversation, with Richard showing insight and sensitivity when they talked of the minor trouble Jerry and his girl of the moment were having. He recalls: "Richard and I were both rather young and romantic and without personal experience, but it showed the quality of his mind. He didn't use typical teen-age language and was extremely idealistic when he talked about the girl he said *he* was going with."

The girl Richard spoke of was Marcia Frankel (pseud.) whom he had met earlier in the year at a dance connected with a B.B.Y.O. leadership-training institute. At the affair Marcia had decided he was a very good dancer. When Richard learned that Marcia (with petite figure and impish eyes) had just recently returned from Holland where she had been an exchange student during her junior year and was full of ideas of her own "for saving the world" as a result of her "broadening experience," he decided she was just what he had been looking for. He promptly asked her for a date to see the Bergman film *Wild Strawberries*.

"Neither of us really understood the movie," says Marcia, "but we were very moved by it. Richard was very emotional about the movie, but I always tended to react negatively to his emotional and intellectual excesses, usually throwing cold water on them." They went out for egg rolls afterward and talked long and hard about the film and related topics. Richard drove ten miles an hour back to the suburb where Marcia lived, apparently not wanting the evening to end. Marcia couldn't wait for him to get her home. Richard wanted to kiss her good night; instead he got a stern lecture on the sorry state of teen-age morality from Marcia, who simply didn't want to kiss him. Richard was probably even more impressed than if he had gotten the kiss, and he called her every night thereafter. Says Marcia: "I didn't really know what to do with him. I hadn't really enjoyed myself and didn't want to go out with him again. I did finally accept an invitation for a dance because he was such a good dancer." That, according to Marcia, was the extent of their relationship in high school.

Richard's first and perhaps only declared high-school romance began in his senior year with Judi Lockman (pseud.), a small cute brunette, intense, bright, and independent. Richard had numerous female acquaintances at Mumford, but Judi was the first to become a full-fledged "girl friend," a development that was the topic of interest, gossip, and giggling around the school. As might be expected it was a very heady affair for a time, with much ardent intellectual talk punctuated by some experimentation with the teenage kiss and hug. According to Judi, however, Richard would not permit the experiment to go too far. At one point he informed her that he had made a promise to his mother that he would not indulge in sexual relations before marriage.

For a while Judi seemed in some awe of Richard; he, according to Fred Baskin, seemed to consider himself a bit superior to her. Early in the summer they fought, and their relationship was terminated. Both were considerably disappointed, but they were soon heading for different colleges and their paths would not cross again.

As for the other girls in Richard's life, Debbie Rossman and Julie Lieberman, for example, still have his graduation photo: a three-quarter view, closely cropped hair brushed neatly up from the crown of his prominent forehead, scanty brows over wide-set eyes lifted in a resolute gaze off camera, mouth opened slightly with the hint of a grin. The great American high-school tradition of exchanging wallet-size photos with messages on the back prevailed at Mumford and Richard proved no exception. On the back of one of his pictures he wrote in small and careful blue script:

> June '60. Debbie, Everything soft and lovely reminds me of you. That which is soft and lovely must also be genuine for you too are genuine. When so many are false and deceptive it's a relief and a joy to know someone like yourself. I know that one day you'll make a great man greater. Save a place in your heart for me. Yours, Richard.

On the back of another:

> June '60. To Julie, We've known each other for seven good inconsistent years. I've always respected you for what you have said and done.
>
> You're part of a frightfully small minority of girls who are sincere and genuine. Don't change. I'm certain that we'll share a good many more years together.
>
> Save a place in your heart for me. Richard.

He didn't explain to Julie his use of the word "inconsistent." Perhaps he meant they had not always seen a lot of each other over the seven years. Said Julie with a sad smile: "Richard was always so enthusiastic and so exuberant, almost overexuberant. You couldn't believe how exuberant he could be. He would come in and pick me up and swing me around. He seemed so joyful, it was really disarming sometimes."

When Richard's work at Mumford was finished, it was clear that he had performed very well indeed, but perhaps not quite as well as he had hoped. He took an award as the outstanding student in the social sciences, but, then, Henry Shevitz had won two such departmental awards. His class ranking was certainly high, but he was not listed near the very top as Henry had been. Though he had thought he probably would, he did not win a National Merit Scholarship as Henry and Fred Baskin had; he was disappointed in fact that he received no mention at all from the foundation.

Ironically Richard's interest in science had waned about the time that cries of an "education gap" went up after Sputnik I was orbited during his sophomore year. He took all the science available at Mumford, biology, chemistry, and physics, plus four years of math, and continued to do well in these courses. But his concern had shifted distinctly to the humanities in his four years of English, three of history, two of French, and courses in government and politics. In addition after-school classes were offered at Mumford in the Hebrew and Russian languages and Richard had spent time diligently studying the latter and attending class once a week from four to six in the afternoon.

His plans now were to study political science at the University of Michigan and then move on to Georgetown and its traditional training for work in the foreign service. It had become almost customary for Mumford graduates to proceed with their education at the University of Michigan, and more than a third of Richard's graduating class of over seven hundred had made the choice to go on to Ann Arbor (only an hour away by car, train, or bus). First, however, Richard had graduation ceremonies to execute, summer camp counseling to perform, and B.B.Y.O. conventions to attend. His speech to his classmates and their families at graduation was by all reports eloquent and forceful, and many an impressed parent asked his son or daughter afterward about the boy who had delivered the extraordinary valedictory address. Mrs. Wishnetsky proudly accepted praise for her son from another mother in the happy crowd, then added lightly, "But you don't know what it's like to have to live with a genius!"

Winning acclaim for his public speaking was nothing new for Richard. He had frequently entered and won contests at B.B.Y.O. assemblies and during his senior year had done particularly well. In December at the regional convention held in Detroit for state chapters, he had "won hands down," despite the efforts of a number of excellent speakers, in both the interpretive reading contest and the oratory contest (including a five-minute prepared speech on a topic of Jewish interest and a three-minute extemporaneous talk on current events). Later in the school year it was the same story at the district convention for six Midwest states and four Canadian provinces at Elkhart Lake Camp outside of Milwaukee. Richard again won both contests easily and, according to one observer, "had the audience of kids simply spellbound."

In the summer in which he was a senior counselor at Camp Farband and before starting his college work in Ann Arbor, Richard, along with six of his friends from the Brandeis chapter, traveled to Starlight Camp in Pennsylvania for the national B.B.Y.O. convention. For the interpretive reading he presented a story (apparently his own), the delivery of which he had polished at the previous conventions and at chapter meetings. It was a melodramatic first-person account of an heroic Israeli soldier who is under heavy fire yet runs from foxhole to foxhole to aid and encourage his mates before describing his own death at the end of the story. Said one of Richard's friends on the trip, "He was able to establish a rapport with a large audience very quickly, easily, and effectively, the kind of rapport which he rarely achieved with an individual or small group." This time, though his delivery again made a strong impression, he managed to place only second in each contest.

"What is a Jew?" was the convention theme, and along with the problems of Zionism and other Jewish questions, was debated in seminars in which Richard took an active part during the five-day meeting. As gregarious as ever, he made a number of new friends, but the impression he made was not always positive. Though he was not a delegate, he offered a proposal on the convention floor to give all the money in the national service fund (two thousand dollars raised by members from all over the country) to only one philanthropic cause, UNICEF, instead of spreading it thinly over a number of charities. Despite a clear-cut defeat when his proposal was voted on, Richard continued each day to bring up the idea and espoused it fervently, until some of the convention were laughing in ridicule. Said one of his new friends: "He did get on your nerves with his rigidity, certainty, and arrogance. Still he talked more interestingly on one track than most people do in general on a variety of subjects." Many in the convention group including Richard moved on afterward for a brief stay in New York City. On a visit to the United Nations and while the others took the official tour, Richard hiked all over the building hunting for more information on UNICEF.

Richard became old enough to fight and die for his country at the close of the quiet fifties, when for the moment his country was not asking its young men to fight and die and the Great Society was only a wicked gleam in the eye of one of Lyndon B. Johnson's prolific speech writers. Yet it seems clear that Richard at this time was more intensely concerned with social, political, and cultural realities than were most of his generation. While the heroes of most of his peers in the city played professional football for the Lions, Richard's great men were people like Chester Bowles, Hubert Humphrey, Plato, and Dostoevski. He was too busy reading *Foreign Affairs Quarterly* to be bothered with school politics and student government, which he considered toys. Generally he held himself aloof from the glut of popular culture in which most of his generation seemed to be happily immersed; while many American high-school seniors worried about whether their new cars would have wraparound windshields and power brakes, Richard spent exceedingly long and tedious hours with his books, marking out for himself humanistic ideals of a high order.

Richard's most memorable and engaging quality in high school, at least to those who could share it, was his intense involvement with life. His was an ardent, restless life style designed to prepare him for the greatness that he seems often to have dreamed about. In retrospect the hints of self-righteousness, grandiose conceit, and self-absorption, the moments of arrogance, rigidity, obsession, and ill-temper, take on a significance that they apparently did not seem to have during the years when Richard grew into tentative manhood. Said Mumford High School principal Bert Sandweiss, in words that were echoed by Percy Prey, the counselor who saw Richard in every term of his four-year stay, "There was no indication at all of future trouble for Richard when he was here with us."

SIX

During his high-school years Richard only rarely attended synagogue services and had little or no concern with a formal profession of faith. His interest in the meaning of Jewishness and the cultural heritage of the Jews was strong, however, and was often expressed in the A.Z.A. and elsewhere. Thus on at least a couple of Saturday afternoons, he attended cultural luncheons sponsored by the high-schoolers of Congregation Shaarey Zedek where his parents had recently taken membership. Occasionally Morris Adler would speak to the young people, and this may have been where Richard's first significant contact with the rabbi occurred.

In the summer after his twelfth-grade year, Richard proudly informed Julie Lieberman that he had gotten to know Rabbi Adler and had talked with him personally at some length. He was full of praise for the rabbi; he liked him very much as a man and thought him possessed of true greatness. The kinship Richard felt stemmed in large part from the fact that the rabbi spoke with insight about Jewish religious and social institutions and at times rendered trenchant criticism. For example:

> The nebulousness of our youth's idea of what "Jewish" means even when they so designate themselves reflects their unsureness of their Jewish identity. One of the central forces in establishing a concept of self is the home. (Psychologists speak of the home as a "crucible of identity.") Through rebellions or emulation the young acquire an awareness of their own identity and selfhood. But the Jewish parent is a shadowy and unclear figure as a Jew, arousing neither great admiration nor intense opposition. He serves neither as "target" nor "model." . . .
>
> Neither is the synagogue effective in helping the young Jew define his role as a Jew in American society and in the contemporary world generally. It represents a religion that is detached not only from the religion of the majority of Americans but also from the young person's life. Indeed, it may not even be related to the life he sees in the Jewish community at large. The organized Jewish community represents a mechanism more than an idea; a system of techniques more than a spirit. Its standards are too often shoddy and poor. Its leadership and programs often do not stimulate a positive response in those who come to it fresh and open-minded.

The group at Shaarey Zedek included a few of Richard's friends from Mumford and other area high schools, and to them he seemed fairly knowledgeable in their discussions about Judaism. Their favorite topic was the apparently irreconcilable trinity of belief, practice, and mode of living. If one really believed in the religion of Judaism as divinely instituted and ordained, it was argued, how was it that many practices set down by Jewish law seemed impossible or distasteful to observe? And even more important, how could one reconcile the supposed belief in traditional Jewish values by synagogue-going Jews and their frequent rejection of these values in their everyday lives? Hypocrisy was thus a favorite subject, and one in which Richard could become intensely involved. It was imperative, he insisted, that people lived what they said they believed. And he would always bring up politics in this connection: how could politicians, who were supposed to be leaders of their communities, constantly betray the principles they urged their constituents to practice?

Richard's religious training as a third-generation American Jew contrasted sharply with the education Morris Adler had received as he grew up in the preceding generation.

Two of the rabbi's earliest memories, his most vivid recollections of the time in Russia before the journey from Slutsk to New York City, were connected with the beginnings of his religious education. He was a very small boy when one spring day after Easter he heard the noise and raucous singing of soldiers in the street. Curious, he went to investigate at a window in his home but was quickly snatched away by his grandmother, who pulled a shade down tightly over the scene in the street. The boy did not understand what a pogrom was, but realized something was wrong when he saw the terrible fear in his grandmother's face. It was a look he never forgot.

The other, quite different, memory involved his first school days in Slutsk, and the rabbi often spoke of it humorously. Jewish children were barred from the schools of Slutsk, but at the age of four or so he had traveled daily to a Hebrew school in the town and could remember having his own taxi service. His parents would hire a strapping young lad from the town and pay him to carry their son Morris to school on his shoulders through the Russian snow and mud.

Joseph and Jenny Adler had previously lived in a smaller Russian town, but when they learned they were going to be parents, they had moved to Slutsk, which was large enough to claim a doctor. Their life in Slutsk was quite comfortable, indeed affluent by comparison with most of their neighbors. Slutsk was especially renowned for its grinding poverty and for its Jewish inhabitants' great pride and dedication to learning, which made the town a scholastic center. On March 30, 1906, the Adlers welcomed their first son, and from an early age the boy was steeped in the East European rabbinical tradition of his father. His mother was a businesslike woman, well educated for her time and place, and helpful in the rabbinical work of her husband. Thus from both parents Morris Adler inherited love and respect for an energetic life of the mind. In 1907 a second son was born, and a year before the outbreak of hostilities that were later to be known as World War I, the family made its move to America. Morris Adler would never again see his native land.

In New York they went where most East European Jewish immigrants went at the time—to the Lower East Side, a way station where Jews scrimped, sweated, and saved enough to move on to the Bronx, Harlem, Brooklyn, Cleveland, or Detroit. The sweatshop and the peddler's cart were livelihood, miserably overcrowded tenements were home, the fire escape and the street were playgrounds. But the schools taught English to desperately eager students, the libraries were jammed, workers read Tolstoi and applauded Shakespeare at the Yiddish theater. It was a buzzing intellectual center and it spawned successful businessmen, attorneys, professors, writers, and rabbis.

The girl who would marry his son Morris would recall of Rabbi Joseph Adler: "My father-in-law became a citizen as quickly as he could. Before election day he would read the platforms and he would know them by heart. He'd read everything and then, of course, he'd vote socialist! But election day he treated like a holy day; he'd put on his top silk hat and his cutaway when he went to the polls. And he would say certain prayers that we say on a holiday: 'Blessed are Thou, O Lord, our God, King of the Universe, Who has kept us alive and enabled us to reach this day.' It was a duty for him and he made it a most beautiful thing."

In writing of the role of the rabbi in America during this "period of adaptation," Morris Adler no doubt used his father as a model:

> The American rabbi of those days stressed the value of integration into American life—integration that would introduce the new immigrants not only to baseball, to social dancing, to movies, but also to Whitman, Thoreau, Emerson, and Emily Dickinson. The rabbis incorporated into their sermons examples of American culture, and often gave lectures upon American ideas and American books. They said to the Jews who came here in such large numbers at the turn of the century: "Enter American life fully; enter it with your tradition; do not remain outside of it; do not isolate yourself from it; overcome the apprehensions which centuries of enforced alienation have bred in you."

Morris Adler had arrived in America in time for his seventh birthday and took his elementary education in a Hebrew parochial school. In the meantime he mastered the English language sufficiently to start his secondary work at De Witt Clinton High School. English would become his favorite language, the richest and most flexible of languages, he felt. Rabbi Adler liked to quote

Lincoln Steffens's *Autobiography* which describes Jewish boys "sitting hatless in their old clothes, smoking cigarettes on the steps outside, and their fathers, all dressed in black, with their high hats, uncut beards, and temple curls, . . . going into the synagogues, tearing their hair and rending their garments."

But there were no similar scenes acted out between Joseph and Morris Adler. Today Mrs. Adler says of her husband: "He was extremely fortunate. Whereas many of his friends rebelled at that precise time as most of us did, Morris did not. The boys would play ball on Saturday afternoon, handball in the backyard. And then later in the afternoon when services would start, a father would come down and pull one of the boys away by the ear. And another would get dragged away. And when Morris got older he told his father, 'You know, I was very lucky. You never caught me playing ball.' And his father said, 'You foolish young boy! Don't you think I knew you were playing ball? I just never wanted you to have the feeling that religion was always in your way of a moment's recreation.' He went to school six days a week, so there really wasn't any other time to play."

At the instigation of mutual friends, Goldie Kadish met Morris Adler in 1924 when he was eighteen and she two years younger. "He was a very shy young man, extremely shy and a real bookworm, in the good sense of the word," recalls Goldie Adler who met her future husband for the first time, appropriately, in the library of the Hebrew Teachers' Institute. She continues: "I'd walk home from the institute with boys in my class and he would walk two blocks behind—there was this beautiful shyness about him, constantly, even in the rabbinate. I think it had to do with an innate modesty. Morris was a proud person—he wasn't humble, but he was a man of great humility.

"I had many friends at the time, and we always looked up to Morris as the most mature. It was strange, he was younger than all the other boys, yet we always on any issue would consult him. I could see right away his leadership qualities. For example, if we all went to a dance or to a show, if Morris were reading a book he wouldn't come with us. He would beg off and maybe meet us later for a cup of coffee—if he finished the book."

Goldie Kadish's parents had come to the United States from Grudna in Russia on their honeymoon in 1898. While visiting her mother's sister they ran out of money and, "thank God, were too dead broke to go back." Mr. Kadish had studied for the rabbinate in Russia, but in America took up bookbindery instead. Goldie was born in New York a decade after the arrival of her parents. The Kadish children finally numbered six, and according to Mrs. Adler, the family was very closely knit:

"I had a great deal of love for my father. My father knew Hebrew very well, and he was such a devoted husband, such a good kindly man, that I had made up my mind as a child that I could only marry a man who knew Hebrew. This was stupid and I met some wonderful boys as I grew up, but somehow I felt that if he didn't know Hebrew he wouldn't have that kindliness of spirit."

When she finished at Washington Irving High, Goldie attended Hunter College until she received from the state board of regents a scholarship to study kindergarten teaching at the Ethical Culture Normal School in New York City. At the same time, Morris Adler continued his work at City College of New York but also attended the Isaac Elchanan Yeshiva for Orthodox seminary studies (the school is now known as Yeshiva University). The courses he had taken at the Hebrew Teachers' Institute involved the study of modern Hebrew and its literature. Now at the Yeshiva he was dealing primarily with the Talmud and in the legal and biblical language of Judaism.

About this time, at the age of twenty or twenty-one, Morris Adler took a position as principal of a Hebrew school connected with a synagogue in the area. Goldie Kadish was hired as one of the staff who taught Hebrew to children of the congregation from four to six every day after their public-school sessions. "Actually our deep friendship started then," says Mrs. Adler, but even so Morris Adler moved very slowly as a suitor.

For a while he watched as other boys picked Goldie up after her two hours of teaching at the synagogue, but gradually her vivacious wit and cheerful warmth moved him to action.

"Our dates," she recalls, "were mostly at the public library on Forty-second Street and Fifth Avenue. Oh what a delightful place! When you speak of adventures, that was the place to go. We'd meet there and do our work, and then if we could afford it we would take in a show. We'd rush down to Gray's Drugstore on Broadway and Forty-third Street, and if you were willing to wait to the last minute you could get tickets to the best shows at half price. They had an agency in the basement and we'd watch the board and see which tickets were available. Then we would race across the streets and get to the theater just in time. We saw George Bernard Shaw—all the good plays—that way.

"One summer we wanted to take some extra courses especially in English so he found that he had one that was required and one that was an elective—he wanted to take the elective in a literature course, so he had his girl friend take the required course in government in a large lecture hall with the seats numbered. So for ten weeks one summer I was Morris Adler. And he got angry because he only got a B in the course. I hated it!"

Poverty abounded in the area, but the neighborhood took care of its own. Women like Goldie's mother formed an organization, for example, that would prepare a full Sabbath meal and leave it anonymously at the back door of a large and needy family so that the family wouldn't know who had sent it and suffer embarrassment. Says Mrs. Adler: "Morris was always very conscious of social welfare and the needs of people. His favorite phrase was, 'You cannot have the awe of Heaven without loving your fellowman.' "

Morris graduated from City College in 1928 with a B.S. degree and a heavy concentration in psychology, philosophy, and English. Writing was his first love. He had dreamed of being a writer, and he did a considerable amount of writing during this period most often on themes that were not strictly Jewish, such as social justice and the plight of the mentally disturbed. "I think," says Mrs. Adler, "if he hadn't chosen the rabbinate he would have chosen psychiatry." He later spoke often and with pride of his years at C.C.N.Y.—a time of great intellectual ferment at the university. He implied humorously that if one hadn't gone to City College in the late 1920's, one had never really been engaged in an intellectual debate.

Upon graduation Morris had decided not to enter the rabbinate, not at least for a while. It had been only because of the great yet subtle and indirect influence of his father that he had seriously considered studying for the rabbinate: he wanted very much to please and emulate his father. At the same time, he had also noted that his father's profession had brought some dissatisfaction and unhappiness to his home, particularly to Morris's mother. She was "a good wife, a marvelous woman, and a very fine Jewess," but as a cultured and educated person she found it difficult to mingle with the poor, often uneducated immigrant women of her husband's congregation. Morris noticed the unhappiness and took it to heart. There were other problems as well, such as what kind of a rabbi his modern intellectual perspective would allow him to be.

The year Morris finished at City College his family moved from the East Side to Brooklyn, where Joseph Adler took a position with another congregation. The romance with Goldie Kadish had to be carried on from a greater distance, and it was decided that since there would be nine at the Kadish table and only five at the Adler, she would make the trip to Brooklyn for dinner once a week. In the summer after his graduation they found themselves even farther apart when Goldie served as a counselor at a camp outside of New York City and Morris traveled to Paris and spent the summer months becoming enthralled by the old city. "His last dance on the mountaintop, I told him," says Mrs. Adler with a chuckle.

When they met again upon his return in the fall, he was full of plans: after they were married they would go off to Paris and live there like Bohemians for a year. Goldie Kadish was willing enough, and after she became Mrs. Morris Adler on June 12, 1929, the day after she had finished her final college exams, the newlyweds readied themselves for their trip. They had already secured their passports and were about to leave when suddenly Joseph Adler became ill. The trip to Paris was off, said Morris; he would stand in for his father and would minister to his father's congregation until the older man became well enough to take over again. The young man of twenty-three officiated at funerals and other services for the congregation, and though the experience had come as a disappointment since his heart had been set on Paris, it was also a kind of introduction to the rabbinate. The people of the congregation turned with considerable reverence to his combination of youth, earnestness, and intelligence.

But Morris Adler had wanted to use the year in Paris to explore himself further and to chart his future course; he was still not sure in which educational direction to turn. Then his new wife recalled that at camp in the previous summer she had met a rabbi who had spoken of a small Orthodox congregation (for the most part immigrants) in St. Joseph, Missouri, which needed the services of a rabbi. Morris applied for the job, was accepted, and took it for one year only. He told his wife, "Well, since we can't go to Paris, I'll have my fling at this."

The year in Missouri proved to be a pivotal one. "It was a delightful experience for him," says Mrs. Adler. "He began to feel that in terms of service towards mankind this was a million miles removed from any other profession. You were dealing with people! You were involved in their lives day in and day out. You saw their weaknesses; you also found their strength. And he fell in love with the rabbinate in that year."

But he was also now confronted with a problem that he would continue to face in one form or another for the rest of his life. He could not wholly accept the Orthodox faith of his father and therefore could not be honest with his congregation. He might appear strictly Orthodox in his practice, but in his thinking he simply could not accept the uncompromising traditional approach. His conscientious practice at the time was the result of habit, of respect for his father, of the feeling that this was a heritage which he ought to continue; but Orthodoxy, he decided, was not viable for American Jewish life and did not meet his own understanding of Judaism.

Goldie Adler, perhaps more rebellious about her religion, had once brought her complaints to her father-in-law. He had replied: "Goldie, anything that offends your reason is not Judaism; it's not really a part of Judaism. It's been tacked on and it's not important. A lot of people have tried in a lot of ways to establish something lasting in their religion. It has gathered a lot of dust, a lot of detachable elements along the way." Now Joseph Adler brought the same kind of tolerant understanding to his son's dilemma when Morris and Goldie returned to Brooklyn.

"I remember," says Mrs. Adler, "Morris's frank discussions with his father and his father's colleagues who advocated sending him to ultra-Orthodox yeshivas in Europe and in Israel. But my father-in-law had a great deal of respect for his son's mind. And he also knew that his son would not be lost to Judaism even if he wasn't strictly Orthodox."

Joseph Adler had taken a position as principal of a staunchly Orthodox parochial school in the Williamsburg section of Brooklyn, and it was with perhaps a good deal of courage that he brought his son for enrollment to the Conservative Jewish Theological Seminary in upper Manhattan: he might well have lost his position as the result of such a "treasonous" act. In St. Joseph Goldie Adler had learned that she was pregnant, and on the day Morris entered the seminary, October 13, 1931, he became the father of a baby girl.

The daughter was named Shulamith and her first home was a Brooklyn apartment rented by her parents while her father attended classes at the seminary and served as a principal and teacher at an afternoon school connected with a nearby Conservative synagogue. Goldie Adler, when her baby was six or seven months old, hired a young girl for five dollars a week plus meals ("We never called her anything but 'Miss Klappenstein,' a fine German girl") and also taught at the school.

Morris Adler's four years at the seminary were not a desperate struggle for the family but demanded a considerable amount of discipline and hard work. In the last years of his studies they moved from Brooklyn to an apartment in Manhattan across the street from the seminary. In the evenings after her baby was asleep and her husband immersed in his studies, Goldie and Miss Klappenstein, a graduate of Hunter College, would attend classes at nearby Columbia University.

Morris also frequently took courses at Columbia while he continued his work at the seminary. At the seminary he was strongly influenced by Mordecai Kaplan, the patriarch of the Conservative rabbinate in America and founder of the Reconstructionist movement, which some view as a fourth branch of contemporary Judaism and others place in the liberal wing of Conservatism. Though he could not agree with Kaplan's rejection of the traditional concepts of God and the Chosen People, Morris Adler continued to revere his former teacher as "the great bridgebuilder between Judaism and the thought of our day; between the pre-Emancipation outlook and the new and vastly changed universe of ideas in which we now live, between the Jew of yesterday and the Jew of tomorrow."

SEVEN

In 1935 at the age of twenty-nine Morris Adler was graduated from the Jewish Theological Seminary of America and ordained a Conservative rabbi. Says Mrs. Adler: "He took the prize for homiletics, which is the art of preaching, every year he was at the seminary. And when he graduated with honors they hoped he would stay on as an instructor or lecturer." But one day the young rabbi was asked to host a man looking for someone to lead a congregation in Buffalo; the two liked each other immediately, and Morris Adler eventually accepted an invitation to address the congregation. In Buffalo he spoke on Friday night and Saturday morning. On Saturday night the officers of Temple Emanu-El elected him their new rabbi. "But gentlemen," he said, "I suppose you think I'm flattered. Why, you take more time in selecting a hat than you took in selecting a rabbi."

"He didn't realize it," says Mrs. Adler, "but that just endeared him all the more. So we moved to Buffalo in 1935.

"The man who had preceded Rabbi Adler at Temple Emanu-El was a Reform rabbi, and the elderly gentlemen—the grandfathers of the children of this congregation—couldn't comply with Reform Judaism. They would have their own services, and when Morris came, he found a small congregation really divided. For the first month he was there he attended services with the elderly gentlemen; every day he went to their minyan and then on Saturday he'd go with them to the early service. Then at ten o'clock he would have a service for the men and women and children who wanted a Conservative service. After a month, these elderly gentlemen realized that this young man was serious-minded and very sincere, and they came to him and said, 'Rabbi, we feel that we want to be one congregation. And we would like to disband our minyan and join with yours and be, as we should be, one family.' "

Subsequently Morris and Goldie Adler and Shulamith, who was now in school, spent three pleasant years in Buffalo. They might have stayed longer if more challenging plans for them had not developed. Congregation Shaarey Zedek—a large, well-established Conservative congregation in Detroit—was in need of an assistant and had applied (as all Conservative congregations in the United States must) to the Jewish Theological Seminary for the names of three possible candidates. Morris Adler was the seminary board's unanimous first selection, and he went to Detroit for a trial sermon. The congregation's decision was in his favor. Mrs. Adler recalls, "It took six months for us to decide to leave Buffalo because in the three years we were there it was such a happy union. It was very difficult to say good-bye."

Before making their move, the Adlers arranged to spend their vacation in the summer of 1938 at the senior Adler's summer home at Rockaway Beach. Morris Adler proudly hoped to be installed at Shaarey Zedek by his father. The night they arrived at Rockaway, everyone in the family came by to offer Morris congratulations and to talk about his new position. It was three in the morning before they all had gone to bed. Goldie Adler knew that her father-in-law liked to go swimming at 6 A.M. during the summer, getting out even before the beachcombers so as not to have people laugh at the spectacle of a sixty-year-old man with a beard engaging in calisthenics. She asked if she could join him and he, noting the late hour, said, "If you're up, wonderful, but I won't wake you."

Later Goldie woke with a start for no discernible reason, doubted that even her father-in-law had gone swimming in the hard rain that was falling, and went back to sleep. Still later she woke again, this time to the news that Joseph Adler couldn't be found anywhere. Goldie got up, quickly searched the house, and then went to the beach. There she found his robe and slippers. "Then these beachcombers told me," she recalled, "that they had seen the man go in, that they had marveled—it was early in the morning and it was cold—and they kept on sweeping. Then it seemed as if he clutched the rope—we had lifesaving ropes around—and he clutched the rope and then they didn't see him anymore." The speculation was that he might have had a heart attack; in any case he wasn't found until four o'clock, before the start of the Sabbath on a Friday afternoon. He was almost washed out to sea when he was spotted and his body brought in.

In the wake of this personal tragedy the Adlers moved to Detroit, and once again they found themselves in the midst of controversy which threatened to divide their congregation. This time, however, the stakes seemed a little higher: the congregation was a nationally prominent one and its disagreement seemed at times to involve much of the Jewish community in Detroit.

In its development, conflicts, and achievements, Congregation Shaarey Zedek (the name means "Gates of Righteousness") has reflected many of the patterns of religious conduct and thought in the American Jewish community over the past one hundred years. Previously Shaarey Zedek had been the oldest and most prominent Orthodox congregation in the city, having been formed in 1869. Then, twenty-five years before Rabbi Adler's arrival in Detroit the congregation had officially shifted to Conservatism, though in fact it had remained quite close to the traditional approach.

The Conservative movement in this country gained its major impetus from the desire of many newly successful American Jews to avoid the wholesale changes wrought by the Reform movement and at the same time to worship in a fashion that was within the norm set by their fellow middle-class Americans—Protestant and Catholic. Thus, women, whose position in Orthodoxy had always been strictly subordinated, were ushered into much fuller and more active participation in the life of the synagogue, and mixed seating, strictly anathema at an Orthodox service, was adopted. Behavior during worship was made much more decorous, replacing the often spirited informality of the Orthodox service. Other changes included the elimination of "commercialism," such as fund-raising and the auctioning of certain religious privileges during the service, and various shifts in the program and content of worship.

Morris Adler's senior at Congregation Shaarey Zedek was Rabbi A. M. Hershman, who had come to the congregation in Detroit in 1907, the year after Rabbi Adler was born. With the formation of the United Synagogue of America in 1913, Shaarey Zedek had joined the new national Conservative organization, yet Rabbi Hershman and much of his congregation had largely remained in the Orthodox mold. Having arrived in America at the age of eighteen with no knowledge of English, the rabbi still found his weekly sermon in English a chore after more than thirty years at Shaarey Zedek; often his audience felt the sting of a fire and brimstone scolding. Finally, after Shaarey Zedek had moved in 1932 into a large new synagogue on Chicago Boulevard in the heart of the city, some of the leaders of the congregation began to talk of the need for a bright young rabbi.

Most of the membership at Shaarey Zedek, like the majority of Conservative congregants across the country, are business owners, executives, or managers, and a large portion of the remainder are professional people—doctors, dentists, lawyers, accountants—though few from the academic or intellectual world are involved. In other words, they are generally among those who have taken the greatest advantage of the upward mobility possible in an affluent America. But when the Adlers arrived in the summer of 1938, some of the prominent and old-line "Hershmanite" leaders, whose perspective was still quite similar to that of most Orthodox Jews in the city, saw the appearance of the young rabbi as evidence of a push for broad change which they felt threatened the congregation's own Judaic soul.

Compounding the issue was the fact that Sharrey Zedek was still the only Conservative congregation in the state. The move further away from Orthodoxy spurred by the arrival of Morris Adler, a graduate of the seminary and a genuinely Conservative rabbi, had caused commotion in Detroit's Jewish community and had been attacked by some elements as pretentious, hypocritical, and corrupting. There were times in that first year when he thought about leaving. "The first year I was packed a few times," recalls Goldie Adler. "In fact it took Buffalo about eight months to find a new man and when they heard Morris wasn't happy, they came and said, 'Look, Rabbi, you can always come back, to us. We don't want you to be unhappy.' But I guess Morris was just determined enough to make a go of it."

In spite of his initial misgivings about stepping in as a strong advocate of Conservative Judaism, it became clear soon enough to Morris Adler that he had made the right choice. "One of the things he liked about Shaarey Zedek," says Mrs. Adler, "was that the president was not the richest man in the congregation but a learned man. Also there was a maximum amount a member might pay as dues so that no man's resignation would constitute a threat." With a nucleus of intelligent support in the congregation there existed an opportunity to perform as a reconciling force, as a unifier and a builder in the congregation and in the community. Furthermore, says Goldie Adler, "The rabbi was not afraid to fight for his beliefs, and he used to say, 'No job will make me give up my convictions.'"

Over the next five years, increasing numbers of Detroit Jews came to know Shaarey Zedek's new assistant rabbi. Thirty-two years old when he arrived in Detroit, he was a broad-shouldered, barrel-chested man with an athletic build and a strong yet sensitive face showing both discipline and generosity—a black moustache over a full sensuous mouth, a broad nose, brown eyes brooding darkly or twinkling behind the scholar's rimless spectacles, heavy brows, and black hair thinning away from a high forehead. His voice was resonant and well controlled, his laughter hearty and thoroughly enjoyed. His extensive knowledge of the tradition and reverence for the past brought him into warm friendship with many of the city's Orthodox. For years he was the only Conservative rabbi on Detroit's council of Orthodox rabbis. At the same time, his concern with the social, political, and economic problems of the day and his consistent attempt to make his Judaism relevant and responsive to contemporary reality soon made him a popular figure with many Reform Jews, Zionists, intellectuals, and ecumenical-minded Christian groups in the community. A Jewish professor at the University of Detroit who met the rabbi soon after the Adlers arrived in the city said simply, "Morris Adler was the only rabbi in the city I could talk to."

Wasting no time in those early years, Rabbi Adler quickly established himself as an articulate voice in the community by penning articles and essays on a variety of often "secular" subjects, addressing various groups in the city, often non-Jewish, and presenting radio talks on matters like brotherhood and the character of religion. During his first year at Shaarey Zedek he wrote an essay on "Free Speech" (first published in Rabbi Kaplan's periodical, *The Reconstructionist*). He begins by posing the argument for suppression: "The American scene is full of panacea peddlers, Utopia salesmen, salvation mongers, wild-scheme brokers—all serving as the 'pied pipers of hysteria' to befuddle and befoul democracy. Never was there such a flood of words in behalf of what are basically undemocratic doctrines.

". . . Hitler states in *Mein Kampf* that if a lie, no matter how impudent, is stated and restated with unflagging emphasis, something of it remains with the auditors. Words thus become the very dynamite which may blow democracy to pieces."

Subsequently the argument is effectively dismantled and an eloquent plea made for social reform and the vigilent protection of civil rights. "We start at the wrong end," he wrote, "when we seek to curb the voices and pens of propagandists. We ought to think in terms of the audience, and concern ourselves with the conditions that make people willing listeners and converts."

As the war at the center of Europe stoked itself into a global battle, Rabbi Adler found it increasingly difficult to justify working with a congregation which had sent over three hundred of its sons into the armed forces. In 1943 he enlisted, attended chaplaincy school, and was assigned to an army hospital in Utica, New York. Mrs. Adler and Shulamith, now twelve and in the seventh grade, stayed with him in Utica until Thanksgiving of 1943 when he received his overseas orders.

In the Philippines with the 11th Airborne, the rabbi's tasks were typical: ministering to his men, writing to a family in English, Yiddish, or Hebrew about the death of their son. Later when he became the first Jewish chaplain to arrive in Japan, he quickly set out to assemble its Jewish population and during his six months there traveled all over the country in a jeep searching for the stateless Jewish refugees, many of them in dire straits, who had fled east into Manchuria during the war and then found themselves in Japan. The rabbi arranged care for these people and paved the road for many of them to come to the United States. "When I was in Hiroshima," he said later, "I felt myself in the presence of a fury and a doom which filled me with foreboding and fear. I know what one of the great scientists meant when he said, 'I am a frightened man.' "

Morris Adler came home to Detroit with the nightmares and resolutions of most sensitive men of the time, and wrote of cultivating an uncompromising hatred of war:

> I mean a determined, impassioned fury, a deep, implacable hatred. Never again must we permit it to be pictured in romantic or glamorous fashion. We should give the lie to every poet who casts a halo of beauty over its grime and blood, and nail to the pillar of shame every pseudophilosopher who extols its virtue. . . . There is nothing beautiful in destruction, nothing heroic in a man crouching behind a gun whose mouth spouts death, or in a flyer dropping ruin from the skies. Foxholes, sinking ships, disfigured bodies, gaping wounds, burning cities are the epitome of cruelty and ugliness.

The rabbi took up without hesitation where he had left off in Detroit. His oft-stated sense that every crisis carries with it the opportunity for new achievement brought him before numerous church and civic organizations across the state preaching "Alternatives to the Atom" such as the harnessing and wise use of power, the "enlarged loyalty to a world order," and education for moral and social maturity. He continued to press for social tolerance and justice for blacks in frank and forceful terms.

The years following the war saw a new surge in synagogue membership—the beginnings of the much heralded "return" of third-generation Jews, most often to Conservative congregations like Shaarey Zedek. The growing reputation of Morris Adler no doubt added to the steady increase in the congregation's rolls, and in his ministry, the rounds of funerals, marriages, births, sick calls, and counseling. He was quickly becoming known as one of the brighter intellectual lights of the Conservative movement, and in

1947 a two-volume collection prepared by the rabbi was published under the title *Selected Passages of the Torah.*

Sociologist Joe Fauman, the Wishnetskys' neighbor and a long-time member of Congregation Shaarey Zedek, feels that Rabbi Adler had an amazing capacity for empathy (a natural gift developed through an enviable self-discipline, thinks Fauman) with an intellectual and emotional range broad enough to move with ease into the minds and hearts of a wide variety of people:

"The sheer force of his intelligence, personality, and vitality was constantly remarkable and tremendously impressive. When this man talked to you, you felt you were the only person in the world who existed for him at that moment. . . . And it made no difference who you were, from the president of the congregation to the caretaker at the synagogue. Nothing that is human was beyond his concern."

EIGHT

Morris Adler said once, "A rabbi practices the most unspecialized profession in the universe. But my association with the young people is, for me, the most satisfying part of my work." Frequent visits to the afternoon school classes at Shaarey Zedek, talks before the young members of the junior congregation, personal chats with the Bar Mitzvah boys, private counseling, appearances before youth groups—all these activities provided Rabbi Adler with the chance to assume his favorite rabbinical role.

The little ones, four and five years old, vividly perceived him as an enormous man of powerful voice and manner, yet also as a warm and tender father- or grandfather-figure who always gave them special attention when he visited their home and loved to have them come to his home at the Feast of Tabernacles to view the sukkah booth constructed in the backyard. As they grew older and began to attend services with their families, they would hear him speak with such intensity that the Bar Mitzvah boys would warn one another to beware of the spittle which might fly from his lips. Many of them coming into more personal contact with the rabbi found him "an easy man to talk to" and, advancing in their studies, became "more impressed with him as a dedicated intellectual." When their achievements in school or in the community won them special recognition, they might receive a personal note of congratulations from their rabbi.

In 1954, the year in which Congregation Shaarey Zedek elected him their chief rabbi for life (Rabbi Hershman had retired after nearly fifty years of service), Morris Adler took a sabbatical year's leave of absence. In November he and his wife left on their first trip to Israel, an experience of importance for both as ardent Zionists. They remained in Israel until January when they returned to spend the next six months in New York City, where Rabbi Adler taught for a semester at the Jewish Theological Seminary as a visiting professor of homiletics.

He continued his intellectual and pedagogical work with his confreres in the rabbinate while serving for a time as chairman of the Law Committee of the Rabbinical Assembly of America and helping to write responsa, or judgments, that affected travel to the synagogue on the Sabbath and the marital status of a woman whose husband has left her.

In 1958 Rabbi Adler's *The World of the Talmud* was published, a small but helpful book which has since gone into a second edition including a printing in paperback. A clear and concise guide to the compendium of Jewish law and its commentaries, the book often sounds one of his favorite themes, the reconciliation of the present with the past. In the late fifties and early sixties he frequently contributed to a new periodical called *Jewish Heritage* published by the B'nai B'rith's Commission on Adult Jewish Education, an organization formed in 1954, which he later served as chairman. He also served on the editorial committee of *Jewish Heritage* helping to shape the magazine's content and direction; he and editor Lily Edelman also collaborated to produce the *Jewish Heritage Reader*, a collection of pieces taken from the periodical. Of her coeditor Lily Edelman has written: ". . . Morris Adler seemed, with every energetic step and gesture, to attack the world-as-it-is. . . . Unlike many professing men of faith, he really did believe, with evey fiber of his being, that man is created in the image and likeness of God and as such has the potential and the obligation to do good and 'to act brotherly.' "

In 1957 Rabbi Adler was named chairman of the United Auto Workers' newly formed Public Review Board, established as a watchdog agency concerned with labor-management disputes. He served as chairman of the board for the rest of his life while also speaking frequently before national and state bodies on church-and-state, intergroup, and interfaith relations. He accepted repeated invitations to serve on boards, panels, commissions, and committees by a variety of agencies, organizations, and institutions on the city, state, and national level. Some of these included the Zionist Organization of Detroit; the Detroit Round Table of Christians and Jews; the Jewish Welfare Federation, the Jewish Community Council, the United Hebrew Schools, and the National Academy for Jewish Studies; Wayne State University's Department of Near Eastern Languages; the Rabbinical Council for the United Jewish Appeal; the Clergy Panel advising the management of American Motors Corporation on moral and ethical matters; the state's Cultural Commission, the Fair Election Practices Commission, the Commission on Ethics in State Affairs, and the Citizen's Committee for Equal Opportunity; the governor's committees on higher education and on problems of the aging; and the U.A.W. backed Community Health Association. Largely because of this public service and his continuing attempt to extend the synagogue's influence deep into the community, in 1960 he was awarded an honorary doctor of laws degree from Wayne State University.

Not everyone was entirely pleased with the rabbi's extensive involvements, however. Said his assistant at Shaarey Zedek, Rabbi Irwin Groner: "'A man is known by his enemies,' he used to say, and he was proud of his enemies. For example, we have over a hundred doctors in our congregation and some of them were not very happy when the rabbi accepted a position on the board of directors of the U.A.W.'s Community Health Association. But while there might be criticism of the rabbi on one score or another, usually it was couched within a great respect for the man himself. Some friends and congregants used to criticize him for being so heavily involved in secular affairs in the community—'What do you need this for?' they used to ask—but he would go right on with it."

Some of the young people of the congregation were especially ambivalent on this point. One young woman formerly active at the synagogue said: "Some people began to think of him as a little king, running the synagogue with unquestioned authority while enjoying the adulation of the community. At the same time we were proud of his reputation, but he had less and less time for the young people, and this was upsetting to some of them."

Most agree, however, that Rabbi Adler did not neglect his rabbinical duties to his congregation. Innumerable notes and letters written in his own longhand (as was all his personal and pastoral correspondence) are still treasured by their recipients. His sick calls and visits to the bereaved were frequent. Said a close friend: "He was a remarkable listener. When he listened he was actively involved with you and you had the feeling that he was totally absorbed in what you were saying. Counseling he enjoyed and did a great deal of. Nonetheless, he was very cautious in his counseling and he had respect for and knowledge of the field of psychiatry. He referred many people to psychiatrists and social-service agencies. But as he used to say, 'When people say they know about psychiatrists and social services and they want to talk to a rabbi, you don't send them away. . . .'"

He had gained the reputation of being "the best man in the city in the pulpit," "a charismatic speaker who when deeply moved could have a tremendously powerful effect on his audience." Though he generally spoke without notes and gave the impression of great facility, he agonized at length over his sermons. "I have a feeling of love and tenderness for words," he said once. "I cannot forget that they are among the greatest gifts the past has given us."

Unlike most Conservative rabbis, in addition to conducting the weekly Sabbath service Rabbi Adler usually took part in daily morning services. "That was another phenomenon," said Rabbi Groner. "He somehow managed to find the time." Harold Schachern, a religion writer for the Detroit *News* and a good friend of Rabbi Adler's, once noted: "Like most busy men, Rabbi Adler has had difficulty saying no to those who would have imposed on his time. His desk, about which visitors often joked, has always been piled high with correspondence, pamphlets, magazines, and other literature which he always insisted on reading before disposing of. At each visit to his office, he always insisted on teasing visitors that the pile was a new one."

Sleeping an average of five hours a night, "the rabbi crammed two hours of work into every hour he lived," said Goldie Adler. "Morris Adler thrived on work," said Rabbi Groner, "and he liked to be very busy—he wanted the telephone ringing, people calling on him, asking for his help. If there was a lull and these things weren't happening, he would get a little restless. He wanted to be busy. I know he said he didn't like it, but I think he did."

Rabbi Groner came to Shaarey Zedek from Arkansas in 1959 in the wake of some unhappiness in the congregation over the fact that Rabbi Adler's preceding assistant had been dismissed. The former assistant rabbi, a talented young man especially popular with the young people of the congregation, had apparently felt that he was not being given sufficient responsibility or authority. For his part, Rabbi Adler thought the younger man was trying to establish his position in an overly ambitious and a not always appropriate fashion. The result was a clash of personalities which led a number of congregants to attempt a reconciliation. Finally the younger man left. As Rabbi Adler explained to one member, "It's just like a marriage that has turned out badly. When two people are incompatible they should not stay together." The episode contributed to the notion held by some that Rabbi Adler was a man with authoritarian instincts in a position of considerable power.

Questions put to Rabbi Adler by young people concerned with the meaning of observance and at times with the basis of Judaism itself were insistent and becoming more so. Said one girl, "Some were disappointed when he refused to give hard and fast answers." At such times the rabbi might say as he once wrote:

> Judaism has never developed an official statement as to what one must believe to be accounted a Jew. . . . The Jew is not taught any catechism and is not bound by an ironclad formula. The Talmud, whose interpretations, applications, and enlargements have shaped Jewish deeds and practices even more than the Bible, records the clashing views of differing schools and scholars, preserving minority opinions along with the binding majority dicta. Even the thirteen articles of faith drawn up by Maimonides in the twelfth century, which are still printed in traditional prayer books, have not gained universal acceptance.
>
> To be sure, profound affirmations are implicit in the tradition. But these have never been formalized as an authoritative creed. . . . Being the culture of a community rather than the faith of a church, Judaism never found it necessary to make uniformity of belief its central cohesion.

Rabbi Adler knew well the difficulty of producing "hard and fast answers," but he also felt that the young especially needed something firmer than what they were getting as an explanation of the faith being urged on them. "Rabbi Adler spoke often of the need for a rationale for Judaism," said Rabbi Groner. "He said,

'We're dealing with a generation which faces an intellectual challenge to religion.' But he was not yet a system builder like Kaplan. His was a mind that dealt in sharp insights which it refined and deepened but he had not as yet synthesized his ideas into a larger structure."

Of course the young people were not the only ones asking hard questions. A matron in the congregation demanded of Morris Adler one day, "Rabbi, convince me I should keep a kosher home." The rabbi replied, "Sara, if I have to convince you, then you shouldn't do it. Only if you do it because you want to do it will it be good for you." The divisions he had found on his arrival in 1938 had not disappeared twenty years later, though his sympathetic and politic personality had brought considerable reconciliation and mitigated much of the harshness. Many of the same questions were still being asked; many of the same arguments were still being raised.

"Actually we have an Orthodox service," says Mrs. Adler, "all the way except for men and women sitting together and the sermon in English. And so Morris had hoped that it would really become a Conservative congregation in that the services would be more modernized and would appeal more to the young people. To cut the time down, there are ways a rabbi knows what one could and should leave out. But we still had groups of people who had a memory of a father and the way he worshiped, which is also a very sweet attitude that one doesn't tear apart. And he used to find fault with his colleagues who would come into a congregation and wipe the slate clean and start off. You can't build a tradition overnight."

The underlying question that Rabbi Adler confronted in attempting to reconcile those in his congregation unwilling to move and those wanting change was always this: If one cannot accept as do the strict Orthodox that biblical Jewish law was divinely ordained for all time, on what intelligently consistent basis does one choose to observe one ritual, rite, or practice in the home or synagogue and not another? As early as 1948 the rabbi had spoken of the problem before a national convention of his associates in the Conservative movement; ". . . we must face the truth that we have been halting between fear and danger; fear of the Orthodox and danger of Reform. . . . The time has come for our emergence from the valley of indecision. For one thing, there is a growing grass-root demand for . . . clarification of our position. There is a growing impatience on the part of our people. . . ." Milton Steinberg, the highly respected Conservative rabbi, put it perhaps most succintly: "Truth to tell, Conservatism has still not formulated the philosophy on which it stands."

Morris Adler said once: "Conservative Judaism is a religion that seeks wholeness and completeness. It wants to embrace all of Judaism. It rejects the way of those who seize upon one aspect and regard that as the whole. It sees Judaism as unifying tradition in which life's polarities and diversities are joined in a great symphony of faith." But he as well as anyone knew that the search and the wish are far from being satisfied, and the form of the symphony remains undetected and unexplained.

As he entered what would be the last decade of his life, many thought Rabbi Adler's concern for the young was growing even stronger. In 1960 the parents of one of his young congregants told the rabbi that they felt it was not right that their son was about to be Bar Mitzvahed without really knowing his rabbi. They felt that whatever else he had to do, this was at least as important. "Tell him to poke his head in my door when he sees it open," said Rabbi Adler. The boy did and thenceforth had occasional half-hour talks with the rabbi, who later reported that the young man was also making it a habit to come around after Sabbath Services with a critique of his sermon. When the parents promised to speak to their son about the matter, Rabbi Adler said quickly, "Don't you dare say a thing. At least I know he's listening! And besides, you'd be surprised how often he's right."

PART II

The mind that centers on learning will imbibe a definite morality as a consequence. Love of truth, precision, the humility that comes from an awareness of the infinite scope of knowledge, respect for the minds of others—these are qualities that the devotee of study will develop. To be sure, now and then, as the Rabbis were fully aware, a scholar of undoubted learning exhibits petulance and arrogance. Two answers may be given. The first is that these undesirable traits might have appeared in an even more aggravated form had this individual remained uneducated. The second is that his approach to learning was faulty at the outset. The need is for more study, not less.

—RABBI MORRIS ADLER

NINE

Replete with gently rolling hills, parks, wooded areas, and tree-lined streets in front of well-kept Victorian homes with their amazing gables and turrets, Ann Arbor is an excellent place for what was probably Richard's favorite pastime, the long walk. It is also a place where many talented and resourceful students have felt excited by an infectious sense that in numerous corners of town at almost any hour things vital, intelligent, or somehow important are being said, read, performed, or observed. There are those who say it can be overstimulating. There are others who call it the home of a cold and impersonal educational factory.

Even before World War II, the University of Michigan was overcrowded and stamped with the characteristics of one of the nation's multiversities; in little over twenty-five years its total enrollment has more than doubled to 38,000. Its campus has spread outward and across the Huron River to the new North Campus, but numerous new buildings have also appeared where there seemed to be no main campus space at all, producing a sometimes ugly, sometimes attractive mixture of Classic, Gothic, Victorian, and Modern. The proliferation of bureaucratic machinery has prompted some students to speculate that a few hard-line secretaries are actually holding the whole contraption together. The hum one hears in Ann Arbor, they maintain, is actually the Machine systematically decimating individual dreams and gifts.

U. of M.'s president Robben W. Fleming, widely noted for his effective dealing with militant radicals, feels that the increasing size of the university "has been vastly overrated as a problem.

Once you're enrolling more than 1,000 students, this business of knowing everyone is nonsense. It's not a question of how big you are but of whether you can manage your size so people can find identity in their own groups."

Though recognized as one of the most distinguished American academies primarily because of what occurs in its classrooms, the university is often epitomized in the minds of its students and alumni by the basement grill of the Michigan Union where the acid and pot heads, the hung-up and hangers-on, the dropouts, hippies, and revolutionaries of subterranean Ann Arbor meet and mingle with their more legitimate collegiate counterparts. The pale-faced girl with Indian costume and waist-length hair eyes a rosy-cheeked co-ed in plaids and penny loafers with the remark "That's how I looked four years ago when I first came here." Small clusters of students from Nigeria, Egypt, India, or Thailand talk politics in English and stare in their native tongue at American girls in short skirts. Harried professors of philosophy or history write their books on pads of yellow paper amid the pleasant languor of Bohemians, the lively polemics of earnest young law students, and the domestic cackle of university secretaries on their coffee break. The lonely ones who have forgotten or lost the ability to be alone with themselves remain until the gloomy ceiling fixtures (which seem to cast more shadow than light on the tiny print of paperback books) are finally turned off at midnight.

Into this variegated university world came Richard and his freshman class in September 1960. Freshmen arrive with various kinds and degrees of sophistication; most, however, seem to find doors newly opened, lifelong restraints suddenly relaxed, old unexamined values now disputed or plumbed deeply, and the intimate confrontation of myriad variants of the human personality. The intensity of competition and the constantly increasing amounts of knowledge to be accumulated are alone enough to cause many students considerable difficulty. When the experience is viewed as a whole, it is not hard to believe recent figures indicating that one out of every ten freshmen in American universities will require professional help with disruptive emotional problems before he finishes his college days.

For many young Jewish students living for the first time in an environment not predominantly Jewish, the college experience can be even more complex and significant. Alfred Jospe, one of many

Jewish commentators concerned with the state of the faith among these young people, has said:

> The Judaism which a young person brings when he enters college frequently tends to evaporate under the pressure of mature intellectual challenge, exposure to new ideas and new human contacts. He frequently discovers that what he knows of his religion does not seem to present a live intellectual option. At the very moment when, for the first time, he is removed from his previous intellectual, emotional, and social context, he encounters an entirely new world of ideas and people of different races, culture, religions and social classes.

He does not, it seems, often turn to Hillel, the Jewish religious affiliate on American college campuses, as a kind of home away from home. Of the five thousand to seven thousand young Jews at the University of Michigan, for example, only five hundred or so are described by Hillel director Herman Jacobs as "fairly active," coming at least once a month to Hillel-sponsored religious activities, mixers, lectures, discussions, and classes.

Richard attended a few Hillel functions during his freshman year but did not come to services and apparently lost interest rather quickly. Said Dr. Jacobs: "We thought for a while Richard was going to pitch in with his freshness, humor, insight, and intelligence but he just stopped coming around. Once in a while I would run into him and he would say, 'I'm going to come and see you,' indicating that he would like to talk about really essential matters —what we call today the 'nitty-gritty'—but this never happened."

In his orientation group and with him during their first few days of acclimation in Ann Arbor, Julie Lieberman found Richard enthusiastic about starting his college work. "He was very ambitious and wanted to take large steps very quickly," she said. It would be the best experience of his life, he expected, one which would shape or alter him, perhaps change him profoundly.

The beginning of the college year 1960–61 almost directly coincided with the opening of the American presidential campaign. Earlier in the year—to be precise, on February 1, 1960—the quiet fifties had come to an end on campus when four Negro college freshmen staged the first lunch-counter sit-in at Woolworth's in Greensboro, North Carolina. The *Michigan Daily* had for its 1960–61 editor New Left leader Tom Hayden, for whom Richard reportedly had high regard and who issued as one of his first tasks a student manifesto for the 1960's:

> Such world wide student participation, taking all forms from sitting-in to peaceful lobbying to mob violence, has been conditioned by the critical world context within which students live. It is a world apparently without leaders, a world of vast confusion, changing cultures, strained by the nearness of total war, and it has been in such shape throughout the life of almost every student. This is the environment the current freshman class inherits—a confused, irritated world in which the classical educational process has taken on a vigorous new emphasis because the student himself has taken on a new, more active, rebellious, militant orientation.

In addition to the many other friends and acquaintances who were with him now in Ann Arbor, Richard's roommate in the Hayden House section of East Quad was John Samuels (pseud.), a good friend from Mumford and the A.Z.A. John and Richard had asked for and received permission to live together during their first year. A slim six-footer with dark hair neatly combed, his eyes framed with glasses, John is intelligent and articulate, but in high school he seems to have been in some awe of these qualities in Richard. "I was not knowledgeable in politics," he says, "but I liked to listen to Richard talk because I could learn a lot from him."

From the start, according to John, Richard concentrated intensely on his studies; being a university student was serious business and generally he didn't enter the frivolity many freshmen enjoy. Up each morning at 6:30, he would study until it was time for his 8:00 class. Except for classes, labs, meals, and the one night out he allowed himself each week, Richard remained in the small room studying almost constantly, sitting at his desk with his elbows resting on the top, often with his hands over his ears to muffle any clatter. Once in a while he would stretch out on his bed if he was reading something he particularly liked, and occasionally he would play background music on the radio when the dorm was especially noisy. At mealtime he would slip on a coat and tie as required, head for the dining room where he would "eat like a horse . . . as if he were feeding a furnace," and return quickly upstairs to study.

Richard's primary concern, John contends, was to win the best possible grades by meeting or topping his teachers' highest standards. He worked only with course texts, reading only what was required and nothing for his own pleasure. The conception of pursuing knowledge for its own sake was only secondary for him. "I didn't blame him for that," says John. "A freshman at U. of M. has to start that way to establish himself academically." Complaining of being a slow reader, Richard spent forty to fifty hours a week studying outside of class because, he said, he was afraid he would fall behind. He never cut a class except in dire emergency.

With such a schedule Richard was almost of necessity considered a loner by most of his floormates, the majority of whom were engineering students. There were only two other Jews on the floor besides Richard and John. The new roommates rarely spoke at length or in depth to one another, shared in few bull sessions, and in fact saw very little of one another. John did little studying in the room and could not relax there while Richard was studying, which was most of the time. Said John: "He had more or less taken over the room. Once in a while I would remind him that I had paid for half of it, and it would be nice to use it occasionally." On Richard's desk was a UNICEF ashtray which usually contained a few coins: John and Richard fined each other for various infractions of the room rules they had mutually established, the money going to UNICEF. On Jewish holidays Richard lit candles in the room, a token religious gesture in which John refused to join him.

As the candidates and campaigners came to town, Richard allowed himself the first few breaks in his study routine. Hubert Humphrey arrived first, and Richard brought Debbie Rossman along to hear the passionate speech of one of his political heroes. On October 14 John Kennedy came to Ann Arbor and Richard was one of the ten thousand people out after midnight to greet him. At 1:40 in the morning Kennedy stood on the steps of the Michigan Union and gave a short speech in which he mentioned the possibility of forming an overseas Youth Corps and called upon the students to offer themselves to the cause of the United States and its role in the world. Returning to the dorm afterward, Richard, with a glowing smile, told Jonathan Rose (one of his two Jewish floormates), "I touched him. He shook hands with me and I said, 'Good luck' and he said, 'Thank you.' "

On October 20 Chester Bowles, stumping for Kennedy, came to talk in the main ballroom of the Union. Richard was again among those who jammed the room to capacity as Bowles spoke casually and effectively, at one point describing the service work that his own son was currently finding so satisfying in Nigeria. The talk caused considerable comment on campus.

In the crowd was a young married couple, Alan and Judith Guskin, doing graduate work at the university. Afterward the Guskins went home and drafted a letter to the *Daily*, suggesting the formation of a group to promote the Kennedy-Bowles idea of a Youth Corps. The letter was published three days later, from which time the Guskin phone "never stopped ringing." Within two weeks a newly formed organization calling itself Americans Committed to World Responsibility (A.C.W.R.), with Mrs. Guskin as its president, had collected eight hundred signed petitions, with thousands of names including Richard's, each pledging years of service abroad. Said Jon Rose, "Richard came in one day and said quietly but happily, 'I think this is going to be something big.' "

Through a friend who was in on the founding of the group, Richard was soon involved in the business of making the new organization function. Mrs. Guskin remembers him well:

"Richard seemed very concerned with being bright and intense and committed. This is the image he seemed to want to project. During the first couple of months he was always in the office, always working, always concerned about the projects of the group and willing to do anything. At the same time he did not seem to be forming friendships within the group, perhaps because he seemed so overbearing and insistent—you had to give him all your attention all the time. He was willing to work, but he wanted to be heard and to be in the limelight."

Richard was in the limelight to some extent for the first month or two. On the front page of the *Daily* for November 5, 1960, is a photo showing Judith Guskin handing a sheaf of petitions to John Kennedy at the Toledo Airport. Behind Mrs. Guskin with a group of three or four A.C.W.R. members is Richard with his large grin. On November 4 he had traveled with the others some sixty miles to meet briefly with JFK in Toledo. According to the *Daily* story: "Top Democrats have confirmed that the Youth Corps had as its main inspiration the activities of the A.C.W.R. here at the University."

Actually, though he had wanted to, Richard did not play a leading intellectual role in the A.C.W.R. According to one member, Richard's presence was simply tolerated among the leaders of the group as long as he was willing to address envelopes and compile book lists for study groups. "You were never quite sure," he said, "if you were offending Richard. People would put him off, not take his ideas seriously, or reject them in an ungentle way. Yet he was always controlled and restrained and never seemed to react badly to such treatment."

At the same time, Richard appeared to the Guskins and others as somewhat self-conscious and affected, a bit stuffy and self-righteous about the importance of his opinions and academic achievements. He did play a part in a symposium on the Youth Corps plan sponsored by the A.C.W.R. in December, but thereafter he more or less dropped out of the group. From the start the A.C.W.R. had wanted the corps to be an international organization. When it actually became an arm of American foreign policy, Richard and many others were disappointed and no longer enthusiastic. At one point in his second term in Ann Arbor he apologized to Judith Guskin for no longer being involved in the activity of the group, but said this was necessary because of the demands of his academic work.

Richard had enrolled in the honors program at U. of M., a specially administered curriculum including a nucleus of courses intended to challenge particularly talented students. A study of the program released by the university that fall maintained that "honors students feel more satisfied with their overall college experience than do comparably bright students" and "feel less overwhelmed by the size of the University" because of closer ties with classmates and teachers. For the first two years Richard would receive the usual assortment of basic liberal arts and science courses.

Though he did well in all his first-term courses, Richard got off to a rather inauspicious start in honors English with Alan T. Gaylord, then an instructor in his third year of teaching and subsequently one of Richard's best faculty friends. In the first week of the term Richard wrote an in-class theme which earned what must have been a very disturbing D. Below his title, "Awareness," the bluebook read as follows:

> "Pilot Com. 4 and Contemporary Affairs," I repeated for the third time with a mixture of expectancy, doubt, and wonder cracking in my voice. Undoubtably I had challenged myself

with the two most demanding courses Mumford High School had to offer.

I had been considering an adventure of this nature for some time. I finally resolved that I would request pilot comp. 4, a class requiring the reading of twenty novels with an impromtu [*sic*]—the most insidious method for relating one's thoughts in a literary endeavor—following each novel. In addition, I would request contemporary affairs. Contempt, as it was affectionately labeled by its victims, was reputed to be a fascinating study of current events which required exhaustive readings. I shuddered when considering the demanding nature of these two classes and genuinely doubted whether they would actually make a positive contribution to my intellectual development.

My fears finally crystallized when I discovered that after hesitantly applying for admission into these two mammoth courses, my requests had received a positive response. I vacillated between ecstacy and grief when I was informed of this, but proceeded courageously to assume the responsibility of the courses.

That was my attitude upon entering pilot comp. and contempt. Upon completing the classes, I clearly recognized that I did not tremble with one emotion which I had once thought would dominate my sentiments upon finishing my eventful semester—that emotion being regret. But, to be more specific, regret was present at that moment of termination, but it was a positive regret for I truly felt sad that I would be required to leave these two classes behind.

The reason for my complete reversal in attitude can be discovered in the nature of the two classes. Unbearably demanding they were, but they were also wonderfully productive. In the process of my last high school semester I became aware of two worlds—one of literature and the other of contemporary man struggling to improve himself. A great awakening occurred within me—an awakening for which my two fearful, overbearing classes were responsible.

Key sentence: That which is most demanding in life is the most productive in making a substantial contribution to the development of the individual.

As required, Richard wrote in response to Professor Gaylord's extensive comments (for example, "Language up on stilts eight feet high. C'mon down to earth."):

I'm afraid I tried to create an impression in too short a time, and failed miserably. I should have concentrated upon a description of my time in these classes elaborating on their intense nature, causing the reader to feel the awakening I felt, and thereby proving my point.

The language of the essay is too meaningless and affected. A revised version would have vocabulary and phraseology which would be on stilts only two feet high.

Almost a decade later, Gaylord has this to say about the bluebook: "One does not wish to make these exercises oversignificant, but there are at least themes here you will recognize: the intense concern with self, discovery of self; the intellectual intensity expressed in a kind of emotional self-caricature."

Two and a half weeks later Richard handed in a three-and-a-half-page typewritten theme entitled "Know Thyself":

> There was a foreboding despair inherent in the night's silence. The clouds blanketed the black sky denying the moon and stars their accustomed pleasure in guiding man in his nocturnal travels. The sharp coolness of the summer air stung the sensitive flesh, and one sought warmth from the uninviting atmosphere. The hollow shrill of an occasional bird rang in the blackness with a melancholy tone. The ground was damp and soft, and one felt unusually uncomfortable by being a victim of the night's mugginess.
>
> Suddenly the silence was shattered by the harshness of a human voice. The sounds possessed an almost eerie quality. Responding to my name, I turned and saw in the distance the large familiar outline of the head counselor, Murray. I quickly noticed that he was not in a congenial state of mind. Mechanically placing myself on the defensive, I approached him in a cautious silence.
>
> "Dick, I want to speak to you for a second," he said in his usual commanding tone. He motioned for me to sit on the bench next to where we were standing. I could recognize the fact that a reckoning was swiftly approaching, and, dropping my defenses, I allowed myself to succumb to the inevitable.
>
> I stared at the shapeless ground while he spoke. When it was required of me, I nodded in indifferent agreement. The drone of his words began to assume form and substance in my mind. They quickly conjured forth vivid recollections of my summer as a counselor.

"Dick, I'm afraid to say that you've been neglecting your responsibility lately. It's unfortunate that I have to tell you this almost at the end of the camp season, but you must be made aware of it. Now of course we all know you began as a successful counselor, but you . . . ," and the rest of his words lost themselves in the bleakness of the night.

"Began as a successful counselor" resounded in my memory. I instantly recalled the enthusiasm and dedication I possessed when I was given my first group of campers. I was responsible for only four boys. They were young and easy to handle. The wonderful and wholesome relationship which developed between the boys and myself was the hallmark of my success. I developed an understanding of the faults and inhibitions, the virtues and desires of each boy, and through an understanding, gained their respect and love. We did many things together—we learned from common experiences and were able to laugh at our mistakes because we were one group.

Then my reverie was pierced by the name of Barry Sands [pseud.]. Murray mentioned the boy in a harsh tone, but I recognized that his voice was tinged with a little sympathy. Barry Sands was a name that struck fear in the hearts of the counselors. The rigors of army basic training were dwarfed by the difficulties and frustrations one encountered in caring for the demon. Actually it was an unfortunate situation. The boy had been undergoing psychiatric treatment. Although he desired to be friends with the other campers, he ultimately antagonized them to a degree of unimaginable ferocity. Barry Sands was a bomb that could wreak havoc, and one never knew when he would explode.

After my initial success at camp, my ego was fortified enabling me to accept with confidence the challenge of almost any situation. I therefore requested that I be given a larger, older group of boys and that Barry Sands be placed under my care.

The dilemma that ensued was a veritable hell. It was necessary for me to be with my group twenty-four hours a day. Excitement, frustration, and antagonism never appeared to diminish in intensity during this period. Fights and petty jealousies alternated with suspicions and ridicule. The boys never seemed to understand each other, and because of the number in the group and the complexity of the situation, I was powerless to improve the atmosphere. I tried hard to do well and be just. But even the most successful of my efforts was soon disregarded by my campers, and they returned to their previous state of unrelenting antagonism. Ultimately I succumbed to the pressures and frustrations; I assumed an air of indifference and began to neglect my responsibility.

I then focused my attention upon Murray's voice. His mild monotone was being replaced by a harsh angry quality. He listed in quick succession the oversights for which I had been guilty. He described sarcastically the eagerness which had accompanied my request for a more difficult group. He ridiculed the confidence that I had exhibited and how I had assured him of my ability to cope with the new situation.

Then my brain was plagued by self-criticism and condemnation. The misery of the previous three weeks spoke loudly accusing me of creating the undesirable relationships of my group because of my profound lack of experience and maturity. I had been presumptuous and overstepped my limitations; now I was paying the penalty.

The meeting ended. I stood still momentarily and then proceeded to my cabin. Gazing up at the heavens, I saw a lone star shining through the massy cloud-covered sky. I smiled in recognition.

Theme: One must be aware of one's abilities and their limitations in order to succeed in one's endeavors.

Displaying many of the same poses and suffering from most of the same stylistic and organizational faults of Richard's first attempt—stiff, abstract, overformal diction, and a vague illustration of theme—this second effort received a C-minus. Professor Gaylord rightly warns of reading with too much hindsight, but, as he says, "It is typically—and spookily—neurotic." At this point he set up for Richard a rigorous method of analyzing his own writing in order to prune his exaggerated style and become "more aware of this tendency to grandiosity and pomposity."

Apparently Richard took the advice and worked very hard. In January he delivered his final paper, a careful, well-reasoned twelve-page analysis of Alexander Jones's interpretation of *The Turn of the Screw,* Henry James's classic horror tale. Pretension can be found in the title, "James, Jones, and Wishnetsky," but rarely in the text, which is generally straightforward and well worded. Richard concluded:

There is no one explanation; one may be more probable than another but I reluctantly concede even that. *The Turn of the Screw* reeks with ambiguity. It can be read at several different

> levels thereby appealing to an enormous variety of readers. But this appeal may appall when one attempts to arrive at a conclusive interpretation. Such an interpretation does not exist. Perhaps this is a quality that will preserve *The Turn of the Screw* as a great work making it a literary challenge to every generation.

The paper received a much deserved A and carried Professor Gaylord's red-ink comment: "I am overjoyed at your writing. You must tell me how conscious this was—at almost every point, you are not too wordy, you are clear, you are not ponderous, you are sharp, you are the tweedy political scientist of the future."

Richard replied with a penciled note: "I was all too conscious when writing the paper. The agony of rewriting it is good proof. I spent eight hours on the original—another eight in revision. After the ordeal, I felt like chopped liver right after being chopped. I offer genuine thanks for making me feel like chopped liver."

Looking back, Professor Gaylord says: "I thought we had 'won' from the evidence of the last paper . . . but of course the style would continue to reflect the personality, as it oscillated between control and chaos. Dick remembered this class as a 'conquering'—but then, he liked to satisfy his memory with a series of crises which he thought had been victories in personality development."

Not infrequently, Rabbi Adler paid visits to the campus in Ann Arbor, and in December 1960 he gave a Hillel lecture which Richard likely attended. "On Being a Jew" the rabbi once wrote: "Though society is sometimes determined to isolate me, my Jewishness takes me out in the broad places where mankind dwells. The dilemmas which inhere in human life and which all sensitive men share—dilemmas arising out of rationality, loneliness, the search for fulfillment, ambivalence, the choice of values to live by—are in my case refined and deepened as I seek to resolve them in the specific frame of my existential situation as a Jew."

TEN

Encouraged but not satisfied by his first-term success, Richard vowed openly to roommate John an all-out effort in the next semester to win an all-A report, a goal he had narrowly missed on his first try. One of his new courses was the freshman honors seminar in American government, presided over by an enthusiastic and cordial young professor of political science named Norman C. Thomas. Working closely with his small group of students, Professor Thomas soon decided that Richard possessed "a first-rate mind" and could think through a problem thoroughly and rigorously and articulate his answer with great lucidity. Said the professor:

"I was almost a bit in awe of Richard at that time, finding someone so young who possessed such a clear and incisive intelligence. He seemed a potentially excellent scholar, not at all afraid of work. As a freshman he talked to me a couple of times about his future studies and seemed quite sure he would be doing his work in political science. Of course Richard was never one to lay out his life in a practical fashion; he never conceived of Richard Wishnetsky six or seven years hence, a holder of a Ph.D., doing solid scholarly work at a reputable university."

As indicated, Richard's social life during his first year at U. of M. was not particularly active. His "dates" usually involved casual or chance meetings with old friends like Julie Lieberman, Debbie Rossman, and Marcia Frankel, coffee and a lot of talk, and once in a while a movie. There were of course new girls to elicit Richard's interest and one of these was Carolyn Toll, a blond, good-looking Jewish girl, then also a freshman. Carolyn got to know Richard in connection with their work for the A.C.W.R. and for the Young Democrats on the Kennedy campaign:

"Richard was a well-dressed liberal with the manners of a conservative boy. He was always very cordial and polite, but he seemed to me a little pompous. He always carried a great pile of books with him. He would walk across the street to say hello to you and in that sense he was a bit of a charmer, but he seemed concerned with being somebody and taking a leadership role. He seemed very ambitious and a climber and I suppose for all of these reasons when he asked me out a couple of times I didn't accept. His manners and his niceness seemed only half-genuine."

By this time Richard had reached his full height of an inch less than six feet but still appeared slight and unathletic at 140 pounds or so. His hands were small and restless; his nose and forehead were not finely cut. His pale, easily flushed skin was only mildly accented by his reddish-brown hair and bespectacled hazel eyes.

Most of his photographs present a boyish face (usually without the glasses) nearly masked by a spacious smile offering little more than intense affability. Without the smile, the lines around the eyes and mouth become a bit grim and are not appealing. As in high school, his clothes were neat, monotonous, and unstylish; he invariably walked the campus in a three-quarter-length tweed jacket.

He seemed to have an eye for only the more attractive girls, thought Carolyn Toll. This must have caused him some trouble, because Richard himself, though not repulsive or unpleasant to look at, "was not very attractive physically, and good-looking girls are generally going to favor good-looking fellows."

Good-looking Debbie Rossman saw Richard more frequently in the spring term for coffee and conversation filled with politics and social issues, boyfriends and girl friends. While she was cynical about the university, Richard seemed quite pleased with his progress in school. Happily, he had found more people like himself and felt more at home, she thought. One day Debbie called Richard for some quick information on a place called Vietnam, because she had heard vaguely that it was soon going to be important. "I'm intellectually rather lazy," said Debbie. "And Richard was always so well informed I'd just call up and get the word from him." As usual Richard appeared knowledgeable and thought the United States commitment a mistake. He was not, however, a pacifist, she thought, because whenever the subject of Germany came up he could very well justify war. "He had a thing about the Germans," said Debbie. "The first time I ever heard the idea that Jews shouldn't buy German-made cars was from Richard."

On the subject of love Debbie found Richard as idealistic as ever. He was fond of talking about the girls in his life; he was, he said, getting on very well with Marcia Frankel. Their acquaintance had been renewed during orientation week when he took Marcia to another Bergman film, *Virgin Spring*. Again Richard reported being extremely moved; again Marcia reacted to his large response by pretending not to be. The pattern for much of their relationship had been set from the beginning. Marcia says that on their casual coffee or study dates she was always out to undercut what she considered to be his exaggerated passion and idealism.

During their first two years in Ann Arbor, Richard, according to Marcia, seemed to pluck from his extensive reading a new philosophy "every week or so" and would quickly test his ideas on different friends. John Samuels confirms that Richard valued Marcia highly as an intellectual or academic referent. In this role and when Richard would come to her with his latest philosophical system or sociopolitical theory, Marcia would undertake (usually with much success) to poke holes in it. Richard would come back the next week to say, "Yes, maybe you were right about that, but listen to this now." And Marcia would go through the process again. He had a bout with Ayn Rand and was very attracted by her intensely individualistic philosophy. Marcia was also taken with Miss Rand for a time, but they soon found her philosophy a simplistic apology for selfishness.

Richard then moved toward the opposite extreme and went on a "socialist kick," constantly talking about the evils of world capitalism. This was also just a phase, however, and Richard soon went on to something else. He was, according to Marcia, always within the confines of one or another philosophical system encountered in his reading, never in between or alone with his own thoughts. Always embracing one ideology or another, when one no longer worked for him he simply jumped into another, seemingly unable to function intellectually without being within a system.

When they studied together for exams in a political-science course, Richard would ask a question, then close his eyes, tilt his head back, and rattle off his answer. He was only displaying his virtuosity, Marcia thought, and was not interested in exchanging ideas on the material. She criticized him harshly for being concerned only with A's and never really challenging his beliefs by going to books outside the course. At this point Marcia shared some of Richard's romanticism, and they would often read together silently or aloud to each other Gibran's *The Prophet,* D. H. Lawrence's *We Have Come Through,* and Walter Benton's *This Is My Beloved.* Predictably Richard was fond of J. D. Salinger's romantic cast of suffering, sensitive, and intelligent adolescents outraged by rampant hypocrisy.

Apparently Richard was deriving from all of this much more than Marcia then reckoned. He was quite serious about Marcia, but he also knew that she was regularly dating Bob Moss (pseud.), a friend of his at Mumford, a leader in the A.Z.A., and then a sophomore at Wayne State. Tall, dark, and good-looking, Bob met Marcia at the same B.B.Y.O. dance that introduced her to

Richard. Three years later, after her junior year at U. of M., Bob and Marcia were married.

On weekends and vacations at home in Detroit, Richard would often go to Bob's house (a few blocks from the Wishnetskys) for intellectual discussion. Soon, however, Richard would be asking Bob about his progress with Marcia, indirectly at first but later actually pumping Bob for details of his sex life. Bob was not particularly anxious to talk along these lines, so Richard would tell Bob how well *he* was getting along with Marcia, finally announcing toward the end of the spring term that he was quite sure she was more or less committed to him and that he, Richard, had won her.

Both Bob and Marcia describe Richard's conception of this relationship as outright fantasy. Marcia insists that she never gave Richard any romantic encouragement. Yet the Mosses now think they were perhaps not fair to Richard. Says Bob, "We've talked about it since and decided that we were always undermining Richard, always emasculating him, never taking him seriously enough."

During the course of his year in the dorm Richard found he generally had little in common with most of his floormates and, according to John Samuels, disliked most of them. There were exceptions, of course, a handful of friends he respected and could talk to. Jon Rose considered him very friendly and more mature than most. Another old friend from Mumford recalls Richard returning from Detroit on occasion bearing a crate of his favorite brand of seedless grapefruit, some of which he would pass out to friends in the dorm.

Richard, however, was very "forthright," said John, in talking to or about people and would say anything that came into his head. He actually let some people know he detested them. He was not adept at hiding what John termed his "high self-esteem" and would not allow anyone to waste his time. When he did attempt to be one of the boys, he could be amiable but humorously inept at the small talk of a bull session. His use of vulgarity was strained and awkward, his put-downs and retorts to casual remarks were usually overblown failures.

The trouble in part was that Richard abhorred the sexual bravado and pseudosophistication so common in the freshman dorm. With his almost classic Victorian conceptions and idealistic schema, he was prompted to discuss and often condemn the behavior of others in terms of the abstract principles he had set for himself. In this regard, he was extremely dogmatic: "Richard was stone-rigid," said John. According to his roommate, Richard's vocational plans had shifted somewhat to include teaching. He saw himself, said John, as a purveyor of knowledge and wisdom and was anxious to assume this role with friends and acquaintances.

From the start, Richard frequently gave John stern advice and commented on his progress in school, his social behavior, and his friends. As Richard's judgments became severely negative, life in the room became strained. Richard was in effect telling his roommate what to do, where to go, whom to see, and how to act. Finally he demanded that John take his prescription for behavior as a condition for their continuing to live together. Richard gave three ultimatums, each implying that John would have to be the one to move out, none of which John took very seriously.

Toward the end of the year, John announced that he had invited a girl to Ann Arbor for the big spring dance a week hence. John had often been dismayed by the way in which Richard had turned what seemed vicarious pleasure in the reports John had volunteered of his life on campus into self-righteous indictment. A bit of a hoax, he thought, might even the score. He told Richard not to worry if he didn't return to the dorm on the big night, since he was planning to spend it with his guest in the motel room he was about to rent. Richard said nothing. A week later as John spruced in front of the mirror before leaving for the dance, Richard said behind him, "You can't do this to this girl. You have no right to do this. She's a woman!"

John asked what business was it of Richard's. He finished brushing his hair, but in turning to leave, ran into a short quick right to the jaw. The punch had seemed almost involuntary. John pulled himself together and left as Richard warned they would no longer be friends or live together if he carried out his scheme.

After the dance, as he had planned, John dropped his girl off at the women's dorm where he had found a room for her and headed back to East Quad and the spare bed in a friend's room he had arranged for himself. In the morning he carefully maintained a disheveled appearance as he sauntered back into the room he shared with Richard.

He didn't want to be awakened for lunch, he told Richard as he dropped into his bed: the night had been so exhausting he was going to sleep until dinner. Richard told John to leave right then or he was going to hurt him in his sleep. In reply, John asserted that he, too, had paid for the room and intended to use it. He couldn't stop Richard, however, from racing downstairs to tell the whole story to their housemother. The incident, says John, "blew over."

John doesn't recall how the scuffle they had on another occasion started, but he does remember not having his heart in it and thus finding Richard sitting on his chest for a while as friends walked in to ask, "What's wrong with Wishnetsky?" John replied, "I don't know." When they struggled to their feet, Richard shoved him back on his bed and on John's ukulele, a possession he had cherished from childhood. When Richard offered to pay for the smashed uke, John replied that it was not replaceable.

Six weeks from the end of the term, Richard spoke with floormate Cliff Prentice, who occupied a single, about making a room switch with John Samuels. The switch never occurred because the two roommates more or less patched up their troubles. According to John, he and Richard ended their year together on decent terms: both realized that their already large personality differences had been magnified in their living together. "We couldn't bear each other day in and day out," said John. "But there was no real animosity. We knew we could be friends only if we separated to pick and choose the times we wanted to be together."

At the same time, Cliff Prentice decided that Richard would make an ideal roommate and so arranged with him to share an apartment the following September. Cliff was a serious-minded sophomore from St. Louis, in zoology but "acutely interested in religion and theology generally," having recently emerged from a trial run in a Presbyterian seminary.

Richard and Cliff had enjoyed a "fair amount of talk" in the dorm, but they drew especially close during the first week of May after Cliff broke off a relationship of some seven months with Susie Goodman, Richard's friend from Detroit. "Richard spent a week pulling me out of that experience," says Cliff. "The sympathy, even empathy, which Richard displayed was just priceless. He used diversionary tactics, trying to keep my mind off the problem, and we went to movies together and concerts during May Festival. I think I got to know Richard better than I knew anyone else on the floor and we became very attached."

Cliff and Richard added a third roommate for September in the person of Pat Martolino, a quiet, self-possessed junior just over from the Philippines who was in the process of switching from engineering to art school. Richard had met Pat, then a Catholic, in the lunch line at East Quad and struck up a friendship which was never really deep, says Pat, because of what he thought was Richard's "put-on warmth." When asked to share an apartment, Pat inquired about Richard among the people on his floor and was told, "No, you don't want to put yourself in that situation." Pat, however, badly wanted out of the dorm and couldn't afford an apartment alone. Thus the three—Protestant, Catholic, and Jew—leased three rooms for September over Bob Marshall's Bookstore, a block from campus.

When he left Ann Arbor in June for the summer, Richard could reflect upon a very busy and successful freshman year. In the second term he had accomplished his goal of an all-A 4.0 average (an A meriting four points, a B three points, a C two, and a D one); he and other freshmen with better than a 3.5 average for the year received special mention and a book as reward from the university.

Unlike many first-year students, who remain only names or faces to most of their teachers, he had made what would prove to be enduring friendships among the faculty. Though he did not join the more radical of the "Mumford crowd," who were involved in the Fair Play for Cuba group, Richard had put in a short stint as a social activist with the A.C.W.R. He was still an avid newspaper reader, digesting *The New York Times* daily for informed opinions on the issues of the day. While his social life consisted mainly of passionate conversation, his circle of friends who could share his concerns, attitudes, and intensity had substantially widened.

Fred Baskin, who was still attending Wayne State and saw Richard once or twice a month during the school year when Richard spent weekends or vacations at home in Detroit, is convinced of his "basic thesis that Richard had a major change of character" at this time: "Every strong personality he came in contact with made a big impression on him. He thought these people were shaping his ethic. In my opinion, his ethic was changing so much that I didn't think 'shaping' was the right word. He came back from Michigan almost a reformed man. I noticed it right away, maybe within three months, maybe even the first time he came back. It was an entire transition."

Whereas in Fred's experience Richard had previously been

openly unhappy about many things in his life, a sharp-tongued, "reasonably cynical," and short-tempered young extrovert with a "healthy intolerance" and a realistic measure of pessimism, now "suddenly he was bending over backwards to resolve all sorts of conflicts and unhappiness and to see things as good and as optimistically as he possibly could, with any measure of tolerance, relativism, absolutism, or anything else it took to do it."

In their talks Richard explained his shift in idea and attitude in intellectual terms, saying that he had become exposed to some profoundly humanistic ideas which had made him realize it was time he got a bit more serious about things. His high-school intellectualism belonged to a boy, he thought, and it was time he grew up a bit. More importantly this should all be part of a general mellowing, he decided. He should reform himself as well as his intellectual activity; he should in fact make a firm effort to get along better with his parents and grandparents, his sisters, and people in the Jewish community generally.

All of a sudden, according to Fred, Richard took a great interest in his sisters. Once in the spring he came into Detroit to show the girls a sunset and give them a simple taste of the good life, taking them away from what he judged to be their preoccupation with television and cashmere sweaters. "I remember him picking me up first," said Fred, "and rushing over there, really almost literally dragging these kids away from the TV set to hustle us out a few miles to see a sunset which he had prophesied would be beautiful —and which had already gone down when we got where we could see it."

Whereas in Fred's opinion Richard had never taken a great interest in his grandparents, he now began to go to their home for long talks, cultivating a concern for their interests, particularly Israel and Zionism. "It was almost as if he was reexamining his roots," said Fred. And finally he began to speak more positively about his parents, especially his father: "Whereas before if he mentioned his father at all, it was between clenched teeth, he now pointed out that we must understand the background his father came from and must judge him on this relative basis. And we must remember that at least he was giving money to good liberal causes. I remember saying, 'Well, I thought we were supposed to judge people by their motives and not their acts.' Of course he didn't hear and went right on about how his father had not been just a potato peeler during the war but something of a hero, and how he admired him for being a tough soldier."

The reality of a shift in Richard's outlook is substantiated of course by Richard himself who, according to Fred, talked about it at some length, but also by Fred's mother. Richard had previously considered her something of "a nag and a bore." Now he was constantly cordial to her, says Fred, "and would greet her and swing her around and make fifteen minutes of conversation with her which was something even I would never bother to do." Richard had become for Mrs. Baskin "a sweet boy."

ELEVEN

Relaxing a bit from his rigorous freshman-year schedule, Richard as a sophomore, while still working on a tight time budget, occasionally splurged a few hours on a date. He now seemed to have more time for movies and plays in Ann Arbor and even got himself to a football game or two during the fall. Though he might enjoy the pageantry and color and the girl he was with, the game, he told Pat Martolino, consisted of a bunch of stupid people hitting one another.

He was up early every morning, always bright and cheerful, "so jovial it was irritating," according to Pat. Usually Cliff Prentice (who kept a tight schedule of his own) was up first, but occasionally Richard was dressed and out of the apartment by 6 A.M. to run a mile or so before breakfast. He would often come back with a happy description—it was raining slightly and the fog was lifting slowly, "Just like walking in heaven!"—and he finally got Pat, who had been a long-distance runner in the Philippines, to join him a couple of times. Richard ran with stamina, thought Pat, and was quite strong physically.

Cliff usually made breakfast and came back at noon after classes to fix lunch. He and Pat did all the cooking and marketing, and Richard washed dishes and cleaned the apartment. Cliff and Pat spent a lot of their time out of the apartment, so Richard did much of his reading there. Often, when the weather was warm enough, he went out on the rooftop porch adjacent to the bedroom where he commanded a good view of the northwest corner of the campus. The bedroom accommodated all three roommates; Richard's bed was placed under a sloping ceiling to which he had affixed large magazine photos of Elizabeth Taylor and Sophia Loren. On his dresser he kept a piece of embroidery done by his sister Terry and on the wall, a crayon drawing rendered by sister Ellen.

Richard tried to lend a hand with the cooking on occasion, but his results were only humorous: an attempt at soft-boiled eggs with the eggs in a dry pot and a TV dinner cooked in its carton. He observed the Jewish religion's dietary laws to the extent of not eating pork and not mixing milk and meat or their products. Throughout the fall, however, the three regularly enjoyed Canadian bacon under the impression it was beef. Finally, a friend of Richard's over for dinner confirmed Cliff's suspicion that it was pork. Richard was "crushed, brokenhearted, and sick at the thought he had broken the law." One Friday night Protestant Cliff, not thinking, made cheeseburgers and was chastized from both sides.

"Privately and in his own way," says Cliff, "Richard was an observer of things Jewish; they were very important to him." Pat, who found Richard "particularly against the Church" and argued with him about Catholicism, confirms that Richard seemed to adhere to a kind of liberal Judaism, once saying, "A lot of Jews give up their religion, but I want to continue with mine." It seems that Richard had become much more concerned with the Jewish faith while living with Gentiles.

On Friday nights he would light candles and read prayers in the bedroom along with Cliff, who would simply observe—the two of them sitting on the edge of the bed, Richard often in the traditional prayer shawl. Quite interested in converting to Judaism, Cliff got Richard to talk about his religion and on two occasions in the fall to join him at Hillel services. Cliff frequently went alone to Hillel on Friday nights and was often needed to complete the minyan, the ten men required for services. One night in October Richard and Cliff went with some excitement to Hillel to hear Richard's Grandfather Hordes speak on the Jewish National Fund. Says Cliff: "Richard had prepared me, and I was certainly duly impressed. He was an immensely powerful man who made a great impression on me. Richard had great admiration for him, especially his contribution of thousands of dollars in steel to the Israeli war of independence in 1948."

Richard and Cliff generally saw things from the same idealistic perspective. "We both took the world deadly serious," said Cliff, who valued their talks highly and seems almost to have idolized his younger roommate. He especially praised Richard's gentleness in working with people and his remarkable politeness, his tendency to take others' grievances very personally, his ability to forgive and forget.

"Richard was an ardent pacifist," he said. "Violence was everything he was against." With a great fondness for practical jokes, Cliff on occasion tested Richard's pacifism and his sense of humor, and found the former intact but the latter lacking. Once he placed a marble slab from the heat register under Richard's bed pillow; another night he unplugged all the lights in the apartment and covered the floor with pots and pans; a third time he taped a baby-bottle nipple to an appropriate spot on Richard's photo of Liz Taylor after Richard had gone to sleep. Each time Richard became upset and angry but responded only with verbal hostility, somewhat surprising Cliff, who had half expected a physical response.

"A couple of times," said Cliff, "I inadvertently said or did the wrong thing and Richard immediately launched into a sympathetic but severe lecture of perhaps thirty minutes' duration, explaining in great detail the error of my ways. He seemed to be acting almost as a parent to a child."

A measure of Cliff's affection and respect for Richard is the fact that years later his memory still holds a poem that Richard wrote and gave to him during their stay together:

> Who deems that man can't rise
> above the life we lead
> When knows damn well that man
> can give, can love, and breed?
> Who mocks the noise we label
> life?
> The sad and angry—they live
> this strife.

"I'll never understand," says Cliff, "how the man who wrote that poem could do what Richard finally did." The poem proves, of course, only that Richard was not a poet.

Pat Martolino had a different view of Richard. Though he agreed that Richard had a very quick and knowledgeable mind and could be "extremely nice" and was in fact quite sensitive to things that he himself was sensitive to—the beauty of a sunset or a blue sky, for example—Pat admitted:

"I didn't like Richard after two months of living with him. He was all right from a distance, but up close he seemed just too intense about very trivial things. There was a lack of tact about him, a lack of awareness of other people's concerns, a lack of good taste. In some ways he was very naïve.

"His friends who used to come over to the apartment once in a while seemed to think highly of him, but actually a lot of what he did seemed put on. When he wanted something (like my car) he could be extremely sweet and I had to be on guard against questions like, 'What are you doing tonight?' Richard, though he was strong, was uncoordinated physically and was always knocking over something in his awkwardness. When he borrowed my car I knew he was going to grind the gears on it. If he didn't get what he wanted, he'd get very angry and say, 'You bastard, why not?'

"He was often wrestling or horsing around in the apartment, always full of motion, gesticulating, giving you the big slap on the back a bit too hard, for which he'd immediately apologize. If a pretty girl walked past, Richard would be rapturous; he'd stomp around the apartment beet red, all excited. Also any idea he didn't agree with, if pushed, made him very aggressive; he'd turn red in the face and his voice would get louder."

Richard told friends he liked his roommates very much, especially Pat, who in turn attempted to steer clear of Richard as much as possible. Pat met the Wishnetskys a couple of times and found them extremely cordial, wondering to himself, "How can they be so nice with such a son?" They once told Pat that Richard had great respect and admiration for him, particularly for his self-control.

"I suppose he thought it was my Oriental stoicism," said Pat with a smile. "I think it was just that he found it very difficult to control his own emotions. He was like a child following an elder around, and I didn't like it. Richard always focused his eyes on yours with a very inquisitive look, like a cocker spaniel trying to get a bone."

The apartment over Marshall's Bookstore was a popular meeting place for a contingent of Pat's art-school friends, whose general dislike for Richard steadily increased during the first term and became rather ill concealed. When Richard would come from his studies in the bedroom to their front-room bull session to ask politely for quiet, they might or might not agree. If not, Richard would ask again, not politely, then leave in anger. At other times they might hear him on the stairs or in the hall outside and decide to avoid him, making their intention rather obvious by heading out the back way—off the back porch and down a convenient tree to the ground. Within the group Richard was a kind of private joke. "We'd refer to him as a 'shmuck,'" said Pat, "and I'm sure he felt very rejected. I felt bad about him."

Joel Greenberg, one of Pat's chums and a classmate of Richard's, says that Richard seemed to take a great interest in people, was extremely gregarious and outgoing, "always giving you a toothy grin and shaking hands." Yet beneath his bright good cheer, Joel felt, there was another, quite tyrannical Richard: "He was one of the few people I've ever encountered who really deserved to be called self-righteous. He was intensely self-righteous and he masked it by being gregarious. Actually, he was not successful. He had many temporary friendships; he lost many friends."

Richard and Joel first met in a Great Books course they took from Alan Gaylord in the fall term of 1961. Though excited and impressed by the course material, Richard still appeared primarily concerned with his grade point average. Said Pat, "Grades meant everything to Richard. They were his strongest motivating force." "Richard took extremely copious lecture notes," said Joel, "and then he would go back to the apartment and completely rewrite these notes, numbering them carefully and putting them in perfect order."

In this second year, Richard found new intellectual heroes on campus, the foremost being Professor Kenneth Boulding, the prominent economist, whose introductory course he took (Professor Boulding has no recollection of Richard). And he became interested enough in his introduction to anthropology to consider majoring in that subject. The university again honored Richard's scholastic work when it listed him along with a relatively few other sophomores who had managed to achieve two straight semesters of a 4.0 average.

Every six weeks or so he would stop in at Norman Thomas's office in Haven Hall to report on his progress and ask politely how Thomas's own scholarly work was proceeding. Often, though he had never met them, Richard would ask about Thomas's wife and family, almost as might a colleague on the faculty. Said Professor Thomas, "He always seemed interested and concerned in a sensitive, intelligent way about people."

With the A.C.W.R. foundering and his interest in the group long since dissipated, Richard did spend some time with picket signs, but by no means could he be called an activist. If Richard did get involved, it was usually briefly or indirectly, giving mostly his sympathy and good spirits for the cause. One gray and biting-cold midwinter day, Richard crossed the Diag in front of the Graduate Library and came upon a group of some twenty-five students standing in a silent, shivering line. He spotted Susie Goodman in the group, who explained that they were holding a peace vigil for disarmament. He was in accord with the aims and purposes of the group, he said, and stood around comforting everyone, keeping up morale. Afterward he seemed overly solicitous, thought Susie, inviting some of them back to his apartment to warm up with hot chocolate or coffee. He appeared concerned about everyone, almost as if he were a sympathetic father, proud of their idealism but trying to keep it from sending them to the hospital with pneumonia.

Richard's concern about civil rights did prompt him on a few occasions to walk in picket lines, particularly in front of the Kresge's in Ann Arbor because the company was reportedly discriminating in the South. He enthusiastically explained the procedure to Debbie Rossman one day, but she was not entirely convinced about Richard's feelings: "Though he seemed very interested in civil rights, I thought Richard was really rather bigoted. At that time I had started dating a Negro fellow, and Richard became very, very upset and tried to talk me out of it. Perhaps this had something to do, though, with his very strong views about intermarriage for Jews."

Richard often did indict the behavior of his Jewish friends who were dating Gentiles, but generally in his second year at U. of M., his attitudes toward sex, dating, and personal relations had noticeably relaxed. Said Debbie, "By this time I was even trying to convert him to my feeling that virginity at marriage was a very bad thing, and that it might be a very good thing to have some experience."

On Sunday afternoons in the fall, Richard and a girl—older than

Richard, a grad student, and the owner of a car—often drove to the Waterloo or Pinckney recreation areas outside of Ann Arbor. He came back one night to tell Cliff that he had asked the girl to go to bed with him. The girl had replied very firmly that she would rather he kill her first. Richard said he had been very pleased with this answer: it had made their whole afternoon together a great success.

Before John Samuels left Ann Arbor for Wayne State at midyear, he also noted a change in his old roommate; Richard had dropped his puritanical stance and seemed generally more relaxed. Further evidence might be found in a letter Richard wrote to a friend in Detroit during the fall. The apartment, he said, in a light-hearted tone, would be available for the friends' use on Saturday afternoon, since all three roommates, in an unusual, "almost frightening" display of school spirit, were going to the football game. While they were cheering, wrote Richard, his friend would be "whispering sweet nothings—damn you."

Richard and Marcia Frankel still saw each other once in a while, but without the ambiguity and fantasy of freshman year. Richard was now quite aware that she was thoroughly committed to her future husband, Bob Moss, and was always eager to hear how the romantic relationship was proceeding. In their talks, Richard continued to celebrate love as the most important thing in the world; what he wanted more than anything, he said, was someone to love and to help, generally to be of service to others. To Marcia, however, Richard always seemed to be dating girls who were more or less spoken for. When she pointed out this habit, he said, well, maybe there wasn't anything they could give him, but he could still be of service to them. He could talk to them at least and could give to them even without a return.

Curiously, one day during the previous summer Richard had dropped by the home of another old friend, Julie Lieberman, and had told her mother that he was seriously thinking of marrying Julie someday and taking her to a small university town where he would teach. This was news to Julie, who in fact never did hear it from Richard. They had never talked much about marriage and never at all with reference to themselves, until one day when he said out of the blue, "You know, Julie, I really think you're not the type of girl for me to marry." "I thought it was rather odd that he brought the subject up that way," says Julie, "but I suppose this was an indication that it had been on his mind before. I think Richard really did want to find somebody who might pull him out of himself, somebody he could feel strongly about, strongly enough to want to marry. . . ."

In December Cliff Prentice decided to move out of the apartment and back to the dorm; his grades were not what he thought they should be, and he feared he had been enjoying himself too much. Before he left, however, he introduced Richard to Mary Wilson (pseud.), a girl Cliff had been dating but had lost interest in. Their first date was apparently an intensely romantic affair for both; they walked for hours all over campus, talked passionately, and recited poetry to each other. When she returned to the dorm, Mary was impressed with Richard, and he was equally enthusiastic about her. Mary wrote poetry and fiction, had an abiding interest in the arts, and generally seemed a warm and generous girl. Richard thought her lovely. That she was rather buxom and thus did not meet his previously held standard of feminine beauty (the petite grace of his mother); that she was not Jewish; that she was supposedly engaged to a young man in the service and stationed overseas; and that she was generally known to have emotional problems apparently did not trouble him enough to discourage courtship.

As the relationship quickly progressed, Richard spoke often and freely about it to some of his friends, a few of whom, including Susie Goodman, were numbered among Mary's dormitory chums. Thus, the romance was followed with interest on both sides. "I like somebody I can just barely get my arms around," Richard told Cliff, meaning he had developed a penchant for large-busted girls. He was deeply in love, he told Julie, and described Mary as well bred and simple, a plain and wholesome girl who was everything he wanted. For Mary's part she also seemed thoroughly in love, and it wasn't long before they were talking about marriage; she was ready and eager to convert for Richard and, as he requested, to keep a kosher home for him. "At one point everyone in the dorm thought Richard would marry her," said Susie Goodman.

At Christmas Richard and Joel Greenberg drove the latter's car to New York City. On the way Richard spoke with vivid enthusiasm about his new love, describing her for Joel, who hadn't yet met her. Richard was in very high spirits, bursting with energy and optimism; when they stopped for gas on the turnpike, he would quickly jump out of the car and do some running. They parted in New York, and Richard stayed with his paternal grandparents before deciding to hitchhike back. On the way home and on the spur of the moment, he headed for the Pennsylvania city where Mary lived with her family. Arriving past midnight and unannounced, he tossed pebbles at her bedroom window to wake her and ended up staying a couple of days.

For a while a kind of happy spontaneity continued to mark the relationship. When Mary stayed out of the dorm all night a couple of times, it was assumed she and Richard were sleeping together; she was reputed to be a girl who found it difficult to say no. Richard and Mary did in fact sleep together, but apparently that's all. "Richard was a virgin before and after Mary," said Pat Martolino. "He asked me at one point if I thought he should go to bed with her, and I told him no matter what he did, he'd have to take responsibility for it."

Richard agreed they should not make love. They probably never did, but late one night with Pat already in bed, the two of them came in and ended up giggling in Richard's bed. Richard asked Pat if he would mind Mary staying the night. Pat said no, and they all went to sleep.

Richard was very excited about Mary's poetry, and Joel Greenberg, whose own poetry had already won him campus recognition, was asked to read and comment. Says Joel, "When I finally met the girl I was struck by the discrepancy between the description I had received from Richard and her appearance." She was a very sad, awkward, and plain-looking girl, thought Joel, and her poetry he judged to be very poor, "high-schoolish and inadequate."

According to stories around the dorm, Mary had previously been under psychiatric treatment. She was, said Susie Goodman, a girl on an emotional roller coaster, very confused, who seemed warm and giving but was easily upset and always appeared near the breaking point. Richard began to report his concern over Mary's unstable emotions, though saying he still loved her deeply. "Mary was an extremely suicidal girl," said Joel. "She was out of contact and she became Richard's venture. He was going to bring her back, to save her."

Richard persisted for a time, but as spring began to arrive in Ann Arbor, he felt himself less and less able to handle what he termed Mary's emotional dependency. There were other problems, too: he felt there was still a drawback in the fact that she was not Jewish, and indicated that his parents objected even though she was going to convert.

The relationship had lasted little more than three months when Richard decided to break it off. "Well, she's a schizophrenic," he explained to Susie Goodman, "and I simply can't handle her emotional problems." His story was a bit different for Pat and Cliff. He had found himself getting too involved, he told them. He didn't want a sexual relationship with Mary because it would be much too serious and he wasn't ready for it yet. Maybe if it had happened three years hence, he thought, things might have been different. Now he actually cared too much and so had to end it.

The night Richard broke the news to Mary, she "literally cracked up" in the dorm; she had to be cared for by her friends, who were finally forced to take her to the infirmary. "She left in very bad shape," said Susie. "We called Richard, and he helped bring her over to the infirmary while she was still clutching her favorite stuffed animal." Richard paid her visits at the infirmary but subsequently told Pat, "If Mary calls, I'm not home." He finally wrote a letter to her parents saying that their daughter was in serious mental-emotional trouble. Mary subsequently dropped out of school.

After his sophomore year in June 1962, Richard called Emanuel Mark at Camp Farband to say that he would not be able to take the senior counselor job Mark had promised him for the summer. He had just taken another job, he explained, doing conservation work for the government in Provost, Utah. His main purpose, he said, was to build himself up physically. No doubt Richard had many reasons for his trip west, but he mentioned to friends that his primary intention was to learn about the "real world." He was going to mingle with the working class for a change. It would also, he thought, give him time to explore himself while doing some good honest work with his hands.

Richard wrote a number of letters from the West, including news of his fighting forest fires and ecstatic descriptions of natural settings in the western landscape. However, as friends later learned, he was generally not happy. When he finished and had picked up his pay, he headed for Seattle and the World's Fair, employing his favorite means of transportation, the hitchhike. From there he flew to San Francisco. His old friend David Roth was doing summer-school work at Berkeley, and when David learned by chance that Richard was on campus, he looked him up expecting a typically exuberant Wishnetsky welcome. He didn't get one, however: Richard seemed strange and distant, unlike David had ever seen him. Richard wrote at this time to Fred, warning of the immorality of Berkeley–San Francisco and its ambience of mental disturbance, rampant homosexuality, and the carelessness of people living only for the moment.

Back home, Richard seemed quite proud and happy about his physical development, which he demonstrated by flexing his new muscles for Julie and many others and by lifting lightweight Fred Baskin high off the floor in greeting. He was full of wild tales about his trip back: he had been robbed and had hitchhiked all the way home on thirty-five cents just to see if he could do it, sleeping one night in a chaise longue under a motel patio umbrella. He had even tried drugs, he said, while riding in a car driven by a wild group of fellows who gave him a lift part of the way.

But he was also disillusioned and unhappy, he told Julie, with the people he had worked with. He had hated the experience, he said, and couldn't stand these men who were so ignorant and uncommitted. All they really cared about, he thought, was their beer and the itch of their bellies. He did come back, said Fred, rather embittered: "Apparently after a few nights he had discovered that while he loved the Common Man, the Common Man didn't love him. He wanted to talk about the things he thought they were interested in, but they really weren't interested in those things. He had been very unhappy and had more or less stopped talking to them entirely during the last half of his stay.

"The whole thing was almost incredibly naïve and idealistic. I thought maybe he had had some more profound reason for going there, but I never did figure out what it was. Maybe he didn't."

To another friend Richard explained: "I feel I've gained so much from this trip and grown as a man so much from it! I feel I've left behind so many people who stayed in Detroit for the summer." What had he gained? A mature understanding, he said, of what "real life" was all about, having encountered it firsthand. He seemed so taken with having become something new that he was almost apologetic about it. This time Richard may have been in some sense right; the summer of 1962 may have marked the beginning of an end to his previously cherished liberalism.

The "new personality" that some found Richard presenting in his freshman year was based on constant affability, ardent optimism, and a self-sacrificing humility. That Richard hardly achieved these ideals is not surprising. More importantly, in his sophomore year Richard seemes to have taken these notions about himself even more seriously.

More than one of Richard's friends and acquaintances questioned the authenticity of his penchant for the impulsive, spur-of-the-moment trip, his gallant attempts to "save" people, and his academic enthusiasm. "In a way this was very much Richard," said Fred Baskin. "But even then I thought these trips, for example, were just a little too stereotyped to be real, especially since I was always rather suspicious as to who had been influencing him. I just assumed he had read Kerouac's book. I never really trusted anything Richard was or did as being Richard."

Richard's concern for others, his zest for the romantic and spontaneous, and his love affair with the world of ideas seem to have involved genuine feelings, but it appears that he also evidenced increasingly self-conscious and affected overtones in their expression. Richard's most basic and unfortunate naïveté may have concerned himself and not the "real world." The fears and doubts that foster such naïveté and explain how someone thoroughly self-absorbed can remain largely ignorant of himself must naturally run at well-concealed depths.

TWELVE

In his junior year Richard shared an apartment on Division Street, two blocks from campus and behind the Union, with his old rival from Mumford High and Camp Farband, Henry Shevitz. They had met by chance on campus one day during the preceding spring, and Richard had proposed to Henry's surprise their living together the following September. "I guess he regarded me as a serious student," said Henry. "Also, I was Jewish, and he hadn't been rooming with Jewish fellows."

Henry (who after three undergraduate years was working simultaneously for B.S. and M.S. degrees in mathematics) and Richard, who was starting on his political-science major, occupied the ground floor of an old Victorian frame at 413 South Division. Richard had wanted to add a third roommate, but Henry refused; they split the rent of $125 a month. Though he had not previously, Richard now claimed to be living on a rather tight budget. Tuition was apparently covered by a scholarship which he indicated Rabbi Adler had helped to secure for him, but rent, food, and other living expenses had to be met on $120 a month, not an easy task in Ann Arbor. Consequently, says Henry, he was "compulsive" about eating at the apartment and generally refused to eat out. If he did agree, they would always end up at a hamburger stand. Otherwise, Henry cooked and Richard washed dishes.

"It was like living in a rut," says Henry in describing Richard's rigid schedule. "He was on an army routine, very irrational." Up seven days a week at eight in the morning ("After a while he didn't even need an alarm clock"), Richard cleaned up, had breakfast, and was out of the house by 8:45, heading for class or a study session. He would be home again at noon for lunch, out for classes or the library again by one, back for dinner at five, and out for more study by seven. He would stop at midnight. The routine, says Henry, was also adhered to on weekends and rarely broken.

Relaxation was a concept that seemed foreign to Richard. He refused Henry's invitations to football games, and though they did play tennis a couple of times and enjoyed paddle ball, which Henry taught him to play at the Intramural Building on a couple of Saturday mornings, Richard later said he no longer had the time. Though he often went to special lectures on campus, he attended few concerts or plays in his last two years in Ann Arbor. Movies continued as his favorite form of entertainment, but they did not always relax him. Perhaps thinking of Mary Wilson, he reacted strongly to *Tender Is the Night;* with Cliff Prentice he saw *Sundays and Cybel* and debated its problematic ending for a week, convinced that the troubled ex-fighter pilot did not kill Cybel at the end.

Richard began his work in political science with what was probably his most intellectually decisive course, Professor Frank Grace's lectures on the development of political theory. Over the last few years, Richard had become increasingly concerned with the abstract and theoretical area of political science, which ultimately merges with philosophy, and less involved with the workings of practical politics, which he now considered only symptomatic of much deeper problems such as man's plight in the modern world and the direction of civilization. A classmate could say about Richard in his last two undergraduate years: "He paid little attention to current events unless they had some bearing on his world views, and even then he was a lead-pipe cinch to oversimplify and probably misunderstand their significance."

He was eager for a course that would explore the big questions, and with Frank Grace this perspective was supplied on Mondays, Wednesdays, and Fridays in the appropriately classic setting of Angell Hall. Yet Richard was not immediately pleased with the course. For the moment he had settled on a strict philosophical relativism which denies the existence of absolutes, maintaining that there are no eternal principles of right and wrong and that ideals and standards of good and evil are ultimately products of the evolution of a particular society. Because of the fact of constant change, he would argue, we can reason about values only in a limited fashion, if at all, and therefore must cultivate a tolerance of all opinions while focusing on the particular needs of men within a specific frame of reference in the attempt to improve their lot.

This modern liberal philosophy Richard carried into an inevitable clash with the firmly traditional views of Frank Grace. Professor Grace, described variously by his students as a "fine gentleman of insight," "an effective and impressive teacher," and "a man of strong beliefs and attitudes which he presents rather dogmatically in class," is a conservative Democrat and a Catholic with a hint of the South in his soft-spoken and courteous manner. A slender, fine-featured, middle-aged man, he has taught in the political-science department at U. of M. for nearly twenty years. He is in a distinct minority in the department (as he would probably be in almost any non-Catholic department in the country) in his adherence to the classical-Christian natural-law tradition established by Plato, Aristotle, Cicero, and Thomas Aquinas and promoted today by contemporary political theorists like Eric Voegelin, Carl Friedrich, and Leo Strauss. About the current study of politics, Strauss has said: "Looking around us, we see two hostile camps, heavily fortified and strictly guarded. One is occupied by the liberals of various descriptions, the other by the Catholic and non-Catholic disciples of Thomas Aquinas."

Natural law posits all natural beings with a natural end or destiny which establishes their proper function. With the use of his reason, man determines what is right and good in terms of his own natural end. As the classical-Christian theory evolves, natural law is basically held to be an emanation of God's reason and will as these are revealed to all men. Fundamental moral principles are self-evident to "normal" men who with unaided "right reason" are able to distinguish and choose between right and wrong. In this way man perceives the natural law as an eternal and universal moral standard assuring man order and happiness if its principles are applied rigorously to all of his civil laws and customs. Thus man, if he develops his rational powers fully and properly and remains "uncorrupted," has access to a set of absolute values.

One of the problems here is that a society of harmony based on the dictates of "right reason" seems impossible to find in either the present or the past. It is clear then that "right reason" is not easily come by and is available perhaps only to a very few elite, wise, or specially informed men who must interpret the natural law for the rest of mankind and guide them. Finally, of course, the modern world with its new temper of tolerance and individualism and the triumphant rise of natural science has seriously questioned not only the authority of religion but also the intellectual foundations of the natural-law tradition. In sum the modern experience of considerable irrationality and ambiguity has been discouraging to the notion that the world and man's place in it are reasonable enough for him to find his way to absolute values.

Still, as Strauss indicates, the academic battles continue to wage, and Richard in the course of his junior year decided to enter the fray. From Professor Grace he received his first thorough introduction to the political and ethical thought of Plato and Aristotle with generous reading assignments in the primary sources as well as in the course text, Sheldon Wollen's *Polities and Vision,* and in books by a number of contemporary commentators on the Greeks and natural law.

Lecturing to a class of seventy students, Professor Grace would often interrupt or cut short his presentation to throw an issue open to discussion. The most frequent to challenge was Richard, not at all hesitant to stop the professor and present his disagreements in long, occasionally quite spirited, debates. Richard initially seemed rather antagonistic, yet as the term progressed, he admitted to an admiration for Grace's attempt to deal with large and basic questions.

With increasing frequency he began showing up at Professor

Grace's office on the fourth floor of Haven Hall, popping in whenever he found the door open. Grace soon began to wonder if Richard was perhaps "polishing the apple" and said one day, "Wishnetsky, you're not going to learn much from talking here. You should be over in the library reading." He asked the young man what his grade point average was, expecting to hear that he was a C or B-minus student. Richard replied that he presently carried an average of between 3.8 and 4.0 and expected to make Phi Beta Kappa that year.

Indeed, Frank Grace found Richard a conscientious and thorough student. Always dressed and groomed neatly, often with a tie, he was polite and mannerly, quite unlike some of the more disaffected students in the group. In class, said Professor Grace, Richard might burst out once in a while, perhaps simply forgetting that others were there, but he seemed basically considerate. As for their arguments, Grace says, "They were nothing very serious at all. Richard was very easy to slap down in class and would bounce right back up again with a smile."

Nonetheless, their most memorable clash during the fall occurred on the morning of October 24. Professor Grace opened the session in a rather ominous tone, telling his students that they might now be involved in one of the most momentous times of their lives. He had reference to the chilling events of the Cuban missile crisis, then at its height, and a discussion ensued which set the day's lecture aside.

There were certain moments in history, argued Professor Grace, when a nation's commitment to its own values and interest was legitimately of paramount concern. He explained firmly that the United States should not back down in the crisis but should press its case strongly. Richard took hot issue, maintaining that following strictly national interests was indefensible when the continued existence of the human race might be at stake. Said one of his classmates, "Richard seemed to be shaken to the core by his awareness of the possibility of nuclear war." Another friend met him on the street later. Richard was bristling and said as they waited for a light to change, "Well, we've all got our trooper boots on now."

He remained tense for the next few days, inviting friends over for discussions, attending lectures on the crisis, and joining a march on campus to denounce unilateral American action and call for United Nation arbitration. At one point they suffered a pelting with rotten eggs and other rather shoddy treatment—an episode that contributed to Richard's sense of personal outrage. Subsequently, however, he seems not to have marched again, though often pressed by friends to do so. "I'm in sympathy with what you're doing and with your aims," he told Susie Goodman when she approached him about joining one of the peace or civil-rights groups. "But I'm not ready to take on the responsibility of getting involved in these things."

Richard seems to have belonged to a "Jewish intellectual nonfraternity group," not really a clique but primarily a closely knit collection of bright politics majors in the honors program. Their academic focal point was a year-long honors proseminar in political science which met twice weekly under the direction of Professor Karl Lamb. The class consisted of nine or ten students (only two or three non-Jewish, only one or two girls) who were required to deliver five papers each term on topics in general areas covering a wide range of the discipline. Of primary concern were practical political problems as discussed in books like Rossiter's *Political Parties,* Campbell's *The American Voter,* and Neidstadt's *Presidential Power.* The perspective seemed to please most of the group, but not Richard.

Others in the class, including his friends from Mumford, Jerry Levitt and Arthur Gold (pseud.), though idealistic, consistently attempted to root ideas in pragmatic terms. Richard instead remained devoted to the strictly theoretical, was generally not interested in the material covered, and called it "dogwork." His staunch refusal to relinquish his concern for the ideal long enough to examine reality and his tendency to speak at great length with apparently absolute conviction soon brought him under attack from classmates, who often dubbed his ideas "unrealistic" or "far out." The group was friendly and well knit, but also very bright and verbal, not about to be dominated by any one member.

"He would listen," says Ned Weiner (pseud.) from Nebraska, "and he'd carry on a dialogue, but if Richard didn't agree, what you said wouldn't penetrate. He seemed to have assumed a special ability to know and to judge and he would say, 'Well, I expected this from you. Someday I hope you will see my point.'" It seemed that once Richard decided he had an answer, he would discuss it only to convince others of the truth of his position. At such moments, says Arthur Gold, "dialogue and exchange stopped and one listened to a little talk by Richard which one simply didn't interrupt." He often used "exaggerated" sweeping gestures which seemed to plead, as did his voice, for understanding and acceptance. Classmates remember "the edginess that prevented him from ever relaxing in a chair," the knit brow or the flashing eyes or the occasionally disconcerting smile which accompanied his softly deliberate or loud, rapid speech.

Tom Butch, non-Jewish and originally from Michigan's Upper Peninsula, was Richard's major adversary in the proseminar. Though affable and seemingly easygoing, Tom had a number of run-ins with him in class. "You could catch Richard on specifics with practical examples," said Tom, who reportedly did so a number of times, culminating in what one witness termed "a real blowup," out of which Richard came decidedly second best.

Richard also had his difficulties with Professor Lamb, a pragmatic conservative who placed emphasis on clear writing as an extension of lucid thinking. He deemed Richard's performance in the first term worthy of only a B. Unhappy, Richard remarked to a friend, "Well, now I have a lower average in my major than I do in my overall course work."

Professor Lamb found Richard's intensity and eagerness "highly attractive" but recalls him as a loner in class, always following "a unique line of thought or reasoning, never wanting to build on anybody else's ideas. He seemed eager to arrive at truth and to understand justice, regardless of the consequences." Richard was certainly loquacious, said Professor Lamb, but not difficult to handle nor able to outtalk the other articulate class members.

Beyond finding him unrealistic and often intolerant, his classmates seemed genuinely to like Richard as good-hearted if emotional and naïve, an academic perfectionist and a sincere humanitarian. None seemed to mind greatly when Richard, who smoked only an occasional pipe and only rarely drank a beer, gently chided them about their cigarettes or alcohol. In class Richard talked so much that Tom Butch once jokingly put a headlock on him long enough for Sue Koprince, a tall, slim blonde with a fresh intelligent face and gentle manner, to get a word in edgewise. Outside of class, Richard was alone most of the time with his studies, rarely socialized with members of the group, and didn't seem truly close to any while appearing a firm friend to all.

But then intellectual discussion was Richard's staple, and he often seemed to need or want nothing else. Steve Berkewitz, a sophomore a year younger than Richard but similarly precocious, met him in the Union Grill after class where they would talk intensely about what they were reading. Steve found him most concerned with establishing a "mainspring, integrative philosophical conception of the world," into which everything would fit. In the process he seemed to be compiling a kind of intellectual diary—a large black binder into which he stuffed all kinds of notes, everything from thoughts of the moment on small scraps of paper to large sheets with quotes of favorite passages. A goodly sample of the fiction of alienation was included in the wide assortment of books they discussed: Kafka's *The Castle* and *The Penal Colony,* Gogol's *Dead Souls,* Sartre's *Nausea,* Camus's *The Stranger,* and Hesse's *Steppenwolf.*

Richard's favorite was Hesse's classic story of Harry Haller, the wolfman of the Steppes, a man fated "to live the whole riddle of human destiny heightened to the pitch of a personal torture, a personal hell"; a man constantly tossed in and out of loneliness and despair, deeply suicidal yet managing to endure if only by spinning elaborate fantasies of violence, savagely estranged from the mediocrity and depravity of bourgeois materialism. Richard told Steve that he saw himself deeply and vividly in the figure of the Steppenwolf, sharing the essential characteristics of the man described by Haller as caught between two ages:

> "Human life is reduced to real suffering, to hell, only when two ages, two cultures and religions overlap. A man of the Classical Age who had to live in medieval times would suffocate miserably just as a savage does in the midst of our civilization. Now there are times when a whole generation is caught in this way between two ages, two modes of life, with the consequence that it loses all power to understand itself and has no standard, no security, no simple acquiescence. Naturally, everyone does not feel this equally strongly. A nature such as Nietzsche's had to suffer our present ills more than a generation in advance. What he had to go through alone and misunderstood, thousands suffer today."

At a less intellectual moment, Steve once engaged in a friendly wrestling match with Richard, learning in spite of his own considerable weight advantage that Richard was "very strong and impossible to pin." He also drove one afternoon with Richard and another friend to a shooting range outside Ann Arbor where Steve found that "Dick was not at all a good shot and quite disinterested in learning—guns held no particular fascination for him, though I tried to give him some pointers."

THIRTEEN

After his experience with Mary Wilson (and with increased involvement in his academic work), Richard did little dating through the fall. His relations with the opposite sex continued to be less than satisfying. The attractive girls he approached either enjoyed themselves on a date until he wanted to get "warmer" or refused him altogether, thinking him "emotionally immature, almost like a child," or burdened with unattractive problems.

Also, it happened that three of Richard's closest feminine friends in Ann Arbor were married within the space of a month or two at the turn of the year. Julie Lieberman's December wedding, which he attended in Detroit, came first and was followed by Debbie Rossman's marriage in January. He also traveled to Indiana for the wedding of another girl he had been serious about over the past two years and had tried to win away from a previous commitment.

At Julie's wedding, however, Richard's luck changed a bit when he renewed his acquaintance with her former roommate, Linda Kohl (pseud.), a pixie with dark hair and eyes and a mobile face which might turn quickly from sad brooding to vivacious charm. Linda and Richard enjoyed a long lively conversation at the reception, which led to a date upon their return to Ann Arbor after New Year's. Soon they were seeing each other every day for coffee and study dates, and once in a while a movie.

Linda Kohl was immediately taken by Richard's courtly style, his high-minded concern for ideas, and his serious air as he read to her from Scripture, displaying an appreciation for the biblical tradition which she found both foreign to her experience and appealing. Generally Richard would talk and Linda would listen, not really interested in the ideas but enjoying his verbal prowess and the chance to "watch him strutting and spouting." Before long

Linda had decided she was "madly in love" with Richard: "I was quite melodramatic about the whole affair. I never was before and never have been since."

The relationship, however, was not pleasant for long. While Linda expressed her warm attitude toward Richard, he often spoke about Mary Wilson as the love of his life, explaining that he didn't feel for Linda what he had felt for Mary. "Perhaps I wasn't sick enough for Richard, to get him out of himself and committed to me," says Linda. Richard's rigidity also caused trouble, since he strongly disapproved of women wearing slacks and held fast to a number of similar attitudes which got on Linda's nerves.

At times she found it hard to cope with his penchant for the exuberant and dramatic gesture. One afternoon as they were approaching the Union, they met a girl with a suitcase coming in the opposite direction; somehow Richard struck up a conversation with the girl, asked where she was going, and ended up carrying the suitcase to her destination a mile away. Another evening after dinner as they began a study session in the tenth-floor stacks of the Grad Library, Richard excitedly announced to Linda that at nine o'clock he would tell her about a wonderful surprise he had arranged. First, however, they would have to study. Says Linda, "When nine o'clock arrived and he told me his surprise was that he had the apartment free until eleven when Henry would return, I was quite let down."

The relationship lasted two months until March. Linda, though still certain she loved Richard, decided to break it off because he seemed so self-centered. "I doubt if he was ever really involved with me at all," she said. "I couldn't play the maiden-in-distress role, and therefore he couldn't play the Robin Hood role which was so appealing to him."

Richard was quite willing to continue, but did not perceive the breakup as a rejection, since it was obvious to both that Linda's feeling for Richard was much stronger than his for her. To a number of friends, including Debbie Rossman (back in Ann Arbor after six weeks in California and no longer married), he proudly explained that he had experienced his first truly complete relationship with a woman: he was no longer a virgin. And he described his experience in lyrical, idealistic terms—a fantastically satisfying and ecstatic experience, he said, by which he had been totally absorbed.

Within a month after the breakup and with a less illusioned and, she thinks, more insightful perspective, Linda Kohl had become very bitter toward Richard. "I wish I knew," she says, "why I ended up hating him so much, but being disillusioned by him explains part of it . . . maybe being disillusioned with myself for having been taken in." What at times seemed to be Richard's extreme consideration for others was, she decided, only an attempt to cope with a cold and calculating, self-centered drive in his own personality—not a real concern, not really for the purpose of helping others, but rather a "reaction formation" intended to make Richard himself feel better. His exaggerated concern bespoke emotional impotence.

During January and February when he was dating Linda, Richard was still having philosophical disagreements with Frank Grace, but described him, in the words he often used for those he liked, as a "very beautiful person." As the spring term progressed, however, some noticed that Richard was quieter and less argumentative in class; in fact his contentiousness seemed to have thoroughly evaporated. Now he was asking questions which would lead to an amplification of Grace's position for the benefit of the class or, as it seemed to some, to let everyone know he now quite agreed. As a classmate put it, "He came into Grace's course as something of a left-wing brainstormer type and left on the way to becoming a classic scholar in the Catholic tradition."

Jerry Levitt had also become excited about natural-law theory and thought Richard's "conversion" occurred primarily because it seemed to offer the possibility of absolutes, a knowledge of ultimate values like goodness, justice, and beauty. Said another classmate: "Richard sought answers, certainty. If an answer was qualified, he bridled, because he liked to identify and categorize ideas and put them in place, to build philosophical structures of them; and building materials have to be steel and concrete." Tom Butch, who had previously debated against Richard's relativism, now felt there was a kind of missionary zeal about Richard; the change seemed almost the "result of a mystical experience." Professor Norman Thomas thought Richard's new convictions rather unusual in one so young, but he was pleased that Richard had been "provided with the intellectual spark in Frank Grace's course to really get him moving."

Still worried about his reading speed, Richard took a course from the university to improve his skill and went on devouring book after book at an even faster pace. Beyond his course work he was now doing a heavy amount of extracurricular reading (as he proudly informed Marcia Frankel, who had criticized him on this point). In addition to books more directly involved with political and social thought, such as Hannah Arendt's *The Origins of Totalitarianism* and *On Revolution,* José Ortega y Gasset's *The Revolt of the Masses,* Albert Saleman's *The Tyranny of Progress,* Carl Becker's *The Heavenly City of the Eighteenth-Century Philosophers,* and David Riesman's *The Lonely Crowd,* he was reading extensively and with excitement, he said, Catholic and Protestant philosophers and theologians like Jacques Maritain, Etienne Gilson, Reinhold Niebuhr, and C. S. Lewis. Books from some of these men, along with his new natural-law perspective, had prompted him, he told a few friends, to seriously consider converting to Catholicism.

Some, like David Roth, his old Mumford chum who was not in political or philosophical sympathy with Frank Grace, tried without success to dissuade Richard from the notion that he had finally found the road to truth. Professor Grace was aware at this time only of Richard's deepening interest in political theory and his consistently fine work. One day late in the semester Richard showed a classmate his term paper on totalitarianism in eighteenth-century France. Professor Grace had just given the paper an A-plus, said Richard in a terrific glow, and had described it as perhaps worthy of being published.

Richard continued to do well in all his courses. With Professor W. H. Locke Anderson in a highly theoretical course in economics he was one of the top two or three in a class with a number of excellent students. Said Professor Anderson: "Richard was one of five or ten students I've had since I started teaching who was a real pleasure to have in my class. He seemed to be a very smoothly functioning student, always prepared, alive, smiling in class, never disrespectful, and able to grasp the abstract considerations which the course dealt with."

Daniel Weintraub, a young professor of experimental psychology at U. of M. with a high-spirited and casual friendliness, encountered Richard along with ten other honors students in the spring of 1963 in a course called Psychology As a Natural Science. "It's strictly a non-life-adjustment course," he says with a twinkle in his eye, "concerned with areas in psychology like perception." Richard, says Weintraub flatly, was one of the best students he has ever taught. In addition he genuinely liked Richard and enjoyed talking to him about a wide range of subjects, including current affairs, when Richard dropped by his office.

One day in the spring Richard announced to his classmates in psychology that he had been spending some time on weekends at Ypsilanti State Hospital for the mentally ill. On Saturdays and Sundays he would make the fifteen-minute drive with a group organized by the Quakers in Ann Arbor to spend a few sociable hours with some of the patients in the institution. He encouraged his classmates to do the same. For his roommate Henry, he described one of his visits, involving a Negro woman patient who had reportedly refused to talk to anyone or respond to any approach. Suddenly, according to Richard, when he had begun to play a piano in one of the hospital's recreation rooms, she had burst into song with a beautiful voice, and everyone had been amazed at his ability to elicit such a response. (At some time in his life Richard had learned to play the piano well enough to entertain himself and others, though he seems to have rarely done so.)

Richard's course in nineteenth-century philosophy was taught by Frithjof Bergmann, a young European-born professor whose existential approach and warm regard for students makes him widely popular on campus. "Richard," he says, "was a very intelligent young man, but he did not have extraordinary powers of abstract thinking. He seemed to rely more on his sensitivity, on his empathy or feeling for ideas. Richard would sometimes come upon good insights and catch something that others would not see simply because of his intensity of feeling."

Richard's essays were unusual, says Bergmann, but not as polished or as rigorously coherent as some. He could speak in class in a rather powerful way, Professor Bergmann thought, and was probably more impressive when speaking than when writing. Others made this same observation.

The course was Richard's first substantial introduction to Friedrich Nietzsche. And about this time Marty Sharpe (pseud.), a sophomore and Richard's friend for years at Mumford and in the B.B.Y.O., found in an Ann Arbor bookstore a first edition of *Thus Spake Zarathustra,* which he bought for a few dollars. He immediately told Richard about his find, and the two spent hours poring over the text, with Marty reading aloud in the original and then giving a free translation. The boys marveled together at the book, whose blending of rich insight with adolescent emotional excess continues to hold enormous appeal on campus. Nietzsche, the German philosopher who died insane at the beginning of the twentieth century and is perhaps most famous for his announcement that God is dead, provides an invigorating call to arms for those who would effect superior selves:

> And there is nobody from whom I want beauty as much as from you who are powerful: let your kindness be your final self-conquest.
>
> Of all evil I deem you capable: therefore I want the good from you.
>
> Verily, I have often laughed at the weaklings who thought themselves good because they had no claws.

Richard's initial reaction was strongly positive, but this was only the beginning of what would prove to be a highly ambivalent response to Nietzsche's passionate and heroic antireligiousness.

Though most of his friends in political science were sure he was at least an agnostic, Richard and Henry Shevitz were in the habit of lighting candles every Friday evening and saying the Sabbath prayer; they would also celebrate with a little wine once in a while and never ate pork. Henry assumed Richard believed in God, though they rarely discussed such questions. Richard did not attend services or meetings at Hillel, but in the spring he did go to Shaarey Zedek's annual reunion banquet in Ann Arbor, attended by students, some faculty, and parents who came in from Detroit. Rabbi Adler as usual presided. After services and a free meal, the rabbi led a general discussion in which Richard and a few others took a very active part. Said a friend of Richard's: "One girl asked the rabbi the kind of question he could never give a straight answer to—concerning the dichotomy of belief and practices, the observation of dietary laws, or some such matter. The rabbi's reply was as usual generalized and historical in perspective; he gave a few reasons why observance of the practice might be advantageous, but finally left the matter up to the individual. Richard immediately popped up and vehemently accused the rabbi of avoiding the question. When Richard remained insistent, Rabbi Adler got very mad at him and really cut him down. He really took Richard's argument apart and left him without a word."

As was generally the case in his first two years, Richard did not get along well with his roommate. Again it was more a matter of considerable mutual annoyance than an overt hostility. But scant feelings of kinship were produced by Richard's unwillingness to share his friends with Henry (who might begin to engage them in conversation at the apartment only to have Richard say, "You were just going out, weren't you, Hank?") and conversely, his attempt to monopolize Henry's friends; his scrupulosity (in demanding payment of a dime debt or advocating that they search for the owner of a long-lost book found in the closet); his rigid routine and academic boasting ("Look, I've got 145 pages of notes for this course," he would say, pointing to a neat stack which was always in full view on his desk); his complaints (when Henry cluttered the apartment for five days while building an amplifier for a phonograph, which Richard subsequently used oblivious to Henry's feelings; Henry finally loosened a fuse in the back of the amplifier and pretended ignorance).

There were, however, a few more amiable moments when Henry and Richard would buy and share a six-pack of beer, when Richard would offer some friendly advice on whom to date and why. Once or twice Richard confessed to Henry that there were times when he would go to the library to study and find that he simply could not work. He could not concentrate, he complained. He would stare at a page and nothing would come. "Well, of course," said Henry, "your mind simply can't take the constant, intensive study you're trying to do. You've got to give yourself a rest once in a while."

Richard said Henry was probably right, that he would try to take some time off. But the resolution lasted only a few days, and he was soon running on a breakneck schedule again. The sense of competition which had previously marked his relationship with Henry continued to do so, and he finally managed a victory in the spring with his election to Phi Beta Kappa. Henry had missed out in his junior year by "about one-hundredth of a percentage point." Including Richard, there were fifteen junior Phi Beta Kappas at U. of M. in the spring of 1963. He seemed very pleased with the honor, though he was sick to his stomach at the installation banquet and had to leave the room several times.

Richard's academic and intellectual plans for the future were by now quite settled. At a gathering of proseminar members at Professor Lamb's home near the end of the term, Richard explained that he had received permission to do his senior honors thesis under the direction of Frank Grace on a subject concerned with Plato. He had decided to devote the rest of his life to the study and espousal of natural-law principles.

This was Karl Lamb's last term at U. of M. and he would not see Richard again. He still retains, however, a "haunting" memory of a warm spring afternoon on campus:

"The honors proseminar finished at about four o'clock. I packed books and notes into my briefcase and walked out of the building to a . . . parking lot, where I was to be picked up by my wife. Richard followed along. He wanted to ask my opinion about a point in political theory which had been brought up in another class. It was not a question that I was particularly competent to answer, and I told him that. It seemed that he was more interested in explaining his own attitude towards the issue than in listening to anything I had to say. . . . Soon my wife arrived, with our baby son in a playpen in the back of the station wagon. Richard kept on talking, hardly recognizing the fact that it was time for me to go. Every comment on my part seemed to set off a new compulsion on his. I soon grew annoyed and impatient. Finally, I rather rudely said good-bye and climbed into the car to drive away. But I am not sure that Richard was aware of any rudeness on my part.

"I have thought since . . . how difficult it is for a teacher to respond to the . . . demands of a student who is emotionally disturbed. The student does not separate his intellectual interests from his emotional needs, and the teacher is likely to cause more harm than good if he indulges in amateur psychologizing. But it is a shattering experience to tell a student that he should see a psychiatrist."

Richard spent the summer before his senior year talking with friends in Detroit, playing tennis, making himself some pocket money, and, as always, studying. On his twenty-first birthday and the days immediately preceding the Fourth of July he sold sparklers in a Detroit suburb for Marty Sharpe and another old Mumford friend who provided a stand and promised him one hundred dollars. Near the end of August he worked for a few days on a garbage truck at the state fair. Also toward the end of the summer, in a spare office in his grandfather's insurance agency he spent two weeks reading all of Plato in preparation for work on his honors thesis—a very meaningful experience, he reported.

In the meantime, the long-standing friendship between Richard and Fred Baskin had begun to lose some of its meaning, at least for Fred: "We would get together and argue about Plato or whatever, and I mean in your sleep, even using his system, you could run circles around him. And this became more and more of a joke around our little group. And it got to the point that I began to value his friendship less and less, until the only thing left was the memory of an old friend. He had become more naïve than he was in grade school and high school, and he was famous for his inability to hear a counter-argument. He would point out that obviously the reasons he brushed these comments aside were first, that he was so confident and next, that he had such love for me that he couldn't bear to hear these things I was saying! He would say things that corny."

Richard saw the experience of his junior year in Ann Arbor as the turning point of his intellectual life, in the Platonic terms he was becoming so fond of, the "periagoge," the turning about from shadow to light. In one sense there does seem to have been an almost literal turning around: Richard's answers to man's largest questions were no longer to be forged in the future but rather to be found in the past. There was more involved here than simply a shift in intellectual perspective. Richard's idealized conception of himself and his future had clearly changed from that of the heroic liberal who would prove his greatness in a series of successful encounters with the problems of his time, to that of the visionary scholar whose greatness would reside in his possession and dissemination of truth. The content of that truth would continually have an important bearing on Richard's perception of himself and his destiny.

FOURTEEN

There were times when some of his friends in political-science honors simply had enough of Richard and found ways to avoid him. Perhaps this helps to explain why none of them ever became his roommate. In spite of his spoken desire for close relationships, the intensity of his personality was apparently attractive only to a point, beyond which it kept most people from intimate friendship with him. In spite of frequent encounters with numerous friends and acquaintances in his four Ann Arbor years, Richard ultimately seems to have been drastically alone.

David Passman, one of the honors group's most talented members, held Richard in affection and respect and yet was never really close to him: "I valued his friendship, but never his advice, freely forthcoming though it was, because I am sober and pragmatic, and Richard was intense and highly emotional: by my standards and calculations his way of going about things was unreliable, proceeding from a basically mistaken view of life. He did not think subtly, even if he was able to follow the reasonings of Plato and Aristotle which he always understood better than the rest of us in the program, we being students of current events which he misunderstood."

David found a father-son theme running strongly through many of Richard's relationships:

"He advised and protected people like me as if to demonstrate how a father should behave, adopting a gentle and parental tone of voice that spoke of genuine deep concern, even resorting to terms of endearment such as one would employ in persuading a small boy. He was attracted to elitism—to the notion of faceless masses of worthless people (people he did not know) being governed by elites of philosopher-kings (people he knew and liked)—because it would be a vehicle for him to exercise authority. My constant question, 'What if the leaders are people who oppose you?' was irrelevant, because the leaders would be his people, and if they were not then the only possible end could be Armageddon.

"As a student he always had a faculty hero who spoke gospel or else someone whose writings he had latched on to as infallible. These were the figures of authority who could explain life and the universe to him, and give him great thoughts to utter. It should be made clear that Richard's wisdom and brilliance were derivative: he understood terribly complicated ideas very easily, but he never had one major original thought of any merit.

"Thus one can find in Richard, more so than in the rest of us, these surrogate fathers, and his own efforts to be one himself. Reconciling his own freedom with the authority whose lack he felt was, I think, one of the major problems of his life."

Among the younger segment of his friends Richard was especially known as a ready counselor and advice-giver. He would take them in tow, would want to know all about their work, telling the younger ones not to be satisfied with the inconsequential things they were studying in high school. They should really be concerning themselves with college-level material. "C'mon now, let's really get to work on these things," he would say. "Really push yourself to the full effort."

As a senior Richard roomed with two Jewish premed students, Mark Miller (pseud.), a junior from Chicago, and David Drachler, a senior from Detroit. Dave had known Richard slightly from Mumford and Farband and, like Henry Shevitz, had been surprised the year before by Richard's suggestion that they live together. Dave had already made plans, but at the end of their junior year he returned the suggestion for the following fall when he and Mark needed a third man. In September 1963 Dave, Mark, and Richard occupied a one-bedroom apartment in a narrow green house on Washtenaw behind the physics and astronomy building, again only a short distance from campus.

"Richard was a very hard person to live with," said Dave, who seems pleasant and easygoing. There were times when Richard could be very considerate: he might come back to the apartment after studying very late and be almost excessively concerned with not disturbing his sleeping roommates; once he gathered Dave's friends including his girl in from Detroit for an elaborate birthday surprise. Yet more often Richard seemed either oblivious to his roommates or hostile, especially toward Mark. Occasionally Richard seemed to care about Dave's opinions, and they would share what Dave thought were valuable discussions. But he never spoke this way with Mark.

"Richard used Mark as kind of slapping block," said Dave, "and he was very unfairly critical of him. They nearly came to physical blows only once and were parted, but Richard exhibited considerable mental cruelty toward Mark."

A member of the glee club, Mark loved to sing and did so constantly in the rather cramped quarters of the small apartment. He was also fond of playing the radio, but Richard would come in at five for supper, slam down his books, and immediately turn it off. Mark usually did nothing, but Dave, who also had his differences with Richard, would at times snap the radio back on. Dave became particularly annoyed by Richard's habit at dinner of throwing out what Dave came to think were "baited questions," generally philosophical and designed to promote an argument. Says Dave, "He knew he could get the better of Mark or me very quickly, and then he could lord it over us."

"Richard was about as bitter toward Mark as one can be toward another human being," said Dave. "He said a couple of times when Mark wasn't around that he would like to take Mark apart, to 'decimate' him." "I know I'm taking out my aggressions on Mark," he admitted once, "but I just can't help it." Dave told him, "Richard, you're no better than Germany when you lose your temper." Richard agreed that his temper was a problem, but then went on about one of his favorite topics, the fine line between madness and genius, which he seemed to use as a kind of excuse.

Fortunately the roommates saw little of one another; Richard was rarely in the apartment except to eat and sleep and he was not doing much of the latter. His studies now often kept him out until one or two in the morning, but he was invariably up and out again for eight o'clock classes. He rarely slept in on weekends and devotedly followed a daily exercise schedule outlined in a Royal Canadian Air Force pamphlet. He told a friend that he had managed his time so that he was now spending sixty hours a week on his studies outside of class.

The schedule was necessary, said Richard, because of his thesis. Page after page of stationery from his grandfather's insurance agency was filled with notes and grew in a pile on the card table he used for a desk in the apartment. As he explained to friends, his purpose in writing on the *Meno* (one of Plato's most controversial dialogues and the subject of critical debate and speculation for thousands of years) was nothing less than to present a definitive statement on the dialogue and its relation to the rest of Platonic thought.

On the wall near his table he taped pictures of heroes like Goethe, Marx, and Carl Sandburg, along with favorite slogans and quotes. Frequently he would leave a quote for the day on a small slip of paper on Dave's desk before leaving in the morning—a passage from *The Prophet* or perhaps something from a Sydney Harris column.

Through the fall as Richard worked closely with Frank Grace in developing his approach to the paper, his admiration for the professor continued to grow. He told Steve Berkewitz at one point that Grace was the finest mind he'd ever encountered. Steve, like some of Richard's other friends, disagreed and thought that Richard's approach to knowledge had leaped from rational to mystical.

Frank Grace continued to regard Richard as a fine student and a "very considerate young man." Richard would visit the professor at home, occasionally speak with him on the phone, and if Grace was not in, would talk politely and at length with Mrs. Grace; he might even bring candy for the Graces' children.

In both the scope and the content of the paper, Professor Grace gave Richard more or less free rein. In turn, Richard's general philosophical approach relied most heavily on the work of an old teacher of Grace himself, Eric Voegelin, a German Protestant political scientist who had rapidly ascended to the top of Richard's list of unassailable intellectual titans. Voegelin's touchstone is pre-Reformation Christianity, which (he says) teaches "a rational science of human and social order," and establishes as an ultimate truth that "man in his mere humanity," without a faith which links him to the supernatural, is "demonic nothingness." Western civilization, says Voegelin, has come to a moment of deep crisis because it has rejected both of these conceptions. Though at times obscure and difficult, Voegelin's writing is marked by a dogmatic assurance which Richard apparently found extremely compelling:

> In order to degrade the politics of Plato, Aristotle, or St. Thomas to the rank of "values" among others, a conscientious scholar would first have to show that their claim to be science was unfounded. And that attempt is self-defeating. By the time the would-be critic has penetrated the meaning of metaphysics with sufficient thoroughness to make his criticism weighty, he will have become a metaphysician himself. The attack on metaphysics can be undertaken with a good conscience only from the safe distance of imperfect knowledge.

Richard found stimulation in other courses as well during the first term: for example, John Higham's heavily attended lectures on the intellectual history of the United States. Higham, a prominent scholar in his field, took note of Richard rather late in the term when he began following the professor back to his office. "Richard did a lot of talking," said Higham, "but it wasn't a monologue—I always enjoyed talking with him. There would always be a number of students out in the hall waiting to see me and I would let Richard go on for a while and then I'd just have to stop him and kick him out."

Richard was unlike most students, thought Professor Higham, because he seemed really committed to the pursuit of truth. Because he considered the assigned term-paper topics "cut and dried," Richard asked permission to write on his own topic. His paper maintained that James Madison's convictions partook of both pragmatism and natural law, and Professor Higham considered the conclusion quite valid. He called the paper "a work of mature craftsmanship, both detached and appreciative."

Also in the fall, Richard was involved in another course with Frithjof Bergmann called The Philosophy of Literature, dealing with writers like Nietzsche, Dostoevski, Hesse, Camus, and Sartre. In their visits in his office Professor Bergmann became more closely acquainted with Richard: "Teaching the kind of courses I do, I come into contact with a number of young people in trouble, with problems. Richard seemed to be one of these troubled ones, searching with much intensity, but there were others who seemed in worse trouble."

Richard's involvement with Nietzsche had deepened, Bergmann noted with some apprehension. Richard seemed to be reacting most strongly to some of the more declamatory and volatile statements which, in order to avoid radical misinterpretation, must be placed in the proper context provided by the kind of thorough reading which Bergmann feared Richard was not giving Nietzsche. "Of course, I love Nietzsche," said Professor Bergmann, who suggested to Richard and his classmates that they all keep a copy of *Zarathustra* by their bedside at night. "But I am aware that it is easy to misread him, to miss the humor and the playfulness, and to weight too heavily those things which he says for their shock value and their effect on his audience." Nevertheless, says Bergman, "If I had to suggest one person for you to go to and learn about, Richard, I would tell you to go to Nietzsche."

Richard reacted with strong ambivalence to two elements central to Nietzsche's thought: his concept of the *ubermensch,* or "superman," and his insistence upon placing complete ethical responsibility on man's shoulders by cutting all transcendent ties. The superman had, through courage and heroic effort, moved beyond the values of his time, thereby separating himself from the great mass of men who wallow in conventional delusion. Since "God is dead," the superman must carry the burden of his honor alone. Yet perhaps more important for Richard was the image of Nietzsche himself as the suffering, heroic scholar driven mad in his quest for truth. Said one of Richard's classmates, "He probably did more reading *about* Nietzsche than he did *of* Nietzsche."

While walking on campus on a Saturday in late November, Richard encountered Sue Koprince, one of the group in political-science honors. Approaching the tall blonde girl he put a hand on her shoulder and gazed at her somberly and at length without saying a word. Sue later felt it was a moment of "total communication," even though they had said nothing. She was sure that Richard had been extremely moved by the assassination of John Kennedy the day before.

A month later at Christmas Fred Baskin made his first visit home from Berkeley where he had started graduate work, and the two old friends discussed the assassination: "We both pretty much believed it was the act of a madman as opposed to a political plot of some sort. I injected my usual cynicism: 'Look, a great man and he's cut down right at the peak of his powers.' Richard identified with him as a great man who had been persecuted—no identification whatsoever with Oswald, whom he considered a madman. We shared a mutual cynicism that the assassination wasn't going to have much effect on people."

Also at Christmas Richard wrote a lengthy letter to Barry Kriger, a friend from Mumford, the A.Z.A., and Ann Arbor, who was spending his junior year at the Hebrew University in Jerusalem. He wrote with bitterness about the banal, meaningless, anonymous rush of mass education. But also, according to Barry: "Richard said he found fantastic inspiration in the study of Plato. He felt as if he were joining with the gods, almost as if he were one of them. He seemed to feel a kinship with the ancient Greek thinkers and their achievements and felt that perhaps he was close to reaching the heights of human achievement with this paper. He said when he turned to his work on the paper, he thought of the words of David, 'God, look on me with favor.' "

For Richard the fall had also been a time of planning for his prospective graduate program, and among the organizations he applied to for the financing of his work were the Danforth and Woodrow Wilson foundations, the former having some religious affiliation. With the Danforth people Richard got only as far as the submission of his application and references, and was not granted an interview. But in January he chanced upon Alan Gaylord, his former English professor who also happened to be a Danforth liaison officer. When he heard Richard's story, Gaylord immediately sent the foundation a long and extraordinary letter of recommendation, which read in part:

> . . . he has a high intelligence, a catholic and inquiring mind, a very great sensitivity, and a great passion both for righteousness and the Examined Life. Now, on this point for all his writing reform, he may not always represent himself adequately. I have looked at personal statements he has written and can see that one might interpret the righteousness as Puritanism, the search for truth as intolerance. I am quite sure this would be incorrect. He is intense, it is true, and still young enough to be shocked and indignant when he discovers mediocrity, accommodation, or hypocrisy. But with individuals, with his peers, this is not an aspect of his behavior. He respects other people's point of view; as a teacher, I think his only inflexible demand would be that his students take themselves and their work seriously.
>
> . . . He is one of a new breed of campus liberals I rejoice to see, because he is equally a citizen of three worlds: faith, action, and scholarship.
>
> This last is especially important when brought into relationship with what I have already said. It explains why, as an Honors Student, he is interested both in practical politics and political philosophy. It . . . explains how the man who calls himself an agnostic, who has read and loved Homer, Dante, Milton, and Voltaire, has explored Camus and modern existential philosophy, knows and can quote the Bible and could say to me and a mutual student-friend just the other day, without the slightest sense of pomposity but with deference and sincerity, I am man in search of God.

When Professor Gaylord describes Richard as tolerant with his peers, as "The Activist," the tough-minded "Realist," and the informed observer of current events, one might keep in mind that two years had passed since he had worked with Richard for an extended period (the Great Books course in the fall of his sophomore year). In any case, the letter failed to arrive soon enough to change the Danforth decision on Richard. However, prospects for his approach to the Wilson Foundation remained extremely bright.

He had been nominated by Frank Grace, a former Midwest regional director of the foundation, and had also received a strong recommendation from his friend Norman Thomas, a Wilson representative on campus.

As for his choice of institutions Richard was considering schools that included Harvard, Yale, the University of Toronto, the University of Chicago, and the London School of Economics, and seemed assured of acceptance and perhaps some financial help at any of them. Near the end of the first term, however, he announced that he was seriously contemplating the possibility of doing a year of graduate work at the University of Detroit, a Jesuit school located in the northwest end of the city and two miles from his parents' home. Most of his teachers and friends were dumbfounded; next to Richard's other choices it seemed at best a second-rate institution. "When I first heard about his plans," said Frank Grace, "I thought it was madness."

Nonetheless, in January Richard filled out an application for the University of Detroit and ordered his transcript sent along with his references from Professors Grace, Thomas, and Wientraub in psychology. All three were glowing. In his handwritten statement of purpose in the application, Richard said: "I wish to acquire a solid background in classical metaphysics and moral philosophy, study the development of these two fields and that of political theory into the Middle Ages, and then acquire an understanding of the breakdown of civilizational values that has occurred since the Reformation."

It was probably true that as Richard explained, only on a Catholic university campus would he find a climate warmly hospitable to the approach he outlines here. But the question remains: Why the University of Detroit? The answer begins with a fall visit Richard made to Detroit at the suggestion of Ted Wright (pseud.), a U. of M. graduate in political science who was then starting postgraduate work at U. of D. Because he knew of Richard's academic aspirations, Ted encouraged him to attend a class lecture given by a professor whom Ted had found extremely impressive.

Thus Richard met Charlotte Zimmerman, an unmarried woman in her early thirties whose scholarly background included undergraduate work at Harvard, a doctorate in sociology from St. Louis, anthropological work with Mexico's Maya Indians, and graduate study under Eric Voegelin. Dr. Zimmerman, as she is invariably addressed by her students, is a tall large-boned woman with short brown hair framing an angular yet mobile face; she is tomboyish in her mannerisms and often blunt in her speech. Cordially egotistical, she is dramatic and resourceful in the classroom and intensely committed to the virtues of discipline and organization.

At the time Richard met her, Dr. Zimmerman was considered by many the most controversial figure on what is generally a very quiet campus. Her distinctive convictions, scorn for the average or mediocre, and sharp criticism ("Too many here are teaching opinions with no foundation in reality") combined to polarize attitudes toward her. She stayed on at Detroit, she explains, because she was allowed to set up her own courses and work closely with a handful of carefully picked students whose programs she directed. Said one of her students: "Half of her classes thought she was the finest teacher they ever had, and the other half thought she was out of her mind." Her conception of sociology, says Dr. Zimmerman, "has for its basis the study of comparative religion and theology, philosophical anthropology, and philosophy of history." It is this last, her grand overview of history supplying answers to man's biggest questions, that marks her clearly as a disciple of Eric Voegelin and held large appeal for Richard.

According to Dr. Zimmerman's perspective in abstract terms, civilizations move in cycles of growth and decline; there appears to be no sociospiritual progress from civilization to civilization. The human condition must always remain the human condition. Since a unified religion is of central importance, when a civilization reaches a crisis it is because a theological point has been openly disputed; there is always a religious crisis first, followed by an institutional crisis and eventually the internal destruction of the civilization by its own members.

From this perspective, then, having already experienced a religious crisis starting in 1507 with the Reformation, an institutional crisis beginning with the French Revolution and considerable societal disorder fostered by the Industrial Revolution, Western civilization seems to be headed for what can only be described as a very dark future. In Dr. Zimmerman's view, our civilization and its institutions for transferring itself are breaking down so rapidly that large numbers of people within society are becoming empty mass men and cultural barbarians. Thus the scholar as hero in Dr. Zimmerman's terms, the most committed, clear-sighted, and honest of men, must set himself apart from the great mass of men who are pleasantly deluded and must consider carefully the abysmal picture presented by a true vision of the history of Western civilization. He must live with the apocalypse and attempt its understanding.

In a class discussion of the present-day effects of the crisis, Dr. Zimmerman may announce in a resigned yet plucky voice: "It's getting late, students. There's not much we can do now. Just sit tight and save our souls, I guess. There has been an entire moral and philosophic change effected since the Reformation. You must realize that Christianity is dead, and when you do, your mind will clear."

Asked about the "optimism" of another scholar, she admits she hasn't read him but says, "Crisis spawns little people who will say anything to remain optimistic. I too would like to escape and be optimistic, but I'm too much of a realist . . . I have to be dismissed because people can't stand the reality I see and show them."

At the close of the session, however, she may say with a kind of heavily guarded optimism: "One last message for today, and that is: There's hope, students. Maybe, just maybe, if theology really does die, and Christianity finally and philosophy and society, maybe people will be shocked back to their senses. And there'll be a great reaction, a re-creating of the old verities, a return to the old truths of pre-Reformation times."

Richard's impression of Dr. Zimmerman soon began to sweep all other considerations aside. He seemed to think, said Frank Grace, that she held the key to an understanding of moral philosophy; only by studying with her was he going to open the door to true scholarship.

FIFTEEN

Bob Moss and his new wife, the former Marcia Frankel, were now living in Detroit not far from Wayne State, and Marcia was driving to Ann Arbor for her senior-year classes. Occasionally in the fall she brought Richard back to the city with her and at his request dropped him off in the heart of Detroit's black ghetto where (as Marcia gathered) he would search for ways to be of help to some of the people who lived there. One day Marcia did some grocery shopping at an A & P in the area, and Richard toured the store with her. Appalled by the quality of the produce, he was convinced the store was exploiting its customers, selling them left-over produce at Grosse Pointe prices. At times, said Marcia, he would pick out shoppers who looked as if they needed help and carry their packages home for them.

Once Richard and Marcia spotted in the alley behind the store a number of small children playing in and around a large heap of garbage strewn with tin cans and broken glass. Richard asked to be let our of the car and, as Marcia drove on, went to try to get the kids to play elsewhere. When left in the area without a ride, Richard faced a bus trip and a considerable walk to reach his parent's home ten miles away. Marcia thought of him at such times as humble and self-sacrificing.

As for Richard's relations with girls during his senior year, roommate Dave Drachler felt they were a large and serious disappointment. Speaking easily in dire, apocalyptic terms, Richard seemed to frighten girls away with his intensity. He talked of past and possible romances and told Dave he was still looking for the love of his life. Instead, says Dave, Richard "suffered one frustration after another," was romantically involved with five or six girls during the year, but got nowhere with any of them. He would date one seriously for a short time before the girl would call it off, and he, quite hurt, would begin with another.

Often the girls seemed already spoken for, but when Dave Drachler stopped dating Molly Rosen (pseud.), a shy and quiet freshman from Detroit with dark brown hair and eyes and a full-blown figure, Richard decided to try. Early in the winter, after being refused a couple of times, he took Molly to see the film *Tom Jones*. Richard seemed thoroughly engrossed in the picture, losing himself completely in the action of the story, his face, as Molly noted, freezing in a laugh with his chin seemingly turned to stone as his mouth hung open for as long as a minute.

"He loved the hero," said Molly. "He thought Tom Jones was the epitome of everything good in civilization—the kind of young man one couldn't find anymore." Outside the theater it was very cold, but Richard was extremely enthused and started vaulting over parking meters one after another. His exuberance lasted for the rest of their walk back to Molly's dorm on the hill which it shares with the University Hospital Center. He was running up stairs, down inclines, and scaling five-foot stone walls. Said Molly, "I was totally floored."

They dated once or twice a month for the rest of the term, and Richard would call or stop by the dorm every week, often early in the evening so they could watch the sunset and walk on the pleasant hills behind the University Hospital and overlooking the Huron River valley. He seemed enraptured by the natural beauty. Molly marveled at the way he studied French—learning a list of two hundred words with the aid of an alarm clock and daily practice drills, repeating the words as quickly as he could, working until he could rattle off the two hundred in an incredibly short time. But though he pressed his interest and affection for Molly, she could not share his feelings and consistently rejected his advances.

"Richard certainly had his ups and downs," says Dave Drachler. "One day he seemed about to crack he was so tense and bitter; the next day he could be perfectly okay, friendly and fairly easy to get along with." He seemed to be in a depressed state quite often—perhaps most of the time—with only occasional periods of lightheartedness. The subject of suicide came up at least once in their talks when Richard asked Dave if he had ever thought of killing himself. When Dave answered no, Richard volunteered that he had personally considered suicide in the past. He wanted to know if Dave thought himself capable of the act. No, said Dave again, he was quite sure he could never kill himself, but he might, under compelling circumstances (for example, to save a loved one), kill someone else. Richard approved of Dave's attitude and went on to disparage Mark as someone who doubtless could do neither.

Richard seemed particularly happy and satisfied with himself only when he managed to get a lot of work done, when he could return at two in the morning and announce that he had just written ten pages. He still seemed able to lose himself in his books and forget his or the world's immediate troubles. "Books seemed to relax Richard," said Dave. "He could go off to the library in a huff, nervous, tense, and having been in an argument, and he might come back after studying, mild-mannered, pleased with himself and the work he'd done."

On March 13, 1964, Richard learned that he had been awarded a Woodrow Wilson Fellowship. Sue Koprince, herself an unsuccessful candidate, found him "very gracious and humble" about the news and almost as excited about something else: "Dr. Grace called me 'Richard' for the first time today," he said with happy pride. The fellowship meant a grant of $1,600 to Richard and $2,000 (part of which he might also receive) to the graduate school of his choice. By this time he had more or less narrowed his options to Harvard—favored by nearly all his friends, teachers, and family—and the University of Detroit.

On a spring-break visit to Detroit he talked with Charlotte Zimmerman, who at first tried to dissuade him. "Why do you want to bring a Woodrow Wilson to a place like U. of D.?" she asked. "Go to Harvard or the University of Chicago." When he insisted he wanted to study under her, she asked him to realize that he would be making a choice between the glamour which would be his if he went to Harvard and the chance to be a true scholar if he came to her at U. of D. She made her terms clear: If he came to her, he would have to accept her guidance completely as to how he should acquire the background he needed. "It's going to be hard," she said, "and it's going to take time, but if you have patience and work hard, someday you'll write a very important book and it will be worth all the sacrifice." Richard agreed that this was what he wanted.

"If I had it all to do over again," says Dr. Zimmerman, "I would do it all the same way. Brilliant students are always on the edge and you can't just turn them away because of that. When I found out what he wanted to do, what he wanted to learn, there was no place else I could send him. I was the only one who could give him what he wanted in terms of the background he needed. It was a very sane decision he made finally to give up the glory of Harvard for what he could get from me."

Back in Ann Arbor Richard announced his choice to Norman Thomas, whom he had not seen since October when he had applied for the Wilson.

"Why in heaven's name would you want to do something like that?" exclaimed Professor Thomas.

Richard explained that his long-range plans were to go to the University of Chicago to study with Leo Strauss. But because he felt himself inadequately prepared in moral philosophy, he could not expect to go to Chicago and meet the competition he would face there or get from a man like Strauss all that he should get.

Charlotte Zimmerman would give him the background he needed. To Professor Thomas, Richard had always seemed to have a healthy sense of his own talents and potential, but now the young man was seriously doubting himself and his preparation. Thomas launched into a detailed argument against Richard's choice, but Richard seemed generally agreeable and offered no real counter. He finally maintained that the work he was going to do with Dr. Zimmerman was simply something he had to do; he had made his decision.

Professor Thomas argued again with Richard on two or three occasions, sent him to other members of the political-science department, and quizzed Richard's friends about what had happened to him. Others also tried their hand. Dave Drachler asked, "What if Dr. Zimmerman leaves U. of D. or doesn't turn out to be the type of person you think she is?" Richard easily dismissed such questions. Fred Baskin, home at Easter, quickly got into an argument with him: "I accused him of not believing the rather plausible rationalization he'd come up with for his decision, and I wanted to know what the real score was. (I had already, as far as I was concerned, written off his ability to do anything intellectually by about the middle of college, even though it was obvious that the boy was bright.) He pointed out that he was an intelligent person going into the social sciences (which we had always agreed dealt with some of the most important and vital questions which for various reasons they seemed ill-equipped to handle) and was going to try to accomplish something."

Richard found himself explaining over and over that he simply could not go to Harvard because the people there were unsympathetic to his philosophical humanism; the political-science department was full of behavioralists and positivists employing quantitative techniques and social psychology without a vital concern for traditional ideas and values. He was totally opposed to the philosophical climate at Harvard. Nevertheless, said Ned Weiner, "An awful lot of people spent an awful lot of time trying to change Richard's mind."

Among those who tried the hardest were his parents, who strongly favored Harvard and for whom U. of D. made no sense at all. His connections with them had been relatively calm during his college years when he had seen little of home, but now in the face of his decision relations became strained again. Said David Passman: "Perhaps Richard took his nature from his grandparents, as I rather think he did, but he was spiritually a stranger to his mother and father. He had the great heart, the uncommon need for love and intimacy, the impractical and shortsighted reasoning processes —not at all their son, through no fault of anybody's."

"One could see the tender concern he felt as a big brother, and the cool correctness toward his parents, who seemed resigned to being utterly defeated and bewildered by him, while he was so courtly and cordial to them. They were crucially important people to him. It mattered intensely to him that his parents should be the closest people to him, understanding him, approving of him, trusting his judgment, but he was different from them, his plans were often ill-advised, and his judgment was terrible."

Frank Grace favored the University of Chicago and also tried very hard to talk Richard out of U. of D. Finally he decided not to press the issue and wrote a letter to the Wishnetskys saying that he thought Richard was making a mistake but not an irreparable one, and because of Richard's resolve, one he should be allowed to make. To himself Professor Grace expressed the fear that Richard was becoming something of a cultist in his reverence for Charlotte Zimmerman and particularly for Eric Voegelin, as the final bastion of truth. Possibly, he thought, Richard had confused the notion that there is something called truth which is perhaps apprehensible with the notion that he or Dr. Zimmerman or Voegelin or anyone in fact possessed it. "Voegelin is a brilliant scholar and a great teacher," said Grace, "but certainly not the possessor of all wisdom and truth as Richard seemed to think he was."

To Professor Thomas, "A strand of rationality seemed to have broken in Richard some time during that period between October when he applied for Wilson and April when he made the decision to go to U. of D. You simply couldn't reason with him." Much of what Richard was doing in the last part of his senior year seemed to Thomas motivated by a need to call attention to himself.

In the middle of March Richard chanced upon Sharon Thompson (pseud.), a girl he had driven with to a wedding in Indiana the year before. Sharon, an attractive blonde, remembered him as kind, gentle, and sad, a back-seat driver on the trip down but gallant when they got stuck in the snow, a young man who could dance exuberantly but who seemed fragile as he folded himself up and went to sleep in the back seat to avoid the anxiety he apparently felt over a fierce blizzard which drastically cut their visibility on the trip home.

Now back at Sharon's apartment for coffee, he talked about his new fellowship, she about her recent conversion to Judaism. Richard was very pleased, though he would not accept her as a full-fledged Jew. They struck up a relationship, went on several dates during the spring, often to see movies like *Jules and Jim* and *This Sporting Life,* and even went drinking one night. After a beer apiece they danced at Sharon's place to *Swan Lake,* whirling and laughing in a way that made Sharon think Richard capable of real joy. Though generally the friendship was platonic for her, occasionally Richard made passes. He seemed to have increasing difficulty taking No for an answer, and after his most persistent effort had been rebuffed one night, "he completely blew up." He moved off in a rage and screamed at her, "I work hard all week! Why can't I find a little relaxation, a little pleasure once in a while." Sharon retorted, "Well, I work hard all week too and I just don't feel like it." He seemed to presume, she thought, license to take what he wanted.

The relationship continued in platonic style. They talked books and ideas: Richard at the time was especially fond of the Stoic *Meditations* of Marcus Aurelius and said he wanted to live the ascetic, almost saintly life of the true scholar. Once when Sharon was in a low mood, he gave her an article by Rabbi Adler clipped from the Shaarey Zedek *Recorder.* The subject was dependency, the point being that there were good and bad kinds of dependency—the good simply a preparation for an individual's independence, the bad a state that kept an individual from ever becoming independent.

Richard described Rabbi Adler in glittering terms and Sharon said, "Well, he sounds like a great man." "Yes, he is," replied Richard, "but he tears his congregation apart viciously, trying to expose and root out their hypocrisy." He went on at length about how materialistic and hypocritical people in the congregation in fact were. But he became incensed—the expression on his face and his whole demeanor changing abruptly—when he began talking about how the rabbi chastised his congregants.

On occasion Richard also spoke with Dave Drachler about Rabbi Adler. Dave once attacked the rabbi as a man of some petty foibles and found Richard extremely fond of the man and quick to defend him. "He is one of the greatest men I know," insisted Richard.

"If he's such a great man, why does he quarrel with his assistant?" asked Dave.

"All men have such foibles," said Richard, "even the greatest."

As this indicates, Richard's rising concern with the place of religion in modern life had led him to a greater interest in Judaism, Rabbi Adler, and Congregation Shaarey Zedek. The congregation had only recently moved to its new multimillion-dollar synagogue in Southfield, and now Richard might occasionally attend Saturday morning services when he was in Detroit for the weekend.

Throughout the year at Richard's instigation he and Dave and Mark Miller had lit candles and said the blessing on Friday nights before dinner and had observed certain of the dietary laws. They would have their usual disagreements, the usual bitterness would be in the air, but the argument would stop for the candles and the blessing and then start again afterward. Of the three Mark was the least concerned about his own identity as a Jew, and this seemed to disturb Richard. "What do you think of your Jewishness?" he demanded one night. "Is it important to you?" Mark refused to answer.

In mid-April on the train back to Ann Arbor after Passover, Richard told a friend that he had just finished his honors thesis; he was carrying it with him on four hundred pages covered with his careful, back-slanted longhand. It had been shaped from nearly a thousand pages of notes which he had been carting around campus with him for months. Having finished, Richard was pleased with his work and told friends that his hopes for it remained intact: possibly it would astonish the political-science department as the definitive statement on the subject, perhaps to be published and praised as was the work of John Kennedy's student days on a much less profound topic, *Why England Slept*. Some of his friends shared his hopes.

When his typing went too slowly and it appeared he would not finish on time, Sharon Thompson offered to help and ended up doing most of the paper. It came to ninety pages of double-spaced text plus forty-five pages of more than six hundred single-spaced footnotes. Before submitting it to Frank Grace, Richard titled it, *Philosophy: A Portrait of Man in Search*, subtitled it, "A New

Analysis of Plato's *Meno,*" and dated it April 20, 1964. That night Richard and most of the others graduating in political-science honors gathered at the Pretzel Bell to celebrate. Everyone drank freely, and after a few small glasses of beer Richard became extremely loud, friendly, and jovial, at one point climbing onto a table and falling off into someone's arms. Tom Butch helped him home, and Dave Drachler told him the next morning that he had been very funny.

There was, however, one more chore to perform in connection with the thesis. Richard, like each of the others in the group, would be examined on the paper in an oral session before a committee of three professors, the man under whose direction he had written, plus two others in the department. He got a preliminary report from Frank Grace and came back to tell Dave Drachler in a soft, almost awed voice, "You know, Dave, Dr. Grace thinks this is one of the finest papers he's ever read."

Still, on the day set for his oral he was apprehensive. At lunch with Steve Berkewitz he consumed a typical noontime meal of a half bag of potato chips, soup, and milk and talked about a friend who the year before had received a C on his thesis and had been given very poor treatment. The C was completely unjustified, said Richard, but these things happened and might even to him. Later they sat on the steps of the physics and astronomy building and talked about Camus's *The Rebel.* Richard, in dismissing Camus's references to the horror of concentration camps, said, "The real concentration camps are systems of thought." When Steve questioned the validity of the analogy Richard insisted, "We are prisoners of our levels of thought, we are inmates of our own souls, we are prisoners of our selves." The words lodged in Steve's memory, perhaps because earlier in the year his girl friend had remarked that Richard seemed to her obsessive, unapproachable, and quite mad.

Richard's apprehension was justified: he could be sure of a rigorous cross-examination on the approach and content of his paper. While Frank Grace's presence would be generally reassuring, Richard hardly knew the other two men on his committee and had every reason to believe that they would be less than sympathetic to his perspective. Jerry Levitt, who had developed a similar orientation under Professor Grace, had been warned by their department adviser, Martin Needler, to expect a very stiff grilling if he insisted on writing about natural law. About Richard's brand of political theory, Professor Needler has this to say:

"One of the principles of this school of thought is that only certain exceptional people can really understand the important issues of politics, that for these people there is no distinction between facts and values, but that certain moral values are obviously right, although their rightness cannot be demonstrated to people who are not able to appreciate the subtler points of political thought. This was a very unfortunate doctrine for Wishnetsky to be exposed to. He already showed symptoms of a lack of emotional stability in the absolutism of his views and his refusal not only to acknowledge that he could be wrong, but even to listen to any views different from his own. Although he was obviously an extremely able student, his extreme intolerance and the aggressiveness with which he maintained his intellectual position created difficulties for him in his academic work."

SIXTEEN

Richard began his paper with an epigraph from Werner Jaeger:

> . . . there is something of this quality of personal experience in *The Republic*, when [Plato] describes the miraculous preservation of the man meant by nature to be a philosopher from all the dangers which threaten him during his education in a dangerously corrupt environment. That is what makes his description of the life of the philosopher in this world seem so tragic: It seems that only a miracle, a divine chance, can permit a philosopher to grow up in it; and most such natures go bad before they are ever fully grown.

In his dedication Richard wrote, "I wish to express my deep gratitude to Professor Frank Grace, who taught me to respect wisdom."

The text opens with a description of "The Decline of Athens and the Rise of Socrates." Because the soul of Athenian morality was being undermined by a variety of forces, the Hellenic world, says Richard, was suffering a "general 'breakdown of law and order.'" At this critical moment Socrates appeared:

> Armed only with the power of his intellect, he became Man in search of Truth offering hope in the midst of despair, order in the midst of chaos. He began to "[explore] the moral cosmos in the human soul," an investigation which resulted in his "discovery" of the human soul, an "epoch-making" moment "in the spiritual history of Greece." At a time "when all traditions were collapsing," Socrates sought to establish a just and permanent basis for morality. Plunging into the depths of his own soul he discovered a new order for man—the order of man.
>
> Socrates conceived of his discovery and its communication to others in religious terms. He had sought for and found the divine in man and, through his penetrating and incessant questioning of his fellow Athenians, attempted to lead them to the awareness he had achieved; to cease such questioning would be "disobedience to God."

Throughout the remainder of the text, Richard treats the movement of the dialogue in great detail, and in the last few pages of Part IV he relates it to the rest of Plato's work, placing it as pivotal, as "The Periagoge of the Dialogues." Generally the essay exhibits an admirable enthusiasm and a vivid awareness of the dialogue as a living document. But it also shows naïve and simplistic thinking, an intense concern for detail and a sweeping dogmatism, much passionate celebration, and perhaps less than enough cool analysis. Underlying the whole production one senses a strong emotional involvement with the plight of the martyred, pure, and unadulterated saint, Socrates:

> The only truly uncorrupt Athenian, the only man who had courage enough to tell his fellow citizens what they *should* have heard rather than what they wanted to hear, was murdered by those very men for whom he cared so much that he refused to withdraw from public life and retire within his private world.

Overall his language is fluent and coherent, though there are occasional lapses into the florid and the ludicrous: "With these words he reveals the profound simplicity and the great profundity of his approach to life and of his intellect."

Richard twice refers to the fact that man is imperfect and so can never be certain of possessing absolute knowledge. Yet his language almost never indicates that this fact has any reality for him, and there are several moments of condescension and good-hearted arrogance. Perhaps because of a notion that anyone who would wade through more than six hundred footnotes would likely be on his side, his tone becomes even more self-assured and dogmatic in the notes. Genuinely original or stimulating ideas, which would undercut the annoyance caused some readers by his tone, seem lacking, however. Nearly all the content of the paper is attributed to his selected scholars, and when he does attempt to go it alone, he may contradict himself within two sentences. Witness the following note:

> There is nothing in our *sense* experience that tells us that all we can know comes from sense experience. Rather, it is a *spiritual* experience that is the basis of all materialistic philosophies; it is a denial by the soul of any reality higher than matter, most likely because that soul has never experienced any reality higher than matter.

In his oral exam Richard faced two professors in addition to Frank Grace: Samuel Barnes and James Meisel, selected by the department to read his thesis because of their strong backgrounds in abstract political theory. Barnes noted in Richard's interest in Plato and rationalist philosophy a strong desire for certainty. In this Barnes could sympathize to an extent. In his own student days at Duke he had gone through a similar experience, a phase in which he had found Plato and the kind of work Richard was doing to be very attractive—until, he said, he became aware of problems, criticism, and shortcomings.

Professor Meisel, short, vibrant, and affable, and with a slight accent retained from his native Germany, is distinctly unsympathetic to natural-law theory and, unlike Professor Barnes, retains no memory of the episode involving Richard's exam. "I've been trying to place which one he was, but I just can't seem to recall," he said three years later. He added with a smile, "I wonder what Freud would say?"

Jerry Levitt described his own oral as harrowing and was sure the examination had been extremely unpleasant for Richard. Sam Barnes agrees that Richard was probably given "a pretty rough time." He says there were possibly a number of ingredients in the unpleasantness, among them a clash of personalities and convictions. Both Jerry's paper and Richard's came under very sharp attack as the professors insisted upon questioning basic premises in a fashion that, Jerry thought, left little common ground for discussion.

"It was a frank and freewheeling discussion," said Professor Barnes, "without too much concern for one another's feelings. This is more or less to be expected, though, with an honors oral or a Ph.D. oral. In effect the student is being tested under fire."

Although Professor Grace was quite unhappy with much of what happened, there was little he could do for Richard. In addition Grace felt constrained to agree with his colleagues in their criticism of Richard's lack of attention to critical opinion not favoable to his position. Indeed in the entire production, there is only one substantial acknowledgment of the fact that there exists a potent body of Platonic criticism which does not swallow its subject whole. In a footnote to Part III Richard says:

> It may be noted that this paper has embraced the interpretation of Plato of German scholarship, as articulated by men such as Werner Jaeger and Eric Voegelin, rather than the less spiritual and more logic-oriented approach of the English school. This decision has been made on the basis of intuition coupled with a considered judgment not hastily arrived at. Intuition must be recognized as often being a key, if not the key, to an understanding of the truth. I hope this intuitive decision, rather than leading me astray, has allowed me to penetrate to a more insightful perception of the nature of this problem than could have otherwise been achieved.

"There are some very interesting things in the notes," said Professor Barnes, who found them the most fascinating part of the paper and focused his criticism on them. The fact that a number of the footnotes bear little relation to what Richard is talking about in the text, Barnes felt, compromised the validity of the thesis. Richard had smiled and said he thought no one ever read footnotes. "He was making pronouncements on the morning news," said Professor Barnes. For example: "The disturbingly high suicide rate among today's college students is evidence that there may be some truth in describing modern positivistic factory-universities in the same terms as Socrates describes the Sophists."

Professor Meisel's chief objection to the paper, according to Barnes, was that Richard had done an inadequate job of discussing Plato with respect to the sociology of knowledge, of assessing the impact on society of Plato's philosophical message. (According to

Richard, Plato's words were an indispensable factor in determining "the very nature and destiny of man.") To some the thesis would seem to be pervaded by a current of immoderation, which is perhaps why Professor Meisel saw fit to write on Richard's copy, "This is the product of a tortured mind." The paper received an A from Professor Grace, but Meisel joined with Professor Barnes in recommending that Richard be graduated only with honors in political science and not—as Richard and many of his friends and teachers had expected—with highest honors.

Though Richard succeeded in giving the impression to Frank Grace and others that he was quite indifferent to his experience in the oral, friends like Dave Drachler, Sharon Thompson, and Molly Rosen thought him deeply disappointed. To all three he announced that Barnes and Meisel had "screwed" him; Dave found him sulking for days afterward. To Molly, Richard explained that he was an individual who stood up for his convictions and made them known. He could have written what he had known to be acceptable, but he was not about to kowtow and thus had to suffer injustice.

The day after the oral Richard entered Professor Barnes's office, very upset and angry, and began to pace back and forth, insisting that Barnes and Meisel had been completely unfair to him. In spite of Richard's increasing anger, Barnes found him "extremely gentle," and as the tirade rose, the professor found himself taking "quite a bit" from Richard, more than he would have normally taken from a student, because Richard continued to be so gentle. Yet he seemed deeply upset about not being graduated with highest honors and kept returning to the notion that it was simply unfair that he had been deprived, since he had put in much more work and had attempted a much more difficult subject than had any of the others in the program. For an hour Richard paced the small office and decried his fate. Professor Barnes tried to reassure him and reasoned that graduation with honors was an accomplishment to be genuinely proud of—he should not be disappointed with second best. Richard disagreed.

Professor Grace had also been shaken by the experience of Richard's exam and, fearing that he had witnessed a personal attack on his own convictions, reportedly vowed never to allow another of his students to undergo the ordeal. Richard and Jerry Levitt dropped by to assure him that their attitudes and ideas remained intact and that they were proud and happy to have worked with him. Richard said he was resolved to continue his study of natural law and to make it his life's work.

With afterthought, Professor Grace now feels he perhaps made a mistake in allowing Richard such free rein on the thesis. It became clear that Richard had bitten off much more than he could chew. "Perhaps my own egotism was at fault or produced the mistake," said Grace. Never again would he allow a student to work so freely on a thesis. Professor Grace now also feels that Richard was treated quite fairly in the oral, that Richard perhaps needed to be put in his place, that perhaps it should have happened before. The paper, he said, generally deserved the criticism it received, and he agreed with Norman Thomas that Barnes and Meisel were highly reputable men who had presented their considered professional opinions.

For another opinion Richard sent a copy of his paper to Charlotte Zimmerman, along with a note indicating that Frank Grace had praised it and had recommended that Richard try to get it published. Dr. Zimmerman says, "I told him it was a very excellent paper for his background, but certainly not the last word and under no circumstances to be published." Professor Grace agrees the paper was not publishable and does not remember ever discussing the possibility with Richard.

Later Richard received Dr. Zimmerman's advice on his exam experience: "I told him to forget about it, that those men were just out to get him because they disagreed with him philosophically, and what they had to say had nothing to do with the validity of his thinking. I told him he'd have to expect that if he was going to stick to his ideas. He'd have to be strong enough to ignore that kind of attack."

Thus Richard's highly successful undergraduate years, which had seen him compile numerous honors, a 3.83 overall average (he had received six B's in eight terms along with his A's), and ranking in the top one half of one percent of his graduating class concluded with what he considered his first significant academic failure, and what may have been a serious emotional defeat. He was made no happier about this time when informed that the Wilson Foundation had withdrawn his fellowship upon learning that he had chosen to work at the University of Detroit. The foundation explained that Detroit did not have a doctoral program in political science and wondered if Richard had nonacademic reasons for his choice. He immediately appealed and asked Frank Grace to plead his case.

Commencement exercises were held on May 22, and the Wishnetskys came to Ann Arbor for the ceremonies at the football stadium. Richard proudly introduced his parents to Professor Grace, and they all heard President Lyndon Johnson tell the new graduates: "Your imagination, your initiative, and your indignation will determine whether we build a . . . Great Society."

SEVENTEEN

Like other young Jews graduating from American universities in the spring of 1964, Richard had planned a summer trip to Europe and Israel. Unlike most of them perhaps, he had placed himself under extraordinary strain during his undergraduate years and was departing with extraordinary anticipation. The effects of the strain might appear at quite unexpected moments.

One day in May before leaving he stopped by to visit Mrs. Baskin, feeling, according to Fred, that he should pay his respects to the people in the old neighborhood. "I gave him some coffee, and we talked," said Mrs. Baskin, a gentle woman who speaks softly in accented English. She had just received a letter from Fred in Berkeley describing the move he had made into new lodgings, a house shared with five other boys—all Gentiles. When the conversation turned to Fred, Mrs. Baskin gave Richard the letter to read. Says Mrs. Baskin:

"And when he read it, 'Oh, my,' he said. 'Oh, *goyim!*' meaning 'Gentiles!' 'He's becoming a real *goy!*' he said, meaning 'He's becoming a real Gentile!' So I said to him, 'Oh, Richard . . .' You know, he was like my son, like he became so cute and nice and sweet. I said, 'Don't be crazy.' Only in Jewish. I said, 'Don't be *mischugga.*' It's a very beautiful Hebrew word . . . it means 'crazy,' but it's like I would say to my own son. I said, 'Richard, don't be *mischugga,*' and his eyes got awfully big and he pulled on my tablecloth and everything fell on the floor, the sugar and the milk and the cups and everything. And then he apologized right away and he helped me clean it up." Fred adds about Richard's reference to *goyim:* "It was tremendously unlike the Richard I had known."

Before his departure on May 26 Sharon Thompson asked Richard if he feared difficulty on the trip with only a limited background in languages. (His French was passable and he knew a little Yiddish.) "No," replied Richard, "I don't expect to have trouble." Sharon asked how he would communicate. Said Richard quickly, "With a smile! It's the universal language."

The university-chartered flight left Detroit on the Tuesday after commencement, landed in New York, and then headed for Paris. On both flights he sat next to Sue Koprince with whom he had just graduated in the honors program. Traveling light, Richard wore a sports coat and wash-and-wear shirt and trousers, and carried the rest of his belongings in an eighteen-pound duffle bag which he stuffed into the overhead rack. He would be hitchhiking most of the time, he said, and traveling alone. While he had considerable money available to him—perhaps a couple of thousand dollars from his grandparents—he wanted to see how little he could spend.

Sue was going to spend the summer teaching in Germany and wondered if she would see him, but Richard made it clear with a quiet firmness that he did not want to go to Germany. He planned not and wished not to meet any Germans. Instead he was most excited at the prospect of spending a month or more in Israel. He had supported the Zionist movement, he said, and it was important to him to see what was happening there. On the night flight to Paris they flew into the sunrise. "It was an awe-inspiring sight," said Sue, "and Richard went crazy over it. He was intensely excited about it and kept going to the front of the plane for a better look and coming back to get the rest of us to look. He was describing it in almost religious, mystical terms."

In Paris Sue planned to stay a week with a girl friend, then drive down through France before going to Germany. When she offered Richard a ride, he made a rather earthy remark ("As he was wont to do at times") and politely refused. They would meet again in July for the flight home. Richard also stayed a few days in Paris and while there called a girl whose name he had been given by a friend at U. of M. A good Catholic girl—very happy and enthusiastic type—about twenty-one," the friend had said. So Richard rang up Dominque des Mazery. They met at the George V rail station and proceeded to her parents' home. Recalls Dominique:

"At first impression he was neither appealing nor good-looking. Neither his dress nor physique made any special impression, but when he began to speak, he won us over completely with his intelligence. He had an hour-long discussion with my mother on the theology of Augustine and Thomas Aquinas. Also he was very well informed on the progressivist Christian contemporary movement whose head is Emmanuel Mounier, which was amazing, since many people in France are ignorant of his name. Richard seemed passionately concerned with theology. Later we went to a café on the Boulevard St. Germain and again we talked, particularly of American problems such as Cuba, and the racial situation." About certain things, however, Dominique found him sentimental and naïve: "Thus, when I asked for news of a mutual friend, he said, 'I am very pleased because he is well. He's not happy, but he is well. He keeps his balance by devoting himself to his studies.' In contrast to his sentimentality, he was as aggressive as a little boy and he was jealous if I looked at another boy in the street. Later he sent me in the mail, as a souvenir, a box of cards with which we had played Old Maid."

Leaving Paris, Richard began hitchhiking through the countryside of France, carrying only his duffle bag, staying whenever possible at youth hostels, often taking pictures. From France he went into Spain, then to Italy, and finally took a boat to Greece. He was usually alone and later he apparently said very little about his experience in these places. Generally he described Europe as a large disappointment, though he did have some kind words for Greece—the warmth and zest of the people ("They're real human beings") and the natural beauty of the Greek islands. He had been in Europe two or three weeks when he boarded a steamer in Greece and traveled deck-class to Israel.

Richard spent his first days in Israel in and around Tel Aviv, staying at the home of his uncle, Herb Hordes, twenty minutes north of the city. With the use of his uncle's car, Richard did considerable sight-seeing and spent time meeting and speaking with a number of wealthy and prominent Israelis, government and business leaders to whom he had introductions from his grandfathers and uncle. Richard's reactions to these people, he reported later, were generally negative. With no special historical interest or striking scenery, Tel Aviv is a large ultramodern metropolis and was perhaps not the most auspicious introduction Richard's highly critical eye might have had to Israel. With all the virtues and vices of the West it could not satisfy his hope of finding something truly different from the materialistic commercialism he felt he had left behind.

After Tel Aviv, Richard stayed on a nonreligious kibbutz near one of the country's threatened borders for two weeks or so. He witnessed, he later reported, an exchange of fire at the border, perhaps was shot at himself, and "ran like the rest of them." It was an extremely sad and disillusioning episode, he said. He spent some time in the Negev either on a kibbutz or on one of the desert tours of Israel's open frontier to the south—for the most part an arid, lifeless region inhabited only by scattered Bedouin tribes and hardy Israeli pioneers battling nature to carve out livable and productive areas around their small settlements. He probably passed the Mile of Trees planted in the name of his philanthropic Grandfather Hordes on the road to Beersheba.

According to what he told friends, Richard was greatly moved by the strange beauty of this harsh, eroded landscape, with its painted cliffs, purple mountains, and canyons colorful at dawn or dusk. He spoke of the thrill of waking in the morning and going out to see only nothingness, knowing that this nothingness was looked upon by one's forebears thousands of years before. And over a year later back in Detroit he would tell two of his friends, who knew little about religion, that it had been at one of these moments in a beautiful natural setting in the desert that he had learned that he was a prophet. It had just come to him, he said: He had been very deeply disturbed in Israel, and finally in the desert he had found "beautiful words" coming out of his mouth. Richard did not elaborate except to explain for his friends what a prophet was in the biblical sense—a man chosen by God to bring His message to men, to guide the nation in difficult times, and to fight for morality against religious and social corruption.

At the beginning of July, perhaps in time for his birthday on the first of the month, Richard arrived in Jerusalem, which at the time was split into the old walled city in the hands of the Jordanians and inaccessible to Jews, and the new city, modern, variegated, thriving, the capital of Israel.

Richard headed for the Hebrew University to meet his friend Barry Kriger, to whom he had written the preceding December. Barry was just finishing a year of study in Israel; he had always thought Richard admirable and likable. For a day and a night Richard stayed with his friend, but because Barry was in the midst of finals Richard later moved in with Harry Keidan who was also visiting Barry during a summer stay in Israel. Harry had attended MacDowell and Mumford and was a junior at U. of M., but he met Richard for the first time in Jerusalem. They shared a dormitory room for three days, and while Harry was not feeling well and generally confined himself to the room, Richard slept little, got up early every morning, donned his neatly kept shirt, slacks, and sports coat, and was off to explore the city.

To Harry Keidan, Richard seemed always on the move, unable to relax, high-strung, and generally in search. When he was not off sight-seeing or talking to people, he was poring over a textbook learning Hebrew. He found the Biblical and Archaeological Museum fascinating, he reported, and traveled to the the American Freedom Forest outside of Jerusalem, where he planted a tree in Frank Grace's name and sent him a certificate which pleased the professor back in Ann Arbor. Using letters of introduction, Richard reportedly met various government officials including Israel's president, Zalman Shazar, with whom he chatted over tea. He was also formulating, said Barry Kriger, an itinerary of scholarly stops in Germany, Greece, and Israel for future doctoral work and wanted to evaluate a few scholars at the Hebrew University. Though disappointed with the response of one or two of these men, he was most taken with Professor J. L. Talmon, a historian of world prominence. They had dinner together and discussed the possibility of Richard working under him. Recalls Professor Talmon:

"As soon as he started speaking, I realized that Richard was quite an unusual young man. His erudition was truly astounding. There seemed to be nothing that he had not read. . . . He was a Jewish God-seeker weighed down, indeed crushed by the mystery of the Jewish fate, Jewish martyrdom, and the significance of Judaism in the modern world."

Most of Richard's time and that which he seemed to find most rewarding was spent visiting with people in the ultra-Orthodox Hasidic community of Jerusalem. These are East European Jews originally from the native locale and circumstances of Richard's grandparents, among the last remnant pursuing a way of life based entirely on the laws of the Torah and Talmud and preserving intact the customs, dress, and Yiddish language of the Polish ghetto and Russian shtetl of more than a hundred years ago. Living in the closed world of a small and shrinking minority, they remain fiercely opposed to the discarding of traditional ways, to what they consider the godless modernism and corruption of present-day Israel.

Richard had become interested in Hasidism and the Jerusalem Orthodox dedicated to its preservation as a way of life in part through respect for his Grandfather Hordes, who ten years before had become reinvolved in the religious movement of his Russian youth.

In general, Hasidism stresses that all—the rich, poor, scholarly, and unlearned—are welcomed by God and are equally children of God. The cultivation of purity of heart, sensitivity, and generosity are deemed superior to study; the true Hasid, or holy man, strives for an ecstatic communion with his God. The emphasis is on joy, humility, devotion, affection, and enthusiasm most evidently expressed in the happy, fervent, self-oblivious dance as form of prayer. In spite of persecution by other Jewish sects Hasidism grew and flourished in the eighteenth and nineteenth centuries among the masses of Polish and Russian Jews, and then began a sharp decline. The Nazi holocaust destroyed the movement entirely in Europe, and only a few leaders escaped to reestablish their communities in the United States and Israel. The people Richard was visiting in Jerusalem were a tragic remnant, among the very few to survive the efficient Hitler.

According to Barry Kriger and Harry Keidan, Richard seemed stimulated and excited by his contact with these people, and he appeared to want something from them. He was trying to rediscover, it seemed, his past, searching for roots, digging into history to find some sense of identity, some notion of where he had come from. Harry felt that Richard was trying to achieve the kind of faith exhibited by the ultra-Orthodox in order to find some sense of purpose and meaning.

In the evening Richard spent with Barry, the two friends ate dinner together in the dorm, then went out for a walk as the sun set and the dusk gathered. They found a large rock to sit on and gazed out over the quiet city as they talked: "Richard remarked on the beauty he saw and felt, and said at one point, 'Barry, I'm really thinking of settling down here, of living here in Israel. It's a real possibility.' He had the most engaging smile I think I've ever seen, a Walt Whitman smile lighting up his whole face, and at one point we clasped each other on the shoulders in a kind of unspoken good fellowship."

After Jerusalem Richard returned to the coast, then crossed the Mediterranean back to Greece, having overstayed the time he had planned for himself in Israel. He would have to rush to get back to Paris in time to make his flight and so set out to hitchhike on the shortest possible route through Yugoslavia, Austria, and the Germany he had not wanted to see. When he met Sue Koprince at the airport in Paris, he told her he had made it by traveling nonstop night and day and living on bread and cheese.

In the postcards and short letters crammed with information which he sent to friends while on the trip, he sounded pleased and in good spirits. But later he was contradictory and apparently ambivalent. To a few friends and acquaintances he seemed enthusiastic about Israel and excited about conditions there; it was a rude shock, he said, returning to decadent Detroit. To others he seemed wholly disillusioned by the materialism and hypocrisy he said he had found in Israel. He had encountered some warm, kind, and admirable people among the ultra-Orthodox, and he often spoke about the natural beauty of the country, but he seemed otherwise disappointed. Occasionally he talked about returning to study in Israel someday. About Europe he was vague but less ambiguous: he had been disillusioned and quite thoroughly unhappy. At times Greece had been pleasant, however, and he also mentioned one other exception when he visited his old Contemporary Affairs teacher, Aaron Gornbein, at Mumford soon after returning. He had come home with the feeling, said Richard, that he had visited only one really fine country—Spain.

Gornbein was shocked: "Richard, why of all places would you prefer Spain?"

"Well," said Richard, "Spain has tradition and an understanding of the value of tradition."

"What do you mean, Richard?" asked Gornbein. "Spain has produced one of the most cruel, backward, repressive societies in the world."

Well, Richard did not really agree with this assessment. There was something deep, he said, which the Jesuits had contributed to Spain, something one just doesn't find elsewhere. "There's a kind of spiritual approach to the problems of society in Spain which I find very appealing," he said. On a later visit to Mr. Gornbein Richard said he had thought about the teacher's remarks, and though he partially agreed, he was still convinced that Spain was an admirable place which has avoided to a greater extent than have other countries the breakdown in civilizational values occurring since the Reformation.

About three months after his return, Richard wrote to another of his former teachers, Frank Grace in Ann Arbor, and said in part that his summer travels, though exciting, had been a disturbing and disorienting experience, robbing him of the perspective he had achieved "through philosophy" and, even worse, smothering his "zest for life."

It seems safe to suggest that what Richard meant by "philosophy" was Platonism and that, for whatever reason, the answers of the ancient Greek no longer seemed definitive. In fact, when speaking about Plato, Richard seems to have used the convinced tone of his thesis less and less. All the keys were no longer to be found in Greece, and with his trip to Israel he had begun to dig deeper into history. Also, perhaps never in his life had he spent such extended periods of time so thoroughly alone, cut off from the kind of conversation he craved and cherished. He admitted to a few closer friends that he had been extremely lonely. One of them said:

"For some reason his personality wasn't clicking in terms of what his expectations were. Though he had some great experiences, he didn't talk much about them because he hadn't enjoyed the trip as he had thought he would. The really great times he wanted to have just didn't happen."

In the midst of his loneliness, a door to the past may have opened to a sad procession of deep-seated fears, doubts, and anxieties concerning his personal worth, his ability to love and the possibility of his being loved, his ability to make sense of himself and his world—all the old terrors and uncertainties so carefully buried under success-upon-demanded-success and denied or avoided with bravado, bustle, humility, or the small delusion.

PART III

In such periods of stress and disruption, man is forced to face the past consciously, to evaluate and select from it that which appears to be precious and relevant. Such a time is now upon us. Much of the uncertainty and confusion in contemporary life is a consequence of our unwillingness or inability to face our past with adequate wisdom and insight. Uncertain of our past, we are confused about our present and are thus alienated from ourselves. The fantastic rapidity of change in our society and its continuing acceleration make the very ground under us quake with frantic movement, appearing to dissolve all the stabilities upon which we formerly built our lives. There is left for some moderns no terra firma upon which to stand.

—RABBI MORRIS ADLER

EIGHTEEN

On a stormy afternoon in Ann Arbor near the end of July 1964, Professor Otto Graf, director of the Honors Council at U. of M. and a regional director of the Woodrow Wilson Foundation, called Richard at his parents' home on Manor Road to explain that the foundation had decided to allow him to take his fellowship to the University of Detroit. Elated, Richard thanked Professor Graf profusely for his efforts in changing the foundation's decision.

When the controversy arose over Richard's decision to go to U. of D., Professor Graf had asked for and received an explanation from Richard. Later he made a call to the foundation's national director at Princeton asking that Richard be given the chance to carry out his plans. When Frank Grace made a similar call, the foundation reversed its decision and Richard was assured of financial help.

With time on his hands before starting at U. of D. late in September, Richard joined some of his old Mumford cronies like Fred Baskin, Larry Bernstein, and Ron Burns for bull sessions at one of their homes or a local delicatessen. Brimming with enthusiasm, he made Charlotte Zimmerman sound "something like the greatest philosopher of the twentieth century, and only Richard knew about her." More than ever his point of view seemed rigid and narrow, his personality "stereotyped."

As always the group discussed Dostoevski for a while, particularly the old question of whether a person may disobey a law if by doing so he ultimately accomplishes something valuable for society. Richard, as an absolutist, morally opposed any transgression of the law.

They also talked of suicide, another favorite subject, and two or three in the group believed that a man could reasonably and morally commit suicide; it was his own personal decision. Once a person saw that his values were unattainable, in fact he had nothing more to live for and perhaps should kill himself. It was a notion which Richard argued strongly against.

With Baskin, home briefly from Berkeley, Richard went one afternoon to U. of D. to meet with Dr. Zimmerman. "I was doing my best to be tolerant," says Fred. "And I was happy to see that at least he recognized that U. of D. was an inferior institution. We all agreed, he and I and Dr. Zimmerman." But Fred and Dr. Zimmerman, who did most of the talking as Richard sat quietly, found little else to agree on. They were very quickly into an argument over the significance and direction of modern philosophy, and Fred found himself particularly disturbed when the professor mentioned that Richard would do well to stay away from certain books. Would it really hurt him, asked Fred, to read a little Wittgenstein? Dr. Zimmerman explained that she had read the authors he was advocating and had managed with intellectual maturity to see the error of their ways, but someone without very rigorous training was simply not yet ready to approach them. Says Fred, "To me this was the horror of medieval Catholicism all over again, and I couldn't believe it."

Later Baskin was adamant: "Richard, you of all people should not study with this woman!" She was sure to have a narrowing influence on him, thought Fred, and was only going to confirm whatever naïve opinions Richard already held. He felt that Richard should at least give these notions a genuine test: "I didn't give a damn if he came out a Hindu; I was only unhappy in her confirming this particular set of ideas because I felt they were preventing him from wrestling with his problem."

Richard and Fred also walked over to the Hordes's home one day and Fred now found his friend seemingly doting on his grandfather: "At that time I guess he was playing them against his parents a good deal. They differed with his parents as to what he really needed. As his psychological problems got worse their attitude was that he had been studying too hard and all he needed was a little chicken soup and a little time off from school, a little love and a trip to Israel maybe, and he would snap out of it. And of course they became very useful to him because they had money and he could go to them."

During August before she returned to Ann Arbor for her sophomore year, Richard dated Molly Rosen about once a week. She found him cynical the night he took her to see *Goldfinger:* "He was cutting people down right and left and using his favorite terms—the masses, the proletariat, the peasants." As they waited in line, he loudly explained that these people were particularly ignorant and stupid because they didn't *know* they were ignorant and stupid. They were happy, he said, because they didn't know any better. Inside he sat next to a girl whose hose, he announced, made her look like a prostitute.

Afterward as they walked out past another crowd coming in, Richard screamed, "It's wonderful! It's a great movie!" He had been engrossed by the film and found in James Bond the epitome of modern society's ideal man—suave, sophisticated, powerful, effective, and amoral. Molly thought him ambivalent about Bond. Later Richard drove them a few miles out to the spot he had chosen for an evening picnic—the grounds of Congregation Shaarey Zedek's extraordinary new synagogue. He had packed some food and they sat on the grass in the warm August night air while he spoke of his admiration for the beauty of the building.

Completed at a cost of nearly five million dollars in 1962, the synagogue is located in Southfield, an affluent, heavily Jewish suburb northwest of Detroit. It occupies the high ground of a forty-acre tract of well-tended green rolling landscape just north of Eleven Mile Road and overlooking the 696 Freeway which rushes traffic to and from downtown Detroit. The synagogue is a massive stone structure presenting an oblique triangular thrust to the western sky. Designed by Percival Goodman to represent the sacred Mount Sinai, it is a striking piece of architecture hailed by some as one of the country's great religious buildings. At night, flood-lit and jutting into the darkness, it is an arresting sight.

Richard and Molly sat in the darkness doing what Molly enjoyed most with him—talking. When he made an affectionate advance, she would have none of it. She felt, she said, no real closeness to him and little sexual attraction. They had been fighting with increasing frequency over his demands that she be more demonstrative and when Molly refused, Richard, enraged, would "totally withdraw and close up."

After *The Night of the Iguana,* in which Richard identified with the Burton character as a "Christ-figure persecuted and driven by a congregation of hypocrites," they drove past the northern suburbs to rumble down a dark gravel road leading to a village church he wanted Molly to see. As the car rushed over the gravel, Molly sat close to the door away from Richard, who was silent and rigid as he gripped the steering wheel. In the aftermath of another tiff in which he had explained how cold and inhibited she was, Molly felt that if she said or did the wrong thing at that moment he would kill her. She had sensed a deep and powerful hostility contained only with great effort, but when they reached the small white church in the quiet village he seemed to unbend and relax. "Isn't it quaint?" he asked. "It *is* quaint!" responded Molly, and Richard laughed. Later they parted amicably and she kissed him good night—the maximum demonstration he ever received from her. Molly now wondered if she should date Richard again.

One early September afternoon Richard appeared at the old farmhouse which stands at the entrance to Camp Farband. He was calling on his old friend, caretaker Brad Mason and Mason's family with whom he had remained in touch during the four years since his last summer as a counselor at the camp. Richard had visited the Masons a number of times when accompanying his sisters to and from camp, had dined with them, and particularly liked Mrs. Mason's pork chops. "I'd kid him about it, but he'd eat 'em anyway," says Brad. "I asked him, 'Richard, they got pigs in Israel?' and he said, 'Sure. They've got lots of pigs in Israel.' "

Brad was pleasantly surprised now to see his young friend at Farband after the camp had already closed. Richard explained that he had hitchhiked out from Detroit and had spent a good part of the day walking on the grounds. "He said he'd been enjoying the marvels and wonders of nature," says Brad, "and he knew I was tired and resting so he didn't want to disturb me." (Brad had recently been released from the hospital after a tractor accident which cost him a leg.)

"Brad, I've come to say good-bye," said Richard after they had settled themselves along with Mrs. Mason in the roughly appointed living room. "I'm taking a long trip. Brad, I've finally got what I want and I'm really happy. I've finally reached a goal that I set for myself."

"That's wonderful, Richard. Tell me all about it."

"I can't tell you much," said Richard, "except that I'm on my way right now to Oklahoma City for two weeks. I'm going to a secret-service school there."

Surprised and pleased, the Masons congratulated Richard. Brad, drawing on his own army experience, asked if he was going to Fort Sill.

"I can't say," said Richard, "but I'll be in Oklahoma City only for a short time and then they're sending me to a school in Kansas —I can't tell you where."

"What kind of outfit is it, Richard?"

"I can't say."

"Is it the CIA?"

"I can't tell you," said Richard smiling.

Recalls Brad: "I kept pumping Richard about where he was going. I figured if he were really telling me the truth he wouldn't say anything. I kept asking him about Fort Sill and the place in Kansas, but he would just smile and not say anything. Finally, he said, 'Brad, you know I can't tell you anything.' And I said, 'Yes, Richard, I know. I was just testing you.'" Nonetheless, Brad was still curious and asked if he was carrying a gun.

Said Richard, "I've got a gun, but I can't show it to you."

"Have you got a permit for it?"

Richard took from his wallet a small blue card for Brad to examine. Actually, Brad recognized it as a safety inspection certificate similar to the one he had acquired himself a few years before from the county sheriff's office when registering a handgun. It was a certification both that the gun had been tested and found in good condition and that the person whose name appeared on the card was authorized under state law to own the weapon. (To own a handgun legally in the state of Michigan one must properly acquire a certificate in one's county of residence; it is not, of course, a permit to *carry* the gun.) Brad noted the name on the card, Richard S. Wishnetsky, and thinks now the county indicated was Washtenaw, which includes Ann Arbor. "It all seemed in order," he says.

Richard was carrying with him what Brad described as an army musette bag with shoulder straps and worn on the back. "Let's see that little .32 you got in there," said Brad.

Richard cocked his head and smiled: "I'll show it to you if you really want to see it. It's a good gun. It's been all checked out."

But Brad declined the offer and told Richard that he believed him. He says, "I figured he had the gun at the bottom under his personal things and I didn't want to make him pull all his stuff out."

In any case, Richard explained that his trip really wasn't going to be a long one—just two weeks and he would be returning to Detroit to start his university work. "Brad, I finally got what I want," he repeated. "I've got a position with the government and I'll be going to the university."

Talk turned to other matters and as usual Richard got on the subject of religion with Mrs. Mason, a Baptist minister's daughter. Richard wanted the Masons' opinions of his people, the Jews. "Richard, if I didn't think well of them I wouldn't have lived here and worked for them," said Brad. Yes, but didn't they think Jews were terribly hypocritical? "Well now, Richard, isn't everybody?" asked Mrs. Mason. "I mean don't we all have a little of that in us?" Richard explained that he was just back from hitchhiking all over Israel and had decided that "religion is all a farce—here and there."

Mrs. Mason made some sandwiches over which the conversation continued, but about 4:30 Richard said he had to be leaving. Brad took his '53 Buick and drove him to the intersection of Mt. Hope and I–94. He would always come back for a visit, said Richard. "Don't worry about me, Brad. I'll take care of myself." Richard got out of the car and began hitchhiking west on I–94.

After telling his story consistently for the second time, Brad said, "I'll swear on a stack of Bibles that every word I'm telling you is the god's truth." And he's certain that Richard was also being forthright: "I knew Richard and Richard wouldn't lie to me." As for substantiating evidence Brad offers the following: "Some time within a year before this, a guy from the government came around to the camp here after it was closed asking, 'Do you know Richard Wishnetsky?' I said, 'Yea, how do you know?' He said Richard had applied for a job with the federal government and had named Camp Farband as a place where he had worked and so they were just checking on him. He asked if I knew if Richard was in any subversive organizations or clubs. I said, 'No, not that I know of. Maybe at the U. of M., but not around here. You should really talk to Mr. Mark, the camp director. I'm just the caretaker.' I told him, though, how highly I thought of Richard."

With information unavailable from official government sources attempts to authenticate Richard's story have been largely inconclusive. If Richard did show up at the camp *after* Labor Day, as Brad recalls, then he spoke with the Masons some time after September 7, which would give him barely two weeks before the start of the fall term at U. of D. in the week of September 20. Hitchhiking would seem an unlikely and time-consuming way to travel to an appointment at a "secret-service school," but then hitchhiking was his favorite mode of travel. Also, if either the CIA or the FBI was involved, Richard may have been traveling in the wrong direction; according to some sources he should have been heading for the East Coast, where screening or training centers for these organizations are supposed to be located. Still, it is not impossible that the kind of place mentioned by Richard exists in the Midwest. For the most part his movement and activities during the first few weeks of September are not well accounted for. But if all of what Richard told the Masons was true, then the time element may not be overly important, since it's quite possible that he was very quickly screened out of any such program for psychological or other reasons (showing up with a gun would have given him two strikes to begin with).

As for the gun, the central files at State Police headquarters in East Lansing have no record of a safety inspection certificate being issued to Richard for 1963 or 1964. However, the State Police keep track only of a gun's current owner, not its former owner or owners. If Richard subsequently sold or otherwise rid himself of a gun he had registered, and a new owner, another state resident, took out a new certificate, the State Police would have discarded their record of Richard's having once registered the gun.

Perhaps the whole episode was a fantastic lark—Richard, unhappy and disturbed over recent experiences, deciding to pay a nostalgic visit to the scene of an earlier, more pleasant period in his life and at the same time to play a kind of game in which he would manufacture a role and step briefly into it. For one who feels deeply fragmented and frustrated it may seem quite pleasant to arrange consciously or unconsciously a separate, more satisfying identity, at least for a while, and perhaps to show it to someone who, like Brad, would have no reason to question its authenticity.

But if Richard's story is assumed to be a fabrication, one of the first of many questions leading to perhaps endless speculation is,

What did Brad Mason take to be a properly issued safety inspection certificate in Richard's possession? Other questions come quickly: Were Richard's words and actions the result of conscious fantasy and an elaborate hoax, or did they stem from a full-fledged delusion? If the former, would he go to such lengths to play a game that might jeopardize one of the few simple, pleasant relationships in his life? Would he offer to show Brad a gun that he in fact did not have in his bag? The answers can only be speculative with the information available.

On the other hand, Richard's excellent academic record, his acceptable politics (with a conservative philosophical basis and a liberal tone), his reported membership in the National Students Association, his recent trip abroad and his plans for further study in Europe and Israel, the increasing evidence of CIA–FBI connections on American college campuses, the fact that the role would appeal to his secret fantasies of power and sophistication, the visit to Camp Farband by a federal agent asking about Richard—some or all of this might argue that there was perhaps at least a mixture of truth and fantasy in what Richard told the Masons, that he might have had some peripheral connection with the CIA, for instance, which he elaborated upon for the benefit of the Masons and himself.

In any case, whether there is fact or fiction or both involved here, Brad Mason might be considered someone likely to receive it from Richard. Brad was a safe "confidant," sure to react positively to the news and generally isolated from Richard's other friends and acquaintances who, if presented with the idea of Richard as a "secret agent," would probably have found it difficult to believe. Needless to say at this point, no one interviewed besides the Masons indicated any notion of such a facet to Richard's life.

Brad Mason never saw Richard again after his September visit, but he offered a thought on what might have happened to the young man: "Richard, I hear, got caught up studying religion some time after I last saw him, and studying religion can do crazy things to a man. I think studying certain things in religion too much can drive a man's mind crazy. You take my wife's brother, for example. He got to studying over and over some section of the Bible and he finally cracked up. He's right now over at Ionia [state hospital for the criminally insane]."

NINETEEN

The main campus of the University of Detroit is a placid, attractive place. The old gray-stone buildings with their red-tile roofs lending a Spanish air, and the newer structures, more modern in design but blended nicely with the old, are arranged carefully to foster a sense of proximity and warmth. Between the library and the Briggs Liberal Arts Building large trees shade a red-brick walk stretching from a modernistic little chapel at the west to a statue of the Sacred Heart on the east. Behind the pleasant exterior one finds many of the goals, frustrations, and paradoxes evident in most other Catholic institutions of higher learning in America.

Lawrence V. Britt, S.J., president of the university during Richard's stay, wrote a message at the time for prospective students:

> The subject of Jesuit education is man, whole and entire, soul united to body in unity of nature, with all his faculties, natural and supernatural, such as right reason and revelation show him to be. And it is a cardinal principle of Jesuit Education that such education must include the development and perfecting of the total human being. Hence, no education can be considered complete unless it includes the intellectual, moral, religious, and spiritual formation of the student.

Yet in spite of the attempt at a personal approach, Richard could find in walking the halls of the Briggs Building large rooms in which students were listening to television sets lecturing on the New Testament. And since a great majority of his nine thousand classmates did not live on or near campus (only 20 percent were from out of town) and scattered to their homes all over the metropolitan area, their connections with the faculty were often brief and tenuous. For the most part they were graduates of the city's numerous parochial high schools, young people who had been told that their chances of losing their faith (and their key to heaven) would be multiplied if they attended a secular college, students who were used to the feeling that life's largest questions have been answered to the satisfaction of any reasonable man. Generally a bright, cheerful, collegiate air prevailed with few beards, little long hair, and much conventional dress in evidence. Rarely could

Richard find the zealous involvement, gloom, or vivid intellectuality of Ann Arbor; rarely was there a hint of student unrest or faculty protest.

It was at Charlotte Zimmerman's suggestion that Richard shared an apartment with Pat Burke and Bill Winter (pseud.) during his stay at the University of Detroit. Pat and Bill were both members of a small group of graduate students whose programs were being directed by Dr. Zimmerman, and her suggestion about living arrangements was typical of her concern for her students—those she had chosen carefully as worthy of special attention because of their scholarly commitment. These few, usually no more than six to ten, were at times referred to as "her clique" or "her little coterie of disciples," and in fact, she made no secret of her desire to help shape the lives of the young people close to her, and of the necessity to isolate them to some extent from the "corrupting" influence of the mediocrity on campus. "I wanted him to become part of the group," said Dr. Zimmerman, "to have the benefit of their companionship and to be able to learn from them."

Pat, a thin, quiet young man with glasses, is dispassionate and well spoken, and regarded by Dr. Zimmerman as a "real thinker." Bill, another whom she regarded very highly, needs a cane and a brace on his crippled leg in order to get around and like Pat possessed more academic background of the type Richard felt he needed. The three rented an apartment with two bedrooms, a living room, bath, and kitchen on the first floor of an old, rather shabby building on Twelfth Street, a few blocks south of Six Mile in a mixed neighborhood a mile east of campus.

At first Richard appeared affable and gregarious, though an intensely dedicated student. He did not seem overly impressed with himself, though Pat Burke remembers him saying with perhaps a touch of cynicism, "My family thinks I should be the great Jewish scholar of my generation." Generally he got along with his roommates and the others in the group without much evidence of the friction one might expect.

His roommates did not see much of Richard, since his schedule was as usual overloaded and rigid. Up and out by eight he would hike to campus to study in his carrel in the library basement with breaks for class, lunch, and dinner until 10 P.M. when the library closed and he would take a short break at the Student Union before spending another two hours or more studying in the sociology department offices on the second floor of the "Sosh Hut," an old house adjacent to campus. He had been given the key to the house as a privilege to facilitate his study.

He was apparently reading constantly and carefully in the books Dr. Zimmerman had set out, along with those required in the only course he was taking for credit during the first term—a three-hour seminar in comparative religion in which she met with all her special students. He was also auditing her introduction to cultural anthropology for undergraduates and occasionally sitting in on the classes of a few other selected professors. The weekends he would usually spend at home with his family. He mentioned that he wasn't getting on well with his parents but didn't talk about his troubles; he seemed devoted to his sisters and spent a day or two at home consoling Ellen, the younger one, when her dog died.

It seemed impossible to get to know Richard better, thought Greg Leszczynski, "another brilliant boy" in the Zimmerman group. Richard was so busy and so gregarious on his breaks that when Greg did manage to corner him in the Union, Richard would soon be up making new acquaintances. He seemed to be trying (successfully) to make contact with every administrator, professor, and student on campus and would quickly get to very meaty subjects: "Do you have a match? . . . What do you think of Aristotle?" There were some who found his forward manner arrogant and unlikable, but generally he was getting along quite well. Though otherwise tending to dominate any conversation, when depressed he would ask questions and be receptive to advice or ideas, and sometimes admit that he hadn't thought through a conviction he had previously presented dogmatically.

Richard's favorite theme, and one for which the rest of the group showed great sympathy, was the alienation and dehumanization of man in modern society. No matter where a conversation started, it would usually end up tied in with the effect of modern life on the human condition. Says Burke, "The two things on which you could not expect to have a rational discussion with Richard were Israel and its relations with the Arabs, and nuclear weapons."

Nuclear warfare was still, after all, the one concrete current issue over which he might feel compelled to some practical political action. The presidential candidates had been nominated, and for Richard (like millions of other Americans) the choice, though unappealing, seemed clear. "If Goldwater wins he's going to take us straight into war," he told friends. Richard was upset enough at the prospect of Goldwater to work for a short time near the end of September in the Citizens for Johnson-Humphrey campaign.

For the first few weeks of his work at U. of D. Richard wondered aloud about his choice of graduate school. He hated U. of D., he said in letters to Fred Baskin. The students were extremely shallow (even more so than those at U. of M.) and none was interested in ideas. Wrestling with his heavy reading assignments and taking voluminous notes, he told his roommates he was worried that he had perhaps embraced more than he could handle.

Then on the thirteenth of October he wrote the letter to Frank Grace in Ann Arbor in which he mentioned the "unsettling experience" of his summer travels. He began by saying that he was nearing the end of his first successful day at U. of D. His first three weeks of study had been a difficult and depressing time, but the source of his troubles resided, he felt, as much in himself as in his environment. Finally, he had made his "first positive and affirmative step forward." He had been deeply involved in his studies, particularly the work of Mircea Eliade, the "superb" comparative religions scholar at the University of Chicago, and the material had finally begun to make sense to him. Despite its considerable difficulties, he felt himself on the way to becoming a genuine scholar, a goal which, thanks to his experience with Professor Grace, he was determined to achieve.

He was not at all disappointed, he wrote, in Dr. Zimmerman, an excellent and challenging teacher and a "fine and delightful human being." And he had made the acquaintance of another extraordinary person at U. of D., "a Polish aristocrat and scholar" who had fought and traveled all over the world. He had made a few friends at U. of D. (if they were truly friends, he wouldn't need more than a few) and remained in touch with home and his high-school friends.

The goal of his studies, he told Grace, was to acquire a background in philosophical anthropology through the study of comparative religion and to proceed to an in-depth investigation of Greek philosophy. He had decided that his situation at U. of D. was really ideal, freeing him from demands unrelated to his scholarly objectives. It was now up to him to use this "splendid opportunity."

Richard concluded with glowing praise for Professor Grace whose students should, he said, respond positively to him if they wished to "assert their humanity." Of course, he added, modern society's moral and intellectual corruption was reason for "despair," especially when a failure of communication occurred.

The "Polish aristocrat and scholar" mentioned by Richard was Professor S. W. Budzinowski of the economics department. He had been teaching in Israel before coming to U. of D. in 1949 where he has been a popular figure ever since. He met Richard a week after the term opened at a coffee hour held at the Union for honor students and thereafter occasionally saw him in his office for five or ten minutes of conversation or at his home near campus.

Richard had a tendency, said Professor Budzinowski, to speak with the air of authority about matters on which he was not fully informed. He seemed to find it difficult to say about any subject, "Well, I don't know about that, but I'm going to learn," and could only be forced to refrain from making his pronouncements by Budzinowski's sharp criticism. Trying to gobble concepts and ideas so quickly, he was getting only a superficial smattering of knowledge. Professor Budzinowski warned Richard that if he was going to be a scholar, he would have to dedicate himself to a search for all the truth, all the facts relevant to a certain problem, whether or not he found some of them unpleasant or disheartening.

There were a few others on the faculty whom Richard appreciated, but the center of his academic attention was Charlotte Zimmerman. His choice, he felt, was being vindicated, and if his expectations had not been entirely fulfilled it was only because he did not have her exclusive concern. He was just one important member in the group with which she worked. She treated him in a warm and friendly way, but when she found him "trying to play the suave male role" in the first few weeks, asking her out to lunch and dinner, Dr. Zimmerman refused and let him know that she did not fraternize with students. A bit wary from the start, she kept Richard at arm's length and never invited him to her flat to the gatherings of a few of her other students.

In class, however, their relationship generally went smoothly and seemed based on considerable mutual regard. As professor and students sat around a large table for the courses he was auditing, Richard would always place himself to Dr. Zimmerman's immediate right and play the role of monitor, only occasionally joining the discussion by touching Dr. Zimmerman on the arm to stop her and saying something like, "Now don't you think there might be this consideration?" Dr. Zimmerman would frequently ask Richard for a particular date which he would supply quickly, "even if he didn't know it," said a classmate. With at least some of his fellow students Richard seemed to want the same strict propriety that Dr. Zimmerman demanded. When a boy in the class referred to him casually as "Rich," he interrupted to explain sternly, "It's 'Mr. Wishnetsky' to you."

Included in the reading for the seminar in comparative religion were several books by Mircea Eliade, Voegelin's *Israel and Revelation,* Nielson on Greek religion, and the Frankfurts on the Egyptians. Each member of the class was required to give oral and written presentations on one of the books read for the course during the first semester and was to complete the second term by writing a long paper. "The way I was handling it, they were doing just what the graduate boys at Harvard have to do," said Dr. Zimmerman.

Richard had become enthused about the work of Eliade, especially a book entitled *The Sacred and the Profane.* In it Eliade is concerned with the dichotomy between the experience of the religious man in an archaic society, for whom the sacred or the supernatural often manifests itself, and the experience of the modern nonreligious man who feels he lives in a "desacralized," completely profane world. Though desacralized, he says, modern man retains deep within his unconscious a genuine religious impulse and therefore the possibility, if he seeks it, "of reintegrating a religious vision of life."

TWENTY

Occasionally in any course taught by Charlotte Zimmerman, reference will be made to Fëdor Dostoevski. One day near the end of a seminar meeting the subject of *The Brothers Karamazov* came up in discussion. When the class ended, talk had turned to the movie version which opens with Lee J. Cobb biting a squealing Hollywood starlet on the leg. As the group moved out of the building with their professor, Richard began to praise in ecstatic terms

Yul Brynner's performance as Dmitri. Dmitri, said Richard, was a man of passion living life to the hilt with the capacity to stand up to suffering and gain from it. And in the role Brynner was the epitome of virility and zestful masculinity. Dr. Zimmerman disagreed. Brynner reminded her of a "pinball machine with that bald head and those flashing eyes and teeth." When Richard continued to argue the point, she said, "Mr. Wishnetsky, you wouldn't know the first thing about masculinity." Later she felt she had insulted Richard and apologized to him the next day before class. It didn't happen again, she says.

Dostoevski is one of several intellectual figures including the Marquis de Sade, Auguste Comte, Nietzsche, and Max Weber who serve Dr. Zimmerman as keys to an understanding of the crisis of the modern age. The Marquis, for example, following in the destructive wake of the Reformation and the French Revolution, represents for her the absolute negation of Western civilization and the doctrine of Christianity; his profound, blasphemous rebellion was in a sense an attempt to achieve divinity through heroic evil. For a great man it is always difficult to live, but especially in times of great corruption, a great man will rebel in drastic fashion. As seen by Dr. Zimmerman, the Marquis was honest and heroic enough to face the evil in himself as well as the sickening corruption and hypocrisy in the Church and the society he once loved—and was driven mad by this vision.

Nietzsche is a similarly heroic madman for Dr. Zimmerman. Because Nietzsche's will to truth, honesty, and capacity for love confronted him with the scandals of Christianity—its fallacious theology and its hypocritical "virtues"—he wrote a counter-Gospel and attempted to live in a realm beyond good and evil on the shifting sands of nihilism. Nietzsche drove himself to ask the impossible questions and, like the very few men who do so, was forced to the alternatives of madness or transcendence. Dr. Zimmerman suggests that perhaps his final madness was the experience of transcendence.

In a sense Nietzsche is a character out of Dostoevski, says Dr. Zimmerman, and Ivan Karamazov shares many of the German's uncompromising qualities. Ivan drives even further the irony of the modern Christian dilemma by refusing not God but his own salvation because it implies acceptance of the terrible mystery of innocent human suffering; confronted with the implications of his position he goes mad. The greatness of Dostoevski, says Dr. Zimmerman, lies in the fact that he forces himself (and his reader) to face honestly the choice between *amor sui* and *amor Dei,* between the love of self which must end in sadism and the love of God which must end in mysticism. According to Dr. Zimmerman, all great rebels make this decision for either good or evil and pursue their choice so completely that the world must consider them mad.

John Samuels, Richard's freshman roommate at U. of M., and David Roth, a friend also from Mumford and Ann Arbor, were both attending Wayne State now and seeing Richard quite often. David, a philosophy major at U. of M., had found his interest gravitating to radical politics; in the long talks he would occasionally have with Richard, he could find little common ground and "did not take Richard too seriously at times." John, now working in psychology, felt more or less the same way. Richard insisted that his friends sit in on one of Charlotte Zimmerman's classes.

John and David joined him at a couple of sessions of the comparative religion seminar and found him almost in adoration of his professor. Richard would proudly look back at his friends seated away from the table and once slipped a note to John which read: "You are watching a very brilliant woman!" He seemed to consider her a fount of infinite wisdom, and inevitably his friends attempted to tease him out of his reverence. When was he going to take her out? they wanted to know, and he would become upset, call them "bastards," and give them a half-violent, half-playful gesture of contempt. John noted that sex (as always) was a difficult area for Richard and one about which he seemed to fantasize extensively. Richard would boast about the attractiveness of the young women who were supposedly interested in him and at his command. But when John and David used vulgarity to bring his opinions of these girls back to reality, he would become incensed and break off the conversation.

Richard also made important new friends early in the fall. Larry Walters (pseud.) had graduated with Richard from Mumford. But though the two had been aware of each other in high school, they had never met before they started a reminiscing conversation on a study break one night at the U. of D. library. Tall, dark, well built, and athletic, Larry had been Richard's antithesis in high school:

socially minded and popular, pursued by the opposite sex, a letter winner on the swimming team, and by his own admission, "very flighty." He had gone on to major in business at Wayne and was now beginning his studies at the Detroit College of Law. Larry is quick to admit that unlike most of Richard's other friends, he is not an intellectual: "School comes anything but easy for me, and I work very hard for what I'm getting." Nonetheless, he projects a personal warmth, attractive high spirits, and a strong penchant for the sentimental which quickly appeared to strike responsive chords in Richard.

Living in the area at the time, Larry found it convenient to study at U. of D. and he and Richard were soon greeting one another like old friends. Richard invited him to study at the Sosh Hut after the library closed, and when they were finished Larry would drive him back to the apartment on Twelfth Street. Soon Richard had acquired another key to the Sosh Hut for Larry's use, and they were often stopping on their way home at night for a snack and conversation at a Coney Island restaurant. Says Larry, "More and more Richard found me to surprise him a bit because he was so pleased to find somebody who was not nearly as bright as he was, but yet feeling the same things. And if I was feeling these things, maybe there were a lot of other people feeling this way."

Late one night when Richard and Larry were studying, they got started on their favorite topic—how most people refused to live life. "Zombies," they began calling them, "animated corpses." "We kind of interpreted the vast majority of people as being zombies," says Larry, "and we decided to form this Anti-Zombie Movement. We got really silly with it, carried away; in fact, we were almost in a trance." The movement needed publicity and exposure, they decided, so Richard called up "The Les Crane Show" in New York to try to arrange a soap-box appearance in which he would present the philosophy and ideas of the movement in a prepared speech. Richard said he would be in New York soon for a meeting with someone from the television show. Later he took two hours off to write the speech.

"We were making up these fantastic slogans," recalls Larry, "and thinking how even children could get in on this by having Anti-Zombie dolls who would wind up and watch television for you so you could do something else. We got so high just on this conversation that it was about three o'clock in the morning when it all ceased and we were just completely exhausted."

Richard was conducting a kind of informal liberal education for Larry, explaining his own studies in detail, taking him to movies, giving him books to read, trying to give him the insights he felt were so important. "Consequently," says Larry, "I owe such a debt of gratitude to Richard in the respect that he took a sensitivity that was there, that hadn't started to bloom, and just kind of introduced me to it."

One evening Larry joined Richard and his roommates to see the Bergman film *The Seventh Seal.* A great favorite with Dr. Zimmerman and her group, Bergman sets his story in the Europe of the Crusades while a plague haunts the land. At one point he depicts a ghastly procession of flagellants scourging each other to atone for the pestilence which they feel is God's punishment. "When those people were being flogged," says Larry, "Richard was in as much pain if not more. Richard was physically reacting. I honestly think you could have hit him over the head with a baseball bat and it wouldn't have fazed him at all. He was cringing, he was going through all kinds of gesticulations and wild movements."

Larry marveled at the way Richard bought books, spending his last ten dollars and going without lunch to buy a dozen paperbacks, keeping them to read at some later date or giving them away to friends. He gave Larry his copy of *Man Alone,* a paperback anthology on the theme of alienation in modern society, one of his favorite books at the time and a required text for the Zimmerman group. On the first page a blurb explains:

> Modern man, alienated from nature, from his gods, and from society, in an increasingly mechanized, atomized, and depersonalized world, too often is unable to achieve an identity and a relatedness to others. What are the circumstances that have led to this predicament and what are the chances for alleviating it? MAN ALONE forthrightly poses the problem and offers guidance for its resolution.

Above this passage Richard crossed out his own name and address and wrote, "Lawrence Walters: A gift from one non-alienated Anti-Zombie to another."

The book presents a variety of views concerning the origins, extent, and alleviation of the problem, and some of the contributors like C. Wright Mills (greatly respected by Richard) describe the condition primarily as a function of the current structure of society:

> The knowledgeable man in the genuine public is able to turn his personal troubles into social issues, to see their relevance for his community and his community's relevance for them. He understands that what he thinks and feels as personal troubles are very often not only that but problems shared by others and indeed not subject to solution by any one individual but only by modifications of the structure of the groups in which he lives and sometimes the structure of the entire society.

On the other hand, when contributors like psychoanalyst Frederick Weiss get down to the business of analyzing the plight of the alienated individual, they concentrate on the personal development and "inner life history" of their patients:

> The alienated patient is not born alienated, nor does he choose alienation. Lacking genuine acceptance, love, and concern for his individuality in childhood, he experiences basic anxiety. Early he begins to move away from his self, which seems not good enough to be loved. He moves away from what he is, what he feels, what he wants. If one is not loved for what one is, one can at least be safe—safe perhaps by being very good and perfect and being loved for it, or by being strong and being admired or feared for it, or by learning not to feel, not to want, not to care. Therefore, one has to free oneself from any need for others, which means first their love and affection, and, later on, in many instances, sex. Why feel, why want, if there is no response? So the person puts all his efforts into becoming what he should be. Later, he idealizes his self-effacement as goodness, his aggression as strength, his withdrawal as freedom. Instead of developing in the direction of increasing freedom, self-expression, and self-realization, he moves toward safety, self-elimination, and self-idealization.

Though for the moment Richard seemed convinced that he was quite set apart from the poor wretch in need of psychiatric help, Dr. Weiss's article appears to describe much of Richard's thought, feeling, and behavior, and more that was destined to appear over the next several months.

Early in the fall, Richard was introduced by an acquaintance to Sherri Jacobson (pseud.), a tall, slender, friendly girl who describes herself as a Pollyanna. Sherri and Richard hit it off well from the beginning and began dating regularly on weekends, attending movies, parties, and concerts. Sherri found him always very polite and "sweet," fond of doing small endearing things for her, and always the gallant gentleman. On their dates he was always in an elated mood; if a depression struck, he would not see her and would call instead to talk of his troubles.

Introduced to the Wishnetskys, Sherri found them "lovely people" who provided "a very warm home" and gave Richard "all kinds of love." In turn she seems to have been most acceptable to the family. Richard, said Sherri, "really had a very good relationship with his mother. He did have some trouble with his father, but it was nothing extraordinary." While Richard would bitterly denounce the prevalence of hypocrisy and materialism in American society, Sherri noted that he also "liked nice things—he liked to dress well, in nice clothes." And since he had access to the family car only on weekends, "he wanted a car very much."

He seemed to have few modes of relaxation, she thought, and he refused to watch television with her, completely scorning all popular entertainment, though she tried to get him to understand that sometimes it was good just to unwind with something unimportant. Instead, he was constantly writing notes to himself and letters, constantly talking of the degeneration and breakdown of modern society and the necessity for a complete revamping. Sherri waited in vain, however, for the formulation of a plan for change. He took her to a couple of Dr. Zimmerman's classes, and as with many of his friends and his roommates, he spoke proudly of his senior honors thesis without mentioning the trouble his oral had produced. Sherri read the thesis but didn't understand it. Richard also loved to read to Sherri, at times telling her a certain passage was a quote from a famous writer, asking if she liked it, thought it beautiful or insightful. When she answered yes, he'd proudly explain that in fact he had written it himself.

When Brother Antoninus read his poetry at U. of D. in November, Richard brought Sherri to a small party for the poet, attended by several Bohemian types, "very strange, beat people." From the beginning Sherri felt out of place at the gathering and said nothing. But as they were leaving, Brother Antoninus went up to her, smiled, and touched her slightly on the cheek. Later Richard was beaming with pride and said that the poet had honored her. "He must have seen that you're such a good person," he said.

TWENTY-ONE

To Sherri Jacobson, his roommates, and many other friends and acquaintances Richard often spoke of the respect he had for Rabbi Adler as a man of great humanity, intelligence, and genuine wisdom. With Dr. Zimmerman, however, he also maintained that the rabbi could be overpowering in his dealings with others—a "real Machiavellian" on occasion. Extremely anxious for Dr. Zimmerman and Rabbi Adler to meet, Richard made arrangements to bring the professor to Shaarey Zedek for services one Saturday morning. As he and Charlotte Zimmerman sat in the comfortably upholstered theater seats of the large main sanctuary, he whispered explanations and instructions (frequently causing worshipers nearby to turn and glare).

Dr. Zimmerman found herself duly impressed by the spacious sanctuary with its gleaming white walls and dark wood paneling, its high vaulted ceiling peaked over the raised altar, or bimah, from which services are conducted, in front of the synagogue's west wall. The wall's abstract stained-glass windows stretch from floor to ceiling to form an inverted V over the Ark, which, when opened for the reading of the Torah, reveals the bright yellow-gold of the fabric covering the scrolls within. Afterward Dr. Zimmerman saw some of the other parts of the sprawling complex attached to the sanctuary: two smaller chapels, two large social halls, a large modern kitchen, a banquet room, a fully equipped set of day-school classrooms used by thirteen hundred six-to-thirteen-year-olds after their regular school day, and a small store where religious articles and souvenirs are available.

As planned, Richard, Dr. Zimmerman, and the rabbi had lunch at the Adler residence neighboring the synagogue grounds. An excellent meal had been prepared by Mrs. Adler, who had suggested the Sabbath visit to Richard because "Saturday was always a very relaxed day for the rabbi." The Adlers and the Wishnetsky family had come to know each other quite well in the time since the Wishnetskys had joined the congregation some years earlier. Goldie Adler knew Richard as "a sweet boy, a good boy, concerned with conscience, morality, and religion, very proud of his religion and proud of his synagogue and proud of the fact that he knew Rabbi Adler so well and that they were friends."

She had noted, though, that Richard lately seemed to be having difficulty in coping with the ambivalence and ambiguity he found in his life, and as they chatted briefly during the meal, she told him, "You know, all of life is full of contradiction. Even when we say something we don't mean deeply in our hearts, we're not always lying. A child will spill out the direct truth, and it's wonderful, whereas there are times when we can't." She also had words for him on another of his weighty concerns: "There's nothing wrong with material wealth if you don't hurt anyone on the way to acquiring it. The Talmud speaks of it—you're answerable in the world to come for the legitimate pleasures of which you didn't take advantage. Since everything was created for the benefit of man, then you negated something that was God-given. There's nothing wrong with material acquisition if you don't hurt anyone."

For the most part, however, they listened to the discourse of the rabbi and Charlotte Zimmerman. Says Mrs. Adler, "When people came to our home to meet the rabbi and to hear him, it was to hear him, not me, so I sat back quietly, thanked God, served the food, and listened." Dr. Zimmerman clearly recalls the occasion:

"Richard was almost overwhelmed by the situation: here were his professor and his rabbi together at the same table. I liked Rabbi Adler very much. He was genuine and warm and learned—a real man, very masculine, and we got along very well. We got into a discussion of religion and we had a very lively exchange. He said a few things about Catholics—you know, 'You Catholics did such and such to us Jews'—and I came right back and said, 'Well, you Jews did such and such, said we were dirty,' and so on. I really enjoyed myself, and of course we finished on very friendly terms.

"In the meantime, however, Richard had gone into something of a state of shock. According to Richard nobody had ever dared to talk to the rabbi that way, no one had ever said such things about the Jews to the rabbi, and the whole thing had been something of a trauma for Richard. Of course Rabbi Adler and I parted on very good terms. I asked him to come down some afternoon and talk to my class and he agreed and gave me a bottle of wine to take home with me. It was wonderful wine. I enjoyed it very much and I sent him a note to thank him."

Since his return to Detroit, Richard had been attending Sabbath services at Shaarey Zedek with some regularity, perhaps three out of four weeks, usually with his family. Religion had become for him an area of the most vital concern. Like the others in the Zimmerman group, he agreed that, in general, organized religion, secularized, diluted, and hypocritical, held little of value; also like most of them, he felt that a genuinely religious approach to life was essential.

Thus he would often talk of what he saw as the crisis of modern Judaism in which the precious basic tenets of the ancient faith were being compromised, undermined, and lost by most of the American Jewish community. Moreover this situation was especially contemptible, thought Richard, since the Jewish people, the Chosen, had for millennia constituted a kind of moral elite, pointing the ethical way to the rest of mankind, and were now more than ever required to articulate the human conscience.

Barry Kriger was back after his stay in Israel and occasionally spoke with Richard at Shaarey Zedek. He recalls that Richard talked of his work with Dr. Zimmerman as his "spiritual bar mitzvah," a redundancy by which he meant a spiritual awakening. "He thought he was achieving," says Barry, "a kind of insight, wisdom, and spirituality which placed him on a religious plateau above most others. He could feel in this way satisfied and could look down on the others and perhaps more freely criticize." Yet Richard had neither extraordinary knowledge of his own religion nor memories of a strongly established early faith. And so he said he was beginning to examine seriously the basic premises of Judaism, trying to sort out what he could accept for himself. His attempt, some thought, was to intellectualize himself into a belief, and Barry Kriger found him particularly interested in any interpretation which seemed to make religion relevant to today's world. He had been convinced of the absolute necessity of religion; now it was a question of which one.

Through the fall Richard's "search" took him to Shaarey Zedek on Saturday mornings, but his experience there produced considerable ambivalence. Though he admired Rabbi Adler and loved to engage him in conversation, Richard's long-standing contempt for what he deemed the "bourgeois" character of the congregation remained. He seemed to derive inspiration from the building and would often prevail on friends to join him at services, showing them around with an air of reverence. He would also, however, voice his dismay over the materialistic implications of the synagogue and the large amount of money spent for what he called its "opulence." He might even refer to it (with a phrase popular with some in the community) as a "Jewish Howard Johnson's."

After services he might come to the kiddush, or reception, partaking of the wine, cookies, and other refreshments and mingling with the other congregants. Extroverted and sticking mainly with the adults, he seemed to be enjoying himself at these gatherings, talking often about issues like the effectiveness of Jewish education, though more and more often referring to what he called "real religion" and implying that very little of it was to be found at Shaarey Zedek.

Richard's contacts with Rabbi Adler at this time occasionally included a long talk, but usually they were informal after-service chats, one of which was recalled by Barry Kriger: "Richard was trying to drive home a point about Nietzsche's insights into this and that, and I can remember the rabbi saying to Richard, 'Yes, Nietzsche was a great, great man,' and going on this way for about a half a minute. But then he talked about some other ideas which the rabbi said he couldn't go along with, though I don't think he carried this on to some kind of final judgment. At this point this would shut Richard up. He would just listen."

Not really a participant in the service, Richard would sit and observe, at times getting up to move around and talk to some of the other congregants. Says Barry: "He would come over to me in the sanctuary while I was in the midst of something, and he wouldn't let me continue. He would want to talk about some idea which had come to him perhaps from something he had been reading." Increasingly he would leave the building entirely and walk outside on the grounds, explaining afterward that he had needed to be by himself, that he just couldn't take the hypocrisy and superficiality of the sermon, the service, or the people in attendance.

Congregation Shaarey Zedek, like most Conservative groups, has a membership with a variety of perspectives or approaches from Orthodox to Reform; members were thus much more concerned about promoting tolerance than with sharing Richard's passionate desire to hammer out rigid definitions. This disinterest in ideology or theology served only to further antagonize Richard. Said Charlotte Zimmerman: "Richard had a real problem with religion.

He needed a faith he could live with. He wanted a really dogmatic kind of religion, but there was nothing I could do for him there. I told him, 'It's something deeply personal, Richard, and you've got to work it out for yourself.' "

One of Richard's attempts to solve his problem was his continuing interest in Hasidism. On Sunday mornings, most often after having attended services at Shaarey Zedek the day before, he would join his Grandfather Hordes in a class on the Talmud at the Lubavitch synagogue in nearby Oak Park.

Lubavitch was a small eighteenth-century Russian town associated with the founder of a branch of Hasidism known as the Habad movement. A scholar unlike the wonder-working founder of the Hasidic movement, he combined the original emotional, universalist approach with a concern for the intellectual, teaching that both mind and heart lead to God but emphasizing thought above feeling.

The synagogue in Oak Park is an extension of the Habad community in Brooklyn where it transplanted itself from Europe in 1940, thus escaping extermination by the Nazis. With a warm and directly human approach embracing all as children of God, particularly accepting all Jews as Jews (unlike some Orthodox who consider those rejecting Orthodoxy as pretenders), they seek converts within the Jewish community, making them one of the few proselytizing groups within Judaism.

One such "convert" was William Hordes whose interest in the Oak Park congregation began about the time the Wishnetskys moved to Detroit. As one of the sponsors of Camp Farband, he met with the Lubavitch group, which at the time was interested in buying the camp. The sale never went through, but in the process Mr. Hordes met Berel Shemtov, a Moscow-born rabbi connected with the congregation, who reminded him of his own Russian Habad roots. For the next ten years William Hordes showed considerable interest in Lubavitch, and though some interpreted his new concern as a "typical old secular Jew's attempt to sneak into Heaven at the last minute," he made it clear to others that though he was not a believer, he felt that Habad was one valid aspect of Judaism which deserved support because it was a potent means of perpetuating Judaism.

By this time Richard appeared to idolize William Hordes as a vigorous self-made man and humanitarian. There were some who wondered about the real motivation of the old man's philanthropy and liberalism, who saw him as an eccentric bantam patriarch who tended to dominate any group he was a part of and who might rise at various community meetings (at which Richard often joined him) to halt proceedings with a forty-five-minute exposition when only a perfunctory "yea" or "nay" was required. But for Richard, William Hordes was a proud and loving grandfather who made it clear that Richard was his favorite, who probably celebrated his birthday (July 3) together with Richard's (July 1) on occasion, and who shared a facial resemblance with his grandson, especially in the prominent forehead and in the mouth and jawline. In a sense Richard had incorporated into his own precarious identity the conscious image he held of his grandfather, representing many of the tradition-honored qualities he wanted to find in himself.

At the Lubavitch synagogue on Sunday mornings Richard was one of only two or three young people in a class of middle-aged or older men studying the Talmud in the original Aramaic. The classes were conducted by Rabbi Shemtov whose stories of the persecution of Russian Jewry and the heroic sacrifices of his own family in the Soviet Union seemed to impress Richard greatly. Because of his lack of an adequate language background and because the study is an esoteric, complex, and difficult one in itself, Richard's classmates were sure that he would soon drop out of the class. Yet with language help from his grandfather, Richard continued to come back each week and occasionally indicated by an astute response that he was perhaps making some progress. Said Sam Cohen (pseud.), a Detroit attorney who was a member of the Lubavitch congregation, "I thought Richard was beginning to grasp it quite well and once in a while he would show a real understanding."

Richard often spoke with Sam Cohen and revealed a darker side of his regard for Morris Adler: "Richard was very critical of Rabbi Adler to me. 'Rabbi Adler could be a tremendous force for good in the Jewish community,' Richard would say: 'Instead he is using his brilliance as a force for evil.' For Richard, Rabbi Adler was responsible for the perversion and vulgarity of religion."

Richard knew that Cohen was a longtime friend of Rabbi Adler's and so brought up the subject of the rabbi several times in their conversations after class. "We have to be tolerant," Cohen told Richard. "How can any person be certain that he is right and has the truth?" But Richard seemed to look for ways to bring the subject up, and his talk would quickly become emotionally charged. Sam Cohen finally told Jacob Kranz, the young American-born rabbi who leads the Lubavitch congregation and who had befriended Richard, "He's not completely rational on the subject of Adler. You'd better try to avoid the subject. He seems to lose balance whenever he starts talking about Rabbi Adler and every time he seems bitterer."

Actually Sam Cohen felt there was perhaps a kernel of truth in what Richard was saying, but thought Richard's attitude too personal, vindictive, and unbalanced: he should direct his hostility to the attitude not the man. Richard, he said, probably found his point of view shared to a certain extent by others at the Lubavitch synagogue.

Over the years Mr. Cohen, who has a brother in the membership of Congregation Shaarey Zedek, found Rabbi Adler becoming more of a "strong Conservative," while his own preference became Habad; personally the two men had drifted more or less apart. "You see," Cohen explained, "we maintain—the Orthodox Jews maintain—that we can understand the logic of the Reform Jews who say that the Torah is not divine. At least they're being logical; after all if the religion is man-made, then it can be man-unmade. But the Conservatives are neither fish nor fowl. They pick and choose. They say the Bible is divinely inspired, but not the Talmud. And so they make changes and they try to have it both ways.

"And then, of course, Rabbi Adler pushed very hard for that new synagogue, a building which an Orthodox Jew would not even consider a true synagogue. It is not even designed properly inside. I heard Rabbi Adler once presenting his argument for the new building. He reminded the people that their fathers had sacrificed to give them the building they were in as a heritage. And it was still a beautiful synagogue, he said, though now for a number of reasons it was not in a suitable section of the city. He asked the congregation, 'What are you going to leave as a heritage for your children?'

"I couldn't believe I was hearing such a thing from this man. And I used to tell him how I felt. I told him once, 'Rabbi, you're not the same man I met when you first came to this city. You have gone along with all the compromises.' Of course, we would talk, and he would defend what he had done and explain his reasons and describe what he was trying to do, how Judaism had to change if it hoped to speak to American Jews. But over the last few years we saw less and less of each other. I always admired and respected the man even when I disagreed with what he was doing. He was always a warm and wonderful human being, but toward the end, I thought, misled."

Some Orthodox Jews in the city still regarded Congregation Shaarey Zedek and its rabbi as corrupters of true Judaism for having fostered the Conservative movement in Detroit. In the community battle for membership Congregation Shaarey Zedek and Conservative Judaism had shown rapid and substantial growth; with nineteen hundred dues-paying families, Shaarey Zedek represented between 10 and 15 percent of all the synagogue-affiliated Jews in the city.

Yet Rabbi Adler had proceeded with the business of change which he felt was so vital for Jewish survival in America in a slow and careful fashion. "Morris was amazing in this regard," says Mrs. Adler. "While he was the chairman of the law committee that approved riding to the synagogue on Shabbas but nowhere else—the majority opinion held that riding to the synagogue on the Sabbath would be permissible for the Conservative Jew—he never rode, never once rode. And he said, 'As long as there is one member in my congregational family that will not ride, I, their rabbi, cannot ride.' And when the synagogue was built and my house here (within walking distance) wasn't finished yet, for six months he slept at the synagogue. I'd go up for services on Saturday, I'd have a bite of lunch with him on the Sabbath and then rest or read until it got dark, and then we would go home together. And the same when he tried to introduce changes. He felt it was unfair to divide a congregation on a small issue when there are bigger issues that are involved."

In any case, the construction of the congregation's extraordinary new synagogue in the early sixties reconfirmed the feeling of some that Rabbi Adler was leading the city's Jewish community down the road to ruin. There was much talk that the congregation was simply fleeing to the posh suburban confines of the "Gilded Ghetto." An Orthodox rabbi in Detroit was heard to say sadly, "They could take that five million dollars and instead of one grand synagogue they could build a hundred small synagogues all over the city."

Criticism also came from sources other than the Orthodox. Shaarey Zedek has been described in the national media as "a Hilton of synagogues—part school, part house of worship, part pleasure dome." And there were some in the city both old and young who felt the building was a monument to the vanity of its rabbi, Morris Adler. Other Jews who saw themselves as the reserved, aristocratic old guard and who considered pretentious conspicuousness among the most grievous of American Jewish sins talked about ostentation and a lack of taste. Some of the young people who had grown up in the congregation cherished warm and happy memories of the old synagogue and found nothing to love in what they felt was the cold impersonality of the new. There were those who spoke of an overemphasis of the role of the synagogue in the community: Judaism, they argued, was not a matter of going to the synagogue to pray but of living an honorable life. Finally, for the most disaffected young, it was a hypocritical, materialistic extravagance representing everything they felt was wrong with American Judaism.

TWENTY-TWO

In the latter part of the fifties there were some in Congregation Shaarey Zedek who saw no need for a new synagogue. Their present one was, after all, less than thirty years old, and Shaarey Zedek had moved three or four times over the years, each time farther away from the inner core of the city. The Chicago Boulevard area in which the old synagogue was located was once among the most prestigious in the city and was still quite respectable, though there were now black people in some of the large houses on the Boulevard and the surrounding areas had deteriorated rather badly. Another move now into the suburbs might be construed as a shameful flight from the encroaching blacks and would encourage other members to take the same action.

Morris Adler's motives for pressing for a new synagogue are not difficult to identify and explain. The congregation had undertaken studies of its growth and movement and had discovered facts that provided a rather clear picture. In rough terms, it was found that in the early fifties, an overwhelming majority of the congregation had been living south of Six Mile Road in close proximity to the synagogue. Yet by 1958 or 1959, the majority were living north of Six Mile in the northwest Detroit area (where the Wishnetskys had settled) and in many cases were moving outside the city limits at Eight Mile Road into the northern suburbs. Thus with the membership and the Jewish community generally joining in the movement of successful city dwellers, the trend had been clearly established: Jews, particularly members of Congregation Shaarey Zedek, would be living deep in suburbia in the years ahead. If the religious education of their children at the synagogue was important to them, they would be faced with the burden of having to provide transportation three or four times a week over the long unpleasant distance into the inner city. If the synagogue was to play any significant role in the lives of its members, it would have to remain in their midst, and to do so it would have to move with them to the suburbs.

When a large tract of land was acquired in Southfield, the architect decided to utilize much of it by designing a building that spread itself out primarily on one level instead of piling its many necessary components on two or three levels. With the forty acres the rabbi was also able to realize a dream of having the synagogue situated away from the bustle of the roadway. Says Mrs. Adler, "He felt that the congregation should not just walk off the city street into the sanctuary; there should be an approach during which you can attune or prepare yourself."

The combination of the size of the congregation (it had become larger than Rabbi Adler had wanted it to be, says Mrs. Adler) and the many different functions and uses it would serve made it inevitably large and complex. Even if only 10 percent of the members came to Sabbath services on Friday night and Saturday morning, the sanctuary would have to be large enough to accommodate six hundred to eight hundred people (as it now does every week). On the high holy days when most of the membership wishes to be present, thousands would have to be provided for (as they are now when the social halls and smaller chapels are all filled to capacity). Throughout the year the synagogue would have to serve the needs of the afternoon-school children and host the numerous activities of the sisterhood, the men's club, and the junior congregation. Conservative leaders have felt—and Rabbi Adler was no exception—that social and cultural activities contribute to Jewish survival while ultimately increasing religious worship and adult study, the two classical activities of the synagogue.

Prominent members of Congregation Shaarey Zedek are quick to point out that some of those who have been critical belong to congregations that are now in the process of planning or building expensive new synagogues of their own even deeper in suburbia. Says a Detroit attorney and a member of the congregation: "Four and a half million dollars sounds like a lot of money and it is, but building costs have gone up tremendously. Everything is more expensive than it was twenty years ago, and a building that would serve the many needs of this congregation was going to cost money." Agreeing that the "common desire for prestige and status" was part of the motivation for some of the congregants, the attorney added, "Despite all of this Rabbi Adler succeeded in making it a House of God. He served an important role not entirely of his own making, and he was sympathetic. He could joke with the people who had to pay for tickets at Yom Kippur, saying 'Don't throw your tickets away—they're good for the rest of the year.' "

Louis Berry, prominent Detroit real-estate magnate, adds rather tersely, "Yes, the synagogue is impressive, but the Vatican is much more impressive and the old Temple in Jerusalem. . . ."

In an article which he contributed to a 1963 issue of *Jewish Heritage* devoted to an analysis of the American Jewish future, Rabbi Adler discussed his notion of the centrality of the synagogue. Written more in the language of prophetic hope than of hardheaded realism, the rabbi's words indirectly indicate the dream he held of the new Shaarey Zedek becoming a model synagogue for the future, a unifying force embracing and reconciling disparate and sometimes unsympathetic elements in the community. The new Shaarey Zedek was, in the last analysis, the expression of Morris Adler's visionary conception of the American Jewish community's creative survival. Ultramodern in design, yet ancient in its representation of the sacred mount, posed proudly on a crest overlooking the busy freeway, it seemed to signify the modern Jew standing up to be counted as a successful, free, and full-fledged member of American society, saying in effect, "There will be no Auschwitz in America; I have given my gift and taken my place and will continue to worship my God."

Money, power, and influence were what many of his congregants had, and Rabbi Adler had decided that these things were indispensable within the structure of American society if any substantial good were to be accomplished. Said a young Detroit lawyer who had been active in youth affairs at Shaarey Zedek: "Rabbi Adler hoped that by drawing more and more of these people into the fold he would then be able to speak spiritually to a significant segment of the Jewish community. It was a very shrewd, probably very effective way of going about it, but it did involve compromise and appeals to motives which were less than pure or truly religious."

Morris Adler was under no illusions about either the motivation of some of his congregants or the meaning of his success in promoting a large membership. In 1965 he told a reporter, "There's no 'religious revival' among Jews today. The upsurge in synagogue membership means simply that Jews have joined the American middle class, which requires that you identify yourself as a Protestant, a Catholic, or a Jew." And though his approach to the American middle-class Jew had been remarkably successful, he had not been able to draw significant numbers of the most thoughtful and concerned young people of the community into the life of the synagogue. Many had left the synagogue and some of these, with their rebellious, antiinstitutional bent, disliked most what their parents had found most appealing.

According to Barry Kriger, "The thing that upset most of the kids is this impersonal aspect of a highly organized institutional religion. I can see how it comes to dominate the religious thinking of those who are sincerely interested and who simply refuse to endure it. I ask them why they don't go off and form their own minyan as they did in my father's generation, but the last thing they want is to be off on their own."

To the most rebellious of the young people involved in a kind of generational confrontation the congregation appeared as a collection of bourgeois hypocrites who symbolized the corruption of the American middle class, the affluent generation of their parents, and the establishment in whose tainted hands the fate of the nation rested. "The worst kind of activity, the most abominable things go on at Shaarey Zedek," said the young Detroit attorney formerly connected with a youth program at the synagogue. He spoke calmly and continued: "People come to perform rituals and take part in the service for less than valid or truly religious motives, using the synagogue and the social situation to knife each other in the back for reasons of status."

The urge to say such things directly to the face of the congregation itself was apparently strong among some of the young people who were particularly upset by what they felt were the realities at Shaarey Zedek. As a member of the junior congregation, Marcia Frankel Moss, Richard's old flame in high school and at U. of M., had prepared a scathing denunciation of the adult congregation for its hypocrisy and dishonesty. For a presentation she was to make to the adults at Shaarey Zedek she had gone so far as to write out a detailed indictment but finally decided against delivering it. Two other friends of Richard's, who were active at Shaarey Zedek also reported that they had thought seriously about doing the same thing. One of these young men left the congregation in a rebellious mood in the middle of high school and now recalls: "I used to want to rip the babies out of the arms of those mothers with the beehive hairdos and say, 'No, I won't let you poison them.' It was a very frustrating thing." Later, after dropping out of his rabbinical studies at the Jewish Theological Seminary, he paid a visit to the new synagogue for Sabbath services. "I walked out," he said, "feeling like I was in a morgue full of dead bodies. I couldn't stand it in there another minute." He had known a kind of love-hate relationship with Rabbi Adler who had fostered and inspired, he said, his early religious concern. Later he came to see the rabbi as a politician and as "a kind of awesome demagogue whose slightest whim would be law with my family." Yet he never lost the feeling that "under the exegesis, the homiletics, and the politics there was salvation, a capacity to achieve great good, and the power to do it. And this made it all the more intolerable for a young person who could not understand why the power wasn't used."

Yet for a great many others who were also highly critical of the congregation Rabbi Adler remained worthy of their high esteem as a man of integrity, moral insight, and compassion. Richard's friends from Mumford and the honors program in political science at U. of M., Arthur Gold and Jerry Levitt, were typical. Both from families who are members at Shaarey Zedek, they agreed that although some elements of the congregation deserved harsh criticism, it was as a whole not different from any other affluent congregation in the country. Morris Adler, they maintained, was a genuinely wise and good man with a far-ranging intellect, a real concern for young people, and a talent for talking to them. Said Joel Greenberg, the young poet who knew Richard in Ann Arbor:

"Rabbi Adler did much much more good than the sum of any harm that anyone might allege he did. He was not a posturer, not a plaything of the congregation. His was an earned integrity. He was educated in depth, and his wit, intelligence, and the depth with which he comprehended philosophy made him incapable of being a sellout. He wasn't just a big shot. Some rabbis are just big shots, but not Adler. Rabbi and Mrs. Adler have given so much money to poor families in Detroit, they've helped so many people in their lifetime, it would be impossible to calculate the number. He was the last of a breed of rabbis." Added a young woman who also had no affiliation with Shaarey Zedek, "I always thought that Rabbi Adler was the only real rabbi around."

In the opinion of the angriest and most disenchanted of the young people, Morris Adler had two options if he wished to retain his integrity: he must either dissociate himself from his corrupt congregation or use his great power to effect the necessary changes. But just what sort of power Rabbi Adler actually held is a question that calls forth a number of contradictory replies. Said Rabbi Groner:

"He had charisma. He had great powers of personal magnetism and the ability to articulate clearly and movingly the issues of our time with a brilliant wit, a personal dynamism, and a keen insight into most situations and people. . . . His influence reached a large number of people and his leadership guided some of the leading institutions and causes of our time. . . . When you add everything up you see a man with a wide range of tasks, responsibilities, and commitments, but the word 'power' may be inappropriate. He had influence, or could influence people. Sometimes he took an unpopular position and while he couldn't influence others, at least he would preserve the validity and affirm the rightness of a minority position. On civil rights, for example, maybe he couldn't change minds in his congregation but that didn't mean he would sit by silently. He spoke out strongly on the issue."

Rabbi Adler's own vision of his role and its possibilities varied widely according to mood and circumstance. There were times (he confessed to an Orthodox colleague in the rabbinate) when he was frightened of his own gift for language, of his facility with words when speaking to an audience, and he quoted the biblical reference "Life and Death are in the power of the tongue." In the drawer of his desk in his study where he often counseled members of his congregation he kept a small plaque with the words "Remember, Adler, you're not God." Yet there were private occasions of painful doubt in which he was flooded with feelings of impotence. "He had moments of great frustration in the rabbinate," said Goldie Adler. "He'd say, 'You know, the difference between my father and myself in the rabbinate is that they needed my father. They don't need me—they want me. They can lead full lives without me, without religion altogether. My father's generation couldn't live in a city without a rabbi, couldn't live anywhere that wasn't near a synagogue. They don't need me.' And I would say to him, 'Well, you think they don't, and they think they don't, but they do, dear.' " There were those in Morris Adler's congregation who felt "there was nothing humble about the man," and others in the city who called him a "pope." And there was a close friend who along with his eloquent praise of the rabbi also volunteered the suggestion that "he wasn't a paragon of all the virtues by any means. He had his vanities and foibles, he enjoyed living well, and he enjoyed being accepted by people of high status."

Yet most of those who knew him best would probably agree that the kind of power Morris Adler revered most and tried hardest to exhibit in his own life is described in a story he was fond of telling about a man who once came to Descartes and remarked on the youthful serenity of the French philosopher's smooth, unlined face. "A man with a face like yours must possess an extraordinary philosophy," he said. "Please tell me your philosophy so that I too might hold it and perhaps achieve the kind of peace your face exhibits." And Descartes replied, "Live as I live and you'll hold my philosophy."

TWENTY-THREE

The Jewish News for the third week in November 1964 carried a lengthy article which opened:

> When word had flashed Monday afternoon—November 16—that William Hordes had passed away, virtually an entire community went into mourning. Hundreds of his friends and coworkers in many movements flocked to his late residence . . .

to pay respect to him and to honor his widow, Bella, who was at his side for four decades as an associate in many causes.

Mr. Hordes, who was 71, died as he had lived: while expressing his human feelings for his fellow men. He had gone to pay a sick call on Eartha Smith, a laundress who had worked for his family for more than 20 years, and as they exchanged pleasantries, at her home on Richton at Dexter, he died suddenly on the porch of her home.

Later in the article Richard is mentioned as his grandfather's frequent companion at Talmud classes and other community gatherings; ". . . there was a strong tie between the two in their joint religious—Zionist—social motivated ideals." Services were held two days after Mr. Hordes's death, and Rabbi Adler canceled a meeting at Grossingers with officials of the Jewish Theological Seminary in order to deliver the eulogy.

That evening Richard and David Roth listened to Brother Antoninus read at the University of Detroit. Richard, apparently inspired by the experience, told David, "I began the day with death and have finished it with a rebirth." It was, says David, the kind of "superdramatic" thing Richard was fond of saying. In fact, Richard appeared to be very much in command of himself following his grandfather's death. Dr. Sander Breiner, a psychiatrist and family friend who had known Richard since the Wishnetskys moved to Detroit, advised the parents to try to get Richard to cry, since the emotional release would be good for him. But Richard was instead assuming the responsibility of comforting others, particularly his grandmother, of being the strong shoulder to lean and weep on. Yet at the same time, he told Sherri Jacobson that he simply could not fathom why his grandfather was dead. Sherri felt that behind his façade of strength, he had been actually quite devastated.

Still he continued to present the front, and at his grandfather's shivah (the traditional Jewish seven-day period of mourning during which friends visit the home of the deceased and comfort the family) he was able to make an attractive and admirable impression. "He was a brilliant, warm, charming, and enthusiastic young man," said his sister Ellen's former eighth-grade teacher at MacDowell. He talked with excitement about his work and insisted she read some of the "Spanish Catholic theologians, Thomists and neo-Thomists," which he listed for her.

He was carrying with him a collection of about eighty note

cards with an original aphorism written on each, and at one point he took Rabbi Groner aside and read him a sampling. It was a highly serious moment for Richard, who seemed very sensitive to the rabbi's reactions. The aphorisms themselves, attempting to capture in a few lines profound, illuminating insights into aspects of the human condition, were for the most part quite Nietzschean in tone. The rabbi, paying close attention, thought most were couched in high-flown, elaborate, and pretentious language with little significant content. There were a few, however, that reflected, he felt, a maturity of thought and concern, whose phrasing and message lingered in the mind.

Sherri Jacobson felt that some people were placing an unfair burden on Richard at this time when they would come up to him and say, "Well, now that your grandfather is dead, you must take over his role." Richard did attempt to do so, and for a short while continued to go to the Talmud class and various other community meetings, asserting himself and speaking in the fashion of his grandfather. His efforts, however, were received rather coldly. Richard, frustrated and unhappy, soon stopped coming.

About the time Richard was sitting shivah for his grandfather, death and emotional disturbance came to the home of Larry Walters; again Richard became the wise comforter. Larry's grandmother and an uncle had died in quick succession, and his mother had been placed in a rest home. Having just finished with one shivah, Richard came to another. Recalls Larry: "He would come and have breakfast and pray and sit with the rabbis and talk. And he was delightful. Everybody loved him at that point. He was a tremendous source of comfort to me and helped me to understand and cope with what was happening in my family. He assured me that things would be okay, that it would simply take time. It was a little thing but it really showed Richard's true colors. He was a rabbinical opportunist. He took the time with just about everybody to give them some food for thought, some gems of wisdom."

"My grandfather died with his shoes on," Richard told Barry Kriger. He appeared stoical about the loss, but like many others, Barry now feels that the death of William Hordes was a turning point for Richard. In losing his grandfather Richard had been suddenly deprived not only of the human companionship of a favorite person but also of the identity support which Mr. Hordes may have provided in some measure. Additionally Richard was forced perhaps for the first time to cope directly with the physical reality of death, the unfathomable void which had beckoned him at times, and which now had swallowed one with whom he had been intimately connected.

That the loss of a "meaningful other" can have a deleterious effect on the state of a person's emotional life has been frequently documented in clinical literature. In one who is highly ambivalent in his relationships with others and who holds much unconscious hostility, the normal progress of mourning may be blocked because his negative feelings cannot be acknowledged. Powerful aggressive emotions may eventually be turned against the self.

In this case, Richard may have held unconscious, unacknowledgeable negative feelings occasioned by qualities in William Hordes—his dominating ego, for example—that Richard loathed in others. Beyond this, he was (as usual) locked into a repressed, inadequate, and ultimately debilitating emotional response by his idealized conception of what his response *should be*. He had played the role of the wise stoic, but the result, soon to appear, was a drastic shift from stoic to manic-depressive, from sage to frenzied searcher, from kind comforter to alienating cad. These "new" roles had occasionally appeared before his grandfather's death, but now they were increasingly in evidence.

Through most of the fall Richard had seemed to Sherri quite able to carry on a normal conversation, able to listen and relate to others. Now, though still kind and courteous to her, he would often get into violent arguments with others, often announcing that they were stupid and didn't understand (as he did) the horrendous state of the world. They would go to a friend's house and almost immediately Richard would provoke an argument, shattering the harmony of the lighthearted company. Afterward Sherri would say, "Richard, don't you realize what you did there? How you alienated people?" Filled with remorse, Richard would exhibit pained surprise and say, "Oh, yes, I see you're right. I'll never do it again." And the same thing would happen the next time they were out. Once he insisted on reading a diatribe he had written against the Jewish Community Center for wasting its money on the wrong causes; the occasion was a small gathering of adults at the Jacobsons' including a woman who was very active at the Center.

Richard had been asked to take part in a youth-group panel discussion of present-day Israel at Shaarey Zedek. One evening in late

November or early December he arrived at the Jacobsons' in plenty of time to pick up Sherri and bring her to the synagogue on schedule. Instead, however, he decided to arrive a fashionable half hour late; making a grand entrance with the announcement that he was better late than never, he explained that Sherri, a typical woman, had caused his delay. Generally he spoke favorably of Israel but said he had found indications that the Israelis were acquiring some of the worst capitalistic traits. Some of the adults present tried to balance his indictment, but he dominated the rest of the meeting and no one else had a chance to say much.

Also at Sabbath services at Shaarey Zedek, Richard was becoming increasingly more critical and unpleasant. Barry Kriger met him one Saturday after services in the lobby where he was talking to an irritated acquaintance of about thirty. Richard was giving him one of his lectures—speaking very loudly so that others nearby could hear, describing Barry as the only person in the whole congregation with sincere and genuine religious feeling.

Such behavior was quickly disenchanting Sherri Jacobson, but Richard was talking seriously about their relationship. "You know," he told Larry Walters, "I might marry Sherri one day. In fact we might marry soon." But when he spoke about marriage with Sherri, she felt "he was being irrational." Their relationship had been a very proper and conventional one, neither sexual nor platonic. It had been pleasant and friendly on Sherri's side, and warmly idealistic on Richard's. A pleasant, happy girl with largely conventional tastes, attitudes, and perspectives, Sherri was Richard's link to the world from which he felt most estranged, the society of his parents and the Jewish community in general. Sherri's acceptance meant a kind of truce with one of his most hated abstractions, the middle class. At the same time, nearly everything he was doing was making that acceptance more impossible. When he began to get especially possessive and demanding, Sherri decided to break off their relationship.

She simply could not take his "philosophical attitude," she said, his constantly negative and apocalyptic ideas. She had been fond of Richard but did not love him, and so after they exchanged Hanukkah presents in the middle of December (he gave her Saint-Exupéry's *The Little Prince*, and she gave him Dag Hammarskjöld's *Markings*) the relationship was terminated. Richard pleaded against the break and took it very hard. He continued to call Sherri and tried to see her, once calling her three times in one night and begging her to go out with him again. Larry Walters tried to soothe Richard's feelings with the opinion that it was perhaps for the best because Sherri couldn't respond to all levels of his personality. Richard seemed to agree but remained hurt: he felt that he had finally established a genuine relationship with a woman.

He tried to look elsewhere for consolation, but without much success. Over Christmas vacation he enjoyed a Shakespeare production at Wayne State's Hilberry Theater with Molly Rosen, home from Ann Arbor. Afterward when Richard became aggressive, Molly said she had decided it would be best if they simply considered themselves good platonic friends. Richard turned to boasting and mild abuse. He had found, he said, that he could have any girl he really wanted at the University of Detroit or in Ann Arbor and mentioned that he was getting what he wanted quite regularly from a current favorite. "You'd be very nice if you lost ten pounds," he told Molly, and explained that she was inhibited, cold, and immature—someday she might grow up and be a woman. They parted that night on poor terms.

Yet Richard called Molly the next morning as if nothing had happened and said he greatly respected her views on sex. He recommended a book or two and read a short essay printed in the Shaarey Zedek *Recorder* by Rabbi Adler whom he praised highly. He carried a clipping of the essay for a while and showed it to Molly the next time they met. Later he typed out a passage from it and gave a copy to Larry Walters who like Richard carried it in his wallet. Prefaced by the line "And the Lord drew out Moses from the waters," the excerpt goes as follows:

> It has often been pointed out that modern life tends to fragmentize people's lives by imposing upon them multiple relationships and innumerable preoccupations. It were as if one roamed from room to room, but the rooms were so far removed one from the other and so unrelated that one never had the feeling of living in a house. One holds many spokes in one's hand, but they are disjointed and separate and do not form a wheel. There is absent a pattern, a center from which our manifold activities radiate and to which they relate. Perhaps the most severe struggle (definitely the most severe struggle) modern man has to wage is within the confines of his own personal life, since there is always the danger that he will have a cir-

cumference but no center; an abundance but no coherence; movement but no direction; multiplicity but no purpose by which it can be unified. We become like the individual parts of a machine that lie about in a meaningless disarray and are not put together to form a functioning mechanism.

Richard had complained to Sherri that he was not performing up to the capacity he had achieved in his last year in Ann Arbor. But the first real test of his work for Charlotte Zimmerman didn't come until late in the term when he was required to give an oral report on one of the assigned texts. Richard's report referred to the political constitution of Israel during biblical times and was judged by his professor as very good, thorough, and ably presented. "It was," she said, "a good summary of Voegelin on the topic, but that's about all—it contained nothing that was Richard's at all, no new insights. I guess he sensed that I didn't think it was the greatest, that I thought there were others in the group who had managed to come up with some of their own insights and had done better jobs. After all, they had been with me longer. He probably felt this, too, but he wanted me to tell him that his was absolutely the best, and I couldn't. This must have been a real blow to his ego."

In retrospect Dr. Zimmerman feels that her understanding of Richard began here with the first hint that he suffered from what she terms a "real success psychosis." Ultimately she came to feel that Richard had developed a terrible inner sense of worthlessness which he could never quite admit or confront since he felt to do so would destroy him. With even the smallest failure representing a grave threat, he must "rationalize about his worthlessness" in the effort to cope with it. After continuing success throughout his academic career, he suddenly found himself in a situation where he was no longer the best, no longer clearly superior to the others in the group at the University of Detroit.

Thus, in the space of a month and a half Richard had experienced the loss of or a rejection by the three most important people in his life at the time: his grandfather, who had served to ground or bolster his identity; Sherri Jacobson, who was to fill his need for social and emotional connection; and Charlotte Zimmerman, on whom he had, in a sense, staked his intellectual life. In addition another man of great though ambivalent importance for Richard had recently left the city: in December Rabbi Adler departed for Israel, where he would spend the next eight months.

Richard spent part of the penultimate day of 1964 writing out a list of quotations and his own aphorisms on two sheets of loose-leaf paper which he gave to a girl friend of his sister Terry's in Ann Arbor.

> As this is the simple truth—that to live is to feel oneself lost—he who accepts it has already begun to find himself, to be on firm ground.
>
> José Ortega y Gasset
> (*The Revolt of the Masses*)

> The truth of order has to be gained and regained in the perpetual struggle against the fall from it; and the movement toward truth starts from man's awareness of his existence in untruth.
>
> Eric Voegelin
> (*Order and History*, Vol. I:
> *Israel and Revelation*)

> To ascend to life "requires an initiatory effort of a heroic nature."
>
> Mircea Eliade
> (*The Sacred and the Profane*)

> Strait is the gate, and narrow is the path, and few there be that find the way.
>
> New Testament

> We go farthest when we know not whither we are going.
>
> Oliver Cromwell

> Return, O Israel, unto the Lord, thy God.
>
> Deuteronomy

> All men are brothers in suffering; and all men are creatures of God.
> Life is hell for those who cannot love.
>
> Fëdor Dostoevski

> Man is the only creature who refuses to be what he is.
>
> Albert Camus
> (*The Rebel*)

> Forsake ye not my law.
>
> Psalms, or Deuteronomy

> We live in a universe of wondrous and infinite diversity, and the more it is investigated, the more fascinating it becomes.

And man has a universe within him, of which the same can be said."

R.S.W. 10-20-64

Reason without passion is sterile, and passion without reason is meaningless.

The death of spirit is the price of progress.

Eric Voegelin
(*The New Science of Politics*)

God is dead, and we have murdered Him.

Nietzsche

Modern man's most significant problem is not maladjustment to a corrupt society but meaninglessness in a chaotic universe.

R.S.W. 12-10-64

TWENTY-FOUR

As Richard greeted the new year in January 1965, he was embarking on what would prove to be the most frenetic eight or nine months of his life. His roommates and University of Detroit friends who saw him every day noted that his periods of elation and depression, which seemed to emerge during the fall, were becoming increasingly longer and more pronounced. The pattern had started with episodes lasting from one to four days and had shifted now so that a depression might run longer than two weeks. The exuberant manic periods seemed longer, perhaps, said Pat Burke, because Richard was then much harder to take, much more "obnoxious." No longer were there periods of "normalcy"; he was either flying off into exuberance or plunging into the depths of a depression.

In his manic phase Richard would be hypertensive and constantly on the run, often arrogant and erratic but usually lucid and coherent, making contact with a great number and variety of people. He would frequently miss class. When he did appear he might be loud and disruptive, halting the proceedings to make his pronouncements. Depending, however, on the circumstances and the people involved, he could still be charming in his expansive moods, making the acquaintance of everybody in a restaurant, going to the kitchen to say hello to the cook, bantering with the owner or a waitress, walking up to people he didn't know and starting a conversation on the slightest pretext and asking for their opinions about God, religion, and the state of the world.

In an effort to set up future doctoral work he was traveling to campuses in Chicago, New York, and New England and calling on professors of wide repute.

He might visit the homes of friends or acquaintances at eleven thirty or twelve at night with a passionate need to talk, to get something off his chest (or perhaps simply to be with someone). He was using the phone at any hour of the day or night. Said Larry Walters: "Every day he'd have a list, a piece of that long yellow legal paper with hundreds of names of people. He'd say, 'I've got to call this one for this and that one for that . . .' They would be friends or this professor or that statesman, and he'd constantly be in the developing stages of something that would just peter out. There was no stopping him." He was constantly scribbling on scraps of paper which often littered the car he used on weekends: notes to himself about things to do, books to read, information to look up, people to contact. He was frequently writing letters, sometimes six or more in a day, to people all over the country.

Richard's frantic behavior shocked some and charmed others. For a few it only confirmed what they had previously thought or felt about Richard. In the midst of a depression Richard might ask his roomates or friends why he couldn't seem to get along with people. At least during a period of depression Richard would be quiet and friendly, even meek and humble, and would generally seem much more pleasant and easier to get along with. You could talk to him, said Pat Burke, and he would ask for advice, often being self-critical to the point of excess. Yet if he learned anything from the answers he got, it never seemed to show after the depression had lifted.

Few people ever saw Richard in such moods because when he felt this way he would usually keep to himself. He would spend much more time around the apartment and would not go home as frequently on the weekends. Trudging off to the library, he would try to force himself through his work, but he reported that he was finding it very difficult to read or write when depressed. That he was no longer able to lose himself in his work seemed to trouble him more than anything else. As the rigid schedule to which he had always adhered began to break down, Richard might read all night and sleep all day or skip several classes and fly off to Chicago or New York; he seemed to be questioning his whole previous life style.

More than ever Richard wanted a close rapport with Charlotte Zimmerman, but the professor points out: "After all I had six other people whose programs I was directing. I just couldn't give Richard the kind of total attention I suppose he wanted. I loved Richard as a student; I love all my students and get very concerned about them. When I heard how much he was trying to study—twelve or eighteen hours a day—and when he complained of not being able to concentrate, I told him, 'Relax, take time off, jump up and down, go bowling, to the movies, have dates, have a beer once in a while.' But I don't know what he did. The trouble was it wasn't coming fast enough for him. He wanted to be a scholar overnight."

To certain friends and professors, including Dr. Zimmerman, Richard complained of increasing trouble at home. The Wishnetskys had never approved of Richard's move to the University of Detroit and were more convinced than ever that his experience there was doing him no good.

With his visits home on the weekends reduced and Rabbi Adler in Israel, Richard only infrequently came now to Shaarey Zedek for Sabbath services. On one of his rare appearances he got into an after-service talk with Rabbi Groner which lasted until all the other congregants had left. Finally the rabbi said, "Well, Richard, why don't you come home with me for lunch?" expecting the perfunctory "No, thank you." Instead Richard accepted and consumed much of the rabbi's Sabbath afternoon with his nonstop talk. "I don't remember what he talked about," said Rabbi Groner. "His usual—Nietzsche, the Marquis de Sade, Camus. I didn't listen that closely after a while because it was always the same and never quite coherent. I didn't really take him seriously. Maybe I should have. I wish now I had listened more closely to what he said."

Nevertheless, on other occasions Rabbi Groner did take Richard more seriously and Richard once told the rabbi that there were times when he could speak to him more easily than he could to Rabbi Adler. Richard gave him lists of books, telling him that he could not really hope to do his job properly without knowledge of these volumes. "I often got the feeling," said Rabbi Groner, "that the roles were being reversed; that Richard was making himself the teacher and me the student." The rabbi finally concluded that Richard was attracted to any book or philosophy which allowed him to look upon most men as a great mass of inferiors and himself as a member of some sort of elite.

Some time after Saul Bellow's *Herzog* appeared in September 1964 Richard read the novel and, according to Larry Walters, got very involved in it. Larry maintained that when Richard found a person or character whom he cared for, he would strongly identify with him, seemingly oblivious to aspects of personality or behavior that did not match his own qualities or taste. Said Larry: "He would end up acting like that character; he would mimic some of the things that character might do. So if he thought that Herzog was the character he wanted to be, he could go around fooling people. He'd fool me, he'd fool anybody, by coming on in this role. I think he used to play a lot of these roles just for a reaction. And the most attractive one for him was this role of the giant intellectual."

Moses Herzog is a Jewish professor of intellectual history whose chaotic personal life has ground to a halt his promising academic career. On the brink of emotional breakdown, hopping frantically between New York, Chicago, and New England in an effort to pull himself together, writing frantic letters to everyone including "the famous dead," he is "overcome by the need to explain, to have it out, to justify, to put in perspective, to clarify, to make amends." Alienated and aware of the devastating impact of the sociopolitical and philosophical dilemmas of the postmodern age and forcing himself to confront large "piercing" questions, he has been widely acclaimed by critics as a man of our times. Yet Herzog is still enough in touch with himself to recognize and finally reject his neurotic impulse toward death. He finally refuses to glorify or romanticize pain, suffering, or hopelessness: "We love apocalypses too much, and crises ethics and florid extremism with its thrilling language. Excuse me, no. I've had all the monstrosity I want."

Herzog, like many of the books Richard read, might have provided an experience of some insight. Yet, as it seems with so many of the books and movies he got excited about, it pleased Richard to identify with the hero in a way that meant escape from the sad reality of his own personal needs, conflicts, and frustrations—to avoid a genuine confrontation with himself by plunging into wrenching literary encounters with the grand and tragic dilemmas of society, civilization, and the cosmos. Perhaps he felt that one might assume a kind of immortality by stepping into a book or a film, by assuming the roles of passionately admired literary or philosophical figures or authors, ultimately by authoring one's own life as if it were a book, taking the descriptions and analyses of the great and their problems and conflicts as cue and prescription for one's own "story."

Richard later mentioned to several friends that he had suffered through a "severe" depression lasting a week or two at the end of the first term in January. He had managed to finish his seminar term paper which, like his oral report, was judged valid and competent, but again he was disappointed in himself, his work, and the response to it. A letter he wrote to Fred Baskin on January 25 was filled with short simple sentences and a bleak, self-deprecating tone and gives some indication of what Richard was like in a depression.

He opened with the announcement that he had little to say. His studies had slowed to a "frustrating halt." The term paper he had written and was too "lazy" to revise was so bad it needed "burning." The five girls he had been dating were down to two, though he had a friend who supposedly could put fifty at his beck and call. Last week he had spent an exciting day at Wayne State arguing with "some fine professors"—Mark in political science and Drury in Monteith College. Recently he had talked with Fred's mother (who loved every word Fred wrote to her). He himself missed Fred's "company and cynicism" and hopefully would be in a better, more communicative mood when they next met. Next week he would be going to New York to check on doctoral work at the New School for Social Research. The next letter would be lengthier, he promised and wished Fred good luck on his prelims.

The day Richard mentions spending at Wayne State was one of several he spent on the campus. Max Mark, a political scientist with a traditionalist approach, had been recommended to Richard by Frank Grace and Richard had first called on the professor near the end of his senior year. The January meeting was their third. Professor Mark, an open and cordial man of European background, thought Richard an interesting, intelligent, but often puzzling young man who would speak of a large concern for Orthodox

Judaism while his philosophical and theological lights seemed to be Catholic, who would render high praise to the Lubavitch movement but evade the question of whether he might join, who was doctrinaire about the role of religion in an atheistic world but who didn't seem committed to any particular event of revelation.

Professor Mark often questioned Richard closely on these matters, but though Richard was always coherent and dogmatic he never really provided answers. "You are thinking on a very abstract level," Mark told Richard once, "and this is fine, but what about very real and terrible problems like poverty? What about the economic realities which affect directly and immediately the lives of people?" Professor Mark thought he should be brought down to earth and so suggested that Richard write a paper for him on the topic "Why I am not a Marxist." Richard agreed it was a good idea, but never wrote it.

On another visit Professor Mark asked, "What makes your attitude toward religion a commitment? What constitutes your commitment?" But Richard talked around the issue and continued his argument that the religion of most American Jews, including most of the American rabbinate, was a meaningless and hypocritical farce. But, said the professor, this is not a religious age. Perhaps it is deficient in an ethical sense, but it seems doubtful that it will maintain itself via religion. It must, said Richard; there is no other way.

On one of his subsequent visits to Wayne, Richard chanced upon his old friend Bob Moss who was now working on a doctorate in history. "As usual, Richard didn't greet me," said Bob. "He simply accosted me. Richard never said hello, he simply launched into a discussion immediately." In this case Richard announced to begin with that he was studying with the world's greatest scholar —or at least the second most important mind of our time perhaps after Eric Voegelin. Bob, greatly irked by Richard's bravado, fired back with "Isn't that just like you, Richard? Why must you always maintain that you're the only one who's doing anything important? That you have a corner on the most important minds of our time?" A violent and intense exchange ensued ranging from fourteenth-century philosophers (whom Bob was studying) to Max Weber who, according to Richard, had attempted suicide a number of times because he couldn't believe in God.

They parted with tempers still frayed, but soon afterward Bob received a two-page letter from Richard who said he was very upset by their meeting. Says Bob, "The tone of the letter was terribly apologetic, almost abject. I was the one friend he had admired the most over the years, and we had much to learn from each other, much we could contribute to each other's development. We shouldn't allow petty feelings to interfere. He recommended some books and wanted to set a regular time every week so that we could meet and talk and cultivate an intellectual friendship. At the time I thought, 'Oh, what's the use?' and didn't answer the letter. I saw him once or twice on campus after that but we spoke only briefly."

On his trip east at the end of January, Richard stayed with his grandparents in New York and was constantly on the phone trying to set up appointments with some of the prominent scholars on the staff of the New School for Social Research. He also made a side trip to New Haven where he spent a day or two with Jerry Levitt on the Yale campus. Richard, enthused about the New School and his plans for future work, seemed more intense and excitable to Jerry, and again was approaching various scholars including Eugene Rostow (then dean of the law school and later a member of the Johnson administration) whom he described as a relation on his mother's side.

Back in New York for the weekend, Richard and his grandfather paid a call on Aaron Glanz-Leyeless, a Yiddish poet, essayist, and journalist with the *Day-Jewish Journal* in New York. Richard made quite an impression on the old author, who was still writing a weekly column while in semiretirement. The next week Mr. Glanz-Leyeless wrote about "A Pleasant Encounter," and Richard subsequently carried a translation of the article around with him for several months, showing it frequently to friends and acquaintances:

> Last week I had occasion to chat with a Jewish young man, a student of a university in Detroit. I was a bit shaken by the conversation. You may ask why. Because I encountered a different kind of American-born young Jew, than the kind one generally meets or, more accurately: different than our general conception of American Jewish youth.
>
> The twenty-two-year-old young man came to me, by his own volition, to chat . . . to discuss with me rather "meaty" subjects . . . the question of serving society; of integration both with

America and with the Jewish tradition; he wanted to deal with the substance of the questions rather than skim their surface.

He told me that he wanted to be a teacher. Not just as a choice of profession, but a teacher who will be a true guide for the younger generation, who will conduct himself properly, who will satisfy the thirst, deepen the understandings of youth rather than merely fill the younger generation with information which can be used only for practical, mundane, and materialistic interests. . . .

Material positions are of no concern to him. He does not care how long he will have to study just so long as he eventually reaches his goal. He is interested mainly in finding a college where he will best be able to devote himself to the goal of becoming a true teacher, one who will point the way to a generation of youth who lack direction. I observed the thoroughly intelligent young Jew and was almost moved to recite a blessing on the occasion. . . .

I asked my young guest a direct question . . . "What is your attitude to the Yiddish, to Jewish history, to the State of Israel?" His answer was: "I understand Yiddish and can even read it to some extent. I visited the State of Israel and was in a Kibbutz several weeks and did acquire some slight skill in conversational Hebrew. I do fully understand the value to me of my people's history and my people's culture. It is my intent to familiarize myself with that culture in the original, with Yiddish. I never changed my name and have no intention of doing so."

In summation, it was my thought during and after the chat with that young man that here may develop a representative of an entire new intellectual generation who will be simultaneously both American and Jewish.

From New York, Richard headed on to Boston where he stayed with his old University of Michigan friends, Arthur Gold and Ned Weiner, for four days in Cambridge. Once again he was chasing down some of the brightest intellectual lights in the area, traveling to Brandeis to chat with a prominent Jewish theologian and making the rounds of vaious departments at Harvard.

Both Gold and Weiner felt that Richard had definitely changed. There was a kind of frenzy about him; he was hyperactive and "hyperorganized, with a list of everything he was going to do except go to the bathroom." Weiner thought there was something definitely wrong with him; Gold, who had known him through high school, felt that it was just another facet of his personality coming to the surface and being somehow exaggerated.

Their friends found him difficult to get along with and at times embarrassing to be with in public. He was often going up to people on the street and engaging them in conversation, and he might walk down the middle of a street screaming and shouting obscenities and waving his arms, or—as he did one night after a movie—might climb on a flagpole in front of an insurance building and shout, "Here I am. Richard Wishnetsky, son of a Russian Jew, and Woodrow Wilson fellow. Thank you, America!"

The day before he left Boston for Detroit, Richard introduced himself to Thomas Cohen whom he recognized as a former University of Michigan student. They were soon discussing a mutual friend active in S.D.S. These people had it all wrong, said Richard with fervor. The only way to change America was to seize power, not by converting people or by being an example or a martyr, but by infiltrating the establishment. "I had not known Richard Wishnetsky before," says Cohen. "I found his sense of misplaced urgency disquieting." Nonetheless, he brought Richard back to his room in Perkins Hall, made him some soup, and introduced him to friends, with whom, as usual, Richard was soon into passionate discussion.

That same day Richard placed a call to Sharon Thompson in Ann Arbor and asked her to pick him up at Metropolitan Airport between Ann Arbor and Detroit on the following day, a Friday. Sharon had heard little from Richard and was surprised at the request. "He didn't even know if I had a car," she said. The next day at the airport he handed her some live clams which he brought to her as a gift from Boston. He had been in a serious depression before leaving Detroit, he told her, but he was past the trouble now and in good spirits. He had managed to see a lot of important people and was buoyed by the feeling that he had made a favorable impression. Even if it meant sleeping on the kitchen floor in her apartment (which it did), he wanted to stay with Sharon while he spent a few days in Ann Arbor. She was the most human person he knew, he said, and he wanted to talk to her.

And talk he did, almost without stopping and often interrupting her to continue his speech. He spoke of Nietzsche, Hegel, and Voegelin (what Hegel had been to the nineteenth century, Voegelin was to the twentieth), of how deeply he had felt the loss of his grandfather, of his family and the bitter fights he had been having with his parents, of a fellow he knew who was taking drugs (he strongly disapproved), of his future doctoral thesis plans, about which he was very excited. For the first time in Sharon's experience, he was often resorting to "vulgarity and foul language" beyond his usual "hell" or "goddamn." He made a pass at Sharon's roommate and described it with amusement later, saying she had just huddled in a corner apparently very frightened. It all seemed to Sharon quite out of character.

TWENTY-FIVE

Whereas Richard seemed to plunge into a depression through an experience of rejection, isolation, or failure, his roommates and friends noted that he would usually begin to pull out of his misery when inspired by either a book which seemed to provide valuable new answers or a stimulating conversation.

An example of the former was a sixty-cent paperback suggested by Charlotte Zimmerman called *Man's Search for Meaning*, by the Viennese psychiatrist Viktor E. Frankl. "I recommended Frankl's book to Richard very highly," says Dr. Zimmerman. "It was a good book for him because it deals with the problem of the will in relation to mental illness, and it points out that you don't have to submit to this notion that there are these great irresistible forces which you can't deal with. I've had students who have talked about suicide; they come to me and say they don't want to but they're afraid they will. And I tell them about Frankl's book and tell them not to worry, that they can't be forced against their will. If they just make up their minds to endure it, they can. But Richard never understood how suffering can have value."

Whatever Richard understood, he got extremely excited about *Man's Search for Meaning* and stayed up all night to read it through. He had achieved a new level of being with the experience of this book, he told Pat Burke in the morning. At the campus bookstore he bought a half-dozen copies and passed them out to his friends, including John Samuels and David Roth, saying this was a book that might change one's life.

The book is a kind of survival tract for inmates of a concentration camp or for those similarly trapped in suffering. It is intended to inspire people to keep their sanity and their humanity—not an inglorious project in these times. According to the author, neurotic states often arise from existential frustration, a conflict of values, or the lack of a sense of meaning, purpose, and freedom in one's life. Frankl explains that man in modern society, cut off from his animal instincts and turning away from the traditions which have previously supplied his life with direction, is increasingly subject to the suffering of a frustrated will-to-meaning. Many who in the past might have gone to their minister or rabbi are now coming to the psychiatrist, not with emotional conflict, but with philosophical questions like "What is the meaning of life?"

Frankl's theories were shaped by the experience of his three years in Auschwitz and other Nazi camps described in a compelling narrative in the first part of the book. The central insight drawn from the horror of his experience Frankl expresses in the words of Nietzsche: "He who has a *why* to live can bear with almost any *how.*" The key is one's notion of the meaning of life and here Frankl had something to say to Richard: "One should not search for an abstract meaning of life. Everyone has his own specific vocation or mission in life; everyone must carry out a concrete assignment that demands fulfillment." For Frankl unmitigated and unavoidable suffering faced with dignity and courage becomes the highest achievement available to man: "Whenever one is confronted with an inescapable, unavoidable situation, whenever one has to face a fate that cannot be changed, e.g., an incurable disease, such as an inoperable cancer, just then is one given a last chance to actualize the highest value, to fulfill the deepest meaning, the meaning of suffering. For what matters above all is the attitude we take toward suffering, the attitude in which we take our suffering upon ourselves."

Exactly what Richard took from *Man's Search for Meaning* can only be guessed at. Depressed, he might have found renewed hope that he could cope with his problems. Masochistic, he might have considered the description of ultimately meaningful suffering most attractive. Troubled about religion, he might have been reassured by Frankl's assertion that even a man with a "dreadful father image" has the freedom to establish a positive and genuine relationship with God. Certain that his troubles stemmed in large measure from his sensitive perception of the horrendous state of the world and its loss of values, he might have found reinforcement in Frankl's notion of widespread existential frustration. Having staked his idealized identity on the conviction that life has an abstract meaning which he would pass on to others, he might have found it difficult to hear Frankl's warning that trying to discover such a sweeping definition would prove naïve and fruitless.

Richard met Janis Newman (pseud.) through the friend who had introduced him to Sherri Jacobson. Janis, a grad student at Wayne with an excellent figure, pert face, and large black eyes, was supposed to make him forget Sherri. On their first date he took her to Shaarey Zedek to walk on the grounds and view the building. Again he seemed to take some emotional satisfaction from simply being near the place. Afterward they went for coffee and Richard was full of praise for the book Sherri had recently given him, Dag Hammarskjöld's *Markings*. Hammarskjöld, he said, had chosen in a very noble way to live his life alone; this was probably imperative if a man was to achieve greatness. A religious mystic, a man of both contemplation and action, masochistic, narcissistic, and finally a "martyr" for world peace, Hammarskjöld was fond of quoting passages from the New Testament such as this from John: "It is expedient for us, that one man should die for the people, and that the whole nation perish not." He also enjoyed shaping his own aphorisms: "Acts of violence—Whether on a large or small scale, the bitter paradox: the meaningfulness of death—and the meaninglessness of killing." Richard lent *Markings* to Janis asking her not to look at what was written on the first page. Unable to resist, Janis found a few kind lines penned by Sherri Jacobson.

On a subsequent Sabbath Richard took Janis Newman to services at Shaarey Zedek where a guest rabbi spoke on assimilation, underplaying its threat to American Jews. Upset by the sermon, Richard felt that the man had no conception of the dangers of assimilation. There really was a crisis, he told Janis, who confessed she had little or no interest in religion. Richard bought her a postcard picturing the bimah at Shaarey Zedek and asked her to keep it as a souvenir.

Richard would call Janis only when in a good mood because he was "just no good to anyone," he said, when in a poor one. On an average of once every two weeks, they went on coffee dates where

Richard would do most of the talking about his favorite subjects: religion and the dehumanized state of the modern world. Janis was fascinated and thought she had never met anyone so intense, so constantly, passionately concerned with what he was doing. They also attended a couple of affairs at U. of D.: the production of a Spanish dance troupe (Richard went backstage at intermission to offer compliments) and a Carlos Montoya concert during which he seemed to enjoy himself immensely, clapping loudly and shouting "Olé!" Afterward, he told Janis he thought the whole thing was something of a bore.

Always holding her hand very firmly, Richard enjoyed taking walks with Janis. He was "ecstatic" as they strolled one afternoon in February after his highly successful (he thought) trip to the East Coast. It was cold with snow on the ground, but everything seemed to have an amazing beauty for Richard. His reactions were similar to those Janis had read about of people under LSD; with excitement he pointed out myriad details—the shape of an icicle, the design of a naked tree against the sky—all of which he found fantastically beautiful. They returned to the car to get warm, and were soon in the back seat doing their first necking. In some contrast, however, to his passionate attitude on the walk, Janis now found Richard cold, unaffectionate, selfish, and ineffectual. Despondent afterward, Richard told Janis that though she was womanly enough to excite a man very quickly, she had a lot to learn in other areas of life before she'd be a real woman. Janis decided that Richard in his egocentricity was capable of giving her nothing but a few interesting ideas and so resolved that their relationship would be entirely platonic. Some time later when she declined another advance, he got bitterly angry and stalked out of her parents' home saying, "All the girls I know are either engaged or frigid."

On another occasion at Janis's home Richard complained of a splitting headache and sought out a bedroom in which to lie down. In fifteen minutes he was up again, and Janis asked if this had happened before. Yes, said Richard, the headaches would occasionally come and there was nothing to do but lie down and hope the pain would pass. Once in an almost amused tone (as if he were speaking of someone else) Richard told Janis that a year before in Ann Arbor he had suffered an episode of radical regression in which he had curled up in a fetal position on a couch in a friend's apartment for two days. Helpless as an infant, he had to be fed and cared for by his friend. Later he gave Molly Rosen a similar description, but said the episode had occurred during his recent January depression, which seems more probably the case.

One evening when she was in a depression of her own, Janis told Richard that she'd been thinking about the possibility of going insane and felt she could actually dispense with her sanity by choice. She asked if Richard thought she should. No, said Richard with little apparent interest. Janis asked if he had ever had similar ideas, had ever approached a similar decision. Yes, he had, said Richard, and his choice had been to keep his sanity.

Late in February Richard took Molly Rosen to the University of Michigan's Winter Carnival in Ann Arbor and embarrassed her with loud and haughty behavior until late in the evening when they encountered Marty Sharpe, his old friend from high school and U. of M. Marty was standing in front of the Union waiting for a bus to Detroit and appeared to be in tears. Richard took Molly inside and came bounding back out to say, "Okay, now tell me what's wrong." Marty explained that his father was dying in a Detroit hospital. Give him a minute and he would drive Marty in, said Richard, running back into the Union. In the meantime the bus arrived, and Marty stepped on it. In the morning Mr. Sharpe died, and each evening of the shivah Richard arrived to talk with Marty, trying to get his mind off the personal aspects of the death and to see it in a broader context. Another topic came up when Richard announced, "Marty, I've discovered sex!" According to Marty, "Dick said, 'Fucking can be so wonderful!' with a particular emphasis on and relish for the word 'fucking.' " Though they never talked directly about the possibilities of homosexuality, Marty thought that Richard was "coming close to the classical Greek concept of bisexuality."

At the end of the shivah for Mr. Sharpe, Marty's grandfather died, and on the way to Cleveland for the second shivah an uncle was killed in an auto accident. By the end of the second shivah in Cleveland Marty was "emotionally distraught." Back in Ann Arbor to complete his senior year, he remained in his room for nearly a week. But in the next several days Richard made a number of trips to talk with Marty and assumed once again the task of wise counsel. He also wrote to his friend letters filled with passages from Eliade on death and regeneration, and extensive quotes from other sources, poetry and prose on the same themes. He sent to Marty's mother a similar letter, but "very grandiose . . . really out of place and inappropriate," said Marty, since Richard hardly knew the woman.

Richard got Marty to take long walks all over Ann Arbor and would sometimes recite French poetry while strolling over the frigid March turf in his bare feet (because he said in his reverence for nature he loved the feel of the earth). "Little by little," says Marty, "he was pulling me back together again, getting me back into society, encouraging me to get out of the apartment and have some human intercourse." The climax of this effort came five weeks after the death of Marty's father on a wild exhilarating motorcycle ride around snow-covered Ann Arbor in which they ended up falling off Marty's bike into a snowbank and laughing uncontrollably.

It might be midnight when Richard would show up at Tzvi Berkal's home, insisting that he read something to Berkal that would only take a minute. It might be three in the morning when he left. The talk usually involved Richard's raging bitterness over the lack of a genuine religious commitment by American Jews and would often include a drastic indictment of the rabbinate including Rabbi Adler. Berkal was no more successful than were many others who tried to learn from Richard exactly what he meant by commitment, what constituted his own commitment, and why he felt justified in condemning others.

As an assistant regional director of B.B.Y.O., Berkal had come to know and admire Richard in high school. During Richard's junior year at U. of M., however, Berkal began to notice his perspective and attitude becoming increasingly negative, arrogant, and hostile. When he returned to Detroit for graduate school, Richard's visits to Berkal, now executive director of a synagogue near U. of D., became more frequent and more urgent: "You knew he had to talk to get something off his chest and perhaps with the emotional release he would be better off."

Occasionally Richard would talk "glibly" of the number of suicides occurring in the country, especially on its campuses, and said it was very prevalent at U. of M.; you just didn't hear about it much, but he had lived only two doors away from someone who had committed suicide in Ann Arbor. It was just another symptom of civilizational breakdown. As for himself he would ultimately accomplish something great or end up in an institution—one or the other.

In spite of frequent annoyances with Richard, in February Berkal asked him to be the keynote speaker at United Synagogue Youth's regional convention which Berkal was directing in March, when five hundred Jewish teen-agers from the Midwest would converge on Detroit. Says Mr. Berkal, "Richard thought he had something to say and I decided to give him a golden opportunity to say it." He could do a good job, Berkal told him, and could get across to the kids as someone with whom they could easily identify, whereas a rabbi might encounter a negative reaction immediately. Richard seemed highly pleased and agreed readily. Yet after two weeks he had not produced the outline which they had decided he should work out. He had been too busy, he said, and besides he didn't really need it for the speech he was going to give to a youth group at Shaarey Zedek as a trial run.

"On the night of the trial speech, within ten minutes after he had finished," says Berkal, "kids were calling me up and pounding on my door, saying that Richard under no circumstances should be allowed to address the convention, that he had rambled all over without much coherence and talked like a madman." Later Berkal told Richard that the keynote speech idea had been dropped in favor of a dialogue between a couple of rabbis.

Richard was off again at U. of D.'s Easter break, this time heading west to Chicago. He wanted to explore the possibilities for doctoral work at the University of Chicago, particularly in its divinity school (whose faculty included Paul Tillich), and with the Committee on Social Thought, which counted among its members people like Hannah Arendt, Saul Bellow, and Mircea Eliade.

In Chicago he had two conferences with the divinity school's dean of students, William N. Weaver. "I remember him quite well," said Dean Weaver, "and was unusually impressed with his wide range of information, his ability to articulate his ideas, and his tenacity of purpose. He was quite thorough and exhaustive in determining the academic resources that were available to him in the Divinity School and the University and spent some time here in talking to a number of people.

"In my conversations with Richard I had no intimation of the psychic disorder within him that obviously had already begun to possess him."

A somewhat different perspective was gained by Melvyn A. Hill, a student on the Committee on Social Thought, who served in a fashion as Richard's host for the Committee: "His days in Chicago were spent in a relentless quest for interviews with . . . intellectual celebrities—he was always to be found, it seemed, on the doorsteps of the great, and as far as I could tell, this was not an unusual pursuit for him; what was not clear, however, was just how serious he was about it all." To Mr. Hill and other students on the Committee Richard seemed often obnoxious and something of an intellectual faker. "His offensive qualities," recalls Hill, "came from a common psychological trick: he was the little boy pretending to outface big men . . . with both the smallness and the bigness his own invention."

Among the other members on the Committee whom Richard spoke to was one of his intellectual heroes, Mircea Eliade. Along with two girls from the Zimmerman group at U. of D. he paid a call on the scholar and was cordially greeted. Afterward, however, the girls reported that Richard had frequently interrupted Professor Eliade and had generally been forward and inconsiderate. Perhaps he had presented himself in a similar fashion on the phone with Leo Strauss, since Richard later reported that Professor Strauss had hung up on him.

With this trip Richard decided that the University of Chicago and especially the Committee on Social Thought would best serve the extraordinary plans he had been formulating over the past several months. He also applied, however, to the divinity school and was still seriously considering the New School in New York. His application included the following statement of academic objectives:

> I wish to acquire a thorough background in and understanding of the areas of comparative religion, philosophical anthropology, political philosophy, and ultimately, philosophy of history.
>
> I am entertaining an idea for a possible Ph.D. dissertation. The following will be a brief outline of that idea.
>
> The thesis will discuss the significance of Aristotle, Descartes, Hobbes, and Nietzsche in the establishment and destruction of philosophy, and perhaps political theory also, in Western Civilization. Aristotle's works will be used to illustrate what philosophy and political theory were as they became the foundation for much of Western society through integration with the Roman and Christian traditions; Descartes represents the break with philosophy in its classical-Christian form;

Hobbes articulates the break with classical-Christian political theory, breaks which I believe can be interpreted not only as a rebellion against the past but also a rebellion against G–d; and Nietzsche paradigmatically illustrates the logical existential consequences of this intellectual rebellion against G–d. Whereas Descartes and Hobbes only intellectually experienced the death of G–d, Nietzsche really experienced it, and it destroyed him.

Naturally this proposed thesis is somewhat presumptuous in contention, scope, and depth, and I anticipate substantial revisions. I also intend to spend three years in Europe before receiving my Ph.D.; one year in Greece at the American College outside of Athens studying classical Greek, and two years in Switzerland, Austria, and Germany, studying German and seeking out scholars in my own areas of interest.

Ultimately I wish to teach philosophy of history in an evaluative as well as descriptive manner.

The grandiosity of Richard's scheme is clearly established in the first paragraph; its full implementation might, take at least two or three scholarly lifetimes.

Subsequently Richard spent a few of his spring days in Ann Arbor requesting recommendations from his former professors and keeping old friends, both faculty and students, apprised of his progress and plans. He had visited Frank Grace and spoken to him on the phone several times during the previous fall and winter and had always been controlled, lucid, and enthusiastic about his work at U. of D. Now as the professor began to hear about his doctoral plans, a change seemed to have come over Richard. As they sat in Grace's small office, he noted that Richard's attention span had apparently become very short; his conversation would jump from one topic to another very quickly without logical sequence. "He was changing the topic," said Grace, "with almost every sentence, jumping up to get a book off the shelf and back into the chair again. He was very hypertensive."

Richard also paid a visit to Frithjof Bergmann, literally bursting into the professor's office on the second floor of Angell Hall in a highly excited state and presenting a list of fifteen or twenty authors of whom he wanted Bergmann's opinion. After a look at the list, which seemed to contain for the most part Jewish philosophers, political scientists, and economists, Bergmann explained that he was simply not familiar with any of them. At times shouting and yelling, Richard maintained in effect that if Bergmann had not read these people he simply did not have the right to teach the courses he did.

Bergmann guessed that none of his colleagues in the department would be familiar with many entries on the list and briefly defended his own competence, but he was disturbed by Richard's frenzied and insulting behavior. He felt that Richard really needed someone to throw an arm around him and say, "Oh, come on, Richard, it isn't all that important." Nevertheless, it wasn't until Bergmann finally agreed to take a look at some of the books on the list that Richard relented and departed, allowing the professor to join his wife who had been waiting for some time in the hall.

On another occasion later in the spring Professor Bergmann was walking on campus when he heard auto horns sounding vehemently and looked to the intersection of State and Liberty to find Richard running toward him, apparently having left his car in the middle of the street, effectively blocking traffic in all directions.

"I must talk to you," said Richard, rushing up to the professor. "It's very, very urgent. Can we talk now because it's very important to me?"

"Of course, yes," said Bergmann, "but let's first move your car."

Once back in Bergmann's office Richard had little to say of apparent urgency. He spoke excitedly and positively of his experience at U. of D., but Bergmann felt there was something that was troubling Richard deeply which Richard would not or could not bring himself to talk about.

In retrospect the episode strengthened Professor Bergmann's feeling that Richard had suffered some personal trouble which he had translated into a vision of the world in deep conflict. He began to spin a conception, suggests Bergmann, of the world sliding swiftly to chaos—a conception that would justify his own feelings of terror and despair.

Ann Arbor in the spring of 1965 was filled with talk of Vietnam. In February the Johnson administration had stepped up its escalation of the war to include the bombing of North Vietnam, and in April the nation's first teach-in was organized at U. of M. Asked by a friend about the teach-in and the demonstrations on campus, Richard said he generally disapproved: overall he seemed to endorse the United States position in the war. Actually, says Pat Burke, Richard did not exhibit much interest in any political or social issue. Once in a while he would look at a copy of *Time* or *The Atlantic* but generally did not bother with newspapers, radio, or television. Occasionally he might argue in support of the war, but he often had to admit he wasn't informed.

This situation changed somewhat during the spring when Richard's radical friend at Wayne, David Roth, convinced him (with the aid of suggested reading) that the administration's position on Vietnam was untenable. Thereafter, at David's prompting, Richard attended a few antiwar rallies at Wayne and generally expressed a strong feeling against the United States effort. Typically he insisted upon seeing the Vietnam war as an especially horrifying example of the degenerate drift of modern man.

TWENTY-SIX

Sharon Thompson had just graduated from U. of M. when she visited Richard in Detroit on April 29 before leaving on a summer trip to Europe and Israel. As a going-away gift he gave her a copy of José Ortega y Gasset's *The Revolt of the Masses* with the following inscription: "Dear Sharon, may this book give you insights into the kind of person which you wish to become. 'All life is a struggle, the effort to be itself.'—Ortega y Gasset. Bon Voyage! With affection, Richard."

The Ortega book had for some time been among Richard's favorites; it was also required reading for the Zimmerman group at U. of D. According to the conservative Spanish philosopher, the natural and proper order of society is aristocratic, and a genuine aristocracy of superior talent and merit is accorded its rightful place at the top. Today, however, the masses, in their pursuit of pleasure are invading not only the areas of social life and the arts but also —and most disastrously—the realm of politics. Now reveling in their own commonness and refusing to accept any order superior to themselves, the masses crush "everything that is different, everything that is excellent, individual, qualified, and select."

Earlier in the spring Richard had talked to Sharon about trouble in his relationship with Dr. Zimmerman. He kept repeating that Dr. Zimmerman had said that the greatest—the indispensable—quality a man must have is courage. He did not elaborate but said repeatedly, "Dr. Zimmerman doesn't respect me. She doesn't recognize my talents and my capacities."

Richard's problems with Dr. Zimmerman resulted primarily from his failure to exhibit the kind of seriousness and total commitment to his work which he always had before. He had begun to seem much more interested in his future doctoral studies than his present work toward a master's degree, and with his trips to the East Coast, Chicago, and Ann Arbor his class attendance had fallen off considerably. Dr. Zimmerman began to wonder if Richard was perhaps trying to rest on his laurels or find scholarly shortcuts.

In addition she was becoming irked by his habit of seeking out important scholars: "He was using my name as an entrée and acting like a rash young kid who doesn't know any better. I was afraid of the impression he might be making." After she heard about Richard's behavior with Mircea Eliade (who is a "good friend"), she sent a note to Chicago disclaiming any responsibility for Richard and expressing her hope that no harm had been done. Eliade later replied that he understood the situation.

Along with a second term of the comparative religion seminar, Richard was taking two other three-credit-hour courses with Charlotte Zimmerman, Sociological Theory and Philosophy of the Social Sciences. For each he had a considerable amount of reading, yet what reading he managed to do seemed most often to involve people like Nietzsche, Dostoevski, Kierkegaard, and Camus—writers often discussed by Dr. Zimmerman, but not then assigned. Recalls Dr. Zimmerman: "When he came around telling me that he was reading Nietzsche and Dostoevski and these other people, I told him to stop it. I told him, 'Under no conditions should you be reading Nietzsche now. You're in no condition to read these people.' I knew he was not the most stable person to begin with, and I wanted him reading the good, calm scholarly books I had chosen for him. I told him, 'If you won't do what I tell you and won't stick to the reading I've assigned for you, then I can't be responsible for your program any longer.' "

Richard's behavior was also causing him trouble with others on campus, including Robert Peters, the director of student aid. Still in his twenties, and a former student at U. of D., Peters had met Richard early in the fall concerning his grant of $1,600 from the Wilson Foundation. For some reason the money had been held up by the foundation for about two months, during which time Richard, though beginning quite amiably with Peters, had become increasingly belligerent, apparently blaming Peters for his problem. Finally in November after the grant money had arrived, Richard apologized to Peters for any trouble he might have caused; afterward Peters sighed to himself, "That's over with, thank God. I won't have to deal with him again."

But in March Richard appeared again, this time asking for money to finance his terms in the summer and the following fall. He would be finished at U. of D. in December, he said, and would be going on to the University of Chicago. He needed the money now to pay for his trips. Peters explained that of the $2,000 awarded the school by the Wilson Foundation under the terms of the grant, 75 percent might go to a student or students (but not necessarily the recipient of the grant) preparing for a career in college teaching. Richard, he pointed out, had already received $525 from U. of D. for tuition in his first two terms.

Richard wanted more money. Peters checked with Dr. Zimmerman who told him that Richard was not performing as well as she had hoped and was doing only fair work. Increasing his visits, belligerence, and vague threats, Richard seemed to be getting almost "hysterical" on the issue. When Peters called Mrs. Wishnetsky, she explained that Richard was also receiving financial help from home and apologized to Peters for her son's behavior—she had heard about his causing trouble on campus. Finally after checking with the graduate dean, Peters sent Richard a letter on May 24 stating that U. of D. would give him a stipend of $354 for the summer and again wave tuition costs; in August he could pick up a stipend of $808 for the fall term.

When Richard arrived for his $354 he was still unsatisfied. He needed more money for his travels; he should be given, he announced, all of the $2,000 he was responsible for bringing to U. of D. Peters pointed out that Richard had already received or been promised *more* than $2,000 from U. of D. and that he simply could not release more money. By the end of the spring Richard was threatening to get Peters fired and was coming in simply to "rant and rave," with the subject of money hardly touched.

Richard was also having difficulty at the library. In the basement, there are a number of carrels assigned to honor students and some of those in graduate studies. Richard's carrel was always jammed with paperbacks, and on the walls he had taped note cards bearing some of his favorite quotes from Ortega y Gasset, Voegelin, and Dostoevski and a number of photos, including a large poster, of singer Barbra Streisand, whom he seemed to think the most attractive woman in the world. He once registered a complaint about someone having removed or defaced a picture in the carrel.

Richard's arrogant impatience seems to have increased as he became less able to study. He might come to the ground-floor front desk on which he would pound while shouting, "Xerox! Xerox!" when he wanted something copied and wasn't being waited on immediately. If employees were talking near him about library business, he might ask archly, "Do you know this is a library?" In one such case he asked an older woman, "Pardon me, do you work here?"

"Yes, I do," said the woman. "Can I help?"

"Yes, I think you can," said Richard. "In fact I know you can." When the woman asked again what she might do for him, Richard raised his hand and screamed, "For Godsakes, you can shut up!"

In another encounter with a girl who had inadvertently taken the chair from his carrel to sit with her co-workers, Richard informed her that she was occupying his chair. Noting unused chairs within a few feet of his carrel, the girl thought he was joking and said with a laugh, "That's too bad."

Richard growled, "Get out of that chair."

Realizing that he was serious, she replied in kind: "Drop dead. Get another chair."

"No," said Richard, "I want my chair. Now get out or I'll take you with it," whereupon the girl moved.

The incident was reported to the circulation director, but Richard had befriended the man who now defended Richard, saying, "He's a very brilliant student who's probably been under some pressure. He's been studying very, very hard. You'll have to try to excuse his temper."

Richard knew he was making few friends at the library, but if he needed further evidence he got it when he walked down to his carrel one night with Janis Newman on a study date. There on his desk he found a 3 by 5 card covered with swastikas and various pleasantries such as "You dirty Jew! You better watch your step—we're going to get you!" Richard snorted with indignation, then laughed and showed it to Janis who found it vile and vicious. He put it in his wallet to keep, despite Janis's suggestion that he get rid of it. Later he showed the card to a number of friends, a few of whom thought he might well have made it up himself.

Occasionally Richard would forsake the basement for an upstairs room in the library. On one spring Sunday afternoon he and Larry Walters sat studying alone in a large third-floor room which contains a raised platform and is sometimes used as a theater. About three in the afternoon Richard stopped his regular studies and began writing frantically, saying he didn't wish to be disturbed. After two hours or so he had covered several pages and finally placed himself on the platform as if to present a speech. He delivered for Larry's benefit a scathing denunciation of American society as materialistic and sick, of the Jewish community and its institutions as the epitome of that society, and of Congregation Shaarey Zedek as a primary symbol of the decadence of the Jewish community. When he had finished, Richard talked of getting his diatribe published, perhaps in *The Jewish News,* and even of having it printed himself in the form of leaflets to be dropped by the hundreds of thousands from a plane over the Jewish neighborhoods in Detroit.

By this time Larry had become Richard's closest friend and confidant during a period when Richard was often alienating friends and acquaintances. They were a complementary pair, each admiring aspects of the other's personality which he felt lacking in his own. In addition, though Larry admitted that occasionally "Richard would do something to impose himself on you, and you wanted to reject him," he remained intensely loyal to his friend. "I defended Richard to anybody," he says. "There wasn't anything that he did, no matter how terrible, that I didn't somehow find a way to justify."

For the most part, Larry simply liked being around Richard and still retains fond memories of the night in May when they attended the opening performance of the Metropolitan Opera Company at the Masonic Auditorium. Larry had found himself with two standing-room tickets when his date for the evening reneged at the last minute. On their arrival, Richard, dressed in his uncle's tuxedo, decided he wanted to be photographed walking up the red-carpeted steps of the auditorium. He moved down to a Cadillac drawing up in front, assisted a woman in a full-length gown from the car, introduced himself as "Richard Wishnetsky, a Woodrow Wilson fellow," and gallantly escorted the woman up the steps between the rows of "commoners" who annually appear to gawk at Detroit's royalty. Once inside he promptly ensconced himself in a box seat, made the acquaintance of an "Italian Princess," leaped into the orchestra pit to congratulate the conductor at intermission, and finally stood in the main aisle, yelling "Bravo!" and leading a standing ovation for the Met's performance of *The Last Savage.*

One of the numerous letters Richard wrote to friends during his hectic spring described the priests at U. of D. generally as homosexuals and perverts. Needless to say, he refrained from expressing such an opinion during any of his frequent chats with Father James McGlynn, the dean of the graduate school. They often talked philosophy with Richard expressing his admiration for the illustrious Jesuit past and his devotion to the ideals of spiritual humanism. Richard was always so calm and well mannered in Father McGlynn's presence that the dean found it difficult to believe reports he began to receive from others—Mr. Peters at Student Aid and the people at the library—that Richard was behaving badly on campus. Perhaps, said Father McGlynn, he was slow to respond to these complaints because Richard seemed to him so thoroughly in control of himself.

Occasionally after paying a visit to Father McGlynn in the Briggs Building, Richard might climb one flight of stairs to present a rather different face to Mrs. Joyce Smith, a writer and an assistant professor of English whose office was on the second floor. One spring day Richard, well dressed as usual but with a "certain urgent, harassed, slightly embarrassed look," had walked into Mrs. Smith's office and introduced himself:

"Hello, I'm Richard Wishnetsky. I've been hearing things about you, interesting things. I hear you're really a cute chick."

"Please, Mr. Wishnetsky!"

"Oh, can't I talk that way with you?"

"No, you certainly may not."

"Oh, I'm very sorry," he said with a small mocking grin.

Mrs. Smith thought that although she had been visited in the past by a number of "rather weird students, Richard seemed really something set apart." They talked for about an hour in what was to be the first of many similar conversations over the next several months. He seemed to want something from her, she says, "an answer or consolation or perhaps affection, something that—as he was to say in another context—would identify him as a human being."

Mrs. Smith, who writes under the pen name of Joyce Carol Oates, was still in her twenties. Prolific and versatile, she has produced novels, poetry, criticism, and drama in addition to her stories. Fiction remains her passion, however, and her latest novels, *Expensive People*, and *them*, have won critical acclaim. Her characters, she says, are often composites of or imaginative elaborations on the people she meets. Of Richard she recalls:

"It was all there on that first day—the latent violence, the scornful refutations, the sense that the majority of people are somehow wrong and therefore contemptible. But he had flashes of insight and good humor; he was charming. He could recognize at times his own audacity, his table-pounding egotism, and nod in agreement with my sometimes harsh judgments of him—in those occasional tender moments of self-illumination that made him unforgettably human."

Richard's obsession with ideas dominated his personality, thought Mrs. Smith: "With Richard, I was always driven to flippancy in an attempt to offset his seriousness; I told him that ideas have but a tenuous relationship to real life and that one should not become deranged over them; they are not that important. He dismissed this contemptuously. Ideas were the highest creations of man, the only reality. (To compromise with the banal world, Richard said, he would become a scholar, a man of ideas.) He could not, clearly, conceive of my notion that ideas are luxuries in this world, rather than the bases of it."

They talked of Nietzsche, madness and the death of God, and of Camus on suicide. "He told me," recalls Mrs. Smith, "that if God did not exist, life was not worth living and that he would commit suicide. I replied with a casualness I might now regret, that he perhaps believed in God, then, simply to save himself from suicide. But he said that he would never, never commit suicide. It was stupid, a mistake."

As he did for many others, Richard described for Joyce Smith his reactions to the film version of *The Pawnbroker* which depicts the sufferings of a Jew who is trying to run his business in present-day Harlem while tortured by memories of the fate of his family in Nazi Germany. His identification with the film's hero, said Richard, had nearly driven him to hysterics. He had first seen *The*

Pawnbroker with a date and had sat for a while intensely involved. Finally he had become so horrified by the inhumanity displayed in the flashback scenes of the Nazi concentration camp that he simply couldn't take it any longer. Leaving his date in the theater, he had walked out into the night and had found an empty field in which he had lain down on the ground. Breathing heavily, crying, and pounding the earth, he had sobbed over and over, "The inhumanity of it!"

To Mrs. Smith Richard boasted of his extraordinary success with the opposite sex and described himself as a lady-killer of unrivaled effectiveness. Once he told Mrs. Smith, who considered his claims "wholly mythical," "You know, I'd like to take you out."

She laughed.

"What are you laughing at?" he demanded.

"The idea of your taking me out. I'm a married woman."

"Well, really, you're too young for me," said Richard. "I prefer older women."

In spite of such episodes Richard could be very sweet, said Mrs. Smith: "He would come to me after he had been very insulting the day before and be meek and apologetic and say, 'Oh, you know I didn't really mean those things I said. You know I'm not really like that. You know how I am!' "

Yet the sexual bravado which he had begun to display after his breakup with Sherri Jacobson continued as a prominent feature of his personality. He told Joyce Smith about the married woman he had been seeing and described a scene (which she felt certain he was fabricating) in which the irate husband walked in on Richard and the cowering young wife—the girl asking Richard to leave and Richard refusing because, he said, "I heard the pleading in her voice." She was, he told his roommate Pat Burke and other friends, the not overly attractive but flirtatious girl in the serving line at a nearby cafeteria. He had marked her as an "easy lay," had set out to prove it, and claimed he had. Arriving at her apartment one night when her wife-beating husband was home, he had staunchly delivered the cad a warning never to lay a hand on the girl again.

Apparently, however, the affair was not entirely a fabrication. One spring day Richard called John Samuels and insisted, as he frequently did, that he had to see John immediately: he was at a hamburger parlor and would John please come right away? Samuels arrived to find Richard making an extraordinary scene in the attempt to get a girl in a serving uniform to leave with him. Introducing her as his new mistress, Richard went off to the telephone where, he had threatened, he would call her friends and tell them that she used drugs. The girl told John she was married and denied having relations with Richard; she had decided Richard was crazy and asked John to get him away from her. Returning to the table, Richard became very loud and threatened to spill coffee on the girl's dress before John managed to move him outside and away from the gaping patrons in the restaurant. John tried to get Richard to explain what was wrong, but Richard returned to the restaurant, blew the girl a kiss from the door, and departed. Richard then seemed docile, mild-mannered, and in control of himself. He asked John to drop him off at his grandmother's, as if, said John, "we'd just been out bowling somewhere."

Wanting to help Richard relieve his frustration, Larry Walters tried a number of times to line him up with girls who were ready and willing to help this brilliant and socially naïve young intellectual out of his predicament. "Richard seemed game for a while," says Larry, "but then he'd always back off, and I was never able to make connections for him. Richard could have had a lot of girls but he was always in too much of a hurry and too clumsy with them." He might, for example, present his blunt approach after five minutes of conversation to a long-haired girl with a reputation on campus and receive her huffy reply: "Of course I won't go to bed with you. I hardly know you."

"Well, you do it with everybody else, why not me?"

Stories of his appeal and prowess, however, continued to come from Richard, often with a light touch of the bizarre: he was dating a divorced woman, he told Mrs. Smith at one point, and at another he explained to Larry that he was having intimate relations with a buxom Negro girl who lived near U. of D.

One Saturday afternoon Richard stopped by the Goodman residence to chat with Susie Goodman and her parents. Susie and Richard had seen little of each other since their sophomore year at U. of M. when he had been dating Mary Wilson. Since his parents were going out for the evening, his mother had left some food in the oven for him, and he asked if Susie would like to join him for dinner. She agreed happily, and later they went to Richard's house to eat the chicken and rice they found in the oven. He was cordial during the dinner and kept pressing Susie to eat more and enjoy herself, but as they talked in their usual animated fashion about a variety of things, Susie felt that there was something very strange about Richard.

"He was so extremely negative," says Susie, "about so many things, about Gentiles in general and Christians and Catholics in particular. He was particularly vehement about Jews assimilating and embracing intermarriage. When I mentioned Mary Wilson, he said, 'I'd never marry a *shiksa.*' I was really shocked to hear Richard say such a thing." He had recently called Mary and found that she was now married. Her conversation, he said, was very dull and she didn't sound at all like the old Mary. She had obviously adapted, he said, and the marriage had robbed her of her vitality and sensitivity—the things he had liked about her. He seemed disturbed that this had happened to her, but pleased that he had not made a mistake in getting more involved. When Susie mentioned that she would not hesitate to marry a non-Jew if she really loved him, she received a harsh lecture.

In spite of Richard's rigidity, which appalled Susie, they got through dinner quite amicably. Then recalls Susie: "Suddenly about seven or seven thirty after dinner Richard said he was very tired and had to get some sleep. He hadn't seemed very tired, but we got up from the table so that he could go to bed. I went into the den to get my purse and Richard stopped at the stairs and put his foot on the first step as if to go up. Suddenly when I was about to turn around, Richard was in the den behind me. He came over quickly and without saying a word started to kiss me. I was shocked; he had never made an advance before or even hinted at it. I guess I had never really lost that crush I had on Richard from our very first meeting, and for a while as he kissed me it seemed very natural that he should finally want to do this. After a minute or two, though, his insistence, his suddenness, made me stop. I had always found Richard attractive and admired him, but now there was a real desperateness about him. I felt like I was being used by Richard simply because I was there and he was desperate. It was as if he thought he possessed me and could take me anytime he felt like it. When I stopped responding, he finally stopped and said, 'What's the matter? You're a big girl now,' in a very cutting and nasty way."

Staring out a window at the darkness after his rebuff, Richard spoke quietly and sadly about how much the street had changed. He continued to brood as he walked Susie home. "There are so few people you can really talk to," he said as a kind of reproach.

Like many others at this time, Professor Budzinowski at U. of D. found it difficult to cope with Richard's conversation for more than a short while. Because of Richard's intensity and habit of not sticking to one subject or idea for any length of time, their conversations were "about everything and about nothing." While frequently denouncing materialistic desires, Richard seemed to Budzinowski "always after money for one thing or another." The professor finally told Richard that he had better decide just what he wanted. If he really wanted to be a scholar as he said he did, he would have to dedicate his life in a way that would demand sacrifice.

Money had become one of the central issues in the conflict Richard was having at home, and he often came to Professor Budzinowski to talk about the increasing trouble he was having with his parents. Budzinowski had met Mr. Wishnetsky on insurance business and had found him an intelligent businessman worried about his son's future at U. of D. Now the professor tried to play the role of reconciler, pressing Richard to realize the importance of getting along better with his family.

"Even the worst parents are your best friends," the professor would say. "They're very concerned about you; in their own way they would like to protect you, insulate you. A father, no matter how much you might disagree with him, is still your father and he still loves you. You must find a *modus vivendi,* a way of living, with your family. If there is no peace at home you will never be able to work as you want to. You may call yourself a scholar or a genius, but if you don't learn to get along with your family, then you will have accomplished nothing, no matter what you try to achieve as a scholar."

Richard seemed to take this advice to heart and later told Professor Budzinowski that he had tried to relate intelligently to his parents. What he may have referred to was the fact that he had finally bowed to their request that he see a psychiatrist. But Richard was also curious, thought Larry Walters, about the possibilities of psychiatry, "because he was troubled. He had things inside of him which needed to be communicated."

Yet ideologically, Richard was bitterly hostile to psychiatry in general as an atheistic, positivistic, dehumanizing pseudoscience, and he might accept with readiness only a therapist with the philosophical view of Viktor Frankl. He had approached Charlotte Zimmerman on the subject, and she had said that of course the value of the experience would depend on the kind of psychiatrist he went to. "I told him," she says, "'Richard, you need somebody really good and professional who can listen to you and help you sort things out.' And at that point he seemed really troubled by it all and agreed right away. I didn't know anybody to suggest but he said he knew a number of people."

Richard told only a few friends about his psychiatric visits. "You know, Larry, I'm seeing a psychiatrist," he said, testing his friend's reaction before giving him more details. "It would take," says Larry, "many meetings with a psychiatrist before anything would happen, because Richard would have to test him out. Usually the person he could trust was the person he could manipulate. If somebody could figure Richard out, Richard would take off. He wouldn't want any part of him. He would ask the guy: 'Have you read Hannah Arendt? Have you read Saul Bellow?' And if the fellow said yes, well then okay, they could talk, but otherwise no."

He told another friend that he had recently come fifteen minutes late to a session and had asked the psychiatrist for a reduction in the fee. The doctor had replied that it was Richard's responsibility to arrive on time, and therefore no reduction was in order. The man was a thief and a crook, said Richard. He soon reported to Pat Burke that he was now seeing a second psychiatrist. Perhaps, he said, the sessions were helping him, but he and the doctor were really only talking philosophy.

TWENTY-SEVEN

Charlotte Zimmerman left the University of Detroit in mid-May for six weeks abroad, including a period of study with Eric Voegelin in Germany. She would return to Detroit near the end of June to teach her summer courses and to read Richard's term papers required for the spring courses he was taking with her. In the meantime her students took their final exams. Richard, though at the time in a state of depression, still managed to earn a B on the Sociological Theory exam and an A-minus in Philosophy of the Social Sciences.

One night in June after the exams, Greg Leszczynski had a long friendly talk with Richard who was still depressed and therefore in a self-deprecatory mood. Richard asked if Greg considered him a friend, and Leszczynski listed what he thought were Richard's fine qualities. He also explained, however, why he thought Richard alienated people, pointing to his intolerance and belligerence. He must try to temper his exuberance, said Greg. Richard admitted he had a problem and seemed to take Greg's advice seriously, but the next day he was off on another manic period and full of plans for visits to Chicago, New York, and Washington. "Richard," said Greg, "this is just what we talked about last night. This is just what you shouldn't be doing." Richard shrugged him off.

Upon learning that Henry Shevitz's younger sister, Vivian, was driving to Chicago, Richard asked for a ride. Vivian agreed when Richard said he would contribute gas money, as were two other boys she was also driving to Chicago. On the road Vivian kept a steady stream of rock 'n' roll music coming from the car radio. Richard finally asked that the radio be turned off—he couldn't stand the music. Vivian, behind the wheel, refused. Richard continued to ask; Vivian continued to refuse. When they stopped for gas and were getting out of the car, he took the keys from the ignition and walked off, announcing he would throw them away unless Vivian would promise to end the rock 'n' roll for the rest of the trip. Vivian agreed and they returned to the car. When they were driving again, on came the rock 'n' roll. Richard began swearing at Vivian, calling her a "whore" and a "bitch." In Chicago he wanted to be dropped at a particular spot on a certain street. Vivian made an attempt to find the street, couldn't, and finally unloaded him somewhere nearby. Again Richard was furious and warned that he would take his revenge.

Richard's application and recommendations had preceded him to the University of Chicago, and his main purpose now was to present himself for interviews with members of the Committee on Social Thought, particularly its executive secretary, James M. Redfield. Though Richard's letter of application had struck Professor Redfield as "pretentious, verbose, and empty," his admission was considered because of his record and recommendations—that is, until his interview with Redfield:

"Ten minutes' conversation with him was enough to establish to my satisfaction that he was crazy. I choose this word with care; I am not a professional in such matters and I have no idea what the trouble was. But I know craziness when I meet it. He was quite incapable of understanding anything that was said to him; he lived in some kind of private or fantastic world. . . .

"I could understand that some would think him brilliant; he made all the kinds of noises brilliant people make, referred to many books, piled proposition on proposition, and hurriedly improvised a great many statements about a great many things. But there was nothing behind it, no coherence, no real thought.

"Others on the committee had not such a negative impression, but when the case was discussed there was no move to admit him. He was clearly ineducable."

Melvyn Hill, one of the students on the committee who had met him on his previous visit, spoke again with Richard:

"With regard to his own project—'the creation and destruction of philosophy'—it was obvious from his conversation that his notions about philosophy were largely incoherent. Even more telling was the fact that, by his own admission, he had read neither Aristotle ('the creation') nor Descartes ('the destruction'). I recall a discussion we had in which we talked about no less a triumvirate than Freud, Jung, and Mircea Eliade; after only three questions charitably put to him, it turned out he had read none of the works in question. . . ."

Richard also looked up his U. of M. friend David Passman in Chicago. There was a kind of "tunnel vision" in Richard, thought David: "What he probed, he probed deeply, like the classical philosophies—and he understood them very well indeed. . . . But the farther he got into his intellectual holes, the more he lost perspective on what was outside them. As he concentrated his attention on the subjects that interested him, he stopped reading about the rest, but he went on being oracular about them." (At some point he might not have disagreed with this, except to reject the image of being down in a hole in favor of being up on a mountain.)

Before leaving, Richard told David that he was on his way to Washington to lobby for a grant of $500,000 from the Department of Health, Education, and Welfare for the Committee on Social Thought. He spoke, says David, "with the same firm conviction that invested all of his designs with a bit of undeserved credibility."

As Richard set out again for the East in mid-June, he was armed with schemes, plans, and proposals, many of which verged on the ludicrous. In New York briefly, he tried to make contact with Barbra Streisand and her agent for a benefit concert he wanted to promote in Detroit. He needed the money, he told a friend, for the trip he wanted to make later in the summer to Europe and Israel. The money—he wanted two or three thousand—had been a source of trouble at home, he said, and when his parents would not provide it, he had threatened to smash up the family car so that it would cost his father the same amount.

Off to Washington with the intention of returning to New York in a week or so, Richard called an old friend from Mumford and U. of M., Franci Barret (pseud.), who worked in the office of one of Michigan's representatives in the House. Franci had heard from Richard in April when he had called long-distance to ask if she would set up appointments for him with a number of VIP's in Washington, including people at HEW and Vice-President Hubert Humphrey.

Subsequently he called several times before his arrival in the Capital and asked about Franci's progress. She finally explained that the meetings he wanted were out of the question, at least through her efforts. Nevertheless, Richard showed up at Franci's office in the Cannon House Office Building the next morning and was loud, shrill, and insistent. He was warned and then asked to leave by one of Franci's office mates, and Franci, distressed and embarrassed, refused his offer of lunch.

During his visit to the Capital, Richard stayed with relatives in Bethesda and had a number of encounters with friends and acquaintances in the Washington area. He had a weekend date with a friend's friend who found him aggressive and rude, but he apparently did not manage to carry out one of the schemes he had talked about most before leaving Detroit—a date with one of Lyndon Johnson's daughters.

Back in New York he was still running into old friends: on Broadway he met Linda Kohl, whom he had dated for a couple of months during his junior year at U. of M. For fifteen minutes he talked of how he had already lined up Sammy Davis and Danny Kaye for his benefit concert in Detroit and would soon be in touch with Barbra Streisand's agent. He said that had recently been through a very bad time and had been seeing psychiatrists. Though he had once thought Linda was sick, she probably wasn't, and instead maybe he himself was. At any rate she wasn't alone. Linda no longer felt bitter or hostile toward Richard but found herself "really shaken by the conversation." Later he called to ask if she would go with him to see his grandparents in Westchester, which he referred to as "an anxious, free place." Linda didn't know what he meant by the phrase and decided she didn't care to find out.

He arranged to meet Larry Walters, who also happened to be in New York, at Lindy's for dinner and ended up trying to get a fellow patron to pay for their meal. He was still trying to line up interviews with scholars at the New School and later told friends he had spent some time in conversation with Jules Feiffer. He visited the editorial offices of *Time* on a quest which had started at a branch office in Detroit to get the magazine to cover the extraordinary character and activities of the Zimmerman group at U. of D. And on the morning of Friday, June 25, he walked into the office of Werner Dannhauser, an associate editor of *Commentary*, and said he wanted to write a series of articles on the subject of the disintegration of Jewish life in America. Interrupting himself frequently to say, "I know I've got a lot to learn, but I'm learning," Richard finally left with the advice to narrow his topic and the assurance that Dannhauser (who felt there was something not quite right with his visitor) would be glad to read anything he might want to submit.

That same week *Time*'s Essay was titled "The New American Jew" and it concluded: "There is a growing awareness that without the light of religion, neither United Jewish Appeal, nor vacations in Israel, nor psychoanalysis, nor Phi Beta Kappa will keep the word Jewish from watering down in America to something as unspecific as the word Protestant can be."

Richard was back in Detroit before his twenty-third birthday on July 1; he was still wrapped up in the business of raising himself some money and planning his trip abroad. He was again collecting letters of introduction to scholars (including Viktor Frankl) in Europe and Israel and traveled to Ann Arbor to ask for one addressed to Eric Voegelin from Frank Grace. Hearing about Richard's new travel plans, Grace found his doubts increasing about Richard's ability to discipline himself for genuine scholarly work. He mentioned in the letter that it might be helpful if Voegelin suggested that Richard concentrate on languages in which, said Grace, he was "sadly deficient," and that he limit his aims and scope to something he could realistically accomplish. Professor Grace sealed the letter and placed it on his desk to await the return visit Richard had promised.

Shortly before his birthday Richard received a letter from Dean Weaver at the divinity school in Chicago announcing that his application for admission had been approved and that he had been awarded a one-year fellowship worth $3,200. Since he would not be starting until the spring quarter of 1966, however, he would not be able to pick up his first hard-cash stipend of $497 until perhaps some time in April 1966. On his birthday Richard included a copy of the divinity school letter with a note he wrote to Professor Gaylord with whose aid he was trying to win a Kent Fellowship. The Committee on Social Thought was still his first choice, he told Gaylord, but he doubted that, even if accepted, he would receive financial help. Thus he still wished to try for the Kent. Later he added a postscript indicating that he would be leaving for Israel on August 1 and returning from Paris on September 10.

Professor Gaylord, who had seen Richard earlier in the summer, remarks: "I knew nothing at all about his mental or personal troubles. But the new humor and the new aggressiveness I did remark upon. Apparently, I was just blind to the pathology of the situation; in retrospect, the hilarity and happy violence of language, the extravagant dogmatics, add up to a kind of intellectual hysteria, but I didn't see that large kind of danger. I do know he thought highly of Rabbi Adler; the last time we visited he set me straight on all the 'good guys'—that was when I noticed how assertive, how arbitrary he had become."

On the night of his birthday Richard stopped by the home of Sherri Jacobson whom he hadn't seen in months. Pleading with her to go out with him again, he got down on his hands and knees to beg, and even mentioned that he was now watching television as if to prove he was really trying to make himself over into a type that would please her. He was so insistent that Sherri's parents were forced to call the Wishnetskys to get Richard to leave. Afterward Sherri told her mother she thought he was going to commit suicide.

During his year at U. of D. Richard had remained in touch with Henry Shevitz, who was now attending medical school at Wayne State. They would at times meet for coffee and talk after Richard's late-night study sessions at the sociology offices after which Henry would drive him home. Richard would occasionally call to ask for a ride somewhere or might invite himself to dinner at the Shevitz home.

Soon after returning from his June travels, Richard called Henry to ask, "What's the state of your sister's finances?" Henry replied that it was none of Richard's business. When Richard pressed the question, Henry again refused and asked why he wanted the information. Richard explained that on their trip to Chicago, Vivian had been short of money and he had loaned her five dollars. Now he wanted the money back, but Vivian would not pay him. "If this is true," said Henry, "I'll pay you the five dollars. Don't bother Vivian about it anymore."

Said Richard, "I don't want to get you involved in this. I just want to know what her finances are. I don't want you to pay me. I want the money from Vivian."

When Henry refused to accommodate him, Richard later called Henry's parents, asked the same question, gave the same story, and received the same reply. From Vivian they learned that she had not loaned Richard any money at all. Nor had he paid for any of the gas as he had promised. In fact he was indebted to her because she had loaned *him* a dollar when he claimed he was broke upon leaving the car in Chicago.

One day within a week after Richard's original call, Henry walked into the kitchen of his parents' home to find Richard sitting there sipping from a bottle of soda pop. He had apparently walked in the side door without knocking. "Where'd you get the pop, Richard?" asked Henry.

"I brought it with me." This was absurd, thought Henry; the refrigerator was stocked with the same kind of pop.

"What's the matter with you, Richard? You know I'd give you a bottle of pop. All you'd have to do is ask. What's the matter with you?"

When Richard repeated several times that he had brought the bottle with him, Henry, very miffed, asked him to leave. Later, determined to settle the dispute over the loan, he called Richard and set up a meeting on the U. of D. campus. When they met, Henry asked point-blank, "Did you loan my sister five dollars or not?" Richard at last admitted that he had not loaned her five dollars.

"Why did you tell me this big story?" asked Henry.

"Well, I wanted to get back at Vivian, to cause her trouble for the way she acted on the trip."

"I don't want to have anything to do with you ever again," said Henry. "As far as I'm concerned this is the end of our friendship."

"But you're my friend," pleaded Richard. "This is nothing—this shouldn't affect our friendship at all."

Henry felt otherwise.

When Richard returned to his classes at U. of D., they had already been in session for a week. Charlotte Zimmerman, back from Europe and informed of his wild travels, was waiting with displeasure for his reappearance. Walking in late to his first class in Contemporary Problems, Richard yelled, "Hello, Dr. Zimmerman!" from the back of the room. "How are you?" His professor told him to seat himself and be quiet which he proceeded to do. After class as Dr. Zimmerman was leaving, Richard approached her wanting to talk. "I have nothing to say to you, Mr. Wishnetsky, after that display," said Dr. Zimmerman, walking out the door. When she was out of earshot, Richard barked, "Fuck my teacher!"

About a week later Richard appeared in Dr. Zimmerman's office with the term paper required for completion of his two sociology courses in the previous semester. (She had give him permission to write one extended paper to cover both courses.) Dr. Zimmerman could see with a glance at its length, footnotes, and bibliography that the paper would be unacceptable. Before leaving, Richard asked if Dr. Zimmerman would please write him a recommendation for the Committee on Social Thought. She replied that on the basis of his performance, she could not. His class disruption, his wild visits to other schools thus jeopardizing her reputation and those of her students, his frequent absence from class, his failure to do enough solid work, and his general failure to discipline himself and to follow her advice—all made it impossible for her to write a recommendation for him.

The rejection came as a shock, said Dr. Zimmerman, and Richard was angry and rude. Though not vulgar, he continued his discourtesy until she had to ask him to leave her office. The next day she found on her desk a handwritten note on a half sheet of loose-leaf paper: Richard apologized curtly for his "rude behavior." He had come for Dr. Zimmerman's help, he wrote, and felt "very bad" that she had withheld it. He trusted that matters would improve in the future; he would do his part to see that they did.

Richard's term-paper assignment had been to read the works of one sociological theorist (preferably Max Weber) along with pertinent secondary sources and to write an analysis with as much originality as possible. Instead, his paper was titled "The Success of Positivism (A Sketch for an Experiential Explanation)" and listed as its sources only Mills's *The Sociological Imagination,* Whyte's *The Organization Man,* and Voegelin's *The New Science of Politics.* It began as follows:

> The phenomenal success of the natural sciences and technology has so overwhelmed contemporary man that today he dreams of a behavioral science of man and of a human engineering to put that science into practice. In spite of the fact that these dreams will not come true, they are held with reverence and pursued with fervor. This paper contends that the success of modern positivism indicates the degree to which men today desire certainty and seek to escape the insecurities of a world without direction, that this success manifests a real hunger for paradise, the dream of miraculously transforming the human world as the natural world has been transformed.

Richard next presents a brief description of positivism and then declares that what the positivist holds to be meaningful, the concrete fact, "ultimately and essentially is meaningless." He continues:

> The essentially meaningless becomes meaningful because the fundamental verities of human experience are today no longer meaningful, the result of the destruction of religion and philosophy in the West. But the concrete fact is a surrogate, and a poor one at that, for the truly meaningful. Consequently, it cannot last for long. The result of the imminent breakdown of positivism will be despair, nihilism, and utter, tortuous meaninglessness. Out of this existential morass, possibly a religious-philosophical revival will emerge. Thus positivism, we may say, is self-destructive, since it denies the validity of that which is meaningful and makes meaningful that which is not. The ultimate consequence is that sensitive people will first lose interest and then despair, thereby deserting positivism and by their despair and desertion revealing its gross inadequacy and fundamental unreality.

The remainder of the twelve-page paper details the various false and vain appeals of positivism and its faulty methods. With its frequently awkward phrasing, oversimplification, pseudoprofundity, and meager sources and documentation, the paper was obviously a rush job, and Richard subsequently admitted to friends that he had put very little time into it. Much of its argument is nearly undermined by a paragraph which includes the opinion that "false opinionating . . . pervades the academic world." There is almost humorous arrogance in his declarations that "practically all opinions which are advanced today are in error," and that "the 'self' is the source of all understanding." But there is nothing funny about the confused and troubled state of mind which the paper as a whole bespeaks. In his effort to speculate on the psychological motivation of the positivist, Richard seems most often to be projecting his own inadequacies and conflicts.

A week or so after he presented it, Richard's paper was returned with Charlotte Zimmerman's penciled comment on the title page: "Not acceptable as a graduate term paper for completion of Soc 172 & 177." Her remarks in the margins of the text referred to a prevalence of cliché-ridden, undocumented opinion, and a general superficiality of treatment. In addition, she told him, his failure to deal in any direct way with primary sources rendered the effort entirely inadequate; with this paper he could expect no better than two D's.

Again Richard was incensed and impudent and refused to accept Dr. Zimmerman's estimation. Again after making a scene he returned the next day to drop off a note of apology, typewritten this time and quite formal: he wished to see Dr. Zimmerman at her convenience, in order to discuss a revision of his paper that would make it acceptable.

In an effort to be thorough with Richard, Dr. Zimmerman asked Father Lawrence Cross, the chairman of the sociology department and one of Richard's firm campus friends, to read the paper (he agreed that it did not fulfill the assignment) and called Richard into a conference. With the priest in attendance, she presented her detailed criticism of the paper. At this point a break occurred between Richard and Dr. Zimmerman, after which bitterness and hostility were often without concealment.

"Richard was really not a creative person," said Dr. Zimmerman. "He had no insight into himself, so how could he be expected to have any insight into anything else?" The question of whether Richard ever really wanted insight into himself is still very much at issue for Dr. Zimmerman: "In May he started seeing this one psychiatrist, but after a while he came back and said he had started going to another one. This went on and on until he said at one point that he had seen six different psychiatrists. And at that point I thought, well, there's no hope here—he's just running away. . . ."

In Dr. Zimmerman's Contemporary Problems, one of a pair of two-hour courses Richard was taking in the summer term, he and a dozen or so other students were called on to explore the relationship between industrialization and current manifestations of the modern crisis.

"That classroom was hell," said one girl in describing the prevailing atmosphere on the days during July when Richard would arrive and frequently disrupt the proceedings with interminable questions and arguments which seemed hysterical, vague, and beyond logic. His differences with Dr. Zimmerman did not seem to be ideological or philosophical but appeared as personal squabbles over minor, unessential, or unrelated points. He might stand up and scream at his professor, and Dr. Zimmerman might also raise her voice to say, "Wishnetsky, if you're not in this class as a student who recognizes me as a professor, get out!"

Apparently the only argument of memorable substance at this time involved Hitler and the Jews. Dr. Zimmerman maintained that Hitler had put into social and political practice the utter corruption of the Marquis de Sade. Richard protested that the Jews of the time were not simply innocent victims but rather a collection of sinners who had turned their backs on God and their religion and therefore in some measure deserved their fate.

TWENTY-EIGHT

Early in July Richard played tennis with Barry Kriger and talked about his plans for a scholarly journey to Greece, Germany, and Israel and his commitment to a life of scholarship which would exclude marriage but involve a string of piquant mistresses. "Barry, I've been through a very difficult period recently," he said, and described vaguely a series of deep depressions and a number of personal difficulties and problems. "I think I'm beginning to come out of it though," he said. "What I've been going through will enable me to reach a new spiritual level."

One evening a few days later Richard and Barry drove together to the *shivah* for the father of one of their friends. On the way Richard stopped at the home of Dr. Sander Breiner, the longtime family friend whom Richard had always seemed to like. Says Barry: "Richard told me his parents had wanted him to see a psychiatrist—this was the first I knew of it. He said, 'So I've been humoring them. They told me to do something and if I didn't they would cut off money, so I'm doing it.'" Richard and Dr. Breiner talked for about twenty minutes while Barry waited in another room. "Richard and Breiner came out," recalls Barry, "and as we were leaving at the door, Richard was saying, 'I know what you're telling me, I understand it completely but . . .' and Dr. Breiner was saying, 'Richard, Richard, Richard, there's no doubt about it, you have a very fine mind. We're just trying to protect you from that mind.' Richard gave a shrug and said, 'Okay, I'll see ya.' As we got into the car Richard made several comments indicating he didn't think much of Dr. Breiner."

It was an informal visit since Dr. Breiner felt himself too personally involved with the family to treat Richard professionally. The doctor knew how concerned the Wishnetskys were about their son ("They were taking a tremendous beating from him") and how Richard was constantly on the run from the doctors who were trying to help him.

"He enjoyed tricking psychiatrists," said Larry Walters, "and boasted of how he was manipulating them. He became sort of immune to the psychiatrists and he might say, 'This guy's an ass' or 'This guy's incompetent.'" Richard was now frequently to be found at the Walters's home, often eating dinner with the family, offering on their piano very loud renditions of show tunes like "Love Is a Many-Splendored Thing," and playing tennis with Larry at a nearby court or swimming in a neighbor's pool.

Their mutual admiration had continued to grow, but Richard's frantic behavior could put a strain on even this relationship: "One day in a water-polo game with some younger kids at the pool, Richard got into this Tarzanish mood, and I guess while we were wrestling around in the water I might have hurt him without realizing it. Anyway, he said, 'Larry, don't do that!' and while we were running around the pool he picked up this big long pole about ten feet long with a hook on the end of it—it's a device to pull people out of the water—and I thought he was kidding. But he threw it at me and I just ducked it at the last second.

"He wasn't malicious about it—it was a joke for him—but I said, 'Richard, don't do that,' and I was really quite perturbed. Richard at this time was hurting a lot of the people he loved and certainly himself. He was devastating, and some of my other friends were casting aspersions on me because he was my friend. For example, with my sister who's twenty and a lovely girl. Richard used to admire her and he'd come over to the house, and he'd be over-friendly to her and give her a kiss and put his arm around her. It was only done with the best of intentions but she finally had to say, 'Get away from me! You're sickening. Don't touch me.'"

Late one afternoon about this time, Molly Rosen received a call from Richard at her parents' house in Detroit. He was calling, he said, from the Wayne State campus and he had just been beaten up. He hastily explained that he had been having sex with a girl in her apartment that afternoon and her boyfriend had walked in on them. Later, he said, the fellow had cornered him in an alley and had pummeled him in the stomach. He was in "pretty bad shape," he said, and had tried to call Larry Walters and his parents but couldn't reach them. Would Molly drive down and give him a ride home? Richard had been unpleasant and insulting the last time they had been together and Molly didn't want to see him; still she felt it would be inhuman to turn him down.

After a twenty-minute drive from her home in northwest Detroit Molly met Richard at a bus stop near Wayne and found him lying on the ground. Coughing a lot, fingering his stomach, and acting as if he had been in a brutal fight, Richard got into the car. Molly felt he was obviously faking.

Richard said he wanted to take Molly out and suggested a restaurant near the campus for dinner. While they ate, Richard, in a critical mood, spoke derisively of Congregation Shaarey Zedek, its synagogue, and its members, but praised Rabbi Adler and once again pulled out the copy of the rabbi's essay which he carried in his wallet and read it to Molly. He spoke of fighting with his own parents and said he had been arguing with them recently when at one point he had pounded his fist on a glass-top table to emphasize a point and had shattered it. He seemed rather proud of his vehemence. Despite claiming a blow to the stomach, he ate well.

On the way home Richard explained that his parents had forced him to see five different psychiatrists. He was outsmarting them all, he announced very proudly, for he had presented a different face to each one and had given each a different story. Then he would tell each what the others had said about him and in the process completely befuddle and confound them. "I've been playing one off against the other," said Richard. "I've been making fools of them. They're just a bunch of fools, all of them!"

Said Molly, "The only fool, Richard, is you."

Richard replied with bitter insults, declaring her frigid and retarded. Molly, who had reached the point where she would trade insults with him, said, "You are just a total ass, Richard."

"You know," he said, "if I had a gun right now, I would kill you."

"Well, that's really ridiculous. You'd send yourself to the electric chair."

"Well, that wouldn't matter."

"It would. It would be a total waste to society."

"No, it wouldn't," said Richard. "If I killed you, then I'd kill myself."

They drove on for a while in hostile silence, but when Richard became insulting again and another fight ensued, Molly pulled the car over and said sharply, "Get out!"

Richard looked at her, opened the door, and then stopped. "I have one last thing to tell you," he said.

"Don't. Just leave."

"The whole thing," said Richard, "everything I told you on the phone was a lie. The whole story, the girl and getting beat up and everything never happened. It was just a trick to get you down here."

When Molly arrived home, she described the episode for her parents and was advised never to see Richard again. But the next morning when the phone rang and Molly answered it, she found Richard pleading in a pathetic voice for help. "Molly, I want to apologize . . ."

"Don't call me again," said Molly, and she hung up. The phone ran again ten times before stopping, a process that was repeated six or seven times until Mrs. Rosen finally answered and told Richard that if he ever called again or came to visit Molly, they would call his parents or the police.

One day as summer came to Detroit with a sweltering spell of hot weather, Richard returned to the apartment on Twelfth Street bearing an air conditioner. He had somehow made the acquaintance of a couple of young businessmen with whom he seemed highly impressed. They supplied building contractors with rebuilt air conditioners, he explained, and they had let him have one at cost for $120. Richard was excited about the deal and with the help of his roommates put the contraption in a window of the apartment. "The thing worked very well," said Pat Burke, "as a heater."

When his new friends refused to give him his money back, Richard called them several times threatening legal action; he wanted and needed the money, he said. On the U. of D. campus subsequently he approached a friend of Pat Burke's whom he knew to have an Italian name. Did he know anyone in the Mafia, Richard asked, and could he put him in touch with someone in the organization? He wanted to put some pressure on a couple of people who had defrauded him. When the fellow, somewhat incredulous, said he could be of no help, Richard asked, "Aren't you Sicilian?" Later the fellow told Pat, "Your friend is mad!"

On a day early in July, Richard encountered Robert Peters from Student Aid at U. of D. and began trailing him around campus, baiting him, and finally following him back to his office where he accused Peters of being a bigot and an anti-Semite. When Peters responded sharply, Richard told him to go fuck himself and then encouraged him to go ahead and hit him—he would soon have Peters's job, he said. This was a repeat performance of a similar episode and Peters had finally had enough. Get out, he told Richard, and never come back. Afterward he called Dr. Zimmerman who told him that the best way to handle Richard was to tell him that he was going to write a letter to the University of Chicago describing Richard's behavior and advising that they not accept him.

Because of his previous trouble with Richard, Peters had already written (but had never sent) a letter addressed to Father McGlynn advising that Richard not be allowed to enroll for the fall term. When Richard came in again acting belligerently, Peters read him the letter and warned that he might send something similar to Chicago. Richard left but came back days later in a very subdued mood to apologize. He seemed to be under sedation as he had in the past when he would come in to apologize in a meek and humble fashion.

Nearly every day at eleven Richard was meeting for an hour of coffee and talk with Kwitka Diaku, a girl he had introduced himself to soon after his return from the East Coast. She had been sitting at noon one day on a bench next to the red-brick walk at U. of D. when Richard had sat down to say that he had noticed her in the library. Full of questions, he soon learned that Kwitka, a darkly handsome girl, worked there while pursuing her studies as a junior in education. She had been born in the Ukraine during the war and had come to America with her family in 1949. Her family had been D.P.'s after the war and she had lived and gone to school in Germany. "Oh, how could you?" Richard had cried, implying that she had thus demonstrated sympathy with the Nazi cause. But Germany was under Allied occupation, she explained; American soldiers were there. Besides, her childhood had been a very happy one and she still recalled with delight the fantasies she had spun in the lovely woods of Bavaria. Richard volunteered that his own childhood had not been very happy; he felt that he had not been the "chosen one" at home. Kwitka said that as a "foreigner" in America she had frequently found herself not accepted in school and had often been unhappy. Richard implied that he had experienced something similar.

Thereafter through the month of July they met almost daily during the week on the red-brick walk. Usually they moved across Livernois to a diner called Leo's. Richard said he hated the Union and its noisy crowd of students, and described it as "a gray mass of nothingness." Kwitka (who had recently broken up with a boy she had been going with for two years) found him usually good-humored and looked forward to their meetings.

In their talks Richard often spoke of his desire for recognition and success, saying, "Someday I'll do something you'll remember me by." "He wanted to be acknowledged," says Kwitka. "He wanted to get to the top and have people accept him for what he was or what he considered he was." This was part of his trouble, he said; people were not respecting him as they should. At the same time, he could always spot the slightest pretense in others and this was generally why he had so few friends.

"He was not at all a child of the twentieth century," said Kwitka, referring to his religious attitudes. He said he could not accept the verdict that God is dead and talked several times of becoming a rabbi and changing the character of the rabbinate. Christ was a prophet, he thought, but he had been too idealistic and impractical. "What if you were Christ today? What would you do?" Kwitka asked him. First of all, said Richard, law and order had to be established with military discipline. A great percentage of the American people were sick, and their society had to be arranged more rigidly and systematically. There was too much freedom in the United States.

Kwitka tended to agree with him on this point but wondered how it would be accomplished. "With the force of a military dictatorship," said Richard. The violence of the Nazis was evil because their end was evil, but if the end was right and good, then the use of violence would be appropriate if it was the only way to achieve the end. Kwitka says, "I sometimes pictured him as trying to be another Christ . . . and he always said he might well die a violent death. He had an extremely pessimistic view of life. This was such a degraded world, it was not fit to live in. He would say, 'I wouldn't want to bring my children into this world.' "

Richard admitted that he had never had much luck with girls, though he considered himself good-looking and personally attractive. "He had this old idea," says Kwitka, "that the girl was the servant, the slave of the man. I said, 'Well, modern-day girls don't like that idea!' " Still he thought that Jewish women were too dominant and didn't allow their husbands to emerge strongly as men. He had dated non-Jews in the past, he said, and he would do so again. In fact, he seemed to have a crush on two girls Kwitka knew on campus: both were Catholic, both he pined over (insisting that one looked exactly like Barbra Streisand), and both were happily engaged.

From the start Richard had pressed Kwitka to accept a date with him, but she had consistently refused. Her firm Eastern Orthodox convictions ruled out the possibility that anything serious might develop, she said, and they could share as much enjoyment in their meetings on campus. Actually she had been made wary by reports of Richard's erratic behavior in the library and was frightened by the prospect of meeting him off campus at night. Nonetheless, Richard kept asking until it became a kind of joke. One day she replied with irony, "Oh, c'mon, how could you take someone like me out on a date!" implying humorously that she was too good for him. Standing over her as she sat on a bench, Richard became enraged and raised his left hand as if to strike Kwitka in the face. "Richard, don't you dare do that to me!" she said so sharply that it startled him. He apologized and never again threatened or spoke harshly to her.

When he came to meet Kwitka at eleven after studying in the library, he would often have with him Kahlil Gibran's *The Prophet*. Occasionally he would place Kwitka just so on a bench near the chapel and shaded by the large trees along the walk, while he stood on the bench and read dramatically. He urged her to type out sections of the book which they especially liked and talked about, and before she was finished she had copied over a third of the text. He also marked several lines as his favorites:

> For even as love crowns you, so shall he crucify you.
> To know the pain of too much tenderness.
> Your friend is your needs answered.
> Your joy is your sorrow unmasked.
> It is when you give of yourself that you truly give.

Richard was also helping to introduce Kwitka to Nietzsche and marked with a red pen many passages for special attention in her copy of *The Portable Nietzsche:*

> . . . combat is salvation; the cruelty of victory is the pinnacle of life's jubilation.
>
> Change of values—that is a change of creators. Whoever must be a creator always annihilates.
>
> Loneliness can be the escape of the sick; loneliness can also be escape *from* the sick.
>
> But it takes more *courage* to make an end than to make a new verse: all physicians and poets know that.
>
> Who sees the abyss but with the eyes of an eagle; who grasps the abyss with the talons of an eagle—that man has courage.
>
> For evil is man's best strength.
>
> To die proudly when it is no longer possible to live proudly.

Curiously, Richard also underlined several lines in Walter Kaufman's biographical sketch of Nietzsche in the introduction:

> The two great events in this period of Nietzsche's life were his break with Wagner and his departure from the university.

> . . . Wagner, fond of Nietzsche as a brilliant and likable professional ally, had no interest in him as a writer and thinker in his own right and stood in the way of Nietzsche's development. . . . If the friendship had given Nietzsche some of the happiest days of his life, the break was one of his most painful experiences; and if the personal contact had done its share to raise his horizon beyond philology and classical antiquity, the breach spurred his ambition to rival and excell the composer and dramatist as a writer and philosopher.

Kwitka noticed that in his carrel in the basement of the library Richard had arranged his books in a special way. On the right side he kept his "light" books—*The Prophet,* small volumes with titles like *Words of Wisdom from a Chinese Garden* and *Springs of Oriental Wisdom,* and a collection of Japanese haiku—which he would invariably bring up from the gloomy basement to read in the warmth and sunlight of the outdoors. On the left were his "dark" books—his own copy of *The Portable Nietzsche* and volumes from Dostoevski, Camus, and Kafka—which he would always pore over in the basement.

As he did with Nietzsche, Richard seemed to identify strongly with Franz Kafka, a German Jew who was tremendously ambivalent toward his father and the healthy bourgeois banality he represented, who sought without success the security of religion and who is described by W. H. Auden as "important to us because his predicament is the predicament of modern man."

Along with his "dark" books Richard seemed to be immersing himself in the literature of the Holocaust. "He had read all about the Nuremberg trials," says Kwitka, "and *The Diary of Anne Frank* and a book about World War II which actually shows pictures from Dachau, the concentration camp, and several others. There was one section on Nazi concentration camps, and he kept on reading it over and over and over again, and it just seemed to play such an important role in his life. I said, 'If it hurts you so much and you know it, why read about it?' And he said, 'Well, I have to know what happened to my ancestors.' I said, 'But they weren't yours. I mean of the Jewish race, yes, but not your family.' 'But I'm a Jew also,' he said. They were part of him, or vice versa he was part of them. When he talked he got so violent his eyes usually got bloodshot—very red. He really spoke out on this—what he was going to do someday. How he was going to punish these people—the Germans and anyone who was connected with this idea of supremacy. This was always in connection with the idea that someday he was going to do something great."

TWENTY-NINE

Richard's troubles with the staff at the library increased during the summer term. Most of the personnel working in the basement in the area of Richard's carrel were young—freshmen and sophomores—and not likely to deal very well with Richard's eccentricity and arrogance. Further they had a job to do. The library was changing its system of classifying books and, with the tasks involved, a certain amount of talk, movement, and noise was inevitable. Richard, having been on a capricious schedule for some time, might arrive at any hour and would create situations to antagonize the workers. He was not really studying, Kwitka thought, but just brooding over his "dark" books, and he would stop at the slightest noise and complain to those in charge. In turn some of the younger employees might on occasion speak loudly, drop books on purpose, or giggle. Then, too, said Kwitka, "He was so anti-German, so anti-Nazi, and several of the kids working in the library were of German extraction."

One of those who worked in the basement was Bob Fathman, a tall, clean-cut, and affable sophomore in the honors program. Bob had been in a class with Richard during the previous fall and had disliked him. But in May when Richard had acted belligerently one day Bob had courteously suggested that Richard might escape the unavoidable noise in the basement by studying on the second floor. Late one summer Thursday afternoon, however, Richard produced another confrontation by demanding that Bob push his noisy cart loaded with books over another route and not pass his carrel. This time both were belligerent, and Richard was soon flicking books off the cart one at a time saying, "Go ahead, hit me and I'll sue you." Bob went upstairs and reported the incident to his superior, who said he would ask Father Cross and Dr. Zimmerman to speak to Richard.

Richard didn't appear the next day, a Friday, and Bob didn't see him again until he was leaving at 4 P.M. after work on Monday.

There was Richard, spreading his arms across a doorjam and barring his path. When Bob moved to the adjacent door so did Richard, again blocking his path, and accusing Bob of getting him into trouble. He wanted an explanation, said Richard, as Bob momentarily jockeyed for an opening. Instead Bob turned and walked out an employees' door at the rear of the library. In the parking lot (where he found that his car wouldn't start) he subsequently caught a glimpse of Richard apparently waiting for a ride. Bob walked down to Six Mile Road and headed east toward a gas station on the north side of the busy six-lane street. After a minute or so Bob looked up to find a Ford traveling west on Six Mile, coming up over the curb, onto the sidewalk, and heading straight for him. Richard was behind the wheel and had with him a girl who had apparently just picked him up in the parking lot. "I had the hell scared out of me," said Bob, who jumped to the side and pressed himself against the wall of a building so he could not be hit. Richard brought the car to a halt, opened the door, and leaving it open into the curb-side lane of traffic, walked around and headed for Bob. "If he wants a fight, now that I'm off work I'll give it to him," thought Bob. Coming up to him, Richard clasped and shook Bob's right hand with his own two hands and said, "Bob, I'm very sorry for the trouble I caused you with my behavior at the library. I'm really sorry. You won't say anything about it will you, Bob? I was just a little upset—you know how it is." Bob replied shakily that he understood. Richard thanked him and got back into the car. The next day Bob again reported the incident at the library and was again told that the proper authorities would be notified.

One day about this time Richard showed Kwitka a loose-leaf page on which had been scrawled, "Jew: We'll get you too!" or something similar, along with several swastikas. He had just found it taped to the wall of his carrel, he said. Kwitka, going about her work at the library, had overheard some vague talk about such a project and was convinced that employees were responsible. She told Richard it was the work of immature kids who didn't know better, and did not really mean it viciously. Still, she says, "He kept on talking about it—'Well, who did it! Who wants to get rid of me?'—and he was actually afraid for his life."

A day or two later Kwitka received a call from the director of the library (a good friend to both her and Richard) who said that

Richard had reportedly frightened some of the girls working in the basement with a knife. He was going to be told not to study at the library. A few days later at their usual eleven o'clock meeting Richard pulled out of his pocket a hunting knife with a five- or six-inch blade in a sheath and said, "You see this?"

Kwitka gasped and said, "What are you doing with that?"

"This I need for my own protection."

"Not in the library!"

Richard talked again about the note and was actually shaking, said Kwitka. "They're punishing me!" he insisted, and she could do little to abate his violent anger.

Through the month of July after his return from Washington and New York Richard seemed most often to be in a manic mood. The tranquilizers which he said he had been taking since May under the direction of his psychiatrists did not send him into a depression and in fact, said Pat Burke, seemed to contribute to his sense of elation; he said he was feeling better. He was usually sleeping very little at this time, but this would change in a state of depression when he might spend eleven or twelve hours in bed and might nod off right in front of someone who was talking to him.

During this time Richard seemed to want a blanket commitment from all his friends in the Zimmerman group to back him up without question in the maneuvering he was doing on campus; they were his friends, therefore they should support him. His schemes primarily involved three goals: he wanted to get Robert Peters fired from Student Aid; he wanted money for his trip to Israel; and he wanted to undermine Charlotte Zimmerman's position at U. of D. because she had not accepted his final paper. (He never did submit a paper for the comparative religion seminar and received an "Incomplete.")

Richard asked Pat Burke specifically to join him in reporting that Dr. Zimmerman had made certain derogatory remarks about other people on campus, criticizing the administration and other faculty members. Burke replied that he could not do so, since such an accusation, as far as he knew, was not true. Richard implied that Pat was disloyal but said little more on the subject. For his plot to revenge himself on Peters he tried to enlist the aid of Greg Leszczynski, asking him to claim that Peters had also treated Greg unfairly. Greg said he had never had trouble with Peters.

"But you said you're my friend," snapped Richard. "Now you won't help me out. What kind of a friend are you?"

"Well, yes, I said you are my friend and I meant it," explained Greg. "But now you want friendship only on your terms and your terms are unacceptable."

Richard had become more and more quarrelsome around the apartment and much of his ire seemed to attach itself to his other roommate, Bill Winter. Usually Richard's threats were veiled: once in the midst of an emotional argument with Bill he asked, "What would you do if I walked up to you on the street and took your cane away? You'd be helpless, wouldn't you?"

After these incidents and others Richard's roommates and U. of D. friends saw little of him. He was out of the apartment a lot and the group generally tried to avoid him. They had begun to feel that Richard was becoming capable of violence and had wondered whether he should be forced to enter an institution. Says Charlotte Zimmerman: "Richard never threatened me to my face and I was never frightened of him. But I was frightened for the other kids after a while. They took an awful lot from him without saying anything, especially Pat and Bill. But they were really afraid of what he *might* do, and they were all ready to pounce on him every time he came near me. He wouldn't have done anything to me because he didn't have that kind of courage. He didn't really have the courage to face me after a while because he knew he couldn't fool me, he knew I saw through him."

On July 15, 1965, Richard sent materials concerning his application to the University of Chicago to Professor Gaylord at U. of M. along with a note indicating that he still planned to leave for Israel on August 1. Also on the fifteenth Richard typed out a résumé of his academic career which he subsequently carried with him so that a new acquaintance might note at a glance just who it was he was talking to. Richard wrote:

> Mr. Wishnetsky graduated with a Bachelor's Degree in Political Science in May, 1964, from the University of Michigan, graduating in the top one-half of 1% of his class. In his junior year he was elected to the Phi Beta Kappa Honorary Society, and in his senior year was awarded a Woodrow Wilson Fellowship.
>
> After graduating from the University of Michigan he had an opportunity to take a two-year fellowship to the London School

> of Economics, in addition to having been accepted to do graduate work at four universities; Harvard, Yale, the University of Toronto, and the University of Detroit. Because of his humanistic and philosophical orientation he selected the University of Detroit in order to study under one professor Dr. Charlotte Zimmerman.
>
> Mr. Wishnetsky will receive his Master's Degree from the University of Detroit in December, 1965. He has already been accepted to the Divinity School of the University of Chicago for January, 1966, having been awarded a full fellowship. The Divinity School is his second choice.
>
> Presently, he is awaiting notification as to whether he has been accepted by the Committee on Social Thought, also at the University of Chicago. Three members of the Committee are Professors Mircea Eliade, Saul Bellow, and Hannah Arendt. Dr. Eliade has agreed to advise Mr. Wishnetsky on his dissertation which will concern itself with the areas of comparative religion, philosophy of history, political philosophy, and philosophical anthropology.

As he indicates, he was still waiting to hear from the Committee on Social Thought, but within a few days he had decided to make a quick trip to Chicago to find out for himself how his application was faring and to explore the possibilities for employment around the university, perhaps at the Hillel Center.

Though it is difficult to substantiate, Richard apparently went on again from Chicago to New York as he had the month before: he reported several days later that he had been in Brooklyn in the third week of July, making a kind of pilgrimage to the Lubavitcher rebbe, the leader of the Habad movement, who resides in Williamsburg in the largest Hasidic community in the United States. Described by some Jews as "a kind of minor-league pope" because of the great influence he holds over the members of his sect, Menachem Schneerson takes on the legendary quality of some of his ancestors when it is reported that he may speak to an enthralled audience in a crowded hall for eight to ten hours, quoting hundreds of passages from a prodigious memory.

According to Richard, the rabbi advised him not to proceed to a study of comparative religions until he had devoted at least the next thirty years to the study of Judaism.

The night he returned to Detroit Richard found some of the Zimmerman group at Greg Leszczyinski's apartment. They gave him a rather cool reception, but Richard seemed quite happy with his trip. He had talked, he said, with a secretary in an office of the Committee on Social Thought and had tried to get her to let him see his file; he had learned that he was probably going to be rejected by the committee and certainly would not receive any financial help. When the secretary left the room, however, Richard said he got into his file and took from it the two letters of recommendation he was now carrying with him. He presented them to the group with much pride. One was signed by John Higham, professor of history at U. of M. and dated June 9, 1965. It read in part:

> One is almost tempted to think of a student with such breath-taking aims as a freak; but Wishnetsky has a hard-headed quality that may well enable him to make his way effectively across the grain of our culture and the barriers of our disciplines. I have rarely if ever known a student so deeply committed to the classic problems of philosophy and political theory.
>
> Wishnetsky's outstanding qualities are: (1) intense intellectual curiosity and genuine excitement about ideas; (2) strong sense of the importance of philosophical beliefs, especially natural law; (3) great clarity and logical rigor of thought; (4) judicious and scholarly but nevertheless lively way of handling problems. His term paper on James Madison was a work of mature craftsmanship, both detached and appreciative. I will not say that it was profound or massive, but it was very good.
>
> Wishnetsky's general poise and alertness are striking. He has a way of bringing a conversation that began on a particular historical point very quickly toward an interrogation of one's first principles—an experience that can be a little unsettling. Personally, he is polite, likeable, and extremely eager. Although not without some decided convictions, he is keenly aware of not having most of the answers.

The second recommendation was written by Frank Grace and dated June 10, 1965:

> I . . . can say without hesitation that he has given me more pleasure than any student I have had in 17 years of teaching. . . .
>
> In his senior year I directed his honors thesis which in my opinion was a brilliant piece of work but perhaps a bit ambitious for a scholar as young as Wishnetsky. I have never known a young man more eager to learn and more willing to expend

> the effort which learning requires. He is superbly gifted and will in my opinion become an original and creative scholar.
>
> He is a young man of the finest character and tries to the best of his ability to live according to the ideals and values of his religion. In short, I rate Richard Wishnetsky outstanding on every count and I am happy to give him this absolutely unqualified recommendation.

After Richard left the apartment with his recommendations, one of his friends remarked, "He's carrying his ego around in his coat pocket."

Through July Richard continued to call on Mrs. Joyce Oates Smith at U. of D. and to indulge in the long talks which she found "sometimes tedious, sometimes exhilarating." He appeared perpetually harassed, she says, and mentioned once that a good day for him was one in which nothing catastrophic happened.

Suicide remained a frequent topic of conversation. "I told Richard," says Mrs. Smith, "that if he continued in the direction he was going he would end up committing suicide." Richard persisted in his notion that he would never kill himself as long as he continued to believe in God, but did mention once, with a casual smile, that if he ever did decide to destroy himself he would arrange for it to happen in the synagogue of Congregation Shaarey Zedek during a Sabbath service.

They talked about the film version of *The Collector*, and Mrs. Smith found Richard identifying strongly with the young man who collects Samantha Eggar and holds her captive. "She didn't try to love him," exclaimed Richard. "This astonished me," Mrs. Smith wrote later, "because didn't he see—didn't he understand? One doesn't do those things, one doesn't kidnap a girl and force her to love him. One doesn't do that!

"But Richard had no concern for what one does or doesn't do, and I see that he was quite right about that movie: Of course she didn't try to love him. The beautiful young girl, normal and intelligent and artistic all at once, is the privileged world that chooses, quite aloofly, not to 'love' the abnormal, the unattractive. There is a certain horror in this choice, simply because it is done in all coolness, with no passion whatsoever. Passion is on the side of the madman; it enlivens and destroys him. Richard was the unloved, the lonely, the anarchistic Messiah who tells bitter 'truths' about the world and is hated for it. This was his role, a conscious choice. He was a person to whom the absolute was the only reality, and all deviation from it criminal."

Elsewhere on campus Richard, with his projected departure date of August 1 soon to arrive, was still in quest of money. He had tried without success to enlist the help of faculty friends to get what he wanted out of the Student Aid office. Now he went straight to the top and called on then-President Britt with a story apparently convincing enough that Father Britt subsequently asked the graduate dean, Father McGlynn, for an explanation. Finally Mr. M. Joseph Donoghue, the dean of men, called Richard in about the complaints being lodged against him. Richard was always a well-dressed, polite, and soft-spoken gentleman with Donoghue. In the meantime Richard's father had expressed the family's concern for their son on a couple of visits to Father Cross in the sociology department.

Some of Richard's old Mumford friends who had not seen him for a while found him in the summer of 1965 something of a puzzle. One who lived near the Wishnetskys' home noted a black pessimism in Richard during their strolling conversations in the neighborhood. Richard predicted that nuclear holocaust would someday be a reality as would a doomsday machine which might force peace if it didn't bring the world to conclusion.

Near the end of July, Richard and Debbie Rossman enjoyed a picnic on the grounds at Shaarey Zedek and spoke at length. Richard praised Rabbi Adler and the synagogue but deplored the falsity and materialism of the congregation. He had been miserable lately and had been seriously contemplating suicide, but the crisis had passed, he thought, and he was in control of himself. He admitted he had seen psychiatrists but was flippant about the possibilities of treatment. He indicted his friends who were involved in civil-rights or antiwar activity for wasting their time. He boasted of his success with women.

After they had finished eating he told Debbie he had always considered her one of the most attractive girls he had ever known. When asked about her love life, Debbie replied that she was at the moment living with a fellow in Ann Arbor. "Do you love him?" asked Richard. When she answered vaguely, he tried to kiss her. Debbie quietly made it clear that she didn't want to be physically involved with him, and Richard was immediately bitter. "Well, why not?" he asked. "You do it with everybody else. Why not with me?" Richard's scorn, which Debbie had felt obscurely ever since the time back at Mumford when he had accused her of having forfeited her virginity, was unmistakable now.

On Tuesday, July 27, Fred Baskin arrived from Berkeley for a short vacation at home. He had written to old friends Larry Bernstein and Richard, hoping at least one would come to give him a ride from the airport. Larry was there promptly, but Richard was nowhere to be seen as Larry and Fred walked through the terminal. Then up ran Richard to grab Fred's arm. He had apparently been in the coffee shop reading poetry to a girl he had with him. The old friends found a place to sit and talked for about a half hour; Richard, according to Fred, had a strange story to tell:

"Richard said he had just recently flown to Europe, that he had just taken the last of his Bar Mitzvah money or whatever out of his account and had just flown to Germany to talk to some professor . . . had spent only a day or so there and had flown back again. He said he was thinking of becoming a linguist, of going over there and studying German."

Though it is not outside the realm of possibility Richard's story was probably a fiction, since the people who were living with him and seeing him every day seem to have heard nothing about it. Fred was saying to himself at the airport, "Well, Richard has hitchhiked to New York, but this is something new!"

Because Richard had a date, Fred chose to ride home with Larry who was alone: "Richard was extremely unhappy about this. He looked at me as if I had just smashed his idol. Richard was sensitive, but this was peculiarly out of character for the Richard I knew." Richard did come back that afternoon to Fred's home, and the two made plans to have lunch the next day.

Some time later in the evening, according to what he subsequently told friends, Richard got into a violent argument with his parents in their home on Manor. He did not return to the apartment on Twelfth Street until about two in the morning and arrived about the same time Pat Burke came in. Bill Winter was visiting his family in Saginaw. Richard and Pat talked for a while, then prepared to go to bed; as they were going off to sleep, the buzzer rang. Pat left the first-floor apartment and went down the hall to the building entrance. There he found two uniformed policemen and a man in a business suit. One of the police asked, "Are you Richard Wishnetsky?" Pat, greatly surprised, said, "No, I'm Pat

Burke. Richard is inside." He led the men back through the hall and into the apartment where Richard was standing in an inner hall between the bedrooms. He said nothing and seemed genuinely surprised, almost shocked. The police introduced themselves and identified the man with them as a doctor. They said the paper one of them held in his hand indicated that they were to take Richard to Detroit General Hospital for observation. Richard was silent for a moment, then said, "Well, they've finally done it."

Very calm, controlled, and affable, Richard asked the police to wait for a few minutes so he could dress. The doctor left by himself. Richard got out a stack of color snapshots and handed them to the policemen saying, "Why don't you sit down and look at these. They're pictures of my trip to Europe. It'll give you something to do while you wait for me." The officers, who also were cordial throughout, looked through the photos. Dressed and ready, Richard came back to the living room and spent a few minutes pointing out things in the pictures.

He left quietly with the police, saying to his roommate, "I'll be in touch with you."

PART IV

The bullet was aimed at one man. Its target, however, was the human, civilized, free order under which we live. Its target was the discipline, the mutuality, and the law which through centuries of struggle and sacrifice man has built into his collective life. The demented mind that pulled the trigger represents an upsurge of the primitivism that threatens civilization, and betrays the persistence of pockets of feeling and attitude in our land not yet redeemed by American ideals and values.

Great as is our grief, we must retain an alert awareness that there are wild and savage areas in our national life. Our bereavement must not shield us from the recognition of our shared guilt. What bursts forth explosively in the case of the extremist exists in a quiescent and submerged form in the normal. What is a spot in us becomes a clot in the fanatic.

—RABBI MORRIS ADLER *on the assassination of John F. Kennedy*

THIRTY

By 4 A.M. on Wednesday, July 28, Richard had arrived with police escort at the emergency facilities of Detroit General Hospital. The temporary restraining order which had supplied the police with the authority to pick Richard up had been issued at a request made by his parents (reportedly with the advice and support of one or more of the doctors who had attempted to treat Richard) to the city physician's office at the hospital.

The metropolitan area's only emergency facility that must serve anyone who comes to it, the Emergency Room of Detroit General, sees approximately 100,000 patients annually. Richard was one of the 10,000 of these who are referred as psychiatric emergencies, and he would become one of the 3,300 psychiatric referrals who are actually hospitalized each year. Richard had gone quietly with the police, but he told Larry Walters later that he had been held incommunicado at Detroit General and had finally ended up there in a straitjacket.

Ideally, psychiatric patients brought to the Emergency Room are to be seen quickly by a doctor and if hospitalization is deemed necessary, are immediately to be transferred by bus to the Detroit Psychiatric Institute at Herman Kiefer Hospital. In fact, however, there are frequent delays of hours and at times even days resulting from lack of space in the mental wards of city, county, and state hospitals. Apparently in this case it took some part of the day before Richard was seen by a resident at Detroit General. The handwritten opinion of the doctor read as follows:

> Patient is 23 year old male who was brought to the E.R. [Emergency Room] because of recent bizarre behavior. He threatened to burn his parents' home down; steal car & drive it

> over cliff. He had made plans to go to Europe; is in debt and has not made provisions to pay. The patient is hyperactive; very aggressive; and could be dangerous if not hospitalized. He needs closed ward care; as he is considered both a danger to himself and others.

When Richard finally arrived at the psychiatric ward of Herman Kiefer, he was assigned to a tiny bare room with a bed, one of 120 for adult patients on the ward. According to what he reported later, he awoke the next morning, Thursday, and found his door locked from the outside when he tried to go to the bathroom. He had gone wild, he said, and had screamed and pounded on the door until he had been throttled by a large Negro attendant and strait-jacketed. Later in the day he was seen by a psychiatrist on the ward who concurred with the resident at Detroit General and added his name to the certificate containing the resident's opinion on Richard. All of this was for the benefit of the probate court of Wayne County, which would decide on Richard's fate for the next several weeks.

In the certificate the doctors also indicated that it would be "improper and unsafe" for Richard to appear in court on the date of the hearing. Meanwhile, on Thursday Edward Wishnetsky filled out a petition for the admission of his son to a mental hospital. In it he described Richard's behavior:

> He has been extremely hostile, belligerent, and threatening recently. He has threatened to smear his family with "scandal" although in reality there is no "scandal" to spread. He has threatened to burn up his mother's car and the family home. He broke his mother's golf club in a fit of anger. He also broke a large glass table top at home. He threatened to smear the University of Detroit with "scandal" if they did not prematurely release his scholarship funds to him so that he could use these funds to go to Europe instead of the University. He has been extremely hyperactive. Does not sleep. Makes innumerable phone calls day and night. Says he is going to get a date with President Johnson's daughters. He is at times very depressed, alternating with very agitated, frenzied behavior. Although very bright, he uses his intellect to verbally slaughter those around him in a very belligerent and hostile manner.

After Richard had failed to appear for lunch on Wednesday, Fred Baskin had made inquiries and on Thursday he arrived as one of Richard's first visitors. He found Richard in his small room and wearing a rumpled suit and tie. "He was doing his best with decorum," thought Fred, "to preserve his sanity, which is what I, what all of us, would have done in such a situation. Richard was very anxious and very nervous, almost with labored breathing, flashing eyes, and flushed face. I attributed this to his having been arrested and hauled down to that place, because I was plenty upset just having walked down the hallway. The worst cases are there, people staring into corners and people waving their hands around—everybody's in pain. You ask yourself, 'What are you doing in this place?' "

Bitterly angry with his parents for having him picked up, Richard maintained that his father was the one who should be sent to a mental home. Said Fred: "He went from anger to almost crying because he didn't have his books—this was a further injustice they had done to him. He wasn't sure if he were crazy or not, he said, but if he hadn't been crazy when he got there, he was then."

As they talked, Richard pointed out the attendant who had subdued him and said they were friends now (the fellow smiled). Still he thought unnecessary force had been used, though he said he understood why the fellow had felt it reasonable to establish as soon as possible that he was capable of handling a patient. Richard vividly described the fear he felt when he was being straitjacketed.

"He was trying to figure out what he should do to get out," said Fred. "He had been doing a lot of phone calling, trying to marshal his resources. But he was shifting very rapidly from one subject to another and was very, very upset." Richard's case would come up the next day, Friday, at a session of probate court and he wanted his interests represented. To this end he got in touch with a friend named Howard Levin (pseud.), an attorney with a law firm in Detroit. Levin had known Richard from the age of thirteen when Richard had entered the Brandeis A.Z.A. chapter, of which Levin was then a sponsor.

On Friday in probate court on the twelfth floor of Detroit's City-County Building, Levin entered his appearance as Richard's attorney. Either at this time or at some subsequent point in the case, some of the documents Richard had been carrying around with him were placed in his file—the article by the old Yiddishist,

Aaron Glanz-Leyeless, the summary of his academic record and plans, the statement of his proposed doctoral thesis, and his recommendations from John Higham and Frank Grace.

Judge Thomas C. Murphy issued a temporary detention order of sixty days on the basis of the report of the two doctors who had examined Richard, and set September 8 as the date for a hearing on Richard's formal admission to a hospital. Thus, he had a little more than a month before the hearing to prove to the doctors and the court that he was in control of himself. In the meantime it was agreed that Richard would be sent to The Haven, a small private institution where the expenses would be covered by the family. Judge Murphy turned the rest of the case over to Judge Ira G. Kaufman, a friend of the Wishnetskys'.

Also on Friday Richard was seen by a psychiatrist appointed by the court to conduct an examination and render an opinion. The doctor later wrote:

> Patient is a 23 year old male who has exhibited bizarre and confused behavior at home. He was a management problem at home. He was agitated and uncontrollable. Patient is still agitated. He is overproductive and overstimulated. He has grandiose ideas. "I want to study under the greatest scholars in the world. I will absorb their knowledge and carry on further." He has ideas of persecution and blames his family for all of his troubles. "My father and mother do not understand. They do not appreciate and are not aware of my plans." This patient has a manic depressive episode with paranoid ideations. Hospitalization and treatment are indicated.

On Saturday, the last day of July, another psychiatrist appointed by the court examined Richard and made this report:

> This 23 year old man is extremely talkative, going into great detail. He does not permit the examiner to ask more than one question. Often his subject matter is out of logical sequence. He says, "My father had me placed here. I asked the city physician to investigate. They came at three o'clock on Wednesday and I was in Receiving Hospital by four. It's been a conflict in the house over nine hundred dollars. I accumulated one hundred eighty dollars in debt. I asked for the money. I planned to take a trip to Israel but that's cancelled now. I want to approach an outside scholar. I got a scholarship in Chicago. My behavior is impulsive but in a definite direction. My parents

> stress the importance of behavior but they say nothing about direction. I went to Mumford High School and got a Phi Beta Kappa. I went to Woodrow Wilson School, Toronoto University and the University of Detroit." Diagnosis: Mentally Ill. Recommend Institutional care.

Richard had some access to a telephone at Herman Kiefer and managed to inform a number of friends about his situation and to ask for visitors. He spoke twice with Pat Burke and mentioned the brevity of the examinations he had undergone. They were going to put him away, he said, on the basis of the judgment of people who had only known him for twenty minutes. He asked Pat to visit him, but Pat was not anxious to see Richard. Father Cross, however, and at least one member of the Zimmerman group at U. of D. did pay a visit to the hospital.

Both John Samuels and Larry Walters saw Richard over the weekend; in his call to Larry he had announced very calmly, "My fucking parents committed me." He seemed jubilantly happy to see each of his friends on their separate visits, singling out each as the only person he could trust. Describing the brutality of the attendants and the incompetency of the doctors, he explained how he had found a loose bed board to protect himself with in case of further attack, and when they had tried to drug him, how he had placed sleeping pills under his tongue to spit out later. He took each on a tour of the ward and introduced them to the new "friends" he had made. With John he was serious and seemed concerned about the "tragic case" of a man who had been committed, he explained, because the Mafia wanted him out of the way. A brief sketch of the reasons for committal accompanied each introduction.

With Larry he was more flippant. "He made fun of the other patients but sympathized," said Larry. "There was one guy who was totally incoherent and couldn't talk and he had no teeth. He was in a straitjacket just fumbling around with his hands, and Richard introduced me to him as though he were his best friend already. Richard wasn't caught up in his own problem; he thought it was the most absurd thing in the world that he was there. These other people were really out of it, but he knew what was coming off at all times. He was not depressed at all. His attitude was a good one. It was an experience, an adventure. He said he was going to be transferred to The Haven and to him it was a big joke: 'Larry, it's fifty dollars a day! Tennis courts, a swimming pool, private grounds, a big mansion!' "

The Wishnetskys were also on the ward seeing their son during the visits of both John and Larry. When Larry arrived, Richard spoke with loud and bitter disrespect to his parents, saying to his father, "You really screwed me this time!" and finally forcing them to leave. He later told Larry that he was going to make his parents pay for what they had done to him.

On Monday the Wishnetskys drove Richard from Herman Kiefer to The Haven. Because they were afraid he might jump out of the car during the forty-minute trip, he sat in the back seat between Larry and another good friend who is a young businessman in the city and close to the family. Richard had asked that both friends come along for the ride. Upon parting at The Haven, he assured his parents that he would give the hospital a chance. He said he knew they were paying a lot of money for his care.

They would in fact pay fifty dollars a day for his stay at The Haven, located outside the community of Rochester in the northernmost reaches of suburban Detroit. (Originally the hospital had been part of a private estate which was disposed of in the aftermath of the Depression. Recently, because of financial reasons, it has been forced to close.) The air of an exclusive and secluded resort hung about the attractive old English-style manor house set well back from the highway and partially hidden by giant shade trees. The atmosphere was undermined a bit when one found that the screen-door entrance to the house had to be unlocked with a key by an amiable nurse. She ushered one into a large tile-covered foyer containing a circular staircase and perhaps a few of the "houseguests" who paid the visitor too little notice or too much.

The Haven had facilities for fifty patients, but there were only about half that many at the hospital during Richard's stay and only about a half-dozen males. The hospital had a good reputation in the community, and though the cost would seem prohibitive for any except those from upper-income brackets, the patients often represented a broad range of the social spectrum. The U.A.W., for example, had a program for its members which could get them or their relatives treatment at The Haven; thus at a given time, anyone from an auto worker to a bank president might be under treatment at the hospital.

Nonetheless, Richard identified the place as a kind of exclusive bourgeois health spa, existing for a few moneyed, boring, and probably worthless people and closed to the many poor, black, tortured sufferers he had met at Herman Kiefer who really needed help.

In the summer of 1965 Mark Allen was employed as an attendant at The Haven before returning to his senior-year courses in psychology at nearby Oakland University. Mark first encountered Richard on that first August Monday when he found the new patient on the front porch of the hospital "talking like crazy" with one of the other attendants. The tenor of Richard's stay at The Haven was accurately set from the beginning, Mark felt. The word had come through the "grapevine" that they were to expect the arrival of a very brilliant young Woodrow Wilson fellow, near the top of his class at the University of Michigan, with a preliminary diagnosis of paranoid schizophrenia. His parents, it was said, had acted to have him institutionalized because he had threatened to kill them and himself.

It soon became one of Mark's jobs to keep track of Richard, to take long walks with him on the grounds, and to join him in some physical activity like sawing logs. Richard quickly chose Mark as someone to talk to, though he didn't seem to have much use for most of the others at the hospital. Thus the patient and his keeper, the younger by two years, saw much of each other and talked extensively. Richard was tense and hyperactive from the beginning and at first explained his stay at The Haven as a vacation, a time for relaxation. He'd been working too hard, he said, and he needed some time off. This façade did not last long, however, and he was soon expressing violent opposition to his presence in the institution.

Richard always made sense when he talked, according to Mark, and always spoke coherently though very rapidly and with a passion which at times did not fit the import of his words. "He would overwhelm you with his speech," said Mark, "giving you little chance for a reply though he wanted you to listen to him." He spoke most naturally when the two of them were alone and without patients or attendants around. Otherwise, with the others he was constantly moving, gesturing wildly, and shouting. "Richard was a big job," said Mark. "He did not get along well with the other patients and attendants. He was very loud and disruptive, and many patients, being depressive types, found him intolerable."

Most of the patients were described as belonging to either "the old neurotics" or "the young psychotics" by Renah Lamm (pseud.), one of the half dozen or so in the latter group, who had been placed in the hospital at the beginning of summer at the age of sixteen. Her parents were members of Congregation Shaarey Zedek, and she had seen Richard at the synagogue on the rare occasions when she would attend services to hear Rabbi Adler speak. At the age of five she had decided that she did not believe in God and when reprimanded by her Hebrew teacher, had been defended in the right to her convictions by Rabbi Alder, who thereby made a friend for life. "He was the only man I've ever loved," says Renah. She and Richard now spoke about the rabbi, but Richard made it clear that Morris Adler was *his* rabbi; he was closer than anyone to him and knew the man's greatness better than anyone.

Richard's arrogant scorn for the other young people at the hospital and the violence which he often threatened produced considerable animosity toward him among the younger patients and attendants. They were soon returning his threats and taunting him with their pet name for him, "Wishywashy," which enraged Richard and frequently brought him to the brink of violence. He did slap a girl friend of Renah's one day "for no reason at all," whereupon Renah struck him so hard in the neck that he broke into tears and complained bitterly. "What's the matter, Mr. Wishnetsky?" asked a young nurse's aide. "I thought you approved of violence." Richard had argued hotly and at length that violence was the only effective method of dealing with the world's disorder and injustice. He now explained that violence was acceptable only when *he* used it, not when it was used against him.

Patients at The Haven were allowed to use the phone, but only at certain times and to certain people. To make a call one had to fill out a slip, get permission and wait for the proper time. This was always a source of trouble to Richard. Said Mark: "When Richard wanted something he had to have it right now. There were times when he simply had to talk to someone in particular. He had ideas coming to him which he had to get to people immediately."

With Mark, Richard often talked of the necessity for law and order. He realized that law must apply equally to everyone, but even with the law, he argued, certain exceptions were allowed.

Then why not at The Haven? Since he did not consider himself ill, he couldn't understand why exceptions to rules could not be made to accommodate him. One of his most vociferous outbursts came when he was denied the phone to call his lawyer: Richard began to slam large glass doors nearly hard enough to break them. Mark tried to calm him but without success, and Richard was left to just "run out of gas" as he always did after a while.

From Larry Walters's two visits to The Haven he learned that Richard hated everything about the place—the good food, the special care, especially the doctors and his lack of freedom and privacy. As he had at Herman Kiefer, he was making fun of the other patients and passing on gossip about them to Larry. They were really sick and needed help and perhaps The Haven wasn't such a bad place for them. He, however, was being victimized. He had none of his books with him, and only occasionally picked up *Time* or *Life* to leaf through. In occupational therapy they had him using a hammer to pound a design into a tin plate (make-work, thought Mark, satisfying perhaps to an old lady). After a few minutes Richard tossed it out a window.

Richard often praised Mark as highly intelligent and urged him to apply for a Woodrow Wilson Fellowship; he was sure Mark would win one. (Mark was skeptical, but later applied and was successful.) In addition to law, they often talked on their walks about free will; Richard ranted about the great fallacy of all the behavioral sciences in their refusal to see man as a free agent and gave Mark a list of four or five articles in various journals. Richard's favorite topic, however, was hypocrisy, which he extended even to Plato whom he seemed to dismiss as a thinker because the Greek had countenanced a form of slavery.

On one Saturday night walk Richard asked Mark how to get to Rochester and to Pontiac (also nearby) from The Haven, and Mark told him. The next day he attempted an escape. There was only one attendant on duty, and Richard easily eluded him, broke through the locked screen door, and headed for the highway. He might have made good his escape, but instead of stepping over the small decorative fence by the highway, he sat down next to it and waited for the attendant to find him. He told Larry Walters at one point that he was plotting an elaborate break in which he would blow up a doctor's car, set fire to one end of the hospital, and escape out the other. Friends heard about one or two other actual attempts. He had been foiled on one, he said, when a patient with two broken legs had tackled him; on another (or perhaps the same) attempt, he had been chased all over the hospital, finally ending up in the basement where he was subdued by a number of attendants and given a hypodermic. After the attempted breaks, Richard was moved to Room 1A, one of the high-security isolation cells for disobedient or violent patients. He was seeing the psychiatrist assigned to him three times a week but his behavior was becoming only more frenzied. In the briefings given to the attendants and nurses, little or nothing was said about Richard. He was obviously not responding in any positive way, and discussion of his case was avoided.

On Richard's first Sunday at The Haven he had a visit from Janis Newman, the dark-eyed, well-shaped girl he had dated early in the year, with whom he had discussed the possibility of choosing madness. He had called Janis during the week and learned that she had just returned from a six-week tour of Europe. They met in the foyer and Richard, very affectionate, kissed her several times. Most of what he had to say was a diatribe (which seemed understandable to Janis) against the hospital, the doctors, and his parents. He felt like the man in Chekhov's story *Ward #6*, he said, quite sane but trapped in a lunatic asylum. He showed Janis the recommendations he was still carrying with him and said he was in touch with an attorney who was going to get him out.

When Richard's parents arrived with his older sister, Terry, Janis was about to leave. "No," said Richard, "I want you to stay. Maybe you can be a witness for me." He greeted his mother and father, and they spoke quietly for a while about a paper Mr. Wishnetsky wanted Richard to sign thereby turning a bank account over from son to father. Richard vehemently refused and kept asking, "When am I going to get out of here?" He and his father argued in increasingly loud voices until Richard threatened to kill his father. Nothing was settled. He wanted to see his sister, but was told that hospital rules indicated that as a minor, she was not allowed in. Bitter again, he talked to Terry at the front door and kissed her through the screen.

In the week that followed, Richard spoke to Janis on the phone and seemed extremely upset. He was saying "wild things" which told Janis that he was seriously considering suicide. Frightened for him and feeling "quite reckless" at the time, she said if there was no other way for him to get out, she would marry him and have him released. The possibility of marriage had never been mentioned in their talks, but Janis had never entirely dismissed Richard as a romantic possibility. Now she was telling him to make marriage to her and not anything else his last resort. Richard seemed touched and said it was a wonderful thing to offer. He was quite sure it wouldn't be necessary, however, since his attorney was working to have him released. The offer was never mentioned again.

Richard's behavior at The Haven had become more and more impulsive and assaultive: he was throwing Coke bottles around and openly threatening suicide if not released from the hospital, and finally this threat had its effect. On the morning of August 19 Howard Levin, by arrangement with the hospital and the court, drove Richard into Detroit for a meeting with his parents and the probate judge, Ira Kaufman. Richard wanted his outright release, but Levin, Judge Kaufman, and the Wishnetskys agreed on a move to Ypsilanti State Hospital and presented this to Richard as a kind of compromise. If he could begin to control himself, he was told, he would have much more freedom and privacy at Ypsilanti.

Judge Kaufman, a conscientious man with a genuine interest in the problems of mental illness, felt himself somewhat torn by the case. He speaks sadly of the numbers of young people he must see in his courtroom who are often brilliant and talented but whose behavior indicates a desperate need for help. "But we must be especially careful," he says, "in admitting people to an institution, since the experience of the institution might be just what is needed to send a person into madness." On the other hand, Kaufman, as a friend of the family's, fully realized their dilemma: "If parents act against a child to have him committed, you know they're doing so because they have been plunged into the depths. . . ."

Thus, later in the day on August 19, Mrs. Wishnetsky drove her son a few miles south of Ann Arbor to Ypsilanti State Hospital, Michigan's largest mental institution, where little more than two years earlier Richard had spent part of his weekends visiting with patients.

According to what he told a friend later, he asked his mother as they drove, "Why are you doing this to me? Why do I have to go?" He pleaded, "I don't want to be there. You don't have to take me there. Let's just go home." Mrs. Wishnetsky continued to drive and said no, this was the best thing for him. He would get help in the hospital. Whereupon, said Richard, he spat at his mother.

THIRTY-ONE

Ypsilanti State Hospital, at the time of Richard's admission, was in the process of decentralizing its many and varied services in the new spirit of change which has affected public mental institutions in the past fifteen years. At Ypsilanti, as with most other places of its kind, there was at the time a mixture of the old and the new: many of the enlightened, more efficient methods of care and treatment inevitably mingled with the old failures, the sudden violence of the prematurely released, the wretched, blasted lives of the chronic sufferers and disintegrated human wrecks locked and forgotten in back wards.

During the preceding decade, more and more people had been entering American mental institutions each year where they were encountering new conditions and techniques which returned them to society in ever-increasing numbers. Two of the most important factors in effecting the change in patterns were a better understanding of the social dynamics of the hospital community (it became clear that anyone, regardless of the state of his mental health, might become highly agitated by the experience of conditions in many mental institutions) and the development and use of drugs to alleviate symptoms and aid in curative treatment. Tranquilizers and antidepressants, for example, have frequently proved effective in the treatment of manic and depressive patients, and certain complex tranquilizing agents have brought relief and at times apparent cure to numbers of schizophrenics.

With the increasing movement of patients into and out of the mental hospital, the chance that mistakes will be made in admission, treatment, or discharge naturally increases. A few months after Richard entered Ypsilanti, a twenty-year-old patient from nearby Jackson went home on weekend leave from the hospital and used a shotgun to kill his father. At about the same time, an eighty-three-year-old woman who was a former patient at Ypsilanti fell to her death from a Detroit hotel room window. She was reportedly the fourth woman released by the hospital as no longer in need of institutional care who had died in the same way at the same hotel in a period of five months. For a while charges flew claiming the inadequacy of medical care at the hospital and the frequent premature release of patients with suicidal tendencies.

In such cases, says the medical superintendent at Ypsilanti State, Dr. Alexander Dukay, who assumed his position soon after Richard's stay at the hospital, "everyone wants to find someone to blame and it's easy to pin the blame on the mental hospital because it can't talk back and defend itself." As Dr. Dukay points out, "Psychiatry is still a very young science; it is not a mature science. In fact psychiatry today is perhaps 80 percent art and 20 percent science. The psychiatrist today is working really more as an artist. Of course we hope someday, and I think we will be able, to work in quantitative terms which lend themselves to a more scientific approach. But until then we must do as well as we can with the knowledge and techniques we've been able to develop."

Ypsilanti State Hospital was opened in 1931 and now treats approximately 3,300 inpatients along with 5,000 outpatients for all types of mental illness. Bed space is usually at a premium and the occasional result is a period like the one which occurred recently during which the hospital refused to accept any adult male patients. The grounds are ample (fifteen hundred acres) and attractive in the summer, with many lovely shade trees and lots of bright green grass. A nicely kept nine-hole golf course occupies the front yard. Numerous three-story red-brick buildings with barred windows are clustered on the grounds; though everything seems properly tended, on the outside the buildings appear bleak, lugubrious, and aged beyond their years. A four-foot chain link fence surrounds the property, but there are several openings available to anyone wanting in or out.

Richard was assigned to a small dingy room with green paint peeling from the walls; it held a wooden chair, a table, and a bed with a thin mattress. The room was part of one of the large third-floor wards which housed patients who were generally much more obviously ill than he, but with whom he mixed very freely and quickly struck up a number of friendships. Despite the less-than-pleasant conditions or perhaps because of them, Richard settled down very quickly at Ypsilanti. He was kept on tranquilizers from the beginning. The drugs, along with an atmosphere which he described as much more humane, soon seemed to enable him to achieve a measure of calm and control which had been entirely lacking in his life for several months.

He was not placed under intensive treatment with a formal schedule of frequent sessions with a psychiatrist, because it was felt that he would probably react negatively to such an arrangement. Thus, his life at the hospital was not ordered in a rigid fashion and he was more or less permitted to arrange his time as he pleased. Unlike his experience at The Haven his relations with the staff at Ypsilanti, doctors as well as nurses, attendants, and aides, seem to have been generally good.

Alice Gretzler, who was doing casework at the hospital, was on vacation from her studies in social psychology at Eastern Michigan University. Having been assigned to Richard's case, she talked with him at great length, spoke with his parents, reviewed his records, and sat in on consultations. According to Alice, "Richard had special treatment at the hospital; the doctors and the staff took a special interest in him and his case and went out of their way to try to help him. Richard said a number of times that he was going to write a scathing denunciation of The Haven, but I think he knew that he was getting very good treatment at Ypsilanti and appreciated it."

Alice feels that during their long walks and talks on the grounds she got to know Richard quite well. He showed her the recommendations he always had with him ("He couldn't stand up without those things"), and he was always carrying books around—a different one every day—though he didn't seem to be reading them. "Richard was a very sick young man," said Alice, "though in his high moments he could appear normal and in control. In his deep depressions his front would dissolve and all pretense of health washed away." When Richard talked of escape, she argued that he should stay and help himself; he should embrace the chance to rest and refresh himself.

"We got along quite well," said Alice. "When we talked I agreed with some of Richard's ideas, but when I disagreed I told him so. At one point Richard got upset, called me stupid, and said he didn't want to talk to me anymore. But later he talked to another girl at the hospital who happened to tell him that I had a very high grade point average and that I was first in my class. Richard came back and told me that he had misjudged me, that he was quite impressed by my achievements. This kind of status seemed very important to him. I told him that I thought he simply considered anyone who agreed with him a good person, very bright and worthy of respect; and anyone who didn't agree with his ideas he considered a dullard.

"Richard said no, this wasn't the case, that he could respect a man who disagreed with him. When I asked for an example, he mentioned a rabbi—I'm sure it was Rabbi Adler—and said that though he and the rabbi had important disagreements, he still had great respect for him."

Richard apparently liked Alice and asked if they could see one another socially after he got out. Says Alice, "I couldn't, of course, give him my phone number or address. All of us were strictly forbidden to give patients such information."

On one of the first evenings he spent at Ypsilanti, Richard received a visit from Sharon Thompson just days back from her trip to Europe and Israel. She found him reading *The Great Escape,* the saga of a group of Allied troops who engineer their escape from a Nazi German prison camp. He was also, he said, learning how to box from one of his fellow patients on the ward, and seemed in generally good spirits as he demonstrated the techniques he had learned. He didn't want to talk about the details of his commitment at this point but spoke bitterly of his experience at Herman Kiefer and The Haven. "Of course I appeared crazy," he said. "I was picked up in the middle of the night and dragged off to a hospital, my sanity to be determined on the basis of five-minute interviews." He liked Ypsilanti better than the other hospitals (he was treated more like a human being, he said), but he was still talking half-jokingly about his plans to escape, about setting a bonfire in the place and taking his leave.

During the next few weeks Sharon drove in several times from Detroit to see Richard at the hospital. One day as they were walking outside, they approached a woman waiting in a car in front of one of the buildings. As they came up to her, Richard put an arm around Sharon and said, "Now, which one of us do you think is in the hospital?" The woman chose Sharon, and they all had a good laugh. "He was still very lovable," says Sharon. When his parents came for a visit one afternoon with Sharon there, Richard was "very good and gentle with them." Sharon knew that he had previously been violently hostile and later asked why he now had been so pleasant. He explained, "Oh, what's the use? It takes too much energy to hate." Still, as he was parting with his parents with Sharon watching out of earshot, he managed to snap the antenna off his father's car (accidently, he said later). According to Richard Mr. Wishnetsky insisted that they go in to report the incident to Richard's doctor.

Sharon's initial reaction had been that Richard's committal was a terrible injustice, but in their talks at the hospital she began to sense an intensity about Richard which indicated that he had been frustrated in a very fundamental and dangerous way. He spoke vaguely but intensely about how something must be done to change things in the world, how he was set apart from most people and forced to walk the fine line between genius and madness, with the former always mistaken for the latter. Still, his genius, he felt and hoped, would result in something good for the world, making it a better place; his creativity would be enhanced by the suffering he had been undergoing in the hospital. Richard proposed marriage to Sharon a number of times during her visits to him at Ypsilanti. She consistently declined but says, "After a while it came up so often that it became a joke."

One day as they sat talking quietly at a table in a lounge, Richard put his head down on his arm and mused for a time in silence. Finally he looked up and said seriously, "Once in a while I see myself as Jeremiah walking the streets of Jerusalem." He didn't elaborate and Sharon didn't press him. Jeremiah, the tortured prophet who spoke bitter, gloomy truth to a corrupt and hypocritical society, was no doubt a figure of great appeal for Richard.

Richard later reported that the doctors at Ypsilanti had diagnosed him as a borderline schizophrenic with suicidal and homicidal tendencies. Psychiatric reliance on the term "borderline" points up an essential dilemma of the profession. Because psychiatrists are dealing with the dynamic complexity of human behavior, they find the boundary often shadowy indeed between what is thought to be health and sickness, between different depths of sickness (neurotic or psychotic), between organic and psychogenic mental illness (which seems without physical cause).

Thus Karl Menninger suggests that psychiatrists see "all patients not as individuals afflicted with certain diseases but as human beings obliged to make awkward and expensive maneuvers to maintain themselves, individuals who have become somewhat isolated from their fellows, harassed by faulty techniques of living, uncomfortable themselves, and often to others. Their reactions are intended to make the best of a bad situation and at the same time forestall a worse one—in other words, to insure survival even at the cost of suffering and social disaster."

Psychiatry has come to view mental disorder, in its simplest terms, as a moving back to earlier, even infantile, ways of feeling, perceiving, thinking, and behaving. In the less extensive disturbance of neurosis the person still manages some measure of social adjustment and remains in touch, in spite of some distortion, with reality; his symptoms may or may not interfere substantially with his personal relations. Psychosis begins when the "maneuvers" finally leave reality behind. Whereas the neurotic generally realizes that what he is doing is not normal, the psychotic is often unaware that there is anything wrong with him, shows little or no insight into himself, and has lost his grip on reality. This was one of the border lines on which Richard appeared to be living.

In examination and in taking Richard's history from his parents, the doctors at Ypsilanti State were attempting to match his case with one of the classical pictures of mental illness for which methods of treatment have been developed. Many psychiatrists, wary of the damage that careless and insensitive labeling can do to a patient and aware that he may soon exhibit another syndrome, now refer to a *schizophrenic reaction* when faced with one of a number of different syndromes which they used to describe as evidence of a disease called schizophrenia. Schizophrenia, as dementia praecox before it, had become a catchall term applied to nearly any manifestation of mental disorder that seemed particularly puzzling. And even with the new concern for stricter terminology, a wide range of symptoms is encompassed by the different types of schizophrenic reaction currently outlined.

Most often mentioned as characteristic of schizophrenic reaction are (1) a disturbance of thinking ranging from an inability to concentrate, a mild vagueness or a confusion in the flow of ideas, to the elaboration of a private language or the adoption of a kind of primitive, infantile thought process; (2) a disturbance of emotion, which may include the fear, anxiety, despair, or ecstasy brought on perhaps in part in reaction to other symptoms; an intense, incapacitating ambivalence; or the lack of emotion altogether; (3) the presence of delusions, the abnormal beliefs opposed to reality and rigidly maintained despite logic to the contrary (often involving delusions of grandeur which convince the person he is God, a prophet, or perhaps a great scholar); (4) the experience of hallucinations—sensory impressions of external objects without the appropriate stimulus—which are most frequently auditory, the individual hearing strange noises or voices presenting orders or criticism.

The cause or causes of the illness have not been established to the satisfaction of most psychiatrists, but many theories have been presented with various orientations—biological, intrapsychic, interpersonal, and cultural—and notions about heredity, chemical imbalance, rejecting mothers, and neurotic family conflict all have their staunch adherents. In any case the result is often a progressive illness (in spite of seeming improvement at times) in which the personality disintegrates, the ego dissolves, and life is lived most intimately with fantasy and with no firm sense of self. In general the prognosis is not good, but, though a genuine "cure" is rare, many return to some measure of social adjustment.

A few of the different types of schizophrenic reaction seem to blend with symptoms of one of the other major psychoses. For example, the schizo-affective type includes symptoms characteristic of the affective, or manic-depressive, psychosis. In such illness either there is a generalized slowdown of mental and physical activity, accompanied by gloomy and morbid thoughts, feelings of guilt and worthlessness, and a sense of despair which frequently leads to suicide; or there is an increase in activity characterized by excitement, elation, and restlessness—a hyperactive state which often includes boisterous laughter, loud eloquent speeches, wild behavior, dramatic gestures, and a highly exaggerated self-esteem.

Another schizophrenic reaction type blends in elements of the paranoid psychosis. The paranoid schizophrenic generally tends to hold his personality together and to retain his grasp on reality more successfully and for a longer period of time. On the other hand, the fact that he does finally undergo some substantial disintegration of the total personality sets him apart from the individual suffering from paranoid reaction in which such a process is not supposed to occur. Actually many psychiatrists feel that paranoid psychosis should not be considered a separate classification and, if looked at long enough, will be seen to have a schizophrenic basis.

But Richard, though apparently described as schizophrenic in the hospital, was ultimately diagnosed as a paranoid psychotic by a psychiatrist who treated him after his stay at Ypsilanti State.

In the paranoid condition hallucinations are quite common, but the bizarre emotions and behavior which point to the personality deterioration of the schizophrenic are missing. Thus, the intelligence seems to remain intact and the emotions appear more or less appropriate. The paranoid person attributes hostile motives to most of those around him and is highly suspicious, meticulous, rigid, and aggressive; he is excessively sensitive to what he deems an affront, a rejection, or an attack and is at war constantly with unconscious inferiority feelings and often with latent homosexuality.

He relies most heavily on the defense mechanism called projection. Feelings of hostility and aggression too objectionable to consciously accept as his own may be projected onto various persons who are then seen as enemies plotting the paranoid's death, defeat, or humiliation. Such ideas are delusions of persecution, the hallmark of paranoid psychosis, and are frequently joined with delusions of grandeur which allow the individual to believe that he possesses the mark of greatness. In this way he can see himself in the most satisfying possible light—as a visionary, wise man, or prophet, for example, hounded and persecuted by the worthless masses who are incapable of grasping his vision of reality.

His delusions along with his suspiciousness, jealousy, and hypersensitivity make for considerable trouble in his personal relationships, and he may well constitute a danger to himself and others. Often what might be his most important relationship—with a therapist—is rendered impossible because he extends his distrustful and defensive ideas to the therapist himself. His future even with sensitive treatment is quite unpredictable, and he poses for the psychiatrist one of the most difficult therapeutic tasks.

After ten days of good behavior at Ypsilanti State Hospital Richard was given a pass which allowed him the freedom to walk on the grounds more or less as he pleased. Thus, when friends like Janis Newman or Larry Walters came for visits, they were given a tour of various points of interest. Janis and Richard started with the store where patients can buy cigarettes and other small items, after which Richard pointed out several buildings on the grounds, waving at one point to a man in a window who had declared himself, said Richard, a murderer. He had gotten to know the man, he said, and described violence in the backgrounds of other patients he knew. He seemed to take a kind of pride in befriending these people, Janis thought, and to admire the strength they could exhibit in hostility and violence. His friend, the boxing instructor, had complimented him on his strength, he said proudly. In displaying his skill he actually struck Janis with force, but seemed barely to notice that he had touched her.

They met a girl of sixteen or seventeen walking alone, and Richard started a conversation with her. The doctors had told her the week before, she said with quiet sadness, that she was a schizophrenic and that she would have to remain in the hospital at least five and maybe fifteen years. "Oh, don't listen to the doctors," said Richard. "Don't worry about what they say. They don't know anything. You know it's very simple just to walk away from here. It's a very easy thing to escape—no fences, no guards."

To Janis Richard still seemed convinced that he was not troubled in any way, but Larry Walters got another impression: "We talked about the fact that he was realizing his problem. He was realizing that he was sick, that he did need help. He didn't know when or how it would come about, but he was willing to stick it out and do his best. What made it so difficult was that he was so alert, so aware. . . . But whereas he had once thought that he just had extraordinary energy, he now admitted he wasn't normal and his hyperactivity was not right." As they walked on the grounds the two friends pretended they were chasing butterflies with imaginary nets. "As long as I'm in this nut house, I should act like it," said Richard.

Later they moved off the grounds and across a road and Larry asked, "Can you do this?"

"It doesn't matter," said Richard. "I could go right now into Ann Arbor and nobody would know the difference." He talked about possible escape plans—getting to Detroit, picking up money at U. of D., heading into Canada, and later going to Europe and Israel. "Israel was his refuge," said Larry. "It was his homeland, and I was going to meet him there the following summer."

The rates of escape from mental institutions seem to fluctuate in accordance with seasonal conditions as well as with administrative policies of varying stringency. Thus, during the summer of 1965 the rate at Ypsilanti State was at its usual yearly peak, but was also uncommonly high because it was generally known that the temporary administration at the hospital was continuing what had been a very liberal attitude; officials, it was said, didn't seem to care how many patients were escaping. Between forty and fifty people per month were leaving the hospital without authorization.

Since he took over as superintendent at Ypsilanti, Dr. Dukay has brought the average down, but he still believes it important that patients be given as much freedom as possible: "We're not running a prison or a concentration camp; we're running a mental hospital and we're trying to maintain the most humane conditions possible. The patients must feel that they are being treated as human beings in order to develop the self-esteem that so many of them lack." Richard, he pointed out, was not felt to be acutely homicidal and not a danger to himself or others while on the grounds of the hospital.

With his new freedom Richard had access to a public pay telephone of which he made considerable use. In three days at the end of the month he made eleven toll calls (three of them to the Southfield home of Rabbi Adler who had just returned from Israel) and charged them to his phone in the apartment on Twelfth Street before his former roommates told him they could accept no more tolls. Richard's parents had come to pick up most of his belongings at the apartment—a couple of end tables, his clothes, books and papers—and Pat Burke and Bill Winter had little desire to have anything more to do with him. Richard had called a number of times asking for visitors and describing his desire to get out. Pat finally argued that he should really give the hospital a chance because other arrangements had failed. "Some friend you turned out to be," said Richard. He seemed to feel that Charlotte Zimmerman had betrayed him (apparently he wanted her also to visit him). To Larry Walters, he would curse and slander her vehemently.

Marie Miller first met Richard at one of the dance parties she was in charge of at the hospital. Hired by the hospital along with several other young people as a part-time aide, Marie and a few helpers would set up the phonograph, dance with patients, and at times police couples attempting to go off together. Richard also showed up one night at one of the weekly sessions at which Marie had assembled a small group of patients for poetry reading, discussion, and improvisation with the patients acting out simple emotions or inanimate objects like a tree or a rock. Marie, a trim and pretty girl studying drama and education at Eastern Michigan, quickly found Richard likable and wanted to get to know him better. However, she and her fellow aides had been given stiff warning by the hospital that under no circumstances should they become emotionally involved to any significant degree with any of the patients. If they found themselves getting too close to a patient, they were to make very sure that they kept their distance, remained formal, and even to a certain extent, cold.

Marie found it difficult to follow these orders with reference to Richard. When he talked about the catastrophic social and political condition of contemporary society, she found herself agreeing with him and sympathizing because he was being asked to adjust to a society that seemed in a sense not worth adjusting to. At the same time, he was being forced to stay in a place which Marie considered in large measure inhuman.

Richard began talking about meeting on the bus into Ypsilanti after work in the evening. He spoke as though the rules did not apply to him and became so intense that Marie felt vaguely alarmed at the thought of what might happen if that intensity suffered enough frustration. But Marie's connections with Richard were severed finally when he came into the recreation department office one day and demanded that he be given her address and phone number. "I have every right to be given this information," he announced loudly. When he was not given what he wanted, he became enraged and caused considerable commotion. After this scene Marie was forbidden to have further contact with Richard.

"Things became a bit strained and upsetting," she says. "Whenever he entered a room where I was or got involved in a group I was working with, I would have to leave, just drop whatever I was doing and take off. After the incident in the rec office Richard became known among the attendants, aides, and nurses as a hard case and a troublemaker."

On September 1, two weeks after Richard's arrival at Ypsilanti, the resident assigned to his case wrote a letter to Judge Kaufman to advise probate court on Richard's progress prior to the hearing set for September 8, when the petition for Richard's formal admission to the hospital was to be decided upon. The body of the letter read as follows:

I have an opinion in the case of Richard S. Wishnetsky who was admitted to the Ypsilanti State Hospital on August 19, 1965, on a Temporary Detention Order. It is that the Temporary Order be extended.

From the information obtained from Richard, his parents, and other sources, it is evident that the patient has undergone a fairly marked change in character and personality over the past several months. Richard interprets this as the emancipation from emotional bondage to his parents over all his childhood and youth. However, his actions and his words have far exceeded the boundaries of a revolt which in itself might not be considered abnormal. Judging from observations during his period in hospital here, there has been some, and perhaps even fairly marked, improvement in his condition and general behavior. However, there is ample evidence yet of an emotional disturbance of considerable depth, on the borderline at least of a psychotic disturbance. With a patient of such remarkable abilities and capacities it would seem wise to be cautious in his treatment now by keeping him in hospital under supervision and therapy in an attempt to improve his prognosis in the long range view. We feel that if he is freed from all restraints now, there is a definite danger of further significant disintegration of his personality.

Mr. Wishnetsky, in our opinion, is still in need of in-hospital treatment.

THIRTY-TWO

What the doctors at Ypsilanti State were apparently most concerned about was the possibility (suggested by psychiatric evidence from similar cases of patients suffering on the border line of psychosis) that Richard might actually be in more peril now under certain conditions than he had been previously. Studies have indicated that particularly with certain types of schizophrenics, the risk of suicide seems to be greatest when the patient's condition appears to be improving, when he appears calmer, when his personality seems better organized and under more effective control. If such a patient is released prematurely and allowed to return to what is for him a stressful, "unsupportive" environment, chances are that he will be even less able to cope with the difficulties of living his life.

Richard later said that when he learned that the doctors were going to recommend that his stay be extended for another month or two, he decided to take matters into his own hands. On one of Sharon Thompson's visits early in September Richard wrote out a letter of transmittal (Sharon thought it was a will) signing over all of his possessions to her. He had the letter signed by two patient-witnesses and without explanation gave it to Sharon to keep. A few days later she drove him into Detroit to get his glasses fixed; he had broken them accidentally, he said, at the hospital and had been given permission to have the prescription filled by his optometrist in Detroit.

Once in the city Richard had several other visits to make and missions to accomplish. Sharon dropped him at the University of Detroit and Richard went to the Student Aid office of Robert Peters. There were no bitter threats this time: Richard said he was starting the new school term and had come to pick up the $808 stipend promised him for the fall semester. Peters replied that he could not release the money until he had word from Father McGlynn.

Richard went to Father McGlynn, explained to the dean why he was out of the hospital for the day, and said he wanted to enroll for the fall term. Father McGlynn referred to the trouble Richard had been having on campus and suggested that he get a recommendation from his psychiatrist at Ypsilanti. Of course the psychiatrists didn't know anything and were completely wrong about him, said Richard. The dean said finally, "Well, in spite of what you or I think, there are problems. Now get yourself to a psychiatrist you trust, someone you can work with, and then come back to see us when you've been able to solve some of these problems." Before leaving the campus, Richard also spoke with Father Cross and managed to enlist his support. The chairman of the sociology department later argued without success that Richard should be allowed to stay in school, that it would be perhaps therapeutic for him to remain in the atmosphere of the university.

Sharon then drove Richard to the apartment on Twelfth. When they knocked on the door, Bill Winter, alone in the apartment and by now thoroughly afraid of Richard, refused to let them in. "Why are you here?" he asked. Richard explained and said he wanted to get something in the apartment. Bill refused to open the door, and Richard went for the landlady who let them in. Once inside they never saw Bill, who remained in a bedroom. Before leaving, Richard spotted Bill's cane in the living room and bringing it to the kitchen, hid it behind the refrigerator. "What did you do that for?" asked Sharon as they left. Richard said his roommates, particularly Winter, had been unkind to him and had generally ignored him. He felt like doing something in return, he said, and went off to visit some of his other friends or ex-friends in the Zimmerman group.

Later Greg Leszczynski came over to keep Bill Winter company at the apartment lest Richard should return. Instead they received a phone call from him. Greg explained that the remainder of Richard's belongings were all packed and ready to be picked up and asked just what it was Richard wanted. "Money," said Richard: Burke and Winter owed him the twenty dollars he had paid for the August rent. Greg said that it was his understanding that because of a thirty-dollar phone bill, Richard owed *them* money. Richard closed the conversation with screaming and cursing. Later in the evening Sharon drove him back to Ypsilanti.

Within two days, on Thursday, September 9 (Richard's September 8 hearing had been delayed to the fifteenth), Sharon returned to the hospital and found Richard ready for another trip into Detroit, this time with a bundle of clothes. As they drove away, he explained that he did not have permission to leave and was embarking upon his escape. Sharon drove past the I–94 Freeway into Detroit and headed for Ann Arbor on some pretext which would give her time to think. There she met a friend and privately told him the situation; he suggested she call the hospital. When she did, she was told not to worry but to simply drive Richard back to the hospital.

Sharon and her friend got into the car and started back with Sharon driving and Richard in the front seat next to her. When it became clear they were returning to the hospital, he become extremely angry and began threatening to blackmail Sharon ("which was pretty silly since there was nothing to blackmail me about"). Putting his hand on the gearshift, he then threatened to strip the car's gears until Sharon also put her hand on the gearshift. As they turned in at the hospital entrance, Richard released a forlorn scream and asked to be let out of the car. Sharon stopped the car, let him out, and drove on to the building that contained his ward, where she spoke to the resident on Richard's case who assured her that she had done the right thing. As Sharon and her friend drove off, they spotted Richard sitting in the middle of a large green field on the hospital grounds.

That night Sharon received a call from Richard who said he was in Chicago; he gave no details but said he had escaped and would be in touch with her again soon. Also, that night the Ypsilanti State Police post broadcast a teletype report throughout Wayne County stating that a mental patient named Richard S. Wishnetsky had escaped from the Ypsilanti State Hospital and should be considered dangerous.

Beyond simply wanting out Richard seems to have wanted the experience of escape—it had perhaps been a large part of his fantasy life before his actual move—of being on the run, pursued and hounded, but outrunning and outwitting and suffering the exhilaration and despair of the innocent prey.

At 7:30 the next morning, a Friday, David Secter was awakened in his basement apartment in Toronto by a phone call from Richard, who said he had just arrived in the Canadian city after leaving Detroit in a rush and without money. Could he drop by? he wondered. Of course, said David, and gave him street directions.

David Secter was about to become Canada's most celebrated twenty-two-year-old filmmaker. He was doing the final editing on a feature-length film called *Winter Kept Us Warm,* which he had written, produced, and directed on an $8,000 budget with the help of a group of fellow students at the University of Toronto and which would soon win acclaim in festivals at Cardiff, Wales, and Cannes. Five years earlier in the summer of 1960, David had come from Winnipeg to attend the B.B.Y.O. convention in Pennsylvania, where he had met the contingent from Mumford High School. Over the years he had kept in touch with most of them, though not with Richard, so that the call had come as a surprise. David warmly welcomed Richard when he arrived a half hour later: "I didn't question his reasons for coming up here with no money. I have a fair number of friends who are apt to do this sort of thing —just pull up on the spur of the moment and appear somewhere with little money and looking for a place."

From the convention, David remembered Richard as excitable,

eccentric, and attractively intense, and the impression he received now generally matched his memories. He had heard from his Detroit friends about the highlights of Richard's academic career and now learned from Richard that he had hitchhiked in from Detroit, that he carried with him impressive recommendations but lacked visa or passport, that things were going well in his life, that he might be studying with Paul Tillich soon, and that he was in Toronto to take out Israeli citizenship. Says David:

"I thought he was being a bit naïve in thinking that it could be arranged so quickly without any papers or anything. But he looked up the Israeli Consulate and I suggested he get in touch with the Zionists or the B'nai B'rith, and eventually he did and found somebody he could talk to who represented the Israeli government."

This Richard did during the morning while David put in a stint in the editing room. Also during the morning Richard called Sharon Thompson, told her where he was, and asked her to acquire his passport by calling on his parents and using the letter of transmittal he had given her. Instead Sharon went to see Richard's attorney, Howard Levin, who seemed very put out by what she told him. Richard had apparently broken his word to Levin by escaping.

About noon Richard joined David at the editing room: "By this time he had found that he simply couldn't get Israeli citizenship for the asking. He was under the impression that any Jew could demand Israeli citizenship. I think it is true if you turn up in Israel, but not under these circumstances. Anyway, this dashed his hopes in that direction." At this point Richard called and asked for money from a friend in Detroit. David had already learned of Richard's alienation from his family and began to suspect that he was in some sort of difficulty.

Throughout the afternoon Richard watched David and his friends work with segments of the film and appeared excited by it. "He seemed to get involved in the story and theme of the movie very quickly and easily," says David. "It deals with two young people trying to make contact, trying to communicate. For a time they're very successful. Quite a beautiful rapport develops, but it doesn't last."

Later Richard and David rode the latter's yellow Lambretta into one of Toronto's pleasant newer neighborhoods to the home of Samuel Eckler and his family with whom David had something of a standing invitation for dinner on Friday evenings. The evening included an excellent Sabbath meal preceded by the traditional lighting of candles and a brief chant by one of the Eckler boys. Through dinner Richard was amicable and seemed quite taken with the Ecklers.

In the "good, roaring, stimulating discussion" which followed, however, the first rift appeared. Pronouncing on issues, particularly the disintegration of the family in modern society (of which he spoke almost as if it were a dead issue), Richard cited in the argument which ensued his own troubles at home. He had been victimized by his hypocritical parents.

Later when the talk turned to philosophy and religious history the rift widened and the discussion became more heated. Richard's arrogant convictions and sweeping dismissals antagonized his host and soured the atmosphere until Richard rather quickly became quiet and apologetic. "He seemed almost on the verge of breaking down into tears," said Mr. Eckler. "He became very humble and apologetic and even said that perhaps he had been wrong about the point I was trying to make. Finally he said something about people not loving him and always reacting negatively toward him. And I said, 'Well, Richard, you've come into our home and have almost immediately shown contempt and been patronizing. You haven't given us a chance at all to develop an affection for you. How can you expect affection to develop if you behave in this way?' " Richard agreed that perhaps he had been responsible and again apologized. On the way back to David's apartment, Richard explained that he had just escaped from a mental hospital.

"He announced it in a way as if to shock me," says David. "He even made a little game of it and asked me if I was still willing to sleep beside him. I said, 'By all means . . . We all have to go sometime.' At this time he asked me if I thought he was insane and we finally discussed his experiences. Because Richard struck me as having his faculties quite fully intact, I went along with his feeling that he'd been victimized. He told me that the reason he'd had to escape was that he'd felt that he was going out of his mind, and when he described the mental hospital, this again was quite convincing.

"He said, I think, that his parents found him a nuisance, that he was pointing out their failings and their errors and that they found this embarrassing, and this was the reason that they had him put away. The implication was definitely that he was an innocent victim, an embarrassment like the prophet ringing the truth. And yet when I asked him for details and he gave me some, they seemed not out of the ordinary—things which might be mentioned by any young man who felt the gulf between the generations and was having difficulty getting along with his parents."

Before they went to sleep, Richard explained that he had been in touch with his attorney in Detroit who was acting as a go-between. He had been assured, he said, that his parents would ask to have the petition for committal withdrawn and would not act again to have him committed if he returned and promised to see a psychiatrist on a regular basis outside the hospital. In the morning he would catch a train back to Detroit.

At the station on Saturday David loaned him ten dollars which he promised to return—and did by mail a few days later with a note of thanks and the report that a happy solution had been found. "He was full of plans again," said David, "but apparently giving up the European idea in order to go to the University of Chicago in the spring."

To Sharon Thompson Richard seemed happy and relieved when she saw him the day after his return. He didn't talk much about the hospitals or his escape, but that night Richard and Sharon and Larry Walters went out to celebrate Richard's new freedom. Though pleased to have with him two of the friends who had proved most loyal during his ordeal, Richard was unaware of a new element in their relationships. Sharon and Larry had often talked on the phone about their mutual friend, and on their first meeting they had become interested enough in each other to meet every night for three weeks thereafter. The three went out together several times in the first weeks after Richard's return. Larry says: "I'd pick Richard up and then Sharon and then we'd go somewhere, and afterward I'd drop Richard off and spend the rest of the evening with Sharon. And he didn't know this! If we went to a show together he held her hand in the show, he put his arm around her, and Sharon would give me a little look out of the corner of her eye, like 'What can I do?' I would get a little irked, not because of what he was doing, but because he was so blind! He was so public in his affection and it wasn't that necessary. Once Sharon asked him very tactfully to lay off, and he said, 'But why? I love you.' I felt very badly for him."

Richard was talking brightly again about his plans: he would be starting at the divinity school in Chicago in January, and in the meantime he would relax and make himself useful by teaching, going to the University of Detroit, or holding a part-time job. He seemed more in control and on the road to improvement, thought Sharon. Though he referred to his stay in the hospitals as a nightmarish experience, it had been in a way worthwhile, he said, because he had gotten to know the inside of the place and what the people there were like. Still he expressed his horror at the tactics used at Herman Kiefer and The Haven and saw his father as a Gestapo agent in the unhappy episode.

Even here Larry Walters thought he saw some improvement: "Again he was recognizing his problem, but he had more faith in his parents. If you treated Richard with love, you got the respect and cooperation you wanted. And this was a situation where Richard's parents had demonstrated their sympathies, their concern, and their sincerity in trying to help him."

A week after his return Janis Newman drove over to the Wishnetskys' home on Manor in response to a phone call from Richard. They went for a walk in the neighborhood, which had become increasingly integrated in recent years, and Richard explained that his parents were about to move to a home in the upper-middle-class section of Detroit east of Livernois known as Palmer Woods.

When the first Negro family had moved onto the block—in a house next door to the Wishnetskys—Richard's parents had called a block meeting and, with others like the Faumans, had urged that their neighbors not panic. Mr. Wishnetsky asked that everyone on the block sign a statement promising not to move out. Two families, however, immediately announced that they would depart as soon as possible, and when the Faumans became the fourth family to move about two years later, it was clear that the tide would not be stemmed. From the start Richard had been very upset by the idea of his parents moving and argued with them bitterly about it. At least in his conversations, what seemed to trouble him most was the simple fact of change in the old neighborhood he had known and loved as a boy.

At the September 15 hearing in probate court, Judge Kaufman agreed to the request of Richard and his parents that he be allowed to remain out of the hospital. With an eye, however, to the report issued from Ypsilanti State on September 1, the judge extended the temporary detention order for another sixty days past the previous expiration date of September 27, during which time Richard would still be under the jurisdiction of the court and could be picked up and returned quickly to the hospital if his behavior warranted it. All of this was on the condition that Richard get himself to a psychiatrist. Another hearing on the original petition for admission was scheduled for November 10. Two days later, on September 17, Ypsilanti State Hospital placed Richard on convalescent status.

The psychiatrist Richard chose to begin seeing three or four times a week was Dr. Irving Silver (pseud.), European-born and a survivor of Hitler's concentration camps. It wasn't long before Richard was telling friends that he was completely at odds with Dr. Silver philosophically and simply couldn't bear the man.

Their relationship was further strained when Dr. Silver reported to the dean of students at the University of Detroit, Mr. Donoghue, that he could not guarantee that Richard would not cause trouble again on campus if he were allowed to reenroll. Richard had called Donoghue and had asked for permission to resume his studies at the University of Detroit, and the dean had responded by asking him to have three psychiatrists provide reports on his mental and emotional condition. If he got one favorable report, he would heed Father Cross's advice and allow Richard to enroll. Dr. Silver's was the only report received, and thus Donoghue decided against Richard's return.

While most who now encountered Richard noted his new calm and control, his former roommates and friends in the Zimmerman group at the University of Detroit saw little change in him. A number of unpleasant scenes occurred at the apartment on Twelfth Street, on campus, or over the phone during the remainder of September, most of them centering around Richard's notion that he had money coming to him because of the August rent he had paid, and his accusation that most of them, particularly his roommates, had forsaken him in the hospitals.

He was "wild, loud, and shouting" at such times, say Pat Burke and Greg Leszczynski, and would accuse them of not helping him get out of the hospital (quite true and they felt more than ever that he should not have been given his freedom). "You were kicking a man when he was down!" wailed Richard. "Not helping me when I was at Ypsilanti was like killing me. You're all shitting on me." On the phone once he told Pat, "There's a justice in this world!" Pat felt this to be a genuine threat and tried to get Richard to spell it out. Richard, however, remained effectively vague: "You're going to wish you had never been born!"

Pat finally called Mr. Wishnetsky and told him that Richard had been threatening people and acting in a generally menacing fashion. But before their conversation could proceed Richard picked up an extension and shouted, "You'll have to stop calling here and threatening me!" and continued to scream into the phone until Pat hung up. Things were a bit different some time later when Pat met Richard one evening on campus. He appeared calmer but was still tense underneath, thought Pat. At one point, Richard asked if Pat had ever been willing to kill somebody. No, said Pat. "Well, you know," said Richard, "I learned something in the institution—I learned what it feels like to be willing to kill somebody." He had wanted to get out so badly, he said, that he had really felt capable of killing somebody if necessary.

Others on campus were also treated to Richard's feelings on the subject of the hospitals. He had been dealt with as if he were a citizen of a totalitarian state, he told a friend on the faculty. There had been shock treatment and other horrors; it had been as if he were living in Nazi Germany. Professor Budzinowski, as usual, had some stern fatherly advice: "There's something that doesn't click between you and the world. Until you come to terms with your vision of your family, friends, and people in general, you're not going to be able to accomplish anything. You're not an idiot, you're not crazy. You have much talent, but you're wasting it." As always Richard seemed to agree, but when the story of his hiding Bill Winter's cane (it had been found a few days later) finally reached Professor Budzinowski, his words were even stronger: "I never thought you were capable of such a vicious thing."

People didn't understand him and his eccentricities and were trying to make him think he was sick, he told Kwitka Diaku. Still meeting her on campus at the University of Detroit, he continued to ask Kwitka for a date, and she consistently refused. She did, however, drive with him early one afternoon to Shaarey Zedek to view the building. Kwitka was impressed but Richard said, "Yes, but the people who worship here are not so impressive." "You can't condemn these people," Kwitka argued. "They're wealthy businessmen—they have money, and you have to have money to construct buildings." But the only reason they gathered at the synagogue, said Richard, was to talk about money. "I admire Rabbi Adler as a man and as a person," he said, "but not the role he is fulfilling now because he is not fulfilling it as a rabbi. He is too often going along with the people and catering to the nonreligious." When Richard spoke of how he was going to "accomplish a mission," Kwitka thought he meant that he was going to become a rabbi.

At least a couple of times Richard accompanied Kwitka to the 4:30 class in existential literature she was taking on Tuesdays and Thursdays from Mrs. Joyce Smith. Mrs. Smith recalls his first visit quite vividly: "This was the first time I had seen him in a situation involving others. He shocked the class—which probably felt sorry for me—by talking wildly and with dizzying generalizations, wrenching the discussion from 'The Damnation of Theron Ware' to Goethe, Shakespeare, Aristotle. What stays in my mind about that class period is his aristocratic, contemptuous dismissal of the other students—they really did not exist for him. He remarked later that they were all negligible, except for one of them—the only one he knew! All this with good humor, with charm . . ."

Richard seemed almost always in an elated, manic mood when he came to see Mrs. Smith; often his argument bordered on the incoherent. When he asked her to be his thesis adviser (because, he said, she was the only one on campus capable of understanding what he wanted to do) she said there must be many people on campus better qualified. Occasionally she would return from a class, having left her office door open, to find Richard sitting at her desk and going through her books and papers.

The strain of having to deal naturally with Richard finally began to take its toll, and Mrs. Smith came to dread coming back to her office. He seemed more insistent than ever in his demands on her time and concern, and in an effort to keep him at arm's length, she told him that if they were going to talk anymore he would have to buy her lunch. Richard agreed and at noon one day they walked across Livernois to eat at the U. of D. Pizzeria. Afterward he discovered he had no money to pay the bill. He never really said good-bye, says Mrs. Smith, but toward the end of September he just stopped coming around.

One day a bit earlier Richard, on one of his visits to his old apartment, proudly told Pat Burke that he had learned that Mrs.

Smith was writing a short story about a character based on him. Exactly how he came by such information is not clear, but in any case he seemed to feel pleased and honored at the prospect of having himself "immortalized." In fact, Mrs. Smith did write a story based to some extent upon her experience with Richard, including a character modeled substantially on him. It was sold to *The Atlantic,* published in the August 1966 issue, and subsequently selected for the O. Henry Award as the finest short story of the year.

The story, "In the Region of Ice," is told from the point of view of Sister Irene, a young nun who is teaching literature at a Jesuit university and whose self-satisfaction is undermined one day with the arrival of a new student. Allen Weinstein, in his bold, manic, egotistical way, argues himself into her course. In the classroom his long speeches are disruptive, he fails to arrive on time with the first paper assigned, he is irritating and presumptuous. Still her sympathy goes to him because she recognizes "a terrified prisoner behind the confident voice." As they walk on the campus, he tries to explain what is important to him:

> "Sister Irene, think of the significant men in the last century, the men who've changed the world! Jews, right? Marx, Freud, Einstein! Not that I believe Marx, Marx is a madman . . . and Freud, no, my sympathies are with spiritual humanism. I believe that the Jewish race is the exclusive . . . the exclusive, what's the word, the exclusive means by which humanism will be extended . . . Humanism begins by excluding the Jew, and now," he said, with a high surprised laugh, "the Jew will perfect it. After the Nazis, only the Jew is authorized to understand humanism, its limitations and its possibilities.

When she responds to him in even a minimal way, the intensity of his own response is so great that she is "terrified by what he was trying to do—he was trying to force her into a human relationship." Then Allen Weinstein disappears. Eventually she receives a letter from him which explains that he is in a mental hospital and indicates that he is contemplating suicide. Alarmed, the nun makes an awkward and unsuccessful trip to the Weinstein home to warn Allen's parents. A month later Allen comes again to her office and describes his stay at the hospital:

> "Do you know what that is," Weinstein demanded savagely, "not to be treated like a human being? They made me an ani-

mal—for fifty dollars a day! Dirty filthy, swine! Now I'm an outpatient because I stopped swearing at them. I found somebody's bobby pin, and when I wanted to scream I pressed it under my fingernail, and it stopped me—the screaming went inside and not out—so they gave me good reports, those sick bastards, now I'm an outpatient and I can walk along the street and breathe in the same filthy exhaust from the buses like all you normal people! Christ," he said, and threw himself back against the chair.

A few minutes later he is desperate in his demand that she give him "something real" of herself, but when he tries to take her hand, she pulls it away. He mocks her, insults her, and cries, "You bitch!" before leaving for good. Months later she learns without surprise that he has drowned himself somewhere in Canada.

THIRTY-THREE

Wayne State University along with the adjacent Historical Museum, the Institute of Arts, and the main branch of the Public Library constitutes Detroit's cultural center, even as it occupies a portion of the ghetto. As one walks through the campus the eye is often roving over the remarkable, unexpected shapes of the new buildings designed by Minoru Yamasaki. Yet, always visible a few blocks away, particularly to the south, are decrepit and ugly structures, some of the city's worst slums. Perhaps because of this, Wayne State is also part of the subcultural center of Detroit for those most alienated from the money, methods, and men who have made the modern campus come to be.

To combat the problem of anonymity for a large and fragmented student body, Monteith College was established in 1959 as an experimental college-within-a-college offering a broad general education. Monteith, however, enrolls only 800 of the university's 31,000 students. Perhaps no more than 2,000 students live in the campus area primarily in run-down high-rent buildings and dilapidated old houses. Some of these students are among the most serious and committed, living in the area in order to be close to one another and to the bookstores, libraries, and other university facilities. In many cases they have chosen Wayne because they want a firsthand involvement with the problems of the ghetto and urban blight. A number are Bohemians who along with professional non-students, hippies, and various other hangers-on make the area the psychedelic center of Detroit; LSD and marihuana contribute heavily to the character of the subculture, and members of the narcotics squad spend considerable time and effort growing beards, learning the dialect, and poking about.

In the Decanter, a small, nondescript bar on Cass Avenue a few doors down from his apartment, David Roth spent an evening with Richard about the third week in September. They had not seen each other during the summer and most of their six-hour conversation involved Richard talking about the hospitals and of troubles with his parents, his former roommates and friends, and Charlotte Zimmerman— "They're all shitting on me," he said. For the first time David thought he noted Richard contradicting himself on matters of fact. Also for the first time Richard's talk was filled with violence: stories of the cold viciousness of hospital attendants and descriptions of what he would like to do to his parents and others. David was surprised to hear Richard speak this way and to see him get involved in an episode of "The Fugitive" on a television set in the bar (he identified with the man on the run, he said).

Also on the Wayne campus, Richard walked into the Monteith office of Professor George Drury, whose acquaintance he had made through friends a year or so earlier. Confidently, he outlined a plan for a course that he thought he might be able to teach for Monteith and wondered if there were any openings in Drury's department, social science.

Professor Drury explained that quite simply it was too late: classes would start in less than two weeks, and there were no openings for additional instructors. Richard indicated that he was not looking for a job but just wanted to teach and communicate with people. It would be impossible, said Drury, to get the necessary apparatus properly established on such short notice.

"You mean to say," snapped Richard, "that with my gifts and my grades I can't teach a seminar or discussion group at Monteith?"

That wasn't the problem, said Drury; it was simply a practical matter of a lack of time. Why not enroll in the college, he suggested, and participate in Monteith's program of "cooperative self-education" in which a student may gather other interested students into a discussion group? Richard didn't want this. It seemed important to him that his course have formal sanction from the university. He did not mention his hospitalization and said his trip to Israel had been put off. Drury finally gave him the names of two women in the administration at Monteith who could give him an official answer. They suggested that he try his plan with the Religious Affairs Office on campus.

About this time Richard began calling and visiting Harv Stiener (pseud.) whom he had met one year earlier while working in the Citizens for Johnson-Humphrey office. Harv, who was majoring in political science at Wayne, says: "I come from a rather strange home environment with respect to religion—it just never included religious training of any sort, or even a mention of religion. I was eight years old before I knew that I was a Jew or what it meant to be a Jew. I had simply no conception of God. I had always been taught that people who believed in God were unintelligent, superstitious people who were not self-reliant and were dependent on a superstitious faith to support them. Therefore Richard was amazing to me and a bit mysterious. Here was a very intelligent person, one of the brightest people I'd ever met, and he was talking about a belief in God very intensely."

Harv Stiener had been in analysis for a year and a half and had been told by his analyst that he should not lean on religion but should develop some functional self-reliance; Richard and Harv had gotten into heated arguments over this point. Now in the fall it became clear that Richard was interested in Harv's experience in analysis and wanted opinions on various doctors in town. Harv wondered why Richard should be thinking about analysis: "He seemed to be in good shape."

Another reason for Richard's association with Harv Stiener was the fact that he was not allowed the use of the family car, and Harv would occasionally provide transportation. One evening Richard found Harv at the home of Sara Winkler (pseud.), Harv's girl friend. He was driving his uncle's car, said Richard, which he had to return, and he wanted someone to drive him back. Harv agreed but first the three spent some time in Sara's painting studio discussing the corruption of American society. Richard finally asked, "Do you know what it's like to be locked up in an institution and how easily you can get yourself locked up in this country?"

Sara and Harv said they did not. Richard went on to describe what had happened to him in the past two months. He related the details while nearly in hysterics, crying through most of it, wailing, "You can't imagine how horrible it was!" Later, Richard moved on to the American Jewish community, Congregation Shaarey Zedek, and Rabbi Adler whom he described as "just a corporation president." Rabbi Adler, he said, had destroyed the real purpose of Judaism as it should have been embodied in the congregation.

Before they left to take his uncle's car back, Richard also talked about the time he had spent in Israel during the previous summer when he had learned that he was a prophet. How had he learned this? asked Harv and Sara. It had just come to him, said Richard, after he had been very upset in Israel. Harv wasn't sure what kind of prophet he was talking about, so Richard explained that a "prophet" in the biblical sense was a man chosen by God to be an instrument for the announcement of His message.

A week later Richard showed up one morning at the Stiener home and asked Harv for a ride to his appointment with Dr. Silver at the Northland Center. When he came out of the hour session, he was in a fit of rage, railing against Dr. Silver, analysts, psychiatry in general, and women. "Silver keeps telling me I'm sick!" cried Richard, slapping his forehead with the palm of his hand. "But *he's* so sick he can't even see straight! He's so goddamn stupid. He keeps asking me what's wrong with *me*. Doesn't he know that he's sick, that he's got all the problems!" Women in general were bitches, he announced bitterly, and he knew two in particular at Monteith who were blocking his way to a teaching position there. "Listen," he said, "they're so lucky I'd even consider teaching at a place like that! In five years they'll be begging me to come and teach a course for them, and I won't give them the time of day."

In the third week of September the director of the Religious Affairs Office (R.A.O.) at Wayne State, the Reverend Hubert Locke, and his assistant, James Lyons, were discussing the possibility of contacting those students who had marked their R.A.O. preference cards "agnostic or atheist." Their hope was to convene some of them in what was to be called "Skeptics Corner" to discuss the possibilities of religious belief versus agnosticism or atheism. The problem was to find someone to lead the group who would not be immediately tabbed as a member of the "opposition."

At this point, in walked Richard, describing himself as a Woodrow Wilson fellow in search of a teaching position to fill an interim between his work at the University of Detroit and his doctoral progress in the divinity school at the University of Chicago starting in January. In talking with him about his background and interests Locke and Lyons soon decided that Richard was just what they needed to lead the "Skeptics." A few days later Richard supplied a course description and the R.A.O. set up a time and place, sent notices to "skeptics," and placed ads in Wayne's *Daily Collegian.* Richard's course description went as follows:

> An attempt to conceptualize in essentially religious terms the experiences responsible for great creative contributions to Western Civilization and pre-civilizational or archaic societies.
> To be discussed: parts of Mircea Eliade, *The Sacred and the Profane, Myth and Reality;* Plato, *The Republic;* St. Augustine, *The Confessions;* Dostoevski, *Notes from the Underground;* Nietzsche, *Thus Spake Zarathustra;* Camus, *The Rebel;* Ingmar Bergman, *Wild Strawberries, The Seventh Seal.*
> Also to be articulated: the basis for a valid critique of the dehumanization of modern society and the formulation of a philosophical and more-human alternative.

Richard was very pleased and excited about his new opportunity and was spreading the good news. One of those he called was the dean of men at the University of Detroit, Mr. Donoghue, saying that he couldn't understand why it was all right for him to teach a course at Wayne but not all right for him to take classes at the University of Detroit. Donoghue said he couldn't understand it either, but would have to stand by his decision.

Not many days later Mr. Donoghue placed a call to Richard to inform him that he had been banned from the campus of the University of Detroit. He was not to appear on campus again, and if he did, the police would be called to escort him off the campus. The persistence of Richard's vague threats on the phone and in person and his quite evident hostility had convinced most of his former associates of the University of Detroit, particularly his ex-roommates and Charlotte Zimmerman, that he was dangerous and should not have been allowed out of the hospital. Pat Burke, Bill Winter, and Dr. Zimmerman had gone to Donoghue, who decided to take action, again in spite of advice to the contrary by Father Cross.

Richard did appear on campus several times after the ban was issued (reportedly the police were called a couple of times to send him away), but the exclusion must have been a galling development for him. A girl who was on the periphery of the Zimmerman group and had taken two or three courses with Richard met him on one such unlawful visit and found him "nervous, shaking, trembling, flushed in the face—it was embarrassing. He shook my hand twenty times in ten minutes." He was working on a very important project at Wayne State, he said, and pulled out what he said were personal letters from Mircea Eliade.

On another of his visits, Richard happened to sit in on a lecture by Dr. James Spiller (pseud.) of the psychology department on the interrelation of philosophy, religion, and science. Afterward Richard met Dr. Spiller, indicated his basic agreement with the lecture, and wondered if the doctor had a private practice. A clinical psychologist, Dr. Spiller said yes, whereupon Richard told his story and ended with a plea to be taken on as one of Dr. Spiller's patients. But the doctor was afraid that Richard wanted to use a relationship with him in order to skirt issues with Dr. Silver. He said no and advised Richard on the importance of cooperating with Dr. Silver and maintaining an adequate "control system" if he wanted to stay out of the hospital.

Dr. Spiller talked with Richard informally but at length in his office three or four times during the latter part of September, October, and the first part of November and also spoke with him on the phone a few times. He came to the conclusion that Richard was on the verge of a major insight, of achieving a "new level of consciousness," a genuine mystical experience, a kind of direct confrontation with the Godhead. Richard's problem, he said, was bound up with his relations to his father, to God as a father-figure, and to authority-figures generally. Richard's troubles occurred because "he began to use this near-insight psychotically."

On Monday, October 4, Wayne's *Daily Collegian* carried a full front-page headline: "Atheists to Get 'U' Blessing." Below it the story opened:

> Atheists and agnostics may soon become part of the family of religious organizations on campus. Skeptics read on.
>
> With the blessing of the University Religious Affairs Office, the "Skeptics Corner" will get off the ground at 2:30 p.m. tomorrow . . . in 460 Mackenzie Hall.
>
> Heading the six-to-eight-week program will be 23-year-old

Richard Wishnetsky, former University of Michigan graduate and Woodrow Wilson fellow, who will begin his doctoral work at the University of Chicago next year.

After a brief description of the origins of the program the article continues:

It is not known whether similar programs exist elsewhere, but "Announcement of the Corner has been greeted enthusiastically here," said [assistant director] Lyons.

"This is not a conversion attempt but an attempt at dialogue about significant questions," he emphasized. For this reason, what Lyons termed "professional" religious people will not handle the discussion sessions.

The raison d'etre instead is to provide a forum for serious students "who are willing to examine in fullness their own views and those of other students," said Lyons.

"So often, students with these philosophical positions are afraid of open, candid discussion," he said.

"Usually, if one side holds a belief, it's leery of the other side. But our program will be strictly an exploration of ideas; an honest intellectual encounter to relate in terms of human experiences, not a conversion attempt."

The article includes Richard's list of books for discussion and then concludes:

To Wishnetsky, whose major interest is in "a revival of the traditional philosophical concept of man and a discussion of the increasing dehumanization in our society," the Corner will chip off "stilted barriers to discussion and provide an opportunity for dialogue."

He is interested in "real communication" not "a forum for arguments."

Survival of the Skeptics Corner, however, will depend on the interest students show.

On Tuesday, October 5, students showed considerable interest, but there was a large gap between what many of them expected and what Richard had in mind. A *Daily Collegian* story in the October 6 edition provided a good picture of what happened at the meeting and an indication of what was ahead.

Atheists' Report

Although he may be, as quoted in Monday's Collegian, mainly interested in "real communication" not "a forum for arguments," Richard Wishnetsky, discussion leader of the newly formed Skeptics Corner, may have to settle for something less.

Many of the people who attended yesterday's first meeting were more than a little upset that the mainstream of discussion centered on problems which they felt are given more adequate attention in some of the University's philosophy, psychology, and religion classes.

The group was forced to move from room 460 to the Chase room in Mackenzie Hall because of the unexpected large turnout of 56 people. . . .

About one third of the people attending from the beginning left right after Wishnetsky gave out the list of selected readings. . . . The works were picked "on the hope that they would provide a critique by which the superficiality and fraud of modern society could be analyzed."

Wishnetsky followed this by reading a couple of selections that dealt with philosophical problems faced by man as he tries to adjust to an industrial society.

At this point a number of people protested that the readings, and, in fact, the entire discussion by Wishnetsky, seemed to stray from that which was proposed in the Collegian and from their reasons for attending.

In an attempt to call a halt to the dissension which was quite evident, Wishnetsky reiterated that "the purpose was to stimulate the individuals to rehash their experiences in light of the works being referred to in hopes that each person might understand the reasons for his or her beliefs."

In view of the large turnout it was decided to divide the groups into two bodies which will meet at the same time and place but on different days, Wednesday and Tuesday of each week, until the group dwindles.

October 6, 1965, was Yom Kippur, the Day of Atonement, marked in the traditional practice of observant Jews by twenty-four hours of prayer and fasting. At eleven in the morning Richard walked into Harv Stiener's home and announced, "I'm starving! Give me something to eat!" Harv was surprised and asked, "Aren't you going to Shaarey Zedek?" No, said Richard, maybe he would go later. He ate a piece of cake with obvious relish and then sat with Harv around the dining-room table, providing his usual denunciation of Congregation Shaarey Zedek, a description of Rabbi Adler as a brilliant man who was being wasted, and an argument against the Vietnam war (which Harv, as a "hawk," defended).

As usual Harv began to wonder about his own position: "If Richard said something with intensity, I'd always begin to doubt my own views." He brought up the matter with his analyst, and the doctor said in effect, "You're all right and he's not." By now Harv was dreaming about Richard in his sleep—nightmares in which Richard, though he had never in fact threatened Harv, attempted to strangle him or attack him with a knife. "Richard's intensity was always so great," said Harv, "and I was always aware that I shouldn't let our arguments go too far."

Excitement, pride, and optimism reigned for a time as Richard involved himself in the activity he had established as his life's work—teaching. "The course is exciting and provocative, loaded with possibilities," he wrote to Professor Alan Gaylord at the University of Michigan. (He had asked Gaylord to recommend him for a Kent Fellowship and the professor, unaware of Richard's recent troubles, sent off a letter substantially the same as the one he had written for Richard's application for Danforth two years earlier.) His teaching was "just what the doctor ordered," Richard told Sharon Thompson. Apparently not fazed by the opening meeting, he repeatedly invited his friends to attend and always spoke of the project with enthusiasm. He told Larry Walters on the phone one day, "Larry, I'm going to be one of the greatest teachers ever to walk the face of the earth."

On October 14, however, the *Daily Collegian's* third and last report on the doings of the "Skeptics" verged at times on mockery:

'Skeptics' Dwindle; Atheists Are Shunned

> Never let it be said that Skeptics are grim and imposing.
>
> Yesterday's meeting of the "Skeptics Corner" threatened briefly to get out of hand and into ribaldry as Richard Wishnetsky, chief Skeptic, read the lines of Dr. Borg, protagonist of the movie "Wild Strawberries," and a young male skeptic read the lines of Dr. Borg's daughter.
>
> Fortunately, his/her lines were brief.
>
> The "Skeptics Corner," which is "not" a group for agnostics and atheists, held its third meeting yesterday afternoon. "This is to be a new experience in communication," explained Wishnetsky, graduate student, "not arguments about religion."
>
> There were only ten persons in attendance, a sharp drop from the crowd of 56 which attended the first meeting which

> Wishnetsky felt were drawn due to a misunderstanding of the group's purpose.
>
> "What skepticism there is to be found in the 'Skeptics Corner' has to do with organized religion and formal institutions generally." He said, "What we want is discussion, not argument, and a sharing of religious experience."
>
> The next meeting will be held at 2:30 p.m. next Wednesday in 460 Mackenzie Hall. Selections from Dostoevski's "Notes from the Underground" will be read and discussed. The Skeptics provided hot coffee, warm hospitality, and encouraged animated discussion.
>
> Atheists (militant variety) need not apply.

Most of the students had come to the first session expecting to describe their own experiences as agnostics or atheists. Actually Richard wanted to gather around him a number of young people who shared with him the feeling that they possessed a genuine religious faith but who were estranged from institutionalized religion. Together they would achieve a "new level of communication," an inspiring and enriching exchange in which truth would be illuminated and more readily approached. "Richard asked what people wanted to do," said Harv Stiener, who attended the first couple of sessions, "though it was clear that we were going to do what he wanted to do." According to Harv, Richard said, "I want to have dialogue," investing the word with an almost sacred aura, as he moved his hand gently from in front of his mouth and out toward the students. Harv thought the gesture appropriately one-way.

In the seminar Richard was highly enthusiastic about Ingmar Bergman; everything in Bergman's films was "true," *Wild Strawberries* was "true," Bergman's conception of reality was accurate and "true." Feeling the case was being overstated a bit, Harv raised a hand and asked, "Wouldn't you agree that Bergman has a point of view which is relevant to him and perhaps true for him, but that he simply is not the final authority?"

"Richard," says Harv, "immediately jumped on me and started screaming, 'You're turning this into an argument! You're going to upset the seminar. You're not really interested in finding the truth.' " Harv pleaded innocent, said he was interested, and was backed by a few of the students sitting nearby. Richard told him to get out and not come back.

"What do you mean by dialogue?" asked a girl in Levis.

"I mean you have to understand me, and I want to understand you," said Richard. Harv left and did not return.

The session on Dostoevski was the first that Larry Walters managed to attend. On the way he encountered on old friend, "a very sexy little thing who had been drinking all afternoon, wearing very sensual clothing, good figure, blonde hair. When I brought her in, Richard's eyes popped out, and from then on the whole discussion was directed to her. He kept talking to her and she had some very good things to say—she surprised me." When Larry said he wasn't interested, Richard spent considerable time trying to locate her on campus. "This was at a time," says Larry, "when he was sexually really deprived. He really wanted somebody at almost any cost, and his sex life kind of got to be a joke."

Just how much interest Richard really had was something Vicky Kolber (pseud.) wondered about. A darkly attractive, full-figured undergraduate, Vicky was one of those Larry Walters introduced to Richard in hopes of drawing him out of himself. In fact, she found herself rather taken with Richard ("I was going through a phase in which I was very attracted to intellectual boys"), but though she tried to get him interested enough to ask her out, he never did. She chatted with him in the Union and attended meetings of Skeptics Corner; he was invariably pleasant and always called out a friendly hello, but Vicky decided he was "backward" with girls.

Richard was a popular figure with certain frequenters of the Union, almost something of a "legend," said Vicky. When he arrived, there would soon be a gathering at his table. He could always be trusted to turn a discussion of the issues of the day to a view of their larger religious meaning, and he seemed happiest when holding forth with such a group. Vicky Kolber recalls the day Richard and his Union friends were sitting together railing at the state of American society when he announced with a facetious air, "Oh, I'm going out to shoot McNamara and Romney and Rabbi Adler." The crowd, largely Jewish and contemptuous of organized Judaism (of which the rabbi was an automatic symbol), chuckled.

As usual dressed neatly in a coat and tie, Richard generally did not tell people about his stay in the mental hospitals and did not appear deeply unbalanced or out of control. In any case, passions were generally running high on the campus at Wayne: Los Angeles had exploded with the Watts riot and the United States government had escalated its war effort in Vietnam to a point that brought a rising tide of protest. Richard attended a few of the speeches and rallies on campus but did not take part in the demonstrations.

His main concern continued to be Skeptics Corner, but he was forced to work with a dwindling number of students and a decreasing response from those few who did continue to show up. Toward the end of the seven-week period that the sessions lasted Richard seemed more bitter and vitriolic, his statements concerning God, religion, and the church establishment becoming "more outlandish and radical." When it was all over, he blamed the failure on a lack of interest and ability in his students.

THIRTY-FOUR

One morning late in October as Lilo Fauman was raking leaves from the lawn in front of her home in suburban Huntington Woods, she looked up to find Richard walking past. He was three and a half miles from his parents' home in Palmer Woods and seemed to be going nowhere in particular, just out for a stroll.

Mrs. Fauman greeted him cordially. The family's contact with him had been very limited since the days when he used to come home for his vacations from the University of Michigan. Then, recalled Mrs. Fauman, he used to enjoy playing with the younger children in the neighborhood including the Fauman kids, who loved him and giggled with delight when he would hold them up high in the air. The Faumans had heard nothing of his recent stay in the hospitals.

Richard had hardly opened his conversation when he accused the Faumans of having caused the disintegration of the old neighborhood by their move to the suburbs; if they had stayed the others would have also. Mrs. Fauman treated Richard's accusation with a ready sense of humor, thanking him for attributing to them so much power and influence. When he insisted on pursuing his notion, she invited him in for a bottle of soda pop.

Inside they found Professor Fauman, a member of the sociology department at Eastern Michigan University. Richard quickly repeated his charge for Joe Fauman's benefit, thereby launching a lengthy and spirited conversation, which lasted over lunch when they moved to the kitchen table for some sandwiches. To each of Richard's questions about the move, Professor Fauman responded with what Richard finally agreed was a reasonable and compelling explanation—before launching into new objections which the professor handled the same way.

Richard then started in on Congregation Shaarey Zedek. If Rabbi Adler hadn't agreed to move the synagogue out of the city, he said, Jewish neighborhoods in northwest Detroit would have remained intact. Fauman quoted studies of the congregation which indicated that the movement of members out of the city had clearly *preceded* the move of the synagogue.

Professor Fauman told Richard that there were of course things which one might like to see the Jewish community do for race relations. For example, one might suggest that the Jewish community buy up housing in all the area suburbs and move one hundred Negro families into each suburb. But you just don't move people around at your own will in this country. This is a democracy, reminded Professor Fauman, and you can't make people move someplace, and you can't make their neighbors accept them or stay put if they don't want to. But, we must do something, insisted Richard. Reasonable explanations were all well and good, but something had to be done somehow.

During their long talk, Richard asked to use the phone over a dozen times, repeatedly trying to make connections with certain parties. When he was finally successful with one of his calls, he announced that he had to leave to meet someone. He refused Professor Fauman's offer of a ride and said he would prefer to walk. Vaguely troubled by his attitudes and behavior, the Faumans said good-bye and did not see Richard again.

About this time Sharon Thompson decided to leave Detroit to seek a job in Washington. Richard came over the night before she left to help her pack and seemed quite subdued. The subject of Richard as prophet had come up again in one of their conversations after Richard had departed the hospital; he had said at one point, "There were times when I used to think of myself as a prophet." Now, he told her that he had recently taken a job selling pots, pans, and dinnerware door to door. It was really quality stuff, he said, and asked if she was interested in buying some. "What the heck are you doing selling this kind of thing?" she asked, almost angry with him for what she thought was a waste of his talents. "Well, I need the money, of course," said Richard. After he had wished her well in Washington and took his leave, Sharon later noticed that he was sitting alone in the dark on the Thompson's front-porch swing, and remained there by himself for a long time.

In Washington, Sharon received letters from Richard, one of them saying that he felt as if his emotions had been knocked back and forth on a tennis court by "the sluggers." Richard was writing a lot of letters at this time, ranging from a rather perfunctory newsy note in reply to a New Year's card from an old friend, to an alternately bitter and buoyant letter to Fred Baskin. And there were other letters which he wrote but apparently did not send, reflecting perhaps his more private feelings throughout the fall and winter months.

On October 20, Richard wrote to Arthur Gold at Harvard and thanked him for his New Year's card. An "incredible amount" had occurred since he had last seen Gold, he said. Something had happened to interrupt his plans for Europe—"probably the most fantastic and terrifying experience" of his life. He couldn't explain in the letter but would do so when they met again. He gave Gold a brief summary of his present state of affairs: he was no longer at U. of D. but teaching a series of seminars on comparative religion, philosophy, and literature at Wayne State, and doing substitute teaching in a number of suburban high schools. In January he would be going to the University of Chicago—though he had just learned that one of his future teachers there, Paul Tillich, had just died. Tillich now belonged "to the ages, not the classrooms."

A few days later on October 25, Richard wrote in reply to a letter he had recently received from Fred Baskin at Berkeley. In a jocular tone tinged with bitter irony he advised his friend to enjoy California, that sunny, pleasure-pursuing world of luxury and joy —"and for those sensitive few, despair." California, said Richard, was Eden for the masses and America's future hell, a "glorious whore" whom all were rushing to embrace. He apologized for his "mad diatribe" and his prejudices—though he was quite aware of them. His alienation from American society was growing, he said, and California seemed the epitome of America's most revolting aspects.

Still, he wrote, he felt his life had taken a more positive turn. He was teaching at Wayne State and would begin substituting in several suburban high schools. In a day or so he would purchase his first car, a 1956 Ford with all the extras, a good buy at one hundred dollars. He had learned that day that Paul Tillich, one of his teachers at the University of Chicago, had died a couple of days before—the papers in Detroit had ignored the story, apparently feeling, he said, that the burning of draft cards was more newsworthy. Tillich was the least scholarly of the four professors he had planned to study with at U. of C., said Richard, but was reportedly a man of warmth and fascination. Now he belonged "to the ages, not the classrooms." Richard concluded with the information that outside of short periods of depression, his "psychic health" was "rather good."

The fact that Paul Tillich died of a heart ailment at the age of seventy-nine on October 22—two days after Richard dated the letter to Arthur Gold in which he mentions Tillich's death—indicates that the note was broken off to be completed later. As to the references to Richard's teaching "in several suburban high schools" (he has already started in the first letter but only has plans for it in the second), he was apparently putting on an optimistic face over plans that seem not to have materialized. Larry Walters and others say Richard gave no indication that he was substituting in the suburbs in the fall. David Roth said Richard at the time was formulating a new plan, scheme, or project nearly every week. He seemed to need an elaborate plan, a projection for the future, in order to carry on with the business of daily living. What daily living was like at times for Richard is suggested in an apparently unmailed letter written on the same day he started his note to Arthur Gold, October 20:

> I think too much. I don't think enough. I want to be me—I am only the welter of my anxieties, fears, and superficialities. I do not walk, I stumble. I do not live, I respond to stimuli. I do not live, I exist. I am not a man, just a body. I live, yet I am dead.
>
> The only anguish I experience is that of self-pity and becoming aware of my own horrid, pervasive, unacceptable and contemptible selfishness, my own inability to love. When I am not miserable I am a phony.

In the same letter, Richard wrote this prayer:

Let my life be a testimony to Thy diverse truths, let it be one of beauty and of justice, for its roots shall be in love and reason. Oh, God, I want to live! Let me! And then let my life go beyond justice, beyond vengeance, let it emerge into the pure understanding of mercy.

Richard, now obviously aware that he has a problem with his "psychic health," seems to have become much less able to assume the old delusions of grandeur and fame which had once served as defenses. His lament, "When I am not miserable I am a phony," is a dreadful dead-end. Yet it is still countered by his cry, "Oh, God, I want to live! Let me!"

On occasion during the previous year, Richard had walked into an interior decorator's studio on Livernois near the University of Detroit to visit an old friend who worked there, Rona Lutsky (pseud.), the wife of one of Richard's Mumford classmates. Richard had attended the Lutskys' wedding and had remained in touch with them in Detroit. He had turned down a number of Rona's invitations to dinner, but one October afternoon about five o'clock he walked into the studio and asked if she could give him a ride to Northland on her way home. He was meeting someone (a woman, he indicated) for dinner.

It was a bit out of her way, but Rona agreed. On their arrival Richard asked if she had a minute to talk, so Rona parked at the deserted end of one of the shopping center's large lots and Richard launched into a description of what had been happening to him over the past several months. He spoke calmly but jumped quickly from one time and place to another, from one complaint to another: "The whole world is against me, Rona. All my friends, everybody I know is against me!" The doctors who had been trying to treat him were wrong—he was not sick. "They're trying to take my life away from me," he said. "They're denying me the possibility of doing what I want to do. They're only harming me." The only person who was any help at all was a rabbi, he said. "He's the only person who really understands me. He knows exactly what I'm trying to do and he's really trying to help." They had had a number of long conferences, said Richard, without mentioning the man's name; he felt the rabbi was the only man with whom he had been able to establish a genuine rapport.

When he had finished, Richard said he felt that Rona was a

good friend to whom he could speak in this way. "Yes, I think I am," said Rona, frightened by the fact that they were alone in the gathering dusk at the end of the empty lot.

The memory of her fear prompted her to hide from him when he came into the studio again a month later. Her car was in plain view outside and she was in an inner office when he walked in and asked for her. The girl in front glanced back to find Rona shaking her head and told him that she wasn't in. Richard left a note saying hello. The Lutskys never heard from him again.

Richard was often speaking to friends about his talks with Rabbi Adler. To some he boasted of his closeness to the rabbi and expounded on the greatness of the man (whose special interest in him implied Richard's own importance). To a few others (particularly his disaffected younger friends around Wayne) he indicated that he was regularly engaging in debates with Rabbi Adler. His interest in the Hasidic Lubavitchers was still deep, but he would mock people at Shaarey Zedek for keeping the "superstitious fast" on Yom Kippur. He would come from time to time for Sabbath services at Shaarey Zedek, but would not hesitate to pick someone out from the congregation after services and castigate him for his hypocrisy and empty life.

Once after services Barry Kriger met Richard and asked how he had liked Rabbi Adler's sermon. "I walked out," said Richard. "It didn't seem to me," Barry says, "the kind of sermon Richard would walk out on. It was on individual responsibility and hypocrisy and the need for a more concerted approach on the part of people to make their religion mean something." Thus, surprised and upset, Barry asked Richard why he had walked out. "Oh, it's all talk, talk, talk—just a lot of words," said Richard. Even Rabbi Adler's words, he said, weren't going to have any effect.

Richard apparently did not have any formal arrangement with the rabbi to meet for regular counseling sessions but nonetheless managed to see and speak to him with some frequency during the last months of 1965—by telephone calls to the synagogue and at home, on unannounced visits to the rabbi's study at the synagogue, and by cornering him for chats on Saturday afternoon after service. Rabbi Groner recalls that on at least two occasions Richard spent considerable time in Rabbi Adler's study and that even without the rabbi there, Richard was allowed to remain and make use of the rabbi's very extensive library. Still, Rabbi Groner insists,

"Richard could not have seen that much of Rabbi Adler because the rabbi was just not that available."

"Richard would call here at home in the evenings," recalls Mrs. Adler, "and the conversations were very long. I couldn't from this end gather the gist . . . the rabbi would very rarely say anything. He would just listen because about all Richard wanted then was an ear." The rabbi never spoke to his wife about his conversations with Richard or about the details of any of his counseling. "And I was glad; I didn't want it," says Goldie Adler. "Maybe I would forget sometime and say something I shouldn't." In any case, it was not uncommon, she says, that a rebellious young man might vent his feelings on the rabbi.

Rabbi Groner also talked with Richard occasionally through the fall, often about Albert Camus. Under the tutelage of Charlotte Zimmerman, Richard had become excited by Camus as an example of a thoroughly modern intellectual who nonetheless was able to move toward a kind of religious faith. Rabbi Groner disagreed and sent Richard to a journal article that argued against this idea. Still Richard pointed to *The Rebel* as a landmark of hope for the modern intellectual.

An extended argument with considerable philosophical and historical analysis, *The Rebel* culminates in an indictment of intellectual excess, arrogant ideological fanaticism, and the self-defeating "idealistic" use of violence. There must be, says Camus, a recognition of the logical limits of all thought and action. About murder he finally reasons: "It is the limit that can be reached but once, after which one must die. The rebel has only one way of reconciling himself with his act of murder if he allows himself to be led into performing it: to accept his own death and sacrifice. He kills and dies so that it shall be clear that murder is impossible."

"I didn't notice Richard slipping into a serious depression," says Larry Walters. "Even when he would come and ask me what my thinking was on the subject of suicide—if he committed suicide what would I think? how would I react? I wasn't perceptive enough to see the tremendous torment because he had a kind of smile or smirk on his face when he said it. And he had talked about it before. It was an alternative all along, at many different points. Even at U. of M."

Through the fall and early winter Richard would periodically bring the subject up and Larry would say in effect, "How can you even think of such a thing? You've got such a useful life ahead of you, your potential is so tremendous." Richard would only shrug his shoulders. He never talked in specifics, and his motives would seem to shift, but generally he appeared to be feeling useless and unwanted. "A lot of times," says Larry, "he might have thought of himself in the way, a bother or a burden to his family. What good was he now? He was out of school—well, maybe it was time to end it now. Other times it was because of a state of depression and not because of somebody else's reaction to him. I would tell him—but I don't think he knew—how most people felt about him. He was seeing a psychiatrist at this time but I began to get the feeling that he was growing almost totally immune to their help. He would say, 'What a racket they have.' "

Neither friend spent time on the University of Detroit campus any longer. Larry had moved into an apartment downtown near the Detroit College of Law, and Richard was living in a variety of places around Wayne State, usually without a phone. Once in a while they would make connections when Richard would show up at Larry's apartment or call at a time when Larry was in. Once Richard asked if he could room with Larry in his large downtown apartment but, as Larry explains: "I said no, and the reasons were that he was still very 'hyper.' Not like before—he was toned down considerably—but I just couldn't have him here talking on the telephone at all hours, all the time. And school was still very crucial for me at that point. It would have been just detrimental for both of us." With the end of October and the disintegration of Skeptics Corner, Richard seemed to slide from view. Even his closer friends around Wayne like David Roth and John Samuels stopped hearing from Richard and seeing him around campus except for chance encounters.

For a short while after returning to Detroit from Toronto, Richard had lived at home with his family. Like many parents faced with a similar situation, the Wishnetskys had reportedly been hesitant to accept the psychiatric opinion that their son was in need of intensive care and hospitalization. When it was agreed that he could remain outside the hospital while regularly seeing a doctor, his mother in particular wanted him at home where she could watch him carefully.

However, about the time the family was making its move from Manor Road to the new home in Palmer Woods, Richard lined up his position with the Skeptics and, without the use of a car, wanted to live closer to campus. He had made a new friend in Steven Lewis (pseud.), a young Jew who had reportedly studied archaeology on the West Coast and was now a student at Wayne State while leading a rather psychedelic existence. For a time in October the two shared an apartment near campus. Richard told Larry that he thought Steven Lewis a "terrific person."

While they were living together, Richard and Steven met and befriended Bill Scott, a dark, good-looking young "nonstudent" who was "hanging around Wayne" while holding down a job. Bill Scott took a liking to both Steven and Richard in their chats in the drab, uncollegiate confines of the Decanter Bar and thought Richard very friendly and articulate.

A few months back Bill had been going with an "excessively attractive" girl named Tina Monte (pseud.), a student at Wayne and "a young woman with many problems and hang-ups." Slowly Bill had become aware that Tina was "sliding out into left field," becoming increasingly troubled and unstable; he decided he wanted no more to do with her. When she landed in a hospital with a "nervous breakdown" and a "paranoid condition," Bill decided to do the humanitarian thing and stay with her until she had pulled herself together somewhat. He had done so for a month or two before he introduced her one day late in October to Steven Lewis.

Steven, said Bill, was young, naïve, and inexperienced in his relations with women and also possessed of "a full share of hang-ups and problems of his own." When Tina, who was several years his senior, showed an interest, Steven was quite taken with her. According to Bill's view of it, she found him fresh and unspoiled and still full of a youthful vitality. They quickly had an affair going, and were soon living together.

Richard and Steven had previously made plans to move together to another apartment, but now Richard, after making the arrangements, found himself stuck with an eighty-dollar-a-month apartment he couldn't afford. Somehow he got himself out of the arrangement and into another set of rooms in one of the eyesore neighborhoods near Wayne State. "It was a dreadful place," said

Larry Walters, "an old house converted into apartments. The doors and walls were paper thin, no buzzer on the door, the manager let you in, there was no telephone, every appliance was old and decrepit, the floors squeaked, the shoddiest furniture, it was dirty, it needed a paint job, the neighborhood was full of derelicts. It was just totally depressing and Richard was totally depressed in it. He hated it and all he really did there was sleep." He was often walking around with Dostoevski in hand at this point, said Larry.

Richard stayed in the apartment through November and the first part of December and then moved into a rooming house. Occasionally during this time Bill Scott would run into him at the Decanter Bar where Richard would come supposedly looking for Bill. Often he would just pop in and out of the bar, talking for a while and then leaving abruptly. He usually seemed in high spirits, maintained his appearance, continued to dress neatly and cleanly, and generally spoke with benevolence about others. While Bill drank liquor or beer and Richard sipped a Coke or a 7-Up, they talked, Richard staunchly maintaining that a man must believe in a religion to live a meaningful life and Bill arguing against the existence of God and the need for religion. Richard gave Bill a couple of books on religion, and Bill responded with a copy of Freud's *Moses and Monotheism.*

Richard said nothing about his recent past or his personal life, yet their conversations suggested to Bill that Richard was frightened of homosexual tendencies in himself. He had been down to a gay bar on Woodward a number of times, he said, "just to observe, of course," and his fears seemed to be tied in with his concern for Judaism and the religion's condemnation of homosexuality. Says Bill: "He seemed to almost idolize Steven whose burning ambition was to travel to Israel to have a dig—he and Richard had made tentative plans to go together. There was more between them than just an ordinary friendship. I don't mean to say they had an affair going, but their relationship for a while was very close."

Bill Scott described Steven as a frequent user of pot and LSD, but he was sure that Richard had nothing to do with drugs. To Bill, Richard without Steven seemed alone and without a close personal friend. "If it hadn't been for Tina," says Bill, "Steven, I think, might have been very good for Richard—he might have been able to pull him through."

THIRTY-FIVE

Shortly after Skeptics Corner broke up, Marty Sharpe, Richard's old friend from Mumford and the University of Michigan, invited him to speak before a group of medical students Marty had joined at Wayne State who called themselves the Anabolists and were devoted to the broadening of their cultural horizons with a series of weekly lectures. Marty promised him a goodly number of bright, eager, receptive minds to whom he could speak on the dehumanization of modern man.

Richard agreed readily and so met Marty one day in mid-November at the Lafayette Clinic, a few blocks from the Wayne State Medical School. He had wanted to drive over in his newly purchased red and white '56 Ford, but to his considerable distress the car wouldn't start. After two or three weeks of proud ownership ("He was like a little kid with a toy," recalls Larry Walters) he would learn that repairs would cost about as much as the purchase price and would eventually have to junk it for ten dollars.

When they arrived at the medical school, they found that only about twenty med students had responded, and most were old high-school and college friends of Richard's. On the stage of an auditorium Richard sat on a table in front of the small group, refused a microphone, and spoke very softly so that it was very difficult to hear what he was saying. Nonetheless, all listened patiently and quietly as Richard strung together quoted passages from Eliade, Nietzsche, and Dostoevski.

On November 3, the resident in psychiatry who had been assigned to Richard's case at Ypsilanti State Hospital had written to Judge Kaufman of probate court with the opinion that "the petition for admission be dismissed." "Mr. Wishnetsky," he wrote, "left the hospital on unauthorized leave on September 9, 1965. This was subsequently changed to convalescent status on September 17. It appeared that Mr. Wishnetsky, by arrangement with the court and his parents, was to stay out of the hospital and continue therapy with Dr. Irving Silver. I have talked with Mr. Wishnetsky's therapist, Dr. Silver, on two occasions and it appears that Mr. Wishnetsky is making a reasonable adjustment outside of the hospital.

"It would appear that Mr. Wishnetsky is no longer in need of in-hospital treatment."

Subsequently, however, on November 19, the doctor wrote again to Judge Kaufman suggesting this time that Richard "be placed on a Diagnostic Order" and be asked to submit himself for examination. The doctor explained that in spite of his previous opinion, "the court placed him on an extension of the temporary order. We presume it was felt that it would have a salutory effect on Richard's behavior if he realized that he could be returned to the hospital at any time. For that reason only we have recommended a Diagnostic Order as there are no recent reports from Richard or his therapist concerning his mental condition at this time."

What had occurred in the interim was that Richard had stopped going to Dr. Silver and on November 17 had started therapy with Dr. Harold Issac (pseud.), who, like Dr. Silver, taught in the department of psychiatry at a nearby medical school and had a private practice in Detroit. The court had not, in fact, extended the temporary detention order under which it still retained jurisdiction over Richard's case but had only postponed the hearing on the case from November 10 to November 24. At that time, the petition for admission first filed by Edward Wishnetsky at the end of July was dismissed by Judge Kaufman, after hearing from Dr. Issac, on the condition that the court be regularly informed of Richard's progress and advised of any disruption of therapy.

A few days before the final hearing on his case Richard had called Dr. James Spiller at U. of D. Richard said that he had taken Dr. Spiller's advice, had stayed with a psychiatrist, and had displayed the kind of control that would please the court. Everything had turned out well, he said; he was sure the petition would be dismissed and he wanted to thank Dr. Spiller for his help. Dr. Spiller says, "I felt at the time that I could help him." Yet at this point Richard's telephone calls and visits were discontinued and the psychologist never heard from Richard again.

Richard was apparently getting along well with Dr. Issac, who, in his thirties, was a younger man than Dr. Silver, and possessed of an excellent scholastic record. Richard told a friend that they had been able to establish some rapport because the psychiatrist had "agreed" with him about the source of his trouble being his parents. Reportedly, Dr. Issac found Richard suffering from a paranoid psychosis, though he seemed to be in remission and moving toward health as they began therapy. Still Dr. Issac was aware that while Richard's personality appeared to be intact, his "illness" might occasionally submerge only to surface again unexpectedly.

On December 3, Dr. Issac wrote a note to Judge Kaufman which contained the following:

> I have been seeing Richard Wishnetsky for psychotherapy since November 17, 1965. As you know, he has been hospitalized in the past half year and has experienced some rather stormy behavioral episodes. At the present time he seems very well controlled. He is working well in his relationship with me and I do not anticipate the need for hospitalization.
>
> If any such need does arise I would, of course, be in contact with his parents. Richard Wishnetsky has assured me that he would follow my medical advice if this need for hospitalization should occur.

A persistent feature of paranoid reaction is an unconscious homosexual tendency which a rigid conscience renders utterly unacceptable and which fosters extensive fear and doubt over sexuality. Like Bill Scott, Harv Stiener felt that Richard had a problem in this area. Richard, said Harv, had boasted on occasion that he had "screwed" this or that girl, but was entirely unconvincing. "In fact, I thought he might be a virgin," says Harv. "I also thought he had homosexual tendencies: Richard always wanted to get real close to you and speak softly in your ear and had his arm around you at times. And he could show a venomous hatred of women. 'All women stink and are bitches,' he said once."

One day late in November Harv encountered Richard on a bus traveling from Palmer Woods down to Wayne State; the two hadn't seen each other since the day they had clashed in Skeptics Corner. To Harv's surprise Richard was vague about his future plans. He didn't know now if he would be going to the University of Chicago in January. He didn't really know what he might be doing. On the campus at Wayne when they parted, Harv watched him walk away and was filled with a sense of his lack of purpose. "He'll never do anything," said Harv to himself. Harv's night dreams still occasionally pictured Richard attacking him, and Harv's analyst finally told him not to be involved with Richard any longer.

Richard's plans to attend the University of Chicago had apparently been scrapped because his parents, his psychiatrist, and the court wanted him to remain closer to home. There may also have been a problem with money. He seemed to be living on what he got from a sympathetic cousin for whom he said he ran errands and then in December from the substitute teaching he began doing for the Detroit Board of Education.

Under the terms of the fellowship from the divinity school he would not be able to pick up his first stipend until the end of his first quarter in April. According to Dean William Weaver, Richard had written to the divinity school "stating that he wished to defer his entrance to the beginning of the Spring Quarter [in May], stating generally and quite briefly for reasons of family difficulties at home. I replied that we could not extend his fellowship further, as it was valid only the current year and that he might wait and enter the following Autumn Quarter and reapply for a fellowship for the next year." Dean Weaver never got a reply. Exactly what happened to his plans for the University of Chicago was a very touchy subject about which Richard did not care to talk.

Through December he continued in his often solitary existence still living near Wayne State, first in his dilapidated apartment and then in a rooming house, seeing Dr. Issac on a regular schedule and doing his substitute work in the public schools. Generally, he avoided old friends but from time to time might appear and seem in rather good shape. One night he arrived at his former apartment on Twelfth Street near the University of Detroit to speak briefly with Pat Burke. He seemed very calm and well controlled as he stood in the doorway and explained: "I think I owe you five dollars" (on the phone bill they had wrangled so heatedly about a few months earlier). "I probably owe you more but now I can give you this."

"That's all right," said Pat. "You probably need it as much as I do."

"No," said Richard, "I'm pretty well fixed." They spoke only briefly; Richard didn't come in and never returned.

Sharon Thompson, home from Washington for a short while at Christmas time, felt she noted a "definite improvement" in him: "He was just beautiful. He was in good spirits, delightful and witty, and talked about a number of different plans—he was going to New York City, he said, and in the following September he would be going to the University of Chicago."

On Christmas Eve, Richard along with Larry Walters and Larry's new girl friend, Karen Joseph (pseud.), attended a revival meeting featuring faith healer A. A. Allen at the State Fair Grounds in Detroit. Larry had been anxious for Richard to meet Karen and had suggested the revival meeting as a kind of lark: he had been to a previous meeting and had "thought it was totally interesting just to watch the people there." At the meeting Richard and Karen sat back and watched Larry become "involved" in the proceedings, walking up onto the platform with the afflicted who hoped to be healed. Richard seemed to enjoy the occasion but didn't take it very seriously—a collection of sick people being robbed by a fraud, he indicated later.

Karen had learned a great deal about Richard from Larry and had quickly felt a kinship with him. Afterward when they stopped for drinks at a quiet restaurant-bar, she and Richard dominated the conversation in the effort to get to know each other better. He talked of the trip he was about to take to New York to explore the Lubavitch movement further and of his dislike for the substitute teaching he was doing. Later, as they drove back to Palmer Woods in a snowfall, all three were in a happy, spontaneous mood and sang Jewish songs together. When Richard invited his friends into his parents' home, however, the mood passed. Once inside he seemed to tighten up and become less communicative. In walking them out to the car he took Karen's hand and kissed her and told Larry how lovely she was. "*Boitshick,* you're a lucky boy," he told Larry, using the Yiddish to convey a special endearment. Karen felt a bit depressed afterward and started to cry with a "strange feeling." She says: "He was unreal. I told Larry that I had never met anyone as beautiful—no one has ever affected me like him. I can't really explain it . . . I was thrilled to have met him, but I felt so bad for him. I think I wanted to cry for him. I was just very much struck by his being so beautiful, such a very special person."

Within a couple of days Richard left for New York reportedly traveling with a Lubavitch rabbi from Detroit to an annual year-end gathering of young people at the Lubavitch center in Brooklyn. In New York, Richard stayed for a while with his grandparents but later told Larry Walters that he also spent two or three days in the

Lubavitch community "living as they do." Says Larry: "He thought maybe this was the answer. Maybe Richard Wishnetsky could contribute his best to that movement. He didn't know—it was an alternative, like Chicago or the New School were alternatives, and he explored them." But on his return a few days later Richard, though impressed with what he had witnessed in Brooklyn, seemed disappointed in his own reaction. "Afterward," recalls Larry, "he felt the Lubavitchers were just too much of a traditional group and were so caught up from birth with the practices of the Lubavitchers. He said, 'Larry, it's not for me and I guess I was mistaken.' "

Also upon his return, Richard learned that on Christmas Eve his friend Steven Lewis had married Tina Monte in a suburban church. They had been living together ever since Steven left the place he was sharing with Richard, but the decision for marriage had apparently been made unexpectedly and Richard had been unaware of the wedding until after his return from New York. Now, he seemed more solitary than ever, especially at the cheerful holiday parties he was attending.

At John Samuels' home, Richard showed up without an invitation at a cocktail party for friends of John's attractive sister, who was home from school in the East; he was generally on good behavior but stayed only an embarrassing five or ten minutes. And at a New Year's gathering of his parents' friends in the Wishnetskys' new home, he appeared in time to welcome 1966. Wearing an ascot and suffering an acne attack, he seemed tense and nervous as he offered "rather suggestive and earthy remarks" to and about a number of people at the party.

After New Year's, Richard began living at home with his parents and his fifteen-year-old sister, Ellen; his older sister, Terry, was in her sophomore year in Ann Arbor. The house, just off Seven Mile near Woodward, is a substantial though unostentatious English colonial built in the thirties or forties and not among the largest in an area of tranquil, winding, wooded streets lined with white curbstones. Richard, with his books and papers, had established himself in the basement in what seemed to one visitor a kind of retreat. But occasionally he would serve as host and guide for seminar discussions among a number of his sister Ellen's high-school friends who would come over to the house. At least one of the young men who came to a couple of the sessions found Richard capably handling discussions of contemporary Jewish novelists like Bellow, Malamud, and Philip Roth, and the Hasidic tales of Martin Buber.

Once in a while, Richard would simply leave home for a day or two or three without informing his family, though sometimes calling back to tell them where he was before eventually returning. Occasionally in December and January he spent the night at Larry Walters' apartment downtown, sleeping on the couch and being careful not to disturb Larry when he left early the next morning to reach his job as a full-time substitute or "resource" teacher at Dwyer Elementary in the heart of the ghetto. Larry recalls: "He used to come back astounded with reports of students smoking and getting pregnant and the language they used. Richard was quite disillusioned that he had to spend so much time on discipline—he wanted to give much more. He said he had to hit a couple of them. Some of their homelife, actions, and language was bizarre to the point of being almost comical."

Richard told another friend that he sometimes worked with second- and third-graders and wasn't getting along very well with some of the kids he especially disliked. An indication of the kind of work he was doing can be found in the following note to his superior, a man he addressed as Mr. Stoll, on January 28, 1966:

> I spent part of the morning reading with most of the boys out of one of the Reader's Digest.
>
> The rest of the time was spent at free play.
>
> The boys were quite co-operative and generally agreeable.
>
> The afternoon was a little rowdier, with Charles, Ronald, and Luigi, acting up, in particular—picking on Gil.
>
> The boys did their arithmetic and shop work. They seemed to enjoy the latter in particular, and worked well.
>
> (Resource Teacher—Dwyer)
> Richard Wishnetsky

One woman who then worked in the administration at Dwyer was "surprised" that Richard had been hired as a resource teacher because he seemed "very emotional." "But," she says, "since I've seen what the board of education has been hiring for substitutes over the past couple of years, I'm not surprised anymore."

During January, Richard visited the campus at the University of Detroit a few times and spoke with Kwitka Diaku. He told Kwitka that he was generally content: he liked the teaching he was doing, he said, but it was not what he wished to do in the future. The tone of his talk was perhaps more melancholy and less militant than in their previous conversations: he was talking about a dream trip to Europe where he would study and enjoy the beauty of the Grecian isles, about his "unhappy childhood" (during which he had tried to remain out of his house much of the time), about his success in school ("Teachers can't really give me a bad grade"). Otherwise, he felt himself a failure in his personal life, saying as he had frequently before, "Whatever I try to do I really fail at."

According to Bill Scott, Richard also paid visits to the apartment Steven Lewis and Tina Monte had taken after their marriage. Richard, it seemed obvious, wanted to continue his friendship with Steven, but their relationship had produced a rather troubled triangle. Again according to Bill (who is unfortunately the only source of information on Steven and Tina and their connections with Richard), Tina was paranoid, extremely possessive and domineering, and motivated by a strong penchant for destroying men. She was also a Lesbian ("It was obvious to everyone around except Steven," says Bill), and though she had slept with Steven before they were married, she no longer made herself available and attempted to impose all sorts of limitations on her new husband. "Underneath her sweet surface," says Bill, "she's the most vicious and destructive woman on the face of the earth." In short, she did not want Richard to develop his friendship with her husband and did not care to have him around. Thus, Tina began telling Steven that Richard was a "faggot" and had, in fact, homosexual designs on him. Steven's best course, she advised, would be to rid himself of Richard's perverted friendship.

Though there were apparently few people aware of it, Richard's plight had become quite desperate as he attempted to face the new year in January of 1966. It seems clear now that in his quest to realize an extraordinarily meaningful life he had been thoroughly stymied and was facing a confusing and painful dilemma. It would be nearly a year before he might again take up significant scholastic work. He had talked of being "useful" and of being a teacher, but the work he was doing at Dwyer bore little or no relation to teaching and seemed only to impress on him the hopelessness of his ghetto students. His relations with the opposite sex had degenerated into the shame and bitterness of his failure to love women or to be loved by them. His connections with most of his other friends and acquaintances had been either strained or broken or had atrophied. Religion and its traditional salvation seemed as necessary and as impossible as ever after his pilgrimage to the Lubavitchers in Brooklyn, and his Jewishness was an ambiguous mixture of pride, hope, horror, and guilt. At the age of twenty-three he was still a boy living in the home of his parents with whom he fought out of an infantile rage. The long-cherished dreams of achievement and fame had shattered on the rocks of one crisis after another. And now if the impulse to violence beat up strongly, he might not so effectively turn to his "awkward maneuvers" of the past, perhaps because many of them had been identified, explained, and in a sense taken from him in the course of his therapy.

One night late in January he stopped for a visit with John Samuels who was home alone. Over the past few months, John had seen little of Richard, though occasionally there had been the urgent, often late-night phone calls in which Richard might impose on John with an insistent request for a ride somewhere or a night's lodging (often apparently after some trouble at home). From the time they had roomed together as freshmen at the University of Michigan John had been witness to some of the more rigid and violent displays of Richard's personality. For whatever reason, Richard's capacity for hostility and violence, unnoticed by most others, had not been concealed from John. On this particular January night, Richard apparently dispensed almost entirely with attempts to hold a mask in place.

In a highly emotional condition, Richard quickly proceeded to unburden himself. At times he spoke quietly with a kind of controlled despair, but he could also become highly animated as he pounded with his hand on a table and declared that it was imperative that he find some meaning and significance in life, that it was impossible for him not to live in a meaningful fashion. His troubled monologue rose to a fevered pitch when he described a number of the fantasies and schemes which had been sifting through his mind in recent weeks. He was moving quickly about the room, then sitting in a chair, then getting up again to act out the gestures of a specific act of violence, especially in describing the possibilities of aggression against his parents.

In the course of the evening Richard talked of the possibility of kidnapping the governor and making demands for mental hospital reform as the condition for his release; of kidnapping doctors at Ypsilanti State Hospital for a similar purpose; of setting fire to the hospital or to automobiles belonging to doctors there; and of assassinating Robert S. McNamara, the Secretary of Defense. He recounted each of the fantasies (as he himself called them; they were simply possible courses of action he had recently mulled over) with a kind of drama and immediacy which fostered the impression that he was not simply mouthing wild speculation.

Richard also talked of delivering a sermon denouncing the congregation at Shaarey Zedek and then committing suicide in front of them. He spoke of driving the family car into a sanctuary wall at Shaarey Zedek. (To one or more of his other friends, he claimed that once he had in fact tried to smash the car into the side of the synagogue but had inadvertently turned the steering wheel in the wrong direction at the last instant; he had also, he said, come very close to hanging himself in the sanctuary.) He did not, says John, mention Rabbi Adler specifically but spoke of the congregation in the usual hostile terms.

There was a fairly clear rationale behind all the fantasies, John felt, some notion of what Richard thought he might achieve by their actual execution. First of all, explained Richard, he would, of course, commit an act that would attract attention, that would make him a focal point and a voice that people would have to listen to. But further he wanted to point up and dramatize the direction of modern society by demonstrating for people how far they had traveled on the road to corruption and catastrophe. And so in all his schemes, always when he spoke of suicide, he implicated a personage or an institution of some significant standing.

Though he spoke of violence against members of his family, such action didn't seem to achieve universal significance. He might kill his father and himself, for example, but since his father was a man unknown to most of the world, there would be little chance to give the act the large and vital meaning he wanted it to have for others. In any case, he had settled on nothing, and the possibilities remained for the moment only in the realm of his imagination. When John's parents returned home late in the evening, Richard broke off this line of talk and soon after left John, who kept to himself their extraordinary conversation.

THIRTY-SIX

As he approached his sixtieth birthday, March 30, 1966, Rabbi Morris Adler seemed to be arriving at the end of one period of his career while laying plans for the start of another. As he looked ahead with perhaps the reasonable expectation of at least one more decade in full possession of his talents, the future he saw was still very active but possibly more contemplative and somewhat less public.

"Morris was a lucky man," says Mrs. Adler. "He was able to see fulfilled many of the dreams that he dreamt about Judaism." Yet about the time the new Shaarey Zedek was completed he had asked, "What is happening to the synagogue as these masses of Jews, untutored and undisciplined Jewishly, enter it? Will the synagogue be able to maintain itself as a center of religious life, or will it be overwhelmed by the masses and become a secularized social institution with the Jewish motif muted?"

The rabbi's sermons were most often generalized in approach—many could have been given to a civic group at Ford Auditorium—and would exhort his audience to embrace the ideals of their faith. Aware of the subtleties of preaching to a highly affluent congregation, he might ask: "Are we doing enough in our collective and personal life to preserve the alert conscience, the sensitive heart, the vital human concern? How do we keep from insulating ourselves with our country clubs, hi-fi sets, trips to Miami? How do we reach out from our comfort into the world-at-large and open our hearts to its tragedy and needs?" When the occasion called for it, however, as on Yom Kippur, he might render incisive criticism.

"It is extremely rare that a rabbi attains the stature of Rabbi Adler in the Jewish community alone without considering his reputation in the community at large and nationally," said a friend. Yet, despite his quick rise to such prominence, private effort apparently continued to play an important role in the rabbi's life. "No one will know in how many ways he helped people," said Louis Berry. "He never spoke of such things. Only when another person was needed in order to help an individual would the confidence be broken."

During his last visit to Israel in the previous summer the Jewish National Fund had named a school after him at Gadot on the Syrian border. In December he and a party of fifty close friends had traveled to New York for the ceremony in which he was presented with an honorary doctoral degree by the Jewish Theological Seminary. "Rabbi Adler will be remembered, I think, as one of the two or three great rabbis of this generation," says his former assistant, Rabbi Groner. Lily Edelman, the editor of *Jewish Heritage,* has written, "He has been called by some the most outstanding rabbi of our day, the quality of whose thirty years of ministering to the Jewish people shall not soon be matched."

Though essentially an optimist, Morris Adler could appear to hold a less-than-rosy perspective to those who knew him well. Here again is Lily Edelman: "Despite the great success he enjoyed, however, Rabbi Adler frequently questioned his calling. Moody and sensitive, he often recoiled from the vulgarity and shallowness of Jewish communal life. He was troubled by the difficulty of reaching modern Jews, particularly the more intellectually oriented.

". . . Much of his published work as well as a vast amount of unpublished material records his feeling that the rabbi is trapped in a 'condition of pathos.' Always in a race with time, he resented the hours wasted on useless meetings and hollow public functions. A rabbi could, he once humorously observed, spend his entire career at banquet tables eating 'one long chicken dinner.' 'Eating for God's sake' was too often the order of his day. He sometimes found it easier to communicate with secularists and nonreligionists than with his own colleagues. He hungered for intellectual challenge from which his position of authority too frequently isolated him. In his own words, 'the deepest aspects of his life remained private and lonely.' "

Rabbi Adler had become increasingly aware of the frustrations of his position, observing that his "messages often fall echolessly into an oblivion of indifference, inattention, and preoccupation," learning in his counseling of "the evils which lurk beneath the cloak of respectability," and lately agonizing over a public position on a war he deplored but about which he felt the known facts were as yet insufficient to make a firm judgment on his country's role in it. He once confessed to a friend that despite being highly praised by so many, he still considered himself a failure in not truly reaching the people he served and in being unable to forge a genuine and modern approach to Judaism. According to the friend, an Orthodox rabbi in the city, Rabbi Adler felt very strongly about the "lack of consistency" in the Conservative position, and when the subject came up in conversation, he would shrug and say, "Life itself is not consistent."

"Intellectually and emotionally Rabbi Adler was a very complex man," said his Orthodox colleague. "There was a complex struggle between the mind and the heart in Rabbi Adler—the conflict of the modern intellectual with a strong emotional attachment to tradition. He would overcompensate and deny frequently the power of this attachment, but he also talked frequently about his father and quoted him often."

As he now embarked on a new year in January 1966, Rabbi Adler seemed more than ever concerned about the plight of young people, particularly the much talked about "identity crises" of young American Jews, often the most intellectually committed, who feel that their faith is neither vital nor relevant to their lives. Near the end of January, he wrote a personal letter to Richard's friends Bob and Marcia Moss, expressing his interest and concern and asking if they might consider a return to an active involvement in the life of the synagogue. Bob and Marcia had extended their hostility to include Rabbi Adler as the leader of the "materialists" and "hypocrites" whom they so despised at Shaarey Zedek, and in their written reply explained that even if they had wanted to return, which they certainly did not, the rabbi would be "the last person in the world" for whom they would return.

Yet many remarked on the rabbi's sustained good humor and optimism. "He was no Pollyanna," said a close friend, "but he insisted that in every crisis there's an opportunity and no matter what had happened he would be asking, 'How do we salvage something out of this? How can we build something of value out of this?' He was a builder. I don't think there were many times when we woke up dreading the day ahead. . . . He took himself seriously, but he was not pompous; he was utterly delightful; a magnificent storyteller, he might stay up with friends matching stories and jokes until the small hours of the morning." And the humor was only part of what seems to have been the rabbi's personal impact. Said another friend: "He gave of himself to you. He didn't remain aloof and detached and superior. He let you know that he too had problems and struggles and conflicts."

"He was enriched by his contact with people," said Professor Joe Fauman. "He might come to a home for a meeting looking tired and haggard, and yet, when people would start to arrive—maybe a close friend or a man he hadn't seen in a year—he would come alive." Yet Fauman had noted that the rabbi had often appeared quite lonely at such gatherings recently.

Though his parents had long since passed away and he was only occasionally able to see his younger brother, Benjamin, a restauranteur in New York, with him in Detroit were his daughter, Shulamith, and his son-in-law, Eli Benstein, an engineer, and their three young children, Judith, Jeremy, and Joel. The children were a delight to their grandfather and at family gatherings he was soon down on the floor playing with them in his shirt sleeves.

Goldie Adler, as the rabbi's life partner, in a full sense of the term, was the single most important person in the life of her husband. Friends talked of their "perfect" or "almost ideal" match, of her wit, intelligence, warmth, and energy, "which put her right up there with the rabbi." Said a longtime friend of the Adlers': "I remember an affair at which Goldie was looking particularly well and a man from the congregation came up and said, 'Goldie, you look so lovely, if you weren't a rabbi's wife I think I'd give you a kiss.' To which she replied. 'And if I weren't a rabbi's wife, I think I'd let you.' " A short buxom woman, her fine hair turning white and her dark eyes vivid and frank, Goldie Adler quickly communicates a gracious warmth and a practical, earthy wisdom. Her conversation is peppered with appropriate Jewish proverbs and humorous stories, but her intelligence is wide ranging and her moral indignation quick to surface. On Vietnam: "We send our boys over there and pin medals on them for doing the same things we'd throw them in jail for if they did them here." On a prominent national politician: "I've always thought he talks out of both sides of his mouth."

On a popular "Jewish" novel: "I thought it was a rag, produced purely for profit, and I wrote the author and told him so."

In the aftermath of a joint book-review lecture presented by Goldie and Morris Adler, the rabbi collected his thoughts on the state of the American rabbinate and proceeded to labor intensively over an article which he finished in the first week or so of February and sent off to *Jewish Heritage* to be published. "The Rabbi: 1966" with its dimension of personal revelation was quite unlike most of what he had previously offered for publication. He began:

> Upon no one else in the Jewish community have the hammer blows of change and mutation fallen as forcefully as upon the American rabbi (excepted are those who live in the few communities of refuge from modern life to be found in Brooklyn and Long Island—the Mea Shearim of our continent). None has been more exposed to the "acids of modernity" than he: none as storm-tossed by the multiple revolutions that have worked such havoc with the inherited and hallowed.
>
> It is small wonder that he appears to himself as standing at a crossroad of uncertainty and ambiguity, without a clear conception of his function and baffled as to direction. He does not define himself either as prophet or priest, philosopher or mystic, communal leader or administrator. He may be something of each, and the result is a blurred portrait that is not easily recognizable, and that except for the designation 'rabbi' bears little similarity to that of his predecessors. How easy it is to pick upon the weakness he betrays, the inner contradictions he unites within him, the corrosions his profession has suffered.
>
> He provides a ready target for those who delight in making ironic thrusts at the vulgarities of the organized life over which he presumably presides in their desire to exculpate themselves from their non-involvement in matters Jewish. He has attained a high degree of conspicuousness, a condition which invites critics to heap upon him the guilt for the shallowness, shrillness, and showiness of so much of communal activity. (There may be a psychological basis to the need or desire to level criticism at the rabbi.) Yet, he is more victim than culprit, more the object than the shaper of the forces of Jewish collective endeavor. The real power in the community rests in other hands, while his own influence is more apparent than vital. The Jewish community itself is in the vortex of powerful circumstances that have their origin and locus outside of it.

And he concluded:

> The rabbi is not infrequently troubled by his own inadequacies. He has not resisted what should have been resisted. He has not devoted himself to basic matters with the inflexible single-mindedness they deserve. He has permitted himself to walk

for too long on surfaces and has lived too much with the peripheral and incidental. He has not sufficiently ignored the dais and the limelight. He has failed his tradition and his people. He sometimes feels this most keenly when he is being feted or complimented.

In the rabbi are concentrated the frustrations, ambivalences, confusions, and uncertainties which bedevil the modern Jew, intensified by his greater rootedness in Judaism and magnified by the representative nature of his position.

"In the last few years," said Rabbi Groner, "Rabbi Adler had begun to slow his pace down a little and was beginning to assess his position and his work, to withdraw somewhat into a more reflective life." In fact, the rabbi had a number of literary projects planned and was in the process of organizing some of his own short pieces for a collection. He had also embarked on a biography of Hayim Greenberg, the Labor Zionist theoretician, journalist, and editor who before his death in 1953 had made an extraordinary impression on Rabbi Adler both in his literary work and in their personal contact. Though a "secularist," Greenberg had become for the rabbi "a personal hero of immeasurable impact" as is clear (along with the reasons for it) in the memorial essay on Greenberg which the rabbi had written in 1963. Greenberg, he said, was a nationalist with a universalist view, a "secularist" whose tone was religious, an "aristocrat" at home with "the masses of his people," an ethical and philosophical man thrust into a life of politics and practicalities. The theme of the essay was the "seamless wholeness" which Hayim Greenberg appeared to achieve in his own person, encompassing many of the paradoxes, dichotomies, and ambiguities with which the rabbi often felt himself beset. Greenberg, said the rabbi, had "attained a consummation denied so many of his generation," and the rabbi's question "Whence this completeness and unity?" was no doubt prompted by the central motivation not only for his study of Greenberg but also for his own continuing exploration of world and self.

If Morris Adler had a flaw, it was perhaps a tragic one, fashioned from the virtue of his proud and articulate intelligence which thrust him into the attempt to comprehend and resolve within himself "all of the frustrations, ambivalences, confusions, and uncertainties which bedevil the modern Jew."

THIRTY-SEVEN

After breaking off contact with David Roth for nearly two months, Richard finally called his old friend one day near the end of January and arranged to meet him in the Decanter Bar. He seemed nervous and depressed and began drinking a lot of beer. In the next couple of weeks, David would find Richard doing considerably more drinking than he had previously known him to do. Richard said a number of surprising and disturbing things. He had decided that all the academic and intellectual work he had done over the past few years had come to naught, that he had been duping himself intellectually with the convictions he had supposedly arrived at. He now questioned—perhaps despaired of—his own talents and his ability to achieve any of his goals. He had just been "living with a lot of books" for the past year or so and not really reading them, he said—an admission which David found quite shocking. When Richard said he had been seriously considering suicide, David (though he had often attacked many of Richard's opinions in the past) now found himself rather desperately defending Richard's past optimism, trying to cheer him up and restore some of his confidence.

Richard remained in low spirits. Perhaps the ideas he had been committed to were still valid, he thought, but he had no positive relationship to them anymore: they were, in fact, valueless to him because he could no longer do anything with them. David changed his tack a bit and tried to argue that it was all to the good that Richard had moved beyond his past illusions and could now proceed to achieve whatever he wished, given his obviously great potential. Richard offered little response to David's suggestion that he rest for a few weeks, pull himself together, and try a new start.

On or about January 31 Richard wrote a letter to Sharon Thompson in Washington, D. C. There were no bright plans quoted nor references to the future, and Sharon was so disturbed by the aimless tone of the letter that she immediately wrote back telling Richard that she thought he must very quickly set out realistic goals for himself. He must get himself moving toward something, she pleaded. She didn't hear from Richard again.

On Tuesday, February 1, Richard began to write a tract in longhand which would eventually cover six pages. Titled "Fantasy Regarding an Assassination of Robert S. McNamara," the piece contains an apology for his imagined murder of the former Secretary of Defense along with a bitter, rambling commentary on himself and the world in which he was trying to live. He opened as follows:

> My act was motivated by philosophical and social reasons, not political ones. It is a protest, the registration of an outrage, a dire warning: It's author entertains no illusions as to it bringing about any immediate substantial change in the American scene.
>
> At present I do believe there will be a change in the future —a change for the worse, most likely to a point when it will become too late for my return to a better condition. (i.e. the bomb, the proliferation of nuclear weapons, the development of doomsday machines . . .)
>
> . . . The selfishness, stupidity and vanity of men shall succeed in triumph over whatever goodness there is—the ultimate triumph will bring this obliteration, both spiritual and physical, of this planet. Hail Brave New World! Hail Nothingness!

At one point Richard supplied a mock headline for his fantasized act: "ANTI-HERO KILLS PSEUDO-HERO." About Mr. McNamara he wrote:

> [He] symbolizes that which I despise—the business mentality which is more concerned with material matters than human matters—the kind of mentality (Protestant ethic) which is most responsible for the dehumanization of society, the prostitution of the intellect, resulting in a very bright but neither wise nor profound man. Ford Motor Co., Success, the U. S. Army, Ann Arbor. He who lives by the sword shall die by the sword. How much did Mr. McNamara take into consideration the killing of innocent Vietnamese which has resulted from American bombings, for this killing is murder?

Of America Richard wrote that it "is rapidly disintegrating":

> The church has become a hypocrisy whose structures no longer find genuine residence in the souls of those who hear them. And most importantly and most sadly of all, the family is swiftly becoming—if it has not already arrived there—shot to

> hell. . . . I am part of the bastard progeny of this nation. We are building not men, but a generation of barbarians and mediocrities who recognize and will breed no value higher than their paltry selfish selves. Zombies!

About himself he wrote:

> My life will probably end with a whimper—a depressed whimper. Possibly a manic bang. Since I cannot live like a man, I hope to die like one. I am entering the final stage of unreality. . . . Withdrawn, unable to develop successfully extended, intimate and frequent human relationships. At times terribly self-conscious. An aware . . . man who can see, envision, a promised land of manhood but has become convinced of his inability to enter it. Prefers the easy way out. You say that I am sick—you are right. You dismiss me because I am sick—in that you are wrong. . . . The dark side of creativity is sickness. . . . Anyway, in our society to be normal is to be sick, to be hung up on loneliness, insecure about one's self, overly concerned about pleasing everybody, being 'nice' all the time—damn niceness! . . . not offending anyone, so that one winds up pleasing no one and to boot not knowing who or why one is."

Richard also included advice and instructions to some of his friends about running their lives and arranging their personal relations. He added a "last will and testament" in which he left whatever money he possessed to the Jewish National Fund and the Lubavitcher Hasidim and then concluded: "Judaism in America does not need to worry about anti-Semitism destroying it from without. The American Jewish community is destroying itself from within. Shaarey Zedek is a synagogue which bears witness against God."

For the evening of the Tuesday on which Richard began his tract, Larry Walters had arranged a blind date for Richard. (Larry hadn't called it a date and had only invited Richard "to join the group" to see the Fellini film *Juliette of the Spirits.*) The girl was Leah Kaplan (pseud.), a good friend of Larry's girl, Karen Joseph, and an education major at Wayne State; attractive, with long brown hair and large brown eyes, she had heard a great deal about Richard from Larry and Karen. Richard was standing outside his parents' home without gloves, boots, or hat in twenty degrees of temperature and a steady snowfall when Larry drove up with Karen and Leah. Covered with snow when he climbed into the car, he remarked about preferring to be outside than inside his parents' home. He seemed generally in good spirits and was dressed neatly in sport coat and tie.

At the theater he did not appear to get involved in the film and announced later that he hadn't cared for it; in a movie, he said, he liked a story line that was coherent and easy to follow. Afterward at a restaurant Richard seemed a bit moody—long silences broken by exuberant outbursts—but otherwise quite normal. Leah noticed that he seemed to get on famously with Larry who would playfully call him "Zorba" to elicit an appropriate response. "I've never seen two men so obviously fond of one another," she said. When she mentioned that she was about to decorate her room in her family's new apartment, Richard teased her about buying some of the curiosities sold at the restaurant—commercially produced antique plaques, posters, and prints. He seemed depressed at this point and sank into one of his long silences.

Outside Larry and Richard cleaned snow off the windshield while the girls sat in the car and talked about Richard. Leah had been told that he would remind her of someone and now Karen wanted to know who.

"Jerry," she said, knowing that Karen was thinking of the rabbinical student Leah had previously dated. "But he also reminds me of someone else," she added.

"Who?" asked Karen.

"David," said Leah, referring to a young man she had dated years earlier who had ended his life by hanging himself.

Sitting with Richard in the back seat on the way home, Leah complained that all her belongings were still packed in the basement of her parents' apartment. "I want so much to get them out and into my room," she said.

"I don't have much use for material things," said Richard.

"Well, I do," replied Leah. "I like very much the paintings and antiques and books I have. Books shouldn't be packed away in the basement."

"All of a sudden" recalls Leah, "Richard became very excited and interested when he heard about the books and said, 'I always have books around me. Books are the greatest things in the world.' He seemed more interested after that, and we talked about other things including religion."

For the remainder of the ride home Richard was his old animated self, offering his usual remarks about the truly religious lives of the Lubavitcher people in Brooklyn in contrast to the pretentious one-day-a-week faith of Congregation Shaarey Zedek, though he also rendered praise to Rabbi Adler. When they dropped Leah off, Richard walked her to the door and said he had enjoyed the evening very much. He implied he would call her some time soon, and Leah left him hoping he would. That night he slept at Larry's apartment and reported that he would soon ask Leah for a date.

During this first week in February Richard met David Roth a number of times on campus, often in the Decanter where Richard would occasionally work on different drafts of his apologia for assassination. Richard explained to his friend that he was only working his fantasies out as a theoretical exercise, but sometimes included the hint that he might just carry one of them into reality. He seemed tense and excited in the bar, showed David a number of different drafts, and wanted to know what David thought. Though Richard presented his writing as having some literary importance, David (not wanting to encourage him at all in this direction) tried to belittle what he read, and said it was badly written. "But what of the ideas?" asked Richard. It was all pretty trite stuff, said David. "Warmed-over Dostoevski": why didn't he broaden his scope a bit and come up with something more original?

As he previously had with John Samuels, Richard spoke of the possibilities of suicide or of assassination and suicide, the two always linked in an attempt to dramatize and publicize his ideas and vision. Though he didn't mention Rabbi Adler specifically as a possible victim, he often talked of committing suicide at Shaarey Zedek as an act of protest. He wanted to subject Rabbi Adler to the humiliation of having spelled out for him just what sort of congregation it was that he led.

Richard also talked about the fights he said he had been having with his parents, especially his father, and showed David some of his writing which referred to his troubles at home. He accepted his role in the breakdown, he said, and felt he had caused his parents pain and trouble. Their problems were simply symptomatic of humanity's failures, and they should not be held overly culpable. The same with Dr. Zimmerman, he said; she was really a good woman, he simply hadn't been able to get along with her either.

One day Richard asked David in the course of a conversation, "Do you know where you can get me a gun?"

"No, I certainly do not," said David, quite shocked. "And I certainly wouldn't get you one even if I did. What the hell do you want with a gun?"

Richard explained that he was making plans to kill himself, and he thought the gun would probably provide the best method. David again tried to buck Richard up, but again apparently to little avail. Also about this time their mutual friend John Samuels was faced with a similar task one evening when Richard drove him down to the Traffic Jam, a popular bar near the Wayne campus. Richard had apparently arranged the use of his grandmother's car for the evening and began talking about suicide as they sped sixty miles an hour down the John Lodge Freeway toward Wayne State. How easy it would be, mused Richard, to turn the car into a concrete abutment and end it all very quickly. John, with a vivid memory of Richard's talk in their last conversation, was highly alarmed, but never looked at Richard and kidded him about the notion in an effort to keep a light, rational banter going.

At the Traffic Jam and after a couple of beers, Richard seemed lively and animated but still quite desperate. Most of what he had previously told David Roth about the failure of his academic work he repeated now for John.

In a sense, John was deeply worried about Richard for the first time. Over the past year or two he and David had discussed Richard a number of times and had compared notes. Both had agreed that if Richard was ever forced to admit that his intellectual endeavors were amounting to little or nothing, he would be most certainly in very deep trouble. Richard, they knew, had never been able to take the slightest implication that his academic work was anything less than extraordinary. If you implied that what he was doing intellectually might not be of the utmost importance, Richard would fly into a rage and dismiss you with contempt.

Now John agreed that Richard's sense of identity had been thoroughly undermined and devastated by his hopeless admission of intellectual confusion, impotence, and failure. As they sat in the Traffic Jam, John argued that Richard, though probably right about his work, had in fact gained an insight that could prove very valuable if he could use it as a new point of departure. Still an atmosphere of despair seemed to envelop Richard.

One morning in the first few days of February, Richard came to the synagogue of Congregation Shaarey Zedek, and after the daily services held by some of the men of the congregation along with Rabbi Adler, proceeded to make something of a scene in the hall outside the sanctuary. He spoke in a raised and angry voice, "ranting and raving" at the rabbi, who in reply admonished him (also in a raised voice) and told him to go to the rabbi's study where they would talk in private. After they had been closeted for a while, Richard emerged apparently calmed by his exchange with Rabbi Adler.

Within the past half dozen or so days Richard had stopped keeping appointments with his psychiatrist, Dr. Issac, and was no longer reporting to Dwyer for his duties as a substitute teacher.

On Thursday, February 3, the day he apparently finished the tract on his fantasized assassination of Robert McNamara, Richard called Leah Kaplan. On the phone he repeated that he had really enjoyed their evening together and said he had wanted to see her again over the coming weekend. Instead something had come up, he explained, which made a weekend date impossible. Nonetheless, though he couldn't see her for the next few days, he would definitely call again next week. Leah said she would be glad to hear from him. Just what Richard might have had planned for the weekend is subject to speculation, but one of his activities on February 3 is clearly documented: he traveled some sixty miles to the Michigan-Ohio line at Toledo and bought a gun.

Before it recently passed a city ordinance which improved somewhat on the state of Ohio's extraordinarily lax gun-control laws, Toledo was the place where most of the hoods, thugs, and convicted criminals from the Detroit area bought their handguns. Unlike Michigan, where a license to purchase a handgun must be obtained from the local police and is restricted to those without criminal record and not adjudged mentally ill, Toledo at the time had no such restrictions and welcomed anyone, whether state resident or not, to purchase from their many prosperous gun merchants. As a result, Detroit police reported that a high percentage of the handguns they had confiscated from criminals (upwards of one hundred per week) had been traced back to the Ohio city.

In Toledo Richard walked into the People's Loan Company, a pawnshop four blocks from police headquarters, and selected a twenty-year-old Colt New Police model .32-caliber revolver, chrome-plated, with a less-than-two-inch barrel sawed off from its original five inches and a cylinder which held six shots. He gave his correct name and street address but said he lived in Dayton, Ohio; he paid $69.95 plus $2.10 Ohio sales tax for a total of $72.05. "It was a piece of junk worth not more than $20," a police expert would say later. The pawnshop had purchased the weapon two weeks earlier for $10.

In the evening of Sunday February 6, Richard bought a ticket to see the film *The Slender Thread* at a theater about a mile from his parents' home. As he walked into the lobby, he met Janis Newman, the girl who several months earlier had offered to marry him in order to get him out of The Haven. Janis, who had seen Richard briefly only once or twice over the past few months, had been in low spirits that night and had decided to treat herself to a movie. Now she said to Richard, "Why don't you come down and sit with me?" He accepted the invitation and bought her some popcorn. They watched as a troubled Ann Bancroft was carefully coaxed from the brink of self-destruction by Sidney Poitier whose earnest help she had tapped by calling the number of a suicide prevention center (a service agency which, incidentally, did not exist in Detroit at the time). Richard was apparently so engrossed in the film that he seemed oblivious to the fact that his nose was continually running and in need of blowing. The point of the film—that since the woman really had much to live for, it would have been a tragedy had she killed herself—had seemed obvious enough to Janis. But when she asked Richard for his opinion as they walked out of the theater, he explained that the woman had actually been right in the first place—she really didn't have anything to live for and should have been left to end her life.

When Janis learned that he had no car, she offered him a ride home. As they drove, Richard said he had been walking for hours that evening before ending up at the theater and had been going off on long walks lately at all hours of the day or night. After a few minutes as he sat close to the car door and leaned his head against it, he said, "You know, I've been thinking about the idea of assassination lately, of assassinating someone. Not that I've really planned it out, or that I'm actually going to do something like this —but my victim, you know, would be some great man whose assassination would shock the world."

He went on to describe McNamara as a possible victim, as a man great in the eyes of the world but epitomizing everything evil in man, everything that had gone wrong with modern society. In any case he would choose someone whom most people thought to be invincible and inviolable, thereby cutting people loose from some of their cherished convictions. Janis asked at one point if he was seeing a psychiatrist and Richard said, "No, they can't help me." This time he made no mention of the possibility of suicide.

Richard said he wanted to walk some more and asked if Janis would join him. Janis, however, had become so depressed by what she had heard from Richard that she said it was too cold and too late and she really had to get home. They were still about a mile from his home, but he asked if she would drop him off right there. As she was pulling over to the curb, he explained briefly that he had recently "discovered two new things, two good things in the world." One was movies—he'd been going to all kinds of movies lately, he said. And the other was sex—he'd "discovered" sex, he said, and boasted coarsely about his extraordinary prowess. Janis felt she finally had clear evidence that Richard was disintegrating, that part of him was obviously standing well off to watch as he said things he didn't really believe. Out of her fear and concern she asked him to call her some time soon; he said he would and stepped out of the car for another long walk in the cold dark night.

THIRTY-EIGHT

On the morning of Monday, February 7, Richard reported for a physical examination at the Fort Wayne army induction center. He had lost his student deferment after dropping out of the University of Detroit, and was now, at age twenty-three, eligible for the draft. After test and interrogation he was told to return the following day for an interview with an army psychiatrist.

Later in the day Richard met David Roth on the Wayne State Campus and at one point announced that he had recently gone to Toledo and had bought himself a gun. Yesterday, said Richard, he had waited until he was alone in his parents' home and then had tested the weapon by shooting it into a pile of newspapers in the basement. Shooting the gun, he said, had given him a feeling of power. David was not shown the gun and would never actually see it; though unsure whether he should take Richard's talk seriously, he had begun to think about what action he might take. Before they parted on Monday afternoon, he agreed to meet Richard in the Decanter later in the evening, an appointment Richard didn't keep.

Also on Monday Richard called his friend Larry Walters. "Richard was very upset with me because we couldn't get together," Larry recalls. "And he said, 'When am I going to see you? What's this crap with school? What's more important? He was like calling out to me, but I didn't really pick it up until afterwards. I didn't mean to be like 'I can't be bothered with you now,' but maybe I sounded that way. I can't remember."

Early Monday evening Richard made another call, this time to Janis Newman, and again wanted to set up a meeting. He was downtown, he said, and he wanted Janis to come down from her parents' home on the northwest side to see *Dr. Zhivago* with him. Janis said she was not anxious to drive downtown alone at night, but wouldn't he come out to see her later at her parents' home? Richard said he would.

He had seen *Dr. Zhivago* before, quite possibly more than twice. Intensely romantic in both substance and style, sweeping in scope, and set in the Russia of his grandparent's generation, it no doubt held great appeal for Richard. Zhivago himself was likely a figure of much interest, but he may have been most involved in the story of Pasha, the young student first seen passing out leaflets announcing a workers' rally. Naïve and self-righteous, Pasha is described as one of those idealistic, honest, and pure young men who will invariably ruin the happiness of anyone they become close to. After the war breaks out, he is apparently killed leading a charge but turns up again as the rigid and ruthless Red Guard General Stralnikov when the revolution engulfs Russia. He has become vicious, totally without regard for human feelings, capable of burning a whole village for little or no reason; as he explains to Zhivago. "In Russia, history has destroyed personal feelings." Near the end of the film, one learns that he has been arrested and has grabbed the pistol of one of his guards to shoot himself in the head.

From downtown, Richard took two buses and walked about a mile to get to Janis Newman's, where he found her alone. With him, he brought some of the writing he had worked on earlier in the day, and he was anxious for Janis to read it. They sat at the kitchen table and Janis began to read from four handwritten pages of notes which obviously constituted for Richard an important literary document. Filled with bitterness and hostility, it spoke of the current state of evil in the world and referred to human beings as "bloated insects." At one point, Richard had written in post-factum terms of an event apparently scheduled to occur at Shaarey Zedek. Further on he included some quotes he had copied out from the lines of Camus, Sartre, Dostoevski, and Buber.

In part the notes read:

> My distorted, disoriented voice either barely uttered or tremendously violent, gives you a slight horrifying glimpse into the dehumanizing future that awaits you and your unfortunate children, who will be healthy, comfortable and secure beyond your fondest dreams and just as diseased. . . . Since I feel that I am no longer able to make any significant creative contributions I shall make a destructive one. What happened in Shaarey Zedek happens only once in a lifetime—it happens in Vietnam, it ocurs everyday—the slaughtering of the innocent, except that the Vietnamese are really innocent. . . . Suffer in your frozen hells of apathy, boil in the self-hate of outraged impotence. Listen to my voice, you deaf ones. Listen to how sick, sad, lonely and forlorn it is.

Janis found Richard's writing to be "rather incriminating" and so shot through with bitter hate and frustration that she could only manage to get through a page and a half. She stopped and said, "This is sick! Don't you know how sick this is?"

"Yes, I do," said Richard.

Janis proceeded to subject Richard to the only lecture she ever gave him—about how he was letting himself destroy himself, how his writing concentrated on only one aspect of reality. "What is your evidence," she demanded, "for saying that human beings are basically so evil?" Richard mentioned authors and books which he said substantiated his position. "Well," said Janis, "I'm sure if I were better-read I could find other authors to take the opposite view and argue just as effectively. What other evidence do you have?"

"My own experience," said Richard. "I don't need to cite evidence. I know it to be true."

He really should be taking care of himself, said Janis. He should be seeing a psychiatrist—what had happened with his treatment?

Richard said he had just been playing with the doctors—he hadn't been really telling them his troubles. He and Dr. Issac, for example, had only philosophical discussions and never really got around to his problems. By the way, he said, he had taken the army induction exam that morning and had gone in with the intention of flunking the psychological test. He had told them that he wanted to be inducted, and when they had asked him why, had said because he wanted the opportunity to kill his sergeant. Janis pleaded with him to go back in good faith to his psychiatrist, and Richard, wanting an end to the subject, said perhaps he would.

Finally Janis said she had some studying to do for her graduate courses at Wayne State, and they moved into the living room. She began with her books, and he started to read somewhere in the middle of his copy of *The Brothers Karamazov,* which had lately been his frequent companion. As usual he was soon underlining and writing notes to himself in the margins. For example, near the beginning of the book he had underlined a passage which describes Alyosha, the gentle and forgiving Karamazov; in the margin he had written, "Me." The passage reads:

> . . . Add to that that he was to a certain extent a young man of our times, that is, honest by nature, demanding truth, seeking it, believing in it, and believing in it, demanding to serve it with all the strength of his soul, yearning for an immediate act of heroism and wishing to sacrifice everything, even life itself, for that act of heroism.

The lines that immediately follow this passage incidentally provide an interesting commentary:

> . . . these young men unhappily fail to understand that the sacrifice of life is, in many cases, the easiest of all sacrifices, and that to sacrifice, for instance, five or six years of their seething youth to hard and tedious study, if only to multiply tenfold their powers of serving the truth and the cause they have set before them as their goal—such a sacrifice is utterly beyond the strength of many of them.

Though Richard identified strongly with both Alyosha, the most "religious" of the brothers, and Ivan, the most "intellectual," Dmitri may have been the brother whose plight involved him most intensely. Feeling cursed and shamed by his patrimony of "insect lust" as a Karamazov, Dmitri begins his movement toward the redemption of effective manhood in the scene in which he is hiding beneath the window of his father's bedroom and is about to club his father to death. At the last second Dmitri decides not to kill his father. On his escape from the garden, however, he encounters Grigory, the old servant in his father's home, the man who had actually raised him and acted as a father surrogate. As Grigory tries to stop him, Dmitri clubs the old man nearly to death and goes off fully intending suicide, from which only good fortune and the love of Grushenka finally save him.

Richard, who felt he had neither good fortune nor the love of a Grushenka, got up after five minutes with his book and asked Janis to put on a record and dance with him. Janis tried to discourage him, but he was insistent, so she put her studies aside and started Astrid Gilberto singing on the hi-fi. As they danced, Janis felt uncomfortable with him, and when Richard started to kiss her, she thought to herself, "No, this is just too sick." He looked into her eyes and said, "Please! Just this once," but she broke away saying, "No, Richard, I just don't feel like it." Richard became angry to a point, then stopped and controlled himself. Soon after, she drove him to Palmer Woods and asked if she might come in to see the Wishnetsky's new home. When they went in he gave her a tour punctuated with derogatory remarks about his parents' materialism and spoke of his loathing for their new home.

On Tuesday, February 8, Richard returned to the Fort Wayne center for his visit with a psychiatrist. Though the results of his tests are privileged information, it was announced later that the army had found him to be unacceptable for induction. Unofficially it was said the decision had been swifty and easily made on the basis of the obvious disturbance he had shown under psychiatric examination.

Also on Tuesday, Richard put in a call to his own psychiatrist, Dr. Issac. He hadn't seen Dr. Issac for at least a week and a half, but now he agreed to come in for an hour on Friday, three days away. Later, some time after ten o'clock Tuesday evening, David Roth got together with John Samuels to discuss Richard in David's office (he was now on the instructional staff at Wayne State).

"We sat there," says John, "feeling quite stupid and inadequate, asking ourselves, 'What are we going to do? Wishnetsky is apparently in a rather precarious condition and he says he has a gun. What do we do about it?' " The problem was deciding whom they should call—police, parents, or psychiatrist. They decided that police action might do more harm than good and arouse even more hostility in Richard. Actually the police could do nothing on the basis of the information John and David could supply, anyway. Calling the Wishnetskys might also cause trouble, prompting a confrontation between Richard and his parents, and John and David feared what he might do with a gun at hand. So they decided to call Ypsilanti State Hospital. John managed to speak to the doctor who had treated Richard there and was given the name of Dr. Irving Silver. A call to Dr. Silver produced Dr. Issac's name. About eleven o'clock, David called Dr. Issac and asked if they could come to his home to discuss their concern for his patient, Richard Wishnetsky.

The doctor said it was very late and he was sure the matter could be handled over the phone. David proceeded to describe Richard's recent behavior, his writing, and his talk of a gun. Dr. Issac seemed not surprised nor overly alarmed and said that Richard had been saying such things and acting in this way before. He asked David if he thought Richard was in imminent danger of killing himself that night. David said he hadn't seen Richard for a day or so. The psychiatrist suggested that if they saw Richard they do everything possible to get him to come in for a visit. He indicated there was little he could do until Richard came of his own accord. In any case, Dr. Issac assured them that if Richard acted out his hostility, the result would be directed only against himself.

"I failed to see how this was a comforting thought," says John. Afterward John and David agreed that they had probably done their duty, but they still weren't quite satisfied or sure that the right things would be done. Yet, from what little John knew of Richard's therapeutic relationship with Dr. Issac, it seemed to be his best chance for help. Most of all, John feared doing anything which might undermine that relationship.

This concern was also perhaps a prime motivating factor for Dr. Issac, who apparently decided to wait for Richard to show up at his appointed time on Friday. Since psychiatry today is unable to answer when or why a man's aggressive fantasy will turn to action, the question of the danger a patient might pose is among the most difficult a therapist is forced to confront.

Eleven o'clock Wednesday morning found Richard walking near the middle of the Ambassador Bridge, the giant span connecting

Detroit with the Canadian city of Windsor. It was a bright, lovely morning with the sun sparkling on the water of the Detroit River far below; there was little snow left from the recent storms and the bridge was clear. In front of him was Windsor, behind him Detroit, each city spreading itself away from its front on the river.

Richard wore a long gray coat, walked very slowly, and looked down at the water. Behind him from Detroit came two young college girls hitchhiking from Chicago to Boston by way of Canada, wearing wool pants and high boots and carrying green book bags. In a jolly mood they were walking at an energetic pace and soon advanced on Richard. One of them recalled afterward: "He could have been considering jumping, although this did not occur to me until later. He looked like a student, although I cannot place just what about him made me think this. Anyway, as we were planning to pace him, we said 'Good morning.' This was the entry to start a conversation, and he started asking us what we were doing. We explained in a matter-of-fact way that we were hitchhiking from Chicago—he seemed to approve very much. He had a very friendly, gentle , and a very polite manner. He said that he had lived in Detroit for a long time and had never seen Windsor so he was going this morning. This we also approved of."

Richard said he was a student in political science at the University of Michigan, and it was soon established that in Ann Arbor he knew quite well a sister and brother-in-law of one of the girls. As they walked along together, Richard responded even more warmly and was soon carrying the girls' bags for them. Among other things they talked about the University of Chicago graduate school, Vietnam, and the draft. Said one of the girls. "[He] mentioned that he had no likelihood of going into the draft since he qualified for exemption on a number of counts—including having been in a mental institution and something about homosexuality. The way he worded it I couldn't quite tell whether this was something true or something he had said to be exempted from the draft, or perhaps something flip to get attention . . . The comment might also have implied that he had tried it only once—I can't remember the reference well enough."

When the girls mentioned that at one point in their trip they had run out of money, Richard tried hard but unsuccessfully to make them accept some of his. After about fifteen minutes of talk he left them at a main highway on the Canadian side where they soon got a ride. Quite favorably impressed, the girls quickly wrote down his name so as not to forget it. One of them recalls, "The experience was pleasant, cordial, relaxed, and not seemingly that of a terribly disturbed person."

Later on Wednesday after his visit to Windsor, Richard saw David Roth at the latter's small dingy basement apartment on the campus at Wayne. They hadn't seen each other since Monday and now David pressed Richard to return to the psychiatrist and continue treatment. Richard said psychiatry just wouldn't help and put the question off, but he now seemed in a very calm, pleasant, almost happy mood. He was talking again of plans for the future: he would make himself some money (driving a truck perhaps for his cousin), get himself an apartment, and later on go to school at the University of Chicago. He was vague about all of this but had stopped talking altogether of assassination or suicide. David came to the hopeful feeling that there might be some cause for reassurance.

Wednesday evening, John Samuels spotted Richard's friend Marty Sharpe in the student center at Wayne State and related in some detail what had been happening to Richard in the past few months during which Marty had lost contact with him. John disturbed Marty by accusing him of being a shallow and disloyal friend to Richard, who, he said, had been talking about Marty and about wanting to see him. The next morning, Thursday, Marty called Richard's home and, finding him out, spoke with Mrs. Wishnetsky for about an hour. From her he learned more about Richard's recent history, the hospitalization and the course of therapy; he expressed concern but did not tell Richard's mother about her son apparently owning a gun and talking of assassination and suicide. Mrs. Wishnetsky promised to make a special note of telling Richard to call Marty. She thought perhaps Marty could cheer him up.

But Richard had left home on Thursday and would not return. At four o'clock that afternoon he was walking away from the Briggs Building on the campus at the University of Detroit when he encountered Kwitka Diaku heading for one of her classes.

"Richard, what are you doing here?" she asked, not having seen him for a few weeks.

"Well, I have some business," he said. They exchanged pleasantries. He said he was going to school at Wayne and that it was no better than U. of D., maybe even worse. Kwitka had to get to her class so they arranged to meet afterward at six. She found him at that time waiting at the bench near the chapel where he had read to her from *The Prophet* during the previous summer. Now he seemed calm, natural, and rather content—even happy, thought Kwitka. They walked across Livernois for some coffee at Leo's.

"He said that he had finally decided that he was going to make something of himself," recalls Kwitka, "that he was really going to do something for humanity. He said, 'I have to leave some sort of trace.' It was rather prophetic of him. He was going to do a great deed. He was very decisive but in a calm way. He wasn't upset at all, in fact he seemed so content that I thought maybe he had gotten some sort of scholarship, maybe even that he had decided to become a rabbi. I felt rather happy for him and said to myself, 'He's finally found what he wants to do, what he wants to achieve.'

"He said also that he had been seeing Rabbi Adler during that term and that he was a good friend of the family. He said he saw the rabbi constantly—once or twice a week. And he seemed more positive toward the rabbi. The talks they were having made him feel better, he said. But he also kept referring to the fact that he was going to leave a lasting mark on this world. I thought maybe he was going to write a book or something."

After their coffee they walked back to the other side of Livernois, where Kwitka would catch her bus for home. As he waited with her, he said he was tired and sat down on the curb of the busy seven-lane avenue.

"Richard, you're going to get run over," said Kwitka. He joked lightly that it wouldn't matter, but she got him to move. Before she stepped on her bus about seven o'clock he said, "I'll meet you here again on Tuesday before your class at four." Kwitka agreed and he added, "And maybe we could even have dinner next week." She smiled and said, "Well, we'll talk about it next week."

"He gave no indication at all of being upset or going through some sort of turmoil," she says. "And usually I could tell very easily if something was upsetting him."

After seeing Kwitka off, Richard may have traveled down to the Wayne State campus to pay a call on Tina and Steven Lewis at their apartment. According to Bill Scott, the triangular troubles, which had afflicted Richard's relations with Steven and Tina since their marriage in December, came to a head during such a visit on either Thursday evening or Wednesday evening; Bill was given the details on Friday in a phone call he made to Steven and Tina inviting them and Richard to a party he was soon to throw. From what Bill could gather, Tina, who had been trying to get her new husband to liquidate his friendship with Richard, finally handled the matter with Richard herself, calling him a "faggot" and a "queer" and accusing him of trying to destroy her marriage with his homosexual designs on Steven. She told Richard to leave them alone and never come back. Steven, apparently siding with his wife, agreed with her description of the situation and in effect terminated his relationship with Richard.

Whether the blowup occurred on Thursday night or on Wednesday, Richard spent Thursday night in David Roth's tiny book-filled apartment. David remarked again to himself on his troubled friend's newfound equanimity. Carrying with him a large leather satchel filled with clothes, books, and other belongings, Richard had asked if he could sleep at David's that night because he said he was in the process of leaving his parents' home and finding himself an apartment. As he had on Wednesday, David noted with some relief that Richard's hostile and violent feelings now seemed to have drained from him. Reportedly at some time on Thursday, Richard called his father from a pay phone and said he would not be home that night. Among other things, Mr. Wishnetsky asked him to come to Shaarey Zedek on Saturday because his younger sister, Ellen, would be reading the Prayer for Our Country before the congregation and Richard's grandmother and other family members would be there. Richard told his father he absolutely would not come.

On Friday morning David was up and out early with a busy day ahead. He told Richard about a political meeting scheduled for that afternoon and suggested they meet there. Richard said he would come if he could. Before he left the apartment with his belongings sometime later Richard wrote a note for his friend saying that he didn't need the five dollars David had borrowed from him recently and that David should therefore give it to charity. It was something Richard had done before. Shortly after noon on the street outside MacKenzie Hall Richard encountered Janis Newman. She was with a friend and they spoke only briefly. But Janis recalls, "He was wild-eyed, intense, and nervous—I had never seen him so bad before." Janis asked him to call her and Richard said he would; he was moving out of the house and into an apartment, he said.

By one o'clock Richard had gathered up his tan leather grip and a brown paper bag containing record albums and had traveled the two blocks from MacKenzie Hall to a small cheap hotel at 70 West Alexandrine called the Strathmore House. As usual dressed neatly in a gray suit, white shirt, and tie, he asked the young woman behind the registration desk if he could have a room for the night. He printed in his correct name and address, paid the correct change for the room with a five-dollar bill, a dime, and a nickel, and then carried his things up to 332, a pleasant newly furnished room with a placid landscape hanging over the bed. In his leather satchel he carried a pair of slacks, two clean shirts, some clean underwear, socks, and toilet articles. Also in the grip were four books: *The Brothers Karamazov, The Portable Nietzsche,* Ortega y Gasset's *The Revolt of the Masses,* and a copy of the Holy Scriptures. Of the six record albums in the paper bag two featured the Soviet Army Chorus and Band and the others presented Igor Stravinsky, Arturo Toscanini, Joan Baez, and Theodore Bikel. The Bikel album featured Israeli songs. Richard also had with him much of the writing he had been doing recently, including his unmailed letter dated October 20 which began, "I think too much. I don't think enough"; his six-page tract on his fantasized murder of McNamara; his four pages of notes written at the beginning of the week with reference to "what happened at Shaarey Zedek"; a letter of introduction to certain people at the University of London; and other similar papers. Also in his possession were more than two dozen Smith & Wesson .32-caliber cartridges and his gun. Richard stayed in his room at the Strathmore for fifteen minutes and then left.

How Richard spent the rest of Friday afternoon and evening has not been clearly established. He did not meet David Roth at the political meeting David had mentioned that morning, but later left a note at David's apartment asking that they meet that night at the Decanter. Richard probably did spend some time at the Decanter Friday evening waiting in vain for David who didn't return to his apartment until four o'clock Saturday morning. There is also a report, reliable though unconfirmed, that on either Friday night or Thursday night Richard drove to the synagogue of Congregation Shaarey Zedek with a "tall and willowy" Wayne State co-ed whom he knew casually, showed her around the outside of the building, and frightened her with musings about how shocking it would be if someone were to shoot Rabbi Adler at services on the Sabbath.

When David Roth came home to his apartment at 4 A.M. Saturday, he found not only Richard's note about meeting him in the bar but also a bullet. The first tangible evidence that Richard actually had a gun, the bullet reactivated in David much of the apprehension he had felt for Richard before his reassuring calmness of the past few days. Yet at four in the morning he felt there was little he could do: he didn't know where Richard was, and though he thought of calling the Wishnetskys he didn't relish the idea of waking them to raise a fuss at this hour. He decided to sleep with his fears.

THIRTY-NINE

"When Morris walked out of that door on Saturday morning and kissed me good Shabbas and said, 'I hope I see you but not too much later, dear,' I said, 'I'll be there, darling.' And we said goodbye and he walked down the road. The grandchildren were here as usual on the Sabbath, and we waved to him, and the little girl said, 'See you soon, Grandpa.' "

Goldie Adler stood in the doorway of the Adler's attractive brick ranch with the two older grandchildren, Judith, eight, and Jeremy, five, and watched the rabbi walk through the gray morning toward the large synagogue about two blocks away. It was Saturday, February 12—Lincoln's Birthday—and the weather was unseasonably warm with the temperature near forty degrees. A light mixture of rain and snow would fall much of the morning.

Among the first to arrive at the synagogue before the service were the Robert G. Franks, the family of the boy who was to celebrate his Bar Mitzvah that morning. Leaving Mr. Frank and her two sons to park the car, Mrs. Frank and her nine-year-old daughter, Franci, came in first and found Rabbi Adler walking in the long, spacious foyer. He came over to greet them and kissed Mrs. Frank and then Franci, who in good humor said, "Oh, your beard really feels funny." They all laughed. Mrs. Frank, a slim and attractive woman, had been a little girl younger than her daughter when Rabbi Adler had first come to Shaarey Zedek in 1938. Her father had been one of the old-guard Hershmanite leaders of the congregation back then, and she fondly recalled being consecrated by the rabbi and chosen to show him around the Sunday school when he was home on leave from the army during the war.

As the service began, Mrs. Frank, her daughter, her older son, and her husband sat in the first row of the sanctuary on the right. Thirteen-year-old Steven Frank, primed for his duties on the first day of his manhood in the synagogue, sat to his family's far left on the bimah. A small, bright-looking boy with a shock of sandy hair, he occupied a large chair facing the more than seven hundred people filling much of the sanctuary. Louis Berry, the president of the congregation, sat next to him in the chair to his right and in the chair to his left was Rabbi Adler. About fifteen feet to their left as they faced the congregation was a large lectern, or pulpit, in the middle of the bimah, behind which, a few paces back and three steps up, was the curtained opening of the Ark. Still farther to their left on the opposite side of the bimah in another set of chairs were the two cantors, Reuven Frankel and Jacob Sonenklar. In the audience were 125 visitors, including several schoolchildren from Congregational, Methodist, and Catholic churches in the area.

The service began at nine o'clock and proceeded smoothly through its many phases. The Torah reading for the day involved the chapters from Exodus that include the story of Moses receiving the Ten Commandments from God on Mount Sinai. Young Steven Frank performed well in his tasks, calling out the page numbers in the prayer book in authoritative fashion, reading his prayers and singing his chants flawlessly. At different points he was joined on the bimah by his grandfathers and by his father and brother. Mrs. Frank sat in the first row with tears of pride. "It was a perfect service," she said. "I had such deep feeling . . . it was so perfect and so lovely." Rabbi Adler also seemed especially proud of Steven and said so in a short speech of congratulations, after which he gave the boy his blessing and a book as a memento.

Earlier Mr. and Mrs. Wishnetsky, sitting near front and center with Mrs. Hordes, had no doubt felt pride of their own when their youngest child, fifteen-year-old Ellen, had read to the congregation in both Hebrew and English the Prayer for Our Country:

> May this land under Thy Providence be an influence for good throughout the world, uniting men in peace and freedom and helping to fulfil the vision of Thy Prophets: "Nation shall not lift up sword against nation, neither shall men learn war any more." "For all men, both great and small, shall know the Lord."

Goldie Adler had arrived at the synagogue quite late and sat near the back of the crowded sanctuary. It was well after eleven o'clock, and she had almost not made it to the service at all. Soon after the rabbi had left that morning, Jeremy, the little five-year-old, had wailed, "Baba, I don't want to go," and Mrs. Adler had almost given in to him. But she had remembered her son-in-law's instructions that the children must go to the synagogue if they wanted to stay with their grandparents over the Sabbath. Also she recalled her special promise to Mrs. Frank to attend the service and the kiddush afterward, since she couldn't guarantee that the rabbi would be feeling up to the evening party scheduled for a downtown hotel. Mrs. Adler had called her daughter who had come over quickly to pick up the children, and the rabbi's wife had reached the synagogue just in time for the start of her husband's sermon.

The day before, Morris Adler had as usual shared a Sabbath eve luncheon with his longtime friend and colleague, Rabbi Moses Lehrman of Congregation B'nai Moshe in nearby Oak Park. As was their custom the two men had discussed their sermon topics, common interests, and problems, and Rabbi Adler had explained that he would speak about Lincoln on the morrow. "But then he said something else," recalled Rabbi Lehrman. "He said he was concerned about this age of ours; how difficult it is for everybody and particularly for youth. . . . [He] told me Friday that he was aware of the terrible pressures and conflicts engulfing our youth today."

Now standing on the bimah near the lectern, his chin and upper lip covered with a short gray beard and moustache, wearing his long black robe, the round black rabbi's hat, and with his white tallith, or prayer shawl, draped over his large shoulders and chest, Morris Adler inspected his congregation from behind his dark-rimmed spectacles. He launched into his sermon, as usual without notes, the words flowing smoothly in his powerful voice and seemingly with extemporaneous ease. He spoke of Lincoln, the man who had been a hero to his father in Russia some sixty years before, as "perhaps the greatest American we have ever produced. Perhaps the only American who has become a global symbol, who has become naturalized in the consciousness of the entire world, who can take his place alongside of Tolstoï and Gandhi and Schweitzer." A description of Lincoln's greatness, said the rabbi, must include the compassion of his heart, his sustained affinity with common people, his intensely personal and nonorganizational religious faith, and the courage of his patriotic dissent.

The rabbi had been speaking for about a dozen minutes when he brought his sermon to its close:

> And I hope that in this hour of bitter decision—in this hour where we too stand at a kind of crossroads, and know not which road leads to the lasting peace and which to the sure annihilation of all mankind—may we, as we commune with his spirit and stand for a while in his presence draw something of the greatness of his goodness, the greatness of his plainness and simplicity, the greatness of his faith and his wisdom, into our own minds and hearts so that with something approaching Lincolnesque perception, we too can meet our problems with humility, with judgment, with faith.
>
> This time it is no longer a country divided against itself. This time it is a whole globe, and yet his words are still true. This globe divided against itself must destroy itself. May the love which he had even for his enemies, may the wisdom with which he embraced every situation, may the largeness of his view be ours so that we may know how to walk through the days ahead with that assurance and with that insight which will mean peace and not war, healing and not suffering, understanding and not hostility, brotherhood and not conflict.

Near the end of Rabbi Adler's sermon Richard Wishnetsky walked into the foyer of the synagogue and hung up his tweed overcoat in the adjacent cloakroom. In a pocket of the coat was a small paper bag containing seventeen .32-caliber cartridges. Richard put a yarmulke on his head and walked through the foyer to the sanctuary. He was dressed well in his gray suit, white shirt, and tie; in a pocket of his suit coat were two loose cartridges. Six more were loaded in the little .32 revolver with the sawed-off barrel which he carried somewhere on his person.

Richard had apparently spent the night in his room at the Strathmore House; a maid wanting to clean the room had found him still in 9:30 that morning. Subsequently, Richard had come down to tell the girl at the registration desk that he had left his grip and his records in the room but would be back for them later. He then left the hotel and did not return, but at some point just before or after his departure he had placed a call to the home of Larry Walters' parents and asked for Larry. A maid had answered and explained that Larry was out. When Richard had hung up she had written on a note pad, "Wishnetsky called at eleven A.M." Afterward Richard had traveled from the campus at Wayne State to the synagogue, either driving himself (having again perhaps gained the use of his grandmother's car) or possibly hitchhiking.

Now at approximately 11:40 A.M., Richard walked into the sanctuary, headed down the left aisle, and took a seat on the far left near the front. Nearby but in front of him and to his right sat his parents and his grandmother. Also close-by but unaware of his presence was Leah Kaplan, who had prevailed upon her father that morning to take her to Shaarey Zedek on the chance that Richard might show up at the synagogue and so provide the possibility of another meeting. Leah remained quite surprised that Richard hadn't called her during the week as he had promised.

When Rabbi Adler finished his sermon, he turned to his right and walked to his seat next to Steven Frank. Steven got up to offer the rabbi his congratulations and a handshake. Reuven Frankel, the younger of the two cantors, had moved from the opposite side of the bimah to the lectern and opened a prayerbook to begin the final section of the service: two hymns, two prayers, and the benediction. He now began to chant the Kaddish, which begins, "Magnified and sanctified be the name of God throughout the world which He hath created according to his will."

At this point Richard rose from his seat on the extreme left of the sanctuary and walked quickly down the left aisle to a spot directly in front of the seats occupied by Louis Berry, Steven Frank, and Rabbi Adler on the raised dais seven steps above him and facing the congregation. A doctor sitting behind Richard had felt there was something strange about the young man's appearance and had begun to obey an impulse to follow him down the aisle when Richard stopped and said calmly with his gun in hand, "I have a statement to make. Everybody off the bimah except Rabbi Adler." The doctor stopped and for a moment no one moved. People in the first rows began to notice Richard and his gun. Mrs.

Frank on the far right attempted to explain the impossible scene by telling herself that it must be a clever little skit dreamed up by the junior congregation on the theme of Lincoln's assassination. But then Richard raised the gun in his right hand and shot it once into the high-peaked ceiling.

The sound was loud but had little reverberation with the excellent acoustics of the large sanctuary. Cantor Frankel stopped his chant and there was a moment of stunned silence. Then a commotion began as people started yelling, "What's going on? What's happening? Who is it?" Mrs. Frank yelled, "Leave Stevie alone!" From her seat in the back Mrs. Adler could see little of what was taking place. Some around her thought they had heard the explosion of a firecracker. Leah Kaplan, sitting in the sixth row near the center, noticed Richard for the first time when he fired the shot, and she also thought of the junior congregation. Richard now shouted, "In your seats. Off the bimah." He motioned with the gun.

"At first I had no intention of moving," said Louis Berry. "I wasn't going to be ordered off the bimah of the synagogue by some kook. But the rabbi said, 'Lou, you had better do what he says—this boy is sick. I can handle him but take the boy [Steven] and leave.'" There was no alarm in his voice and he seemed calm, according to Berry. Others close to the front thought the Rabbi looked frightened. Steven needed no urging and was down the stairs and off the bimah as quickly as possible. Mr. Berry followed him into the first rows of the congregation and stood next to Leah Kaplan and her father. "Somebody's got to stop him," said Mr. Kaplan.

"Sit down, Abe," said Berry. "He's got a gun."

"I don't think the gun's loaded," said Leah's father.

Berry replied, "You don't know if it is or not."

Leah kept repeating half aloud, "It's all right, it's Richard. It's all right, it's just Richard . . ."

Mr. Berry said later that he had felt certain Richard only wanted to have his say: "I'm no hero, but if I had thought he was going to shoot that gun at the rabbi I would have done something, gone around in the back and come up from behind him or something. But not by the wildest stretch of the imagination did I think he was going to do what he did."

A few men near the front had in fact begun to move toward Richard, but he waved his gun at them and said, "Everybody in their seats." They sat down and Richard moved quickly and surely up the seven steps of the bimah to the lectern in the center. He seemed perfectly calm and in control of himself; his every move appeared deliberate and thoroughly planned. To the left Morris Adler sat forward in his chair. On the far right Cantor Sonenklar, in his seventies, hadn't moved from his seat; Cantor Frankel had moved away from the lectern and was edging off with the intention of getting to a telephone. A mother sitting in the first row with her children thought in the grip of her fear that Richard "was not Jewish and that something was happening to us as Jews." She felt that they had all been surrounded, that there were others with Richard who were training weapons on the congregation. She found herself paralyzed with the terrified notion that they were all about to be annihilated in the style of a Nazi execution. "Aunt Muriel, Aunt Muriel!" she called out. "Take care of my children."

Facing his audience from behind the lectern, Richard took from a coat pocket a piece of paper and spread it out in front of him. On it was a short speech, the first draft of which he had written on the inside cover of his copy of *The Brothers Karamazov*. He rested his gun hand on the top of the lectern, took a small microphone in his left hand, and began to read. A tape recorder, used, as was the custom at Shaarey Zedek, to record the entire service, continued to turn, thus capturing the speech and the sounds of what followed.

"This congregation," Richard read in a clear and self-possessed voice, "is a travesty and an abomination. It has made a mockery by its phoniness and hypocrisy of the beauty and spirit of Judaism. It is composed of people . . ." He stopped as he noticed a member of the congregation moving toward him. "Off!" he shouted. Eugene Merkow, thirty-seven, had left his seat near the front and had walked up the main aisle almost to the bimah.

Rabbi Adler motioned him away saying, "Get back . . . he has a gun."

Merkow called to the rabbi, "Do you know him?"

The rabbi replied, "Yes, I know him very well . . ."

Merkow moved back and Richard continued: "It is composed of people who on the whole make me ashamed to say that I am a Jew. For the most part . . ." Here the stir of his audience, which had never really subsided, became even louder. One woman said later, "It didn't make sense . . . I thought he was a Communist."

"Everybody quiet," demanded Richard. "It is composed of men, women, and children who care for nothing except their vain, egotistical selves. With this act I protest a humanly horrifying and hence unacceptable situation." After the slightest pause Richard turned to his right, revolver in hand, to face Rabbi Adler, who, according to some, gestured for him to leave the bimah now that he had spoken his piece; others thought the rabbi had beckoned for the gun. In either case Richard moved two or three paces directly toward the seated man, said in a soft, almost tender voice, "Rabbi . . ." and then, with the gun aimed steadily at arm's length, shot Morris Adler in the left forearm. The rabbi was in the process of rising, with his hands braced on the arms of the chair. The bullet ricocheted off the bone, then left his arm and entered the left side of his head behind the ear. Amid loud screams from the congregants, many of whom were ducking behind the pews, the rabbi continued to rise. Richard continued to move toward him. At almost point-blank range Richard fired again as the rabbi was beginning to topple. This time the bullet pierced the rabbi's round black hat and creased the top of his skull. As the screaming from the audience reached a wild intensity, Rabbi Adler fell heavily to the floor. Richard now turned toward the congregation (perhaps catching a glimpse of his father who was moving to the front of the bimah) and placed the gun barrel against his own head. Without hesitation he raised up on his toes and fired a bullet through his brain. He reeled and stumbled backward for seven or eight feet, then fell on his back at the rear of the bimah near the Ark.

The sanctuary was in pandemonium and remained so as men, women, and children continued to scream and wail. Several men close to the front, including three doctors who immediately attended Rabbi Adler, were quickly on the bimah. Arthur Lang, an attorney who had been sitting in the front row, was among the first to reach the bimah and noticed as he glanced at Richard that an envelope had apparently fallen from the young man's coat pocket and was lying next to him on the floor. Lang snatched up the envelope and went out of the sanctuary to examine its contents.

Lying on the bimah, his blood soaking his prayer shawl and the carpet beneath him, Rabbi Adler remained conscious and called for his wife. Mrs. Adler, making her way as quickly as possible from the back of the sanctuary through the nearly hysterical throng, managed to reach the bimah and knelt at her husband's side. "It's only my arm, Goldie," said the rabbi, "so don't worry."

Somewhat reassured Mrs. Adler said, "Relax, darling, and let them fuss over you; I'm standing right by." Afraid that she was obstructing the work of the doctors, she moved away a bit. An old man was standing on the bimah, screaming and pulling his hair. The mother in the first row, still terrified by her idea that there were others involved in an execution plot, refused the aid of a friend who wanted to lead her out of the sanctuary and into the lobby. "Don't go there," she said. "They're out there too." Others had run immediately out of the sanctuary, some going directly to their cars, some to call for police and ambulances. Many remained, shouting their demands to know what had happened and who had shot the rabbi.

"I didn't recognize that it was Richard when the boy went up," says Mrs. Adler. "I really didn't know who it was. Even when he was lying on the floor—after I got up from talking to the rabbi and when I turned and saw this boy lying there—I didn't know who it was. He was lying in a pool of blood and I was so ashamed because there were three or four doctors working on Morris and no one had gone over to the boy. So I said to one of the doctors, 'Go over to the boy.' He said, 'He's better off dead.' I said, 'Look, somebody loved him, he's somebody's child.' But I didn't know that Mr. and Mrs. Wishnetsky were behind me. I didn't know even when I turned towards them, and when she said to me, 'I'm so sorry!' I said, 'Stop. The boy couldn't help it; he was sick.' I didn't even know then it was Richard."

From her seat in the sixth row Leah Kaplan could see Richard lying on the bimah; a number of people had crowded up in front to attend the rabbi but there was no one around Richard. She could see his feet twitching. She decided that if somehow she could make him aware of the fact that she was there and had listened to what he had said, it might be some comfort for him. Leah climbed the steps of the bimah and moved back to where Richard was lying, not far from the Ark. When she got within two feet of him she saw that from the wound in his head there came a pink foam with bits of white matter floating in it. As she stood there he started to vomit, first a stream of yellow bile and then a thick flow of blood. Leah turned and walked back to find her father.

Somewhere in the synagogue Arthur Lang, who had picked up from the bimah the envelope which had fallen from Richard's coat pocket, found inside a few pages of writing similar to that which

Richard had shown friends in the past two weeks, including plans for an assassination whose victim would be part of "the supreme sacrifice," a bitter condemnation of American Jewry, and a description of a dance he had attended in the previous November in which he denounced the unseemly behavior of the young Jewish girls there. After reading it Lang turned the writing over to "authorities of the synagogue."

The Southfield police had received their first call from the synagogue at 11:48, probably within a minute of the actual time of the shooting. Their first units were at Shaarey Zedek within two or three minutes, and with their arrival the emotional scene in the sanctuary began to calm a bit. There were men in front now who were saying firmly, "Will everybody please contain themselves. Will everybody please leave the synagogue." People began to heed the requests, and with a semblance of calm returning the sanctuary began to empty quite rapidly. Within a few minutes two ambulances arrived, one to carry Richard to nearby Providence Hospital, a Catholic institution, the other to bear Rabbi Adler a few minutes farther to Sinai Hospital, where he had so often visited the sick and dying of his congregation. Along with Louis Berry, Goldie Adler rode in the ambulance with her husband, and as he remained conscious and asked about the Frank boy, she reassured him that only he himself and Richard had been hurt.

A call had been placed from the synagogue to Sinai briefly describing the rabbi's condition. His arrival in emergency was met by a hastily called team of eight physicians, including a neurologist, neurosurgeon, anesthesiologist, and internist, all prominent in their fields. A decision to operate immediately was made after a view of X-rays; by the time the rabbi had reached a third-floor operating room, he had lost consciousness. With the reassurance of the few words she had been able to exchange with her husband Mrs. Adler waited in firm hope of his complete recovery. "I sat near the door," she says, "because I was so sure the doctor was going to come out and say he was all right." She and her daughter, Shulamith, and Mr. Berry were soon joined in their vigil by a large number of friends, many with names prominent in the city. Mrs. Adler recalled: "That first day at the hospital I had more concern for others than for [the rabbi]. When people heard, they rushed [over] . . . so that I was afraid that somebody needing emergency treatment might not be able to get into the building." News teams from all the media were arriving at both hospitals and at the synagogue, and the publicity Richard had anticipated began.

Larry Walters, whom Richard had tried to contact earlier that morning at eleven o'clock, was picking up some clothes from a cleaner's in northwest Detroit some time after noon when a woman in the shop said, "Did you hear what happened at the synagogue? Some boy named Wishnetsky or something shot the rabbi." Larry raced his car to Shaarey Zedek, then to the Wishnetsky home, and finally to Providence Hospital. There he found Mr. and Mrs. Wishnetsky, Richard's grandmother, his sister Ellen, and several other relatives and friends. They were all "waiting for word of Richard's death," since there had been no hope from the beginning. According to the doctors at Providence, he had suffered massive brain damage and was completely paralyzed. He had shot himself cleanly through the brain, severing vital connections in a fashion that usually means almost immediate death. Larry attempted to comfort Ellen as he walked her around the hospital, but instead wept uncontrollably himself. During Mrs. Wishnetsky's wait on Saturday she received a message from Mrs. Adler which said in effect, "I am most concerned for you. The rabbi is holding his own."

Actually, despite Goldie Adler's fervent faith to the contrary, the news from Sinai was not good after a two-hour operation. The doctors had found that Morris Adler had suffered serious brain damage from the freakish shot in which the bullet had glanced off the bone of the rabbi's left forearm at just the required angle to send it up into the base of the skull behind the left ear. The bullet had not reached the brain, but had fragmented in the process of shearing off about a square inch of the heavy skull bone and driving numerous and minute bone slivers into vital areas of the brain. The second bullet, actually much more accurately aimed, had only grazed the top of the rabbi's head and had ended up in the heavy brim of his black hat. The rabbi's condition was listed as very critical; the doctors could offer no prognosis.

The first few radio news reports, aired soon after the shooting, were something less than accurate and failed to carry Richard's name. Tzvi Berkal, who had worked closely with Richard as an assistant director of the B'nai B'rith Youth Organization during Richard's high-school years, first heard about it as he walked home from services at Congregation Adas Shalom. A member of the congregation drove by and said: "Did you hear what happened to

Rabbi Adler? He's been killed by a group of people who came into the synagogue. They don't know who they were, but they think it was maybe Rockwell's group [the American Nazi party]. Somebody says a young man came in screaming and ranting anti-Semitic things and shot the rabbi." In the confusion of his thoughts and feelings at that point Berkal speculated to himself that it could have been a young Jew, a member of the congregation, and possibly either of two young men he knew, one of whom was Richard Wishnetsky.

A few others who heard vague first reports also thought of Richard, though often for reasons they could not easily explain. Harv Stiener first learned of the shooting from a friend who was driving him down to Wayne State. "Did you hear that Rabbi Segal has been shot?" said the girl.

"Oh, no, you must mean Rabbi Adler," said Harv, feeling it had to be the most prominent rabbi in the area.

"Oh, yes, I'm sorry: it was Adler. How did you know?"

"And I bet Wishnetsky shot him," said Harv. "If anyone could do it, it would be Wishnetsky." They promptly confirmed his speculation on the car radio.

Later Harv spent most of the night weeping and repeating to himself, "Richard was such a lonely person—nobody liked him, nobody really cared about him—he was never really close to anyone."

After learning details of the shooting on an afternoon broadcast, Bill Scott called Tina and Steven Lewis. Bill spoke to Tina and she seemed surprised at first but then dismissed the matter saying, "I knew he'd do something like that—he was a creep." Two months later Steven and Tina would be divorced.

Local and national radio and television gave considerable coverage to the story on Saturday. "We all sat there and wept and couldn't believe it when they showed Richard's picture on television that night," recalls Brad Mason, Richard's friend and the caretaker at Camp Farband. Debbie Rossman, who had attended the Snowball Dance at Mumford with Richard years back, heard the story first on her car radio as she drove down a freeway. She broke into tears and had to pull the car over. "I usually don't feel very strongly about anything," says Debbie. "But this time I was really shocked. I knew I would never be as surprised or shocked by anything again. I thought, 'Now I know anything is possible.' "

As the news of Morris Adler's plight spread, messages of sympathy and prayer began to arrive from Israel, the Orient, where he had served as a chaplain during the war, England, France, Canada, and many American cities. Michigan's Governor Romney, a personal friend, echoed the public remarks of numerous civic and religious leaders in the community in a statement issued Saturday night calling for prayers for the rabbi's recovery. In the days that followed numerous prayers and services were dedicated to the same intention in synagogues and churches across the country. "I received countless offers of prayers and encouragement," said Mrs. Adler, "and usually from complete strangers. I received exquisite rosaries, mass cards, and novenas for his recovery almost without number."

On Saturday evening the party at the Sheraton-Cadillac Hotel for nearly two hundred formally attired guests of Steven Frank and his family went on as scheduled. The party was held "because the Jewish tradition is that you never cancel—even if there is a tragedy," and because it was felt that Rabbi Adler would want it to be held. Earlier at the synagogue after the shooting, some of the congregants had walked from the sanctuary into the adjacent social hall which had been decorated gaily in red, white, and blue and set with long tables holding hundreds of glasses of red wine and silver trays of honey cake and cookies. Mrs. Frank's father had sung the Kiddush, people had kissed and congratulated Steven and then quickly deserted the hall. "Send the cake to a hospital," Mrs. Frank had told the caterers. Young Steven seems to have come through the ghastly conclusion to his Bar Mitzvah without serious emotional trouble, though months later he was still wondering to himself if he too had been marked as a victim: along with a number of notes of sympathy and good wishes for Steven from friends and strangers in the days after the shooting the Franks received four crude anti-Semitic letters which threatened his life or welcomed the prospect of his death.

On Sunday, as relatives of both the Adlers and the Wishnetskys (including the rabbi's brother and Richard's paternal grandparents and an uncle) arrived from New York and elsewhere, the rabbi's condition worsened somewhat. Artificial devices had to be employed to help him breathe. On Monday late in the morning a second operation was performed, this one lasting three hours, to remove bits of brain tissue swollen with blood and other fluid, and to relieve pressure on the brain. A tracheotomy was also performed to facilitate the rabbi's breathing, and he was then placed in an intensive-care unit. There was nothing more they could do, said the doctors: it might be several weeks before the full extent of the injury could be determined. He continued to give no sign of consciousness.

At the synagogue immediately after the shooting, the Southfield police had played back the tape recording of the last few minutes of the service. It was quickly decided that no one would benefit from a public release of the tape with the sounds of pandemonium and hysteria at its conclusion. The press was gathered, the situation explained, and all agreed to quote only Richard's words and to make no copy as the tape was played through once. On Sunday morning, however, the police were surprised to hear a recording of Richard's short speech and the sound of his gunshots played several times on WCAR in Pontiac. When they tried to contact the station's owner (who had been present at the synagogue with the press corps), they were told he had just left for Florida. Subsequently the recording was played on other radio and television stations in Detroit, and over the weekend was frequently heard on stations all over the East.

The story had nearly covered the front pages of the Sunday papers in Detroit, and also made front-page headlines in some papers in New York and other cities. In general the stories were fairly accurate, though they frequently employed references to a "berserk," "confused" gunman who was "shouting" and "screaming" as he leaped onto the bimah. At least one account in a New York paper had Rabbi Adler protecting the Frank boy by pushing him to the floor and throwing his own body over him.

Over the next few days Detroit's newspapers supplied some of the details of Richard's background in articles with titles like "Attacker: A Brilliant Mind Engulfed by an Inner Hell," and "The Psyche That Got All Twisted Up." Dr. Sander Breiner, acting as a spokesman for the Wishnetskys, was quoted as saying that he didn't think the shooting was simply an expression of Richard's disaffection from his religion or from Rabbi Adler. "His was a disturbed thinking process," said the doctor. "There was something in him—he was going through hell—that was bizarre, something hidden. This inner process expressed itself in religiosity. His act was similar to one burning himself or mutilating himself as a protest. . . ."

School friends of Richard's like Pat Burke and Jonathan Rose were interviewed, his probate court file was opened, and his academic and psychiatric careers traced. Richard was described as "the brilliant, sensitive, and deeply religious son of one of the most prominent families in the congregation and in the Jewish community." His belongings and writing which police found at the Strathmore House were described and quoted at length in both Detroit dailies and were reportedly turned over to the FBI for brief check because of Richard's references to the Secretary of Defense. After the world had learned most of what it was going to learn about him from the newspapers, at twenty-five minutes past midnight, Wednesday morning, February 16, 1966, Richard died at Providence Hospital. He had been unconscious for four days.

"The closest I ever got to looking into his poor, tormented soul," said Fred Baskin later, "was reading in the newspaper those things he wrote to himself at the end. For all the thousands of hours that he and I argued and discussed ourselves and intellectual things, I never considered, even at that time, any of what he said to be much of a reflection of Richard."

Later on Wednesday afternoon about one hundred people attended private services at a funeral chapel in Southfield and a brief graveside ceremony at Clover Hill Park Cemetery. Rabbi Groner, who had been conducting a retreat for young people at the congregation's kibbutz in northern Michigan at the time of the shooting, spoke the eulogy for Richard. He was "intelligent, an outstanding student," said the rabbi, ". . . not only in search of God—he was in search of himself. . . . There was in him fear and anger. There was an abyss of dread. There was malice that flowed like the tides. . . . How could these qualities and tendencies reside within one human spirit? Love and hate. Intelligence and madness. The search for clarity and the acceptance of fantasy. 'The heart's devious—who can know it?' "

Plainclothes police seemed to be at the ready when the Wishnetskys arrived at Shaarey Zedek on the Sabbath one week following the shooting. There as they entered their seats near the front of the sanctuary the family found themselves surrounded by four rows of close friends. The sanctuary was jammed as Rabbi Groner delivered the sermon, part of which went as follows:

> We come to the synagogue to seek a message: we come to the synagogue to find direction in our lost and confused condition. If you listen you can hear a message, a task, a purpose, a duty. Search your hearts and you will discover it. We shall preserve that which madness wanted to destroy! We shall sanctify that which has been profaned! We shall consecrate that which has been defiled! Because there was hate here last week, we shall learn how to love more deeply. Because there was fear here last week, we shall open the reservoirs of courage, a courage which will bring calmness and resolution and stability. Because there was divisiveness and disintegration, we shall reaffirm our shared ideals of truth, of justice, of peace. Because there was aggression here, we shall demonstrate our compassion, a compassion which strengthens and sustains and supports all those who wait by the side of Rabbi Adler, his family who hope and pray for his healing and his restoration.

After the seven days of shivah, the Wishnetskys were anxious to pay a visit to Mrs. Adler, who continued to spend most of her time in her vigil at Sinai Hospital. The rabbi's critical condition had remained essentially unchanged. Mrs. Adler and Mrs. Wishnetsky had exchanged notes of sympathy as they waited separately at the hospitals. After the shivah Rabbi Groner had asked the Wishnetskys to wait another week before approaching Mrs. Adler, but she insisted that they come to see her immediately. "They had to pick up their normal lives as quickly as possible," she says. Thus Mr. and Mrs. Wishnetsky, along with their daughters, Terry and Ellen, came to Sinai one evening before visiting hours. Mrs. Adler spoke at length with the parents but had special words also for Terry and Ellen: "I was trying to convince the girls that their brother loved the rabbi as much as they did, that he meant him no harm, that Richard's illness was like a cancer . . . and I really felt it. I love both girls—they were both in my classes—and I said, 'I know the rabbi's going to get well and I'm sure that when he does he'd love to see you.' "

Mrs. Adler's faith in her husband's complete recovery continued strong despite the fact that he had shown no improvement, his life now depending on equipment in the intensive-care unit which determined his breathing, fed him intravenously, monitored his bodily functions, and corrected his body temperature. After a while she began to speak at times in Hebrew to her husband, who remained unconscious. She explained: "Whenever I spoke Hebrew in Israel and made the slightest error, Morris would admonish me that I can do better . . . So I am speaking Hebrew to him, hoping that a mere error, a *greiz,* will cause some annoyance, will bring a response—that he then will answer me. And I will not give up hope. He *will* reply!"

"Everything is being done that can be done to allow his brain to recover," said a doctor at the hospital two weeks after the shooting. But so much is unknown, he said, in brain injuries involving coma that the mysteries preclude prognosis. Two weeks later, nearly a month after the tragic Sabbath at Shaarey Zedek, Mrs. Adler's anguished vigil finally ended. At 7:42 on the morning of March 11, 1966, Rabbi Adler died, with his wife and his daughter at his bedside. In nineteen days he would have been sixty years old.

Glowing public tributes to the man were subsequently recorded in the city's newspapers from the wide variety of prestigious people who had worked with Morris Adler, including Governor Romney who proclaimed Sunday, March 13, the day of the rabbi's funeral, as a period of statewide mourning. The national president of B'nai B'rith, Dr. William A. Wexler issued a statement which said: "The Jewish Community has suffered the loss of one of its most distinguished scholars, whose passion for righteousness, incisive brilliance of learning, compassion for the troubles of others, and capacity to articulate goodness and wisdom were harmoniously combined in a wonderful human being."

Dr. Henry Hitt Crane, the retired pastor of Detroit's Central Methodist Church and a close personal friend to the rabbi for twenty-seven years, said: "He was the best mind in this city. With him, you had a sense of basic loyalty that was so unquestioned. There was this complete candor and amazing graciousness, and he was incredibly articulate because of his assiduous study and the breadth of his sympathies. He was a total person."

On the bright and sunny afternoon of Sunday, March 13, more than six thousand people attended services for Rabbi Adler at the synagogue of Congregation Shaarey Zedek in what was described as the largest funeral in the history of Detroit. The crowd was so great that many were forced to stand outside the large building. Said one of the mourners in a comment that was frequently echoed, "It was so strange going to his funeral. I had just always assumed that Rabbi Adler would one day officiate at *my* funeral. . . . That's the kind of impression of vitality and permanence the man gave."

Also in the crowd was Leah Kaplan who had come to the synagogue on the day of the shooting looking for Richard. Leah had apparently been deeply affected by the experience. She said she thought it had definitely changed her life and her perception of the world and herself. At the service she was "obsessed with the thought that these two men had died so uselessly." As a child she had attended Hebrew school but had not been much interested; now she felt the need to know more about her faith and to practice it well so that Richard and the rabbi would not have died in vain. After the funeral service for the rabbi had been completed, she waited until she was entirely alone in the large sanctuary. Then she began to say to herself, at first very quietly, then louder and louder until she was nearly screaming, "I promise, I promise, I promise . . . ." vowing to attend services every Saturday from that day forward and to live her faith as fully as possible.

The procession of cars driving from the synagogue to Clover Hill Park Cemetery where Richard had also been buried became so long that many had to be stopped from joining it. Riding with her parents two cars behind the one that carried Mrs. Adler was Renah Lamm, the young girl who had been confined in The Haven during the time Richard had spent there seven months earlier. Renah was still living at The Haven, though she was coming home for the weekend occasionally and was now attending the funeral of the man she described as the only man she had ever loved. On Friday at The Haven she had been listening to a radio in the occupational therapy building when the announcement was made of the rabbi's death. Stricken with a blind panic she had "just started running and running," out of the building and onto the grounds until she was caught by a nurse and encouraged to weep out her anguish.

Now at the graveside service under the large tent covering the freshly dug grave, it was Goldie Adler's time for weeping as she stood with her family next to her dead husband's casket. The crowd of mourners was overflowing the tent and there were still more cars arriving as the family was led away before the lowering of the coffin. Mrs. Adler, finally unable to contain her grief, pressed herself against the casket and wept quiet prayers to her God.

Tossed somewhere in the jumble of Renah Lamm's thoughts and feelings as she stood a few feet away was the memory of a long-ago day when the rabbi had kindly and wisely defended a five-year-old's right to disbelieve in that strange and mysterious God.

EPILOGUE

. . . we do not kill from duty, but pleasure, or much more, rather, from displeasure and despair of the world. For this reason we find a certain amusement in killing people. Has it never amused you?

—HERMAN HESSE, *Steppenwolf*

Richard Wishnetsky was born into what W. H. Auden would soon call "the age of anxiety," a period of rapid, pervasive, and bewildering change, when the structures of social order and significance seem to be shifting or perhaps breaking down. As has apparently happened before at such times in history, a widespread sense of moral confusion and psychological insecurity seems to have accompanied social and cultural disruption.

The world Richard entered was in the process of developing two radically new capabilities: a demonstrated capacity for the mass slaughter of millions upon millions of an appointed group of people and the immediate access to global self-destruction. With its disruption of families and its ironic, surreal quality for most Americans, who learned primarily from newspapers, books, and movies of its remote, incredible violence, World War II seems to have had continuing consequences in the attempts of many young people to find meaning and identity.

Richard and much of his American generation experienced a life style affluent enough to take sustenance for granted and to concentrate on matters less mundane. Growing up in a world of dials and push buttons, some of which were connected to the nuclear hardware which the supernations continued to rattle at each other, and raised with the instant switched-on action of television, they were, in terms of social and political awareness and perhaps impatience, a truly new generation. The generational gap could only widen as the children grew further into their radically new experience, but one of the things they learned early from their elders was the story of how Americans brought law and order to the old West primarily with the use of violence. It was a vicarious, fictional violence which, like the experience of the war, remained in the memory and imagination in a glow of surreality.

Television and other forms of mass media assumed a new and prominent role in the individual quest for identity, prescribing a multitude of contradictory images which merged into an impossible conglomerate personality: physically attractive and effective, sexually and financially aggressive, success-oriented yet companionable, flexible, and easily adjusted. A yearning for the status of a public personage seemed to be fostered by the media's promotion of stars, culture heroes, or villains who always seemed so sure of a self, since one had been so publicly and glamorously defined for them.

Richard's schools, with their extraordinarily competitive atmosphere, perhaps unfortunately reinforcing the notion that personal worth is based on recognized success and the opinion of others, also contributed to the multiple reflections from which he was trying to establish a valid and meaningful self-image. Generally the institutions of modern society seem to have formed a labyrinthian hall of mirrors warped by the pressure of the times, often making it a desperate matter to find a relatively undistorted picture of oneself. Hypersophistication and self-consciousness have added seemingly new and complex dimensions to the ancient problems of self-estrangement and the search for the freedom of psychic health and spontaneity.

The peculiarly American combinations of widespread affluence and spiritual emptiness, of the material well-being of the suburbs and the slow starvation of the ghetto, of the bright shining rhetoric that speaks of freedom, equality, and American moral superiority and the continued degradation of those left out and the astronomical figures on divorce and violent crime—the daily collection of such discordant words and images, the terrible gap between self-idealizing rhetoric and insistent reality, seems to have produced an exorbitantly ambiguous society. One wonders about the confusion and frustration promoted by a society that tells its young people to see their nation as the fount of peace, freedom, and democracy but which sends them through schools most often experienced as authoritarian and denies them access to its political process until three years after they're old enough to die in one of its wars; a society that proudly teaches them its position in the Nuremberg Trials but threatens or punishes them if they take it too seriously;

that glowingly talks about its love for truth but tells obvious lies about its history in high-school texts; that tells them about sex according to Victorian standards but teases and overstimulates them with a constant flow of commercial erotica; that calls itself a nation under God but frequently shows little concern for the principles of any religion.

It should not be difficult to understand why the idealistic young find hypocrisy the most intolerable of sins even though it seems a natural and inevitable *effect* of self-doubt and self-delusion. The charge of hypocrisy implies that the accused recognizes his own duplicity, yet most people, truly unaware of moral contradiction in their lives, are more appropriately described as self-deceptive. The young, like Richard, nevertheless see hypocrisy as a threatening and malevolent force undermining the relations between individuals and groups in society. And in this sense they may be right: widespread moral discrepancy and ambiguity may be inimical not only to their idealism but also to their own identity and equilibrium.

It has been argued that membership in the ethnocentric life of Detroit's Jewish community provides "a viable defense against the anonymity and alienation which plague an increasingly homogenized urban America." This is no doubt true for those who are comfortable in their membership. Richard was not, and his Jewishness became one of the battlegrounds on which he quite consciously chose to fight out the conflicts of his identity. In some ways he seems typical of a certain segment of Jewish youth who readily accept their Jewishness but reject the formal tenets of Judaism, who find it difficult to fill their Jewish identification with meaningful content, who are alienated from middle-class Jewish life and hostile toward the religious establishment.

The events of the 1960's were undeniably important in fostering the apocalyptic temper and the urge to confront and defy authority. The estrangement of increasing numbers of young Americans continued throughout the decade, and its underpinning was a gathering sense that the nation's political institutions had become corrupt and inadequate before the task of effecting the large changes required. The most disaffected of the young viewed the assassinations, civil-rights killings, mass murders, and the Vietnam war as unmistakable symptoms of their nation's complete moral bankruptcy.

Many of these young people became passionately involved in radical politics or joined the psychedelic communion of hippiedom. As his own alienation grew, Richard turned away from his formerly intense interest in the troubling course of world events to the less frantic realm of scholarship. Whatever the psychological motivation for embracing a system of absolute values and an apocalyptic perspective, insofar as these ideas helped to shape his conscious notion of himself and his role in the world, they helped to determine his actions. In this sense his philosophical perspective seems to have helped narrow his vision, rigidify his attitudes, and limit his freedom.

According to Dr. Frederic Wertham, a psychiatrist who has written extensively on violence in America, "No murderer's mind functions in a vacuum. Every murder is an act in the context of history." And clearly the assassination-suicide at Shaarey Zedek involved in significant fashion many of the nation's social dilemmas, from the regulation of firearms to alienation in the multiversity. But while one easily agrees with Dr. Wertham, it is quite another matter to determine the relative importance of Richard's encounters with the larger forces of society and culture. Constantly dynamic, fluid, and enormously complex, these factors can be frozen and dissected intellectually only at the expense of truth. The search for a simple answer can lead only to a spurious kind of understanding.

Focusing more closely on Richard in the last few weeks of his life, one is confronted with the picture of a young man who has come to see himself as a loathsome failure at the age of twenty-three. With frustration and self-disgust grinding constantly within, he apparently could no longer turn to the old ways of coping—the delusions of grandeur or the frantic outburst of a manic episode. The urge to violence continued to grow out of his rage and despair, but the expression of that urge would remain unacceptable unless the act satisfied other levels of intention and purpose as well; it would have to be a meaningful act of violence if he was to be master of his own destruction.

The beginning of Richard's solution was an idea that he may have been toying with for some time as he ran to and from the people who were trying to help him. The idea seems to have taken shape as he came to admit the possibility that he was ill, that he was not simply the healthy and blameless object of malevolent outside forces. And, as it seems, he began in a deceptive and perverse way to indulge his illness, even perhaps to cultivate it in a sense. He apparently began to see his illness as something very special and significant. Just as he had previously (from boyhood, perhaps) considered himself marked for a kind of greatness, so he now began to frame a conception of his illness in similarly exalted terms.

By his own account, Richard suffered through an almost hysterical identification with the hero-victim of the film *The Pawnbroker*, a Jew who decades later is still hounded by his memories of the Holocaust. Richard, with no such memories but suffering instead from a haunted imagination, also felt himself a victim, a kind of suffering survivor struggling with a paradigmatic sickness. He was indeed, he seems to have decided, "a young man of our times"; certainly, with his intelligence and idealism, a worthy representative of his generation. And yet now he was sick, because in a world that he considered corrupt and insane, it was not possible to be healthy. And so Richard wrote: "You say that I am sick—you are right. You dismiss me because I am sick—in that you are wrong. . . . The dark side of creativity is sickness. . . . Anyway, in our society to be normal is to be sick. . . ."

One is reminded of Harry Haller, the Steppenwolf, one of Richard's favorite characters, whose story, says the narrator of the novel's introduction, "is a document of the times, for Haller's sickness, as I now know, is not the eccentricity of a single individual, but the sickness of the times themselves, the neurosis of that generation to which Haller belongs, a sickness, it seems, that by no means attacks the weak and worthless only but, rather, precisely those who are strongest in spirit and richest in gifts."

In his precarious condition, Richard felt that he could not adjust to his vision of the world. But what's more, he saw his inability to do so as something meaningful. For Richard, such a world should *not* be adjusted to, is not worthy of adjustment. Instead he saw himself driven into the disease of his generation, a disease whose symptoms he would manifest and explore to their final consequence.

Previously he had seen himself as one of those very few who understand the world's true nature and who (when given the chance) would teach others its meaning. Now he saw himself as a paradigm of postmodern man, torn by the large and terrible forces that would ultimately deliver all men to his own fate. In a sense he would attempt to conquer his sickness by reaping its worst evil with the world as a witness, so that in the process the world might learn where it was heading. In one of the notes he left for his audience Richard explained this quite explicitly: "My distorted, disoriented voice either barely uttered or tremendously violent, gives you a slight horrifying glimpse into the dehumanizing future that awaits you and your unfortunate children, who will be healthy, comfortable and secure beyond your fondest dreams and just as diseased. . . ."

In Richard's terms, to be sick was to be alienated, immersed in meaninglessness and absurdity, without a clear sense of identity and unable to live according to genuine moral values. In his view most people were leading such lives but without self-recognition. He too was sick, he admitted now, but at least he knew it. And knowing it, he could accept the notion that the only appropriate response to intolerable conditions was what others would call aberration or madness. Finally by elaborating his idea of its paradigmatic quality he seems to have reinforced and exploited his illness, making himself almost impervious to help and at last embracing the possibility of the abnormal, the unlawful, even the violent act as an acceptable solution to his dilemma.

Probably much of what became Richard's final solution had been part of his fantasies for a long time before Lincoln's Birthday, 1966. As he considered possibilities during the first weeks of 1966, what seems new was the development of what he decided was an intellectually acceptable justification for murder and suicide. He had come to the conclusion that he would never be able to live as a wise and prophetic scholar, the role he had chosen as the only way to personal fulfillment. Now in his final attempt to cope with an intolerable world, he would strike the awful, apocalyptic blow which he would not survive—but by which the world would be cast in the bold, cruel light of truth.

Often in his writing and conversation near the end he had mentioned Robert McNamara as a possible victim. McNamara, whose public image for some at the time was the stereotype of the coldly efficient organization man without moral insight or human feeling, symbolized much of what Richard hated in modern society. Yet he finally turned to Rabbi Adler as a victim much more fitting and suitable. Richard knew the rabbi well as the head of a congregation that symbolized for Richard everything that was wrong with the Jewish community, as a leader in a society of pervasive evil, and perhaps most importantly as an eminently good though misguided man; for Richard's plan seems to have demanded someone whom both he and the community considered good and valuable. It had to be so, because the shooting must appear utterly senseless and absurd—until his audience began to get a completed picture of his act and recalled his words on the bimah, ". . . I protest a humanly horrifying and hence unacceptable situation"; until they found in his hotel room the books and records which he would leave as a quick index to his superior taste and intelligence; until they finally heard him saying to them, "Suffer in your frozen hells of apathy, boil in the self-hate of outraged impotence. Listen to my voice, you deaf ones. Listen to how sick, sad, lonely and forlorn it is."

Like a work of art, his final act may have had different levels of conscious meaning for Richard and more than a single possible interpretation. He may well have seen the rabbi as a kind of religious sacrifice, as Mrs. Smith has suggested, a victim of "that old scapegoat mechanism whereby the sins of the community are punished and absolved in a single figure."

In Richard's black sacrifice, however, there seems to have been no absolution intended. His killing of Rabbi Adler as a representative of the congregation seems to have been more a vengeful act of retribution against a wayward group which, in his eyes, had "made a mockery by its phoniness and hypocrisy of the beauty and spirit of Judaism." If he could not punish each of them individually, he would in any case take away their beloved, seemingly inviolable rabbi and desecrate their "opulent" temple in a way they would never be able to forget. It was not purification that Richard was about, but profanation. As Rabbi Groner observed:

"Wishnetsky managed to violate, transgress, desecrate so many sacred laws, dicta, and sanctities with one final action that it's almost unbelievable. First of all he picked the holiest day of the week, the Sabbath; the holiest place, the synagogue; the most sacred place in the synagogue, the bimah; and the most sacred spot on the bimah, near the Ark. He picked the holiest of men, the rabbi; and to compound all of this, he committed this crime before an audience—in public—which in terms of Judaic ethics and law, makes it even more hideous."

Though in Richard's view American Jewry had been chosen to preserve true religious faith in the modern world, by turning its materialistic back on traditional beliefs and practices it was sharing in the dissolution of modern society. That Congregation Shaarey Zedek was leading the way in this direction was an idea that may have been reinforced by Richard's involvement with the tradition-bound Lubavitcher community.

But Richard seems also to have had a grander design in mind. As he explained to his friend, David Roth, Congregation Shaarey Zedek was a collective example of the myriad corruptions of modern society. Thus Rabbi Adler appears to have become part of a microcosmic drama containing what Richard felt was intense and universal significance. In his view the rabbi would play the role of the Innocent who are slaughtered daily and will be inevitably destroyed by and with the Damned in the consummate horror of the final cataclysm.

As the supreme antihero, Richard would then in effect command the world to look and listen. Society must understand his fate; it must see what it had done to one of its most promising young people. He was sick, but only as the rest of society was and would be, for quite clearly he had reached the end of a course that the rest of men were swiftly traveling—the road to a destruction that would spare neither sane nor insane, neither good nor corrupt.

From this perspective, then, Richard employed ritual, symbol, and sacrifice to say that he did not have the will to live and that his death would demonstrate the shape of things to come. Given his premise—that his illness was paradigmatic, that the world was as inevitably doomed as he was—he moved with a kind of terrible logic to make that illness prophetic, playing out its mad and evil promptings until he had provided his own judgment and execution. The assassination-suicide at Shaarey Zedek was, in the terms which I suggest were Richard's, a transcendent and allegorical sacrifice, a demonstration in miniature of global ruin. The congregation too played their symbolic role, as representatives of the renegade race of man.

Dr. Wertham has written:

> In a human being's life, murder is one of the most crucial, experiment like events that can possibly take place. It reveals the innermost springs of the individual's life and is a profound self-revelation of character. Far more than any other act, it re-

> quires an enormously strong impulse, an overcoming of resistances, a conquering of inhibitions, and a building up of rationalizations. It is invaluable, therefore, for understanding the true texture of human personality and of mental mechanisms in general. It might be truly said: Tell me what kind of murder you could or would commit, and I'll tell you what kind of a man you are.

From this viewpoint, with murder and suicide as his moment of ultimate estrangement, Richard's final act became a fully achieved expression of self. He was not only fulfilling his notion of the role he had chosen to play in the world (essentially that of a teacher), but also in the process channeling and releasing all his pent-up frustration and hostility, ultimately playing out many of his fantasies of power and fame.

Clearly Richard's long-standing need for a sense of potency was finally fulfilled as he stood on the bimah with the ultimate power of life and death held firmly in his hand. His careful planning and execution of the act suggest his propensity for rigid self-discipline, and the calculated publicity recalls his dreams of "greatness." His despair spoke of his failure to excell, and in a perverted way, his grandiose rationalization encompassed his desire to perform a creative service for mankind. The actual killing was a final expression of his terrible isolation, and the sweeping indictments he left behind were the final product of his lust for certainty. During his last year Richard had become increasingly interested in the idea of using force to solve personal and societal dilemmas, until, in the last month or so of his life, he appears to have become obsessed with the possibility of a violent solution to his own problems.

In all, Richard displayed the flare for the dramatic and the theatrical, the penchant for the one grand moment of meaning which had always been an important feature of his personality. The ritual setting of the act, its aura of necessity and inevitability, its deep involvement of an audience who were supposed to undergo an experience that would literally change their lives, the subversive quality of the act and its use of the most popular of guerrilla tactics—these and other elements suggest recent developments in the contemporary theater which have appropriated labels like the theater of cruelty, living or environmental theater, and guerrilla theater. If an account of the act seems to read like a stage drama or some other kind of fiction, there may be good reason: in a very real sense Richard seems to have constructed it as one would a fiction and then played out the role he assigned to himself—just as he had occasionally in the past assumed elements of the identities of some of his favorite literary figures. There was nothing original about his construction, since for the most part he was plagiarizing from the authors, books, and films which had held special appeal for him; one can find in his final act and in his justification for it bits and pieces from the novels of Dostoevski, the writings of Nietzsche, books like *Steppenwolf, The Rebel,* and *The Revolt of the Masses,* and films like *The Pawnbroker* and *Dr. Zhivago.* No matter that in the works involved one could find much to undermine Richard's rationalization; as always, he took from art and ideas only what would serve his own purposes.

Actually on the bimah Richard became not what he apparently thought himself to be—a sensitive murderer-prophet destroying out of his tortured concern for humanity—but rather a sick and self-deluded killer. In those last few weeks, in fact, he seems to have been so filled with the impulse to murder that it may have been fortunate that his need to dissimulate and wear the mask prevailed and that many more did not fall victim to his violence. For years he had been running from his real troubles (to larger, more heroic ones) because of an inability to admit weakness, foible, or low impulse. It was no different when he stepped up to shoot the rabbi and himself.

His real motive force, lodged in aggressive hatred, had to be covered over with an elaborate and—in his eyes—almost humane justification. Surely Rabbi Adler was more to Richard than simply a convenient symbol filling a role in an abstract drama of death. First of all he had been a friend to Richard and had confronted him with an honesty and concern that may have shamed Richard's fragmented and role-playing self. It was just such a genuinely open and honest friendship that Richard seems to have felt most threatened by and which he often seemed to undermine. To some extent, the rabbi had been one of Richard's counselors and, like the psychiatrists, had been trying to draw him away from his flirtation with the abyss. As a counselor he had no doubt asked Richard to look at himself clearly and to face life squarely, but each task brought only guilt and anxiety.

The rabbi was the last in a long line of teachers in Richard's life who had occasionally elicited some of his most intense ambivalence. Teachers had been his saviors, he felt, those who had contributed most to his value as a human being. Their work had prompted his reverent resolve to become a teacher himself, yet teachers had also betrayed him: they had not always appreciated his talents nor often enjoyed his efforts to teach *them.* Their unfair criticism, lack of faith, and outright rejection had caused him bitter disappointment. To the finish at Shaarey Zedek Richard carried with him a backlog of largely unvented resentment against his teachers stretching well back into childhood.

Richard's feelings toward his teachers were part of the general ambivalence he displayed in relation to most authority figures. Often in the past (and again with Rabbi Adler) he had assumed either the reverent awe of hero worship or the bitter contempt of rebellious egotism. Quite obviously his father was also represented in the person of Rabbi Adler; indeed a psychiatrist would likely choose to talk first about the rabbi as a father-surrogate. Richard's troubled relations with his parents, had long been the source of much unhappiness, and he had at times openly threatened to take their lives. While in the hospitals, he told psychiatrists that his parents were the cause of all his troubles, and again in his last few weeks he spoke to friends of how he was weighing the possibility of killing his father.

On at least one occasion near the end Richard also talked in a magnanimous and forgiving way about his family. Still, the powerful old hostility apparently remained, and the shooting seems not only a symbolic patricide but also a more direct venting of aggression against his family, especially his father, whose name he would destroy with an act almost more cruel than if he had actually turned his gun on them, for they would now have to live with the memory of horror and shame. In the end he rejected direct expression of the impulse to patricide at least consciously because he could find no grandiloquent rationalization for it. It would not properly serve his larger purpose, he told John Samuels three weeks before the shooting.

Finally Morris Adler seems to have filled at least one more role for Richard. With imposing physique and verbal facility, potent intelligence and magnetic warmth, the rabbi showed an extraordinary ability to be involved meaningfully with others and a capacity for getting things done. Richard had no doubt fancied all these qualities in himself, secretly matching himself against his rabbi, perhaps enjoying a heady notion of parity now and then but also feeling woefully inadequate at times. Also on occasion (for example, the Hillel banquet in Ann Arbor) he had known firsthand the pressure of Rabbi Adler's imposing personal manner. In all, with reference to the rabbi as a successful and effective human being, Richard seems to have felt a confused mixture of respect, awe, fear, resentment, and a large dose of what so often seems to be part of the motive for assassination, old-fashioned envy.

Richard's aggressive impulse, for so long repressed and rigidly covered over with false tolerance, sentimentality, and pacifism, had finally become so insistent that it seems to have included not only the rabbi but indirectly all of those for whom the rabbi stood. Apparently, though, it could not be fully vented unless finally turned on Richard himself; according to psychiatric opinion this seems most often to occur with depression-prone, highly ambivalent, and repressed individuals—like Richard. As also seems to be the case with most suicides, Richard had an extensive history of self-defeating attitudes and actions. He had begun the process of his self-destruction long before its final accomplishment. His long-time fascination with the myth of the hypersensitive hero driven mad by his too-vivid perception of cruel and suffering mankind seems to be one expression of this process, and many others could be listed.

In the past, Richard had turned to words not actions to solve his problems and had appeared quite successful for most of his life. At the end, however, though words were still important to him (one of his friends could argue that if Richard had not been allowed to make his little speech on the bimah, no one would have been hurt), it seems clear that his faith in the power of language had broken down. Over the years, comprehension and communication had seemed vital to Richard, but he had also used the spoken word as an act of aggression, defense, or reconciliation in a way that could foster a feeling of potency. What would have happened if someone in the front of the sanctuary at Shaarey Zedek had somehow had the presence of mind to say in a firm and friendly voice, "Richard, I'm interested in what you're saying. Could you elaborate a bit?"

My own guess is that Richard would not have been deterred: words seemed simply no longer enough to accommodate the complex of hostile needs which he had brought to the bimah. This is not to say, however, that once the decision was made (perhaps earlier in the week) its violent conclusion was inevitable. A carefully planned fantasy is one thing and its execution is quite another; between the two stands the still intact mystery of human volition.

In any case, Richard's words and actions both seem to indicate a perversion of the imagination, from a tool with which one can share the experience of others and thus make compassionate connection to a means for producing a wall of delusion behind which one can hide and announce that there's nothing more to learn. Richard's words on the bimah may have resembled, in his mind, those of Jeremiah, his favorite prophet, but they carry only the crude power of a half-truth told with shocking, terrifying drama. Their self-righteous presumption to judge does nothing to advance the cause of truth. Rather the imagination has severed its connections with reality, and its images have frozen into symbols: Richard was no longer dealing with another human being as he confronted Rabbi Adler, but only with a symbolic presence. Nor was he really interested in influencing the actions of those who would determine the future; in his eyes the future was already determined. In his tract on his fantasized murder of McNamara he explained:

> My act was motivated by philosophical and social reasons, not political ones. It is a protest, the registration of an outrage, a dire warning: Its author entertains no illusions as to it bringing about any immediate substantial change in the American scene.
>
> . . . The selfishness, stupidity and vanity of men shall succeed in triumph over whatever goodness there is—the ultimate triumph will bring this obliteration, both spiritual and physical, of this planet. Hail Brave New World! Hail nothingness!

The imagination has stopped working here in the service of curiosity and hope; Richard has learned all he wants to and has fastened himself instead to the certainty of doom. Instead of the courage which Martin Buber ascribes to the prophet who engages history, no matter how terrible, there is only the false strength of Richard's savage withdrawal. His words reflect the impotence of illness, a kind of spiritual irresponsibility and moral weakness. They carry only frozen rage and bitter despair, and the decision for destruction, though not perhaps inevitable, seems consistently to follow.

All men have the capacity for violence. Whether they will display it or not is determined in part by the society in which they live. The urge to realize violent fantasies is the key to suicide and murder, and a society that contributes to that urge while doing little to provide or support counterforces will be a violent one. As psychiatrist Kenneth Keniston has pointed out, "The issue of violence is to this generation what the issue of sex was to the Victorian world." The fact that we have witnessed and imagined violence on an incomparable scale has made us, says Keniston, "vastly more sensitive to and fearful of our inner angers," which may explain why "post-modern youth, to an unusual degree, remain open to an awareness of their own angers and aggressions, and why this awareness creates in them a sufficient understanding of inner violence to enable them to control it in themselves and oppose it in others."

Whether or not one agrees with this assessment, it should be remembered that until recently American postwar youth have not frequently witnessed real violence, at least of the kind that has apparently kept the manufacturers of war toys from finding much of a market in Europe. Violence, either fictional or real, experienced via the media, may at times heighten stimulation while subverting the reality of consequence. Then too Richard seems a tragic reminder that there are those in this generation who may have grown up apparently with a passionate pacifism, yet who (if they should slip under the shadow of the apocalypse) may come to terms with their anxiety and fear by finally embracing the violent deed and acting it out.

The distinction between acceptable and unacceptable violence might appear quite understandable, but in fact we have been anything but clear and honest in our attitudes toward violence. We have not said, as Rabbi Adler did, that violence in *all* its forms is always vile and abhorrent, though its use may be regrettably necessary to preserve one's life and freedoms. We have instead said in a multitude of ways that violence is exciting, entertaining, effective in solving problems, manly, laudable, and generally quite acceptable as long as it serves our purposes. Just what those purposes may be we have often left rather vague in the cliché-ridden rhetoric of the mayor or the statesman who may talk of defending law and order, the free world, or our national interest but often seems to mean little more than the defense of the status quo and of his own abstract version of the truth.

What really frightens and appalls us is not violence *per se* but violence in league with seeming madness—irrationality, anarchy, or revolution. Thus we are most upset by the specter of the armed guerrilla uprising forecast by the self-styled revolutionary young. We seem much more concerned about street crime, unpredictable and often senseless, than we seem to be about organized crime, whose corporate efficiency appears to fascinate more than disturb. We are deeply upset by the often quiet, seemingly harmless young men like Richard and Sirhan who in a tragic flash turn themselves into assassins, and we are shaken by the mass murderers like Speck and Whitman who wreak their incredible havoc also without warning. Presented with a picture of Oriental revolutionaries attempting a takeover in their own country, we can authorize the massive destruction of a small nation ten thousand miles away.

The ambiguity of our attitudes toward violence may have stemmed in part from our paradoxical experience of having been involved in large-scale violence while not having encountered directly the full reality of its effects. But it has also been fostered by the same sense of anxiety, discontinuity, and self-doubt which has contributed to all our national discrepancies and moral contradictions. The result seems to be that America is in the midst of an identity crisis, appearing to the world by turns as alienated, idealistic, virulent, dynamic, self-glorifying, and paranoid. Not very long ago we thought we knew what America was—one could go to any schoolboy's history book as if to a catechism and learn from its proud satisfaction and doctrinaire simplicity.

The catechetical definition was promoted and accepted by many, despite its elements of illusion and deceit, perhaps because America was still an adolescent with a vague, inarticulate guilt, high idealism, and boundless aspiration, without a sense of history or a genuine self-assurance. But in the years following the end of World War II America has seen swift change and violent upheaval, and in response to these events opinions on the identity of America seem to be increasingly in conflict and confusion.

Now America is told that it faces dissolution and dehumanization as a modern mass society, that its children of affluence are "growing up absurd" amid innumerable social and institutional problems. In no small part the American reality still to be forged in terms of values affirmed and acted upon will depend on how the American people deal with the issues raised by the events that culminated in the black Sabbath at Shaarey Zedek.